Napier and the Peninsular War

WILLIAM NAPIER

Napier and the Peninsular War
Officer of the 43rd Foot in Wellington's Army,
Author of the *History of the Peninsular War*

H. A. Bruce

Napier and the
Peninsular War
Officer of the 43rd Foot in Wellington's Army,
Author of the History of the Peninsular War
by H. A. Bruce

FIRST EDITION

Leonaur is an imprint
of Oakpast Ltd

Copyright in this form © 2010 Oakpast Ltd

ISBN: 978-0-85706-353-3 (hardcover)
ISBN: 978-0-85706-354-0 (softcover)

http://www.leonaur.com

Publisher's Notes

The opinions of the authors represent a view of events in which he was a participant related from his own perspective, as such the text is relevant as an historical document.

The views expressed in this book are not necessarily those of the publisher.

Contents

William Napier's Boyhood	9
Napier's Youth and Early Service	15
The Peninsula	33
Storming of Ciudad Rodrigo	66
Letters to His Wife	74
Offer of Employment in the Portuguese Army	84
The Petite Rhune	105
Battle of Orthes	128
Battle of Waterloo	139
Occupation of France	150
Collection of Materials for the History	175
Bromham and London	227
Marshal Soult in England	280
Lady Hester Stanhope	295
Remarks on the *History of the Peninsular War*	311
Appendix 1	342
Appendix 2	354
Appendix 3	365

By Jove! I do not think such a history has appeared since that of Xenophon. The writing is beautiful, and though entirely free from affectation he says the best things short, pithy, and to the purpose. There never was written anything of more rapid current, and in his course he flings to right and left the dirt and filth of prejudice; lays bare the baseness and corruption of the Juntas, &c, and exposes, alas! the blindness and folly of our military agents—the madness or imbecility of our Government! and all this done with good taste, and from undoubted documents, quoted in the margin.

Major-General William Campbell

CHAPTER 1

William Napier's Boyhood

Born at Celbridge, on the 17th of December, 1785, William Francis Patrick Napier.

Died at Clapham Park, on 12th February, 1860, General Sir William F. P. Napier, K.C.B., Colonel of the 22nd Regiment, aged 74.

William Napier was the third son of the Honourable George Napier, who was sixth son of the fifth Lord Napier. Descended from Scott of Thirlestane, from whom he derived the characteristic family motto, "Ready, aye ready," and from John Napier, the inventor of logarithms, he inherited much of the speculative talent of one ancestor, and the chivalrous loyalty of the other. His mother, Lady Sarah Lennox, was the seventh daughter of the second Duke of Richmond, by Sarah, eldest daughter of Marlborough's famous lieutenant, Lord Cadogan. Of Lady Sarah's sisters, one was married to the first Lord Holland, and was mother of Charles James Fox; another to the Duke of Leinster, and was mother of the unfortunate Lord Edward Fitzgerald: a cousinship which exercised no slight influence on the opinions and career of William Napier.

Of young Napier's early days the details are difficult to obtain, and not very satisfying. It would be interesting to learn the course of training which fitted him for the work of producing a History universally admitted to be excellent, and one which will form a landmark for the literature of our language.

It would also be useful to learn the moral culture which resulted in the formation of a character so remarkable for its enthusiastic worship of everything good and noble, and for its detestation of everything mean, cruel, or crafty.

As regards the last, the moral atmosphere of Castletown, where he spent much of his youth, and his familiarity with the elevated sentiments of his parents, and of his aunt Lady Louisa Conolly,[1] had a large effect in the formation of his mind.

Celbridge House, near the village of that name, was only a mile distant from Castletown; and at Celbridge House lived Colonel and Lady Sarah Napier with their eight children.[2] Their residence was by the country people called "The Eagles' Nest," on account of the remarkable features and high spirit of the Napier boys.

Colonel Napier, the father of heroes, was himself cast in the true heroic mould. He possessed uncommon powers, mental and bodily; his capacity for war, for science, and for civil affairs, was great; he preserved in public life uncompromising integrity and disinterestedness throughout a period when public morality was far more lax than it now is, and was endowed with that presence of mind and rapid decision in difficult or dangerous emergencies, which indicate a master spirit.

In his capacity as superintendent of the Woolwich Laboratory, he conferred important service on the country by altering and improving the manufacture of English gunpowder.

Some years later, when Lord Cornwallis became Lord-Lieutenant of Ireland, he pressed on Colonel Napier the Comptrollership of Army Accounts. "I want," his Lordship said, "an honest man, and this is the only thing I have been able to wrest from the harpies around me." Colonel Napier's labours in this office are faithfully recorded on his monumental slab in Redland chapel near Clifton.

> He restored the military accounts of Ireland to exact order, when years of neglect and corruption had plunged them into a confusion productive of great loss to the country, and great injustice to individuals. He recovered several millions of money for the public treasury, and by his probity and disinterestedness made his office a model for patriotic public servants; his first act was to abolish all fees, thus voluntarily reducing his own salary from many thousands to six hundred pounds *per annum*.

Colonel Napier refused more than once the representation of his

---

1. Lady L. Connolly was the wife of Colonel Connolly of Castletown, in the county of Kildare, and sister to Lady Sarah Napier, William Napier's mother.
2. Charles (Gen. Sir C. Napier, conqueror of Scinde); Emily (married to the late Gen. Sir Henry Bunbury); George (Gen. Sir G., Governor of Cape); William (Gen. Sir William, subject of this biography); Richard Napier, Esq., Q.C.); Henry, Capt. R.N. (author of *History of Florence*); Cecilia, and Caroline, died in youth. Besides these was Louisa, a daughter of Colonel Napier's by a former marriage.

county in the Irish parliament, which was secretly offered him, because factions were so violent and so corrupt that he could not hope without the influence of wealth to steer a proud and earnest course between oppressive power on the one hand and rebellious democracy on the other. And he was called "impracticable" by ephemeral politicians, just as afterwards the epithet was sometimes applied to his sons, because they scorned to bend their principles to their personal advantage.

At a later period we shall find his son William refusing a seat in the English parliament, which was more than once offered to him, from motives very similar to those which governed the decision of the father.

William Napier received his earliest school training as a day-scholar at a large grammar school in Celbridge. The master appears to have been a passionate ill-judging man; and the feeling of the great mass of the scholars, both from birth and on account of their religion—for they were mostly Roman Catholics—was essentially democratic; and this feeling was heightened by the state of Ireland, which was at that time fermenting with the heat of coming insurrection.

Charles Napier, William's eldest brother, organized his schoolfellows as a volunteer corps; and it is no small proof of the influence over his kind with which nature had so remarkably endowed him, that he succeeded in enrolling the scholars in support of a government which they had been taught to consider as the enemy and the oppressor of their faith. On the occasion of one of their drill-parades, William Napier, then a boy of eleven, being insubordinate under arms, was by order of his young commander tried by a drum-head court-martial and sentenced to some penalty to which the culprit would not submit. His brother Charles accordingly ordered in true Roman spirit, for he loved the offender devotedly, that he should be drummed out of the corps.

This was carried into effect, but in a disorderly manner with hooting; and when the mob closed on the young recusant, William—his fiery nature revolting against the insult—whirling a large bag of marbles like a sling, discharged them amid the crowd, and then, charging, broke the obnoxious drum, and forced his most prominent assailant, greatly his superior in age and size, to single combat. Although getting far the worst of it and badly hurt in the fight, William, still refusing to give in, was restored to the ranks by his brother for the pluck he had shown.

His youth had indeed fallen on troublous times. Previous to the outbreak of 1798, the soldiers too often ill-disciplined and brutal, and the yeomanry actuated by sectarian hatred, treated the poor Roman Catholic peasantry with extreme ferocity, and thus aggravated the evil they were intended to allay.

On the other hand, houses were nightly assailed by the disaffected in search of arms; and on both sides the fiercest passions were in full play.

During Colonel Napier's absence in England the younger children, of whom William was one, were left under the care of an old nurse, Susan Frost, at Celbridge House, where it was well known there was a collection of arms. One night several hundred "Defenders" surrounded the house and demanded that the arms should be given up to them. On the first alarm Susan Frost sent a maidservant by a back way to Castletown House for assistance, and collecting the children in one room, she herself stood at the door with a pair of loaded pistols, and in concert with an old manservant refused to deliver the arms or to admit the rioters, notwithstanding their threats of death to all within if they refused to yield. The "Defenders" fired constantly at the windows which they shattered with bullets; and at length procuring a heavy beam proceeded to batter the massive door, which was beginning to yield when the reinforcements summoned from Castletown arrived, and the assailants dispersed.

When the insurrection of 1798 broke out, many families took refuge in Dublin. The elder Napier would not do so. In that time of trouble and terror he fortified his house, armed his five sons,—the subject of this memoir being then twelve years old,—and offered an asylum to all who were willing to resist the insurgents. His house was never attacked, though often threatened; and finally the little garrison removed to Castletown, where Colonel Napier was, from his kinship and military knowledge, invested with the command; and here he remained, scouring the country with some of his sons at his side, constructing field-works for the defence of the neighbouring town, and often standing between the poor and the ferocity of the ill-disciplined soldiers who formed its garrison.

Educated amidst such events, William Napier's mind was early familiarized with scenes of trouble and danger; and the effects he witnessed of the oppression of a people by a dominant faction awakened him to questions of good government.

By nature tender as a woman, he recognised the weakness of every created thing as the strongest claim on his protection, and no doubt his intense natural hatred of oppression and injustice was aggravated by the peculiar horrors he was frequently called upon to witness, as the accessories of that bloody and terrible period. The following recollections of a sister have reference to the Celbridge schooling days.

His only schooling had been received at the village school of Celbridge, of which the pedagogue was a queer old man named Bagnal, who might have been a tolerable Latin scholar for anything I know to the contrary, but who was totally unfitted for the education of such boys as my dear brothers; at all events William learnt nothing from him. He spent much of his time with a vagabond called 'Scully the tailor,' who I dare say was an amusing companion, and something of a poacher, and they used to be out for hours together after some mischief or other. His next dearest friend, and that was a steady one, was the late Lady Londonderry, then a beautiful young married woman, who used to call him her son, delighted in all his scrapes, and always begged him off when my father was angry. She was not our relation, but her uncle[3] was my aunt's husband, and so we were like cousins; and she, who had wild spirits herself, thought us at twelve and fourteen pleasanter companions than the older people. She was a very clever woman too, and she always prophesied that 'her boy' would make a great figure somehow or other, though he did not mind his lessons better than she had done herself, and loved no reading except novels. In that she was, however, mistaken; for though he preferred romances and chivalry, of which Don Bellarmin of Greece was his especial favourite, he read everything he could lay his hands on; history, poetry, travels,—all were devoured with eagerness, and his memory, though not I think at that time very accurate, was unbounded and retentive to a very remarkable degree.

Conspicuous among his favourite subjects at this time were *Plutarch's Lives*, and these imbued him with that passionate admiration for the great men of antiquity which distinguished him through life, and had a signal effect in the formation of his character. During his last illness, when his bodily strength was so nearly exhausted that his medical attendants declared he could not live many hours, unless he could be kept from talking so that he might obtain some sleep, he has

---

3. Colonel Conolly.

talked to the writer of this *Life* for hours together of the great deeds of Caesar, Alexander, Hannibal, and of other heroes of antiquity, whose first acquaintance had been made by him in the enchanting pages of Plutarch.

One hero, not unworthy to be associated with those great names, he saw and conversed with frequently in these youthful days; but Captain Arthur Wellesley, in whom Colonel George Napier saw "the makings of a great general," was then generally considered "a shallow, saucy stripling."[4]

---

4. *Life of Sir C. Napier*, Vol. 1.

CHAPTER 2

Napier's Youth and Early Service

In June 1800, at the early age of fourteen, William Napier received his first commission in the Royal Irish Artillery, was soon after transferred to the 62nd Regiment, and reduced to half-pay by the treaty of Amiens in March 1802.

A few months afterwards his uncle the Duke of Richmond gave him a cornetcy in the Blues, and he joined the troop of Captain Robert Hill, Lord Hill's brother. During his short service in this regiment he composed a mock-heroic poem called the *Blueviad*, of which however the only record is in the statement of his friend Major Hopkins that Sir William frequently repeated passages to him while serving together in the 43rd Regiment.

While in the Blues, Sir John Moore, then forming his celebrated experimental brigade at Shorncliffe, proposed that he should take a Lieutenancy in the 52nd Regiment, at which young Napier caught eagerly; and Moore was so pleased by his readiness to relinquish the pleasures of London, the gay trappings of the household brigade, and fourteen shillings a day (the pay of a cornet in the Blues at that time), for the hard life of a real soldier and six shillings and sixpence a day, out of pure love of his profession and a desire to learn it in earnest, that he soon afterwards obtained a company for him in a West Indian regiment, got him removed thence into a battalion of the army of reserve, and finally fixed him in 1804 ninth captain of the 43rd Regiment, then forming part of Moore's own brigade.

The 43rd had previously been in a bad state of discipline; courts-martial, duels, and insubordination prevailed; some officers had been dismissed, and the regiment was placed under Sir John Moore to stop the mischief. The company to which young Napier succeeded was avowedly the worst in the regiment; the captain had been cashiered, the lieutenant who had charge of the company was about to quit the service, and there were bitter disputes between him and the men about their accounts. Napier was not yet nineteen years old; of the three subalterns under him, the youngest was old enough to be his father, and only one of them either knew his duty or was willing to do it In three months however it was generally allowed that, with the exception of Captain Lloyd,[1] of whom Sir W. Napier modestly said, "he was endowed with natural gifts to which I could lay no pretensions,"—the youthful captain was at least equal in the exercise of his command to any captain in the regiment, and that his company was in orderly conduct and zeal second to none.

The secret of this success is to be sought in the absorbing earnestness with which Napier threw himself into every pursuit, but more particularly into the duties of a profession for which he had an enthusiastic love; also in the high standard he fixed in his own mind as attainable by the private soldier. It is no exaggeration to say that he loved soldiers; his men saw that he did so, that he respected them, that he thought each of them capable of being a hero; they respected themselves in consequence, and the pages of their captain's glowing *History* prove that in many cases they were heroes.

In speaking of this company in after life Sir W. Napier said that it had always maintained its character, in evidence of which he stated the fact, among other circumstances, of its having been with that company that Captain Hopkins performed the brilliant exploit at Sabugal detailed in chapter 4, book 12, of Napier's *Peninsular War*. "I owed them much," he used to say; and his endeavour to pay his debt to them at times straitened his pecuniary resources.

Lady Sarah Napier appears to have inspired all her sons with uncommon veneration and love, and the correspondence between her and the boys when absent from home was constant The following letters refer to the period between the time of our hero joining the Irish artillery and his being appointed captain in the 43rd Regiment. His letters at this early period of his life, and indeed for some years afterwards, are, as regards writing, spelling, and expression, those of a very ill-taught schoolboy. They are here printed precisely and literally as written, in order that the reader may judge of the uncommon labour

---

1. One of Napier's earliest and dearest friends; he was killed in the Battle of the Nivelle, in 1813, when lieutenant-colonel commanding the 94th Regiment, and his character is drawn by the historian at the end of chap, 1, book 23 of the *History of the Peninsular War*.

and perseverance he must have devoted to repair his defective education, and to prepare himself for the task of writing a History, of which the style is universally admitted to be a model of force, eloquence, and correctness.

LETTER TO HIS MOTHER.
[*When 2nd Lieut. in the Royal Irish Artillery.—Age 15.*]
Dearest Mother   Cork Feb. 11th 1801.
I am extreemely mizierable at having made my father uneasy, but as you said you wished me to rite a long letter I thought it was better to wait till Colonel Hydes auction was over that I might send you an account of it. Diamond sold for 660 pounds. Despard is gone off in debt to every officer and every tradesman in Cork or Fermoy. I am very much obliged to Cecilia for her letter. Ought I to answer it or not for I dont know whether it requires an answer. Colonel Baird is better than anybody can expect.
   I am dearest Mother
    Your affect. Son
     W. Napier

The following letter was to his dearest friend Charles M'Leod; they were afterwards in the 43rd together, and his glorious death in the breach of Badajos, as related in the *History*, was the greatest sorrow which up to that time Napier had ever known.

TO CAPTAIN CHARLES M'LEOD.
[*Written while on half-pay.—Age 17.*]
My Dear Charles.   Castletown July 1803.
I am very sorry to hear that you have got into a kind of company from which I have so lately escaped, that is to say, Jockys gamesters and idlers that you have your own set apart from the other officers of the Accademy and that you have got a supercilious haughty manner to all the others, now consider the consequences of it, the Accademy is the Duke of Yorks Hobby horse and should General Jarry write to him that you did not learn anything your promotion is ruined forever, and for what—to be laughed at not only by the sensible men of the army but even by the very people whom you keep company with. You will not I am sure be displeased at what I say to you as it only comes from my friendship and from the knowledge which I have obtained by experience of the unhappiness which

it may hereafter occasion you; that you will profit by it is the wish of your

      Sincere and affectionate friend
      W. Napier.

TO HIS MOTHER.

[Just joined the Blues as Cornet—Age 17. Written after an illness.]

My Dearest Mother,   Canterbury December 8, 1803. Louisa will tell you that I am not low, but what people call as hearty as a buck and as hungry as a hawk she will likewise tell you the reason I was low last week Mr. George being the occation of it, I waited yesterday untill 6 o'clock for Lord Frederick and Boon[2] who were to have come down and see me I had soup a roast neck of mutton masht potatoes and a plumb pudding with a bottle of port a peece and Lo and behold they came not, if they come today they must have it cold as I cannot afford such a dinner every day, having seen the last of 28 guineas in my illness which were to have paid my mess bill for a fortnight about £13 my mess subscription £5.5 my fees to the riding master £5.5 and to pay my expenses for the month of November which as I would have left the mess it would very near have done.

I likewise owe an officer who lodged with me for 4 weeks £3.8 as when he left the lodgings they brought him the whole bill which he paid as I wanted money for my sickness my share coming to the above thus my dear Mother you see I am in debt without my fault £27 bating 2s. George will tell you that I even refused to hire a chaise though ordered by the Doctor untill he George desired me and said you or my father would not mind that expense as it was absolutely necessary for my health I went out 12 times which cost me 6 pound but that is all taken into the 28 guineas I must likewise make a present to my own and the officers servant who lodged with me as before I got my own he did everything for me he likewise sat up two nights with me and gave me my medecins he likewise taught my servant how to give them to me and how to clean my things, he got my coals and candles to when my servant was buisy about me otherwise I should have lost them.

My own servant sat up also two nights before I got a nurse and

---

2. A nickname for his brother Charles.

left his mess to be near me where he got a bad dinner every day about 8 o'clock and it cost him more a good deal than his mess, and I never expressed the slightest wish for anything that he did not instantly run as hard as he could to buy it for me dressed me and carried about into the chaise in short he was just as attached as Gerarty without any of his drunkenness and much quicker I trusted him also with my 28 guineas when he might easily have cheated me but the instant I was well he brought me a bill and reciept for every shilling he had laid out, pray write me word how much I ought to give each of them I am sure your eyes must be better you write so well and strait, pray give my love to Aunt and to my dear Emily and tell her I will write to her soon but you must frank me a large quantity of paper or else no letters as paper is very dear and very bad here as everything else is and likewise send me word who I am to put them under cover to, I hope the Duke of Richmond[3] is not displeased with my conduct, I have not written to him yet as I do not know what to say, nor what to call him Your Grace or My Lord or Uncle or Uncle Duke but if you will inform me and dictate the heads of a letter I will write it. My love to Dodeny and believe me

       Your tired son
       W. Napier

My dear Mother   Canterbury 9th December
I am increasing in stature and in strength as to wisdom and godliness I leave that to other people to talk of I walked between four and five mile this day without being the least tired I could even have walked as much more as the miles seem yards in proportion to the Irish ones, My wisdom comes next I have been bargaining for a poney for the time I am in the Regiment which an officer will sell me for 10 or £12 giving me saddle bridle horse cloth and collar along with him I can go for a whole day at a canter which is excellent exercise for me it costs me nothing feeding I am allowed forrage as for a large horse which is twice as much as he will eat, but I took care to say nothing about him untill another officer who likes him promised to buy him at the same price whenever I chose to sell him so that if you think I had better not have him send

---

3. The duke gave him his cornetcy.

me word directly, I have had the most affectionate letter from George with a present of £10 saying he was sorry he could not give me more and that as long as he had a guinea none of his brothers or sisters should want one as the only reason he cared for it was that he might have the pleasure of sharing it with us, I shall take care that I will not drink any wine at the 52nd mess until I am able to pay him for it is not fair he should lose by his generous disposition. &c. &c. W. N.

Canterbury
My Dearest Mother, December 12. 1803.
The first part of your letter will have been answered long before you read this, and before I answer the second I must put in a word of my own, I cannot have poney as the officer wont sell him now, so there's an end of He. Pray tell Emily that notwithstanding her *sneer* about not understanding such difficult things as to know whether a man was a good officer and so forth &c. General Moore says the same as me, for Capt. Campbell of the Royal Cns. says that at dinner one day talking of the Blues G. M. said there's a young man in them whom I am very anxious to get into the 52nd and he is so to, *for* as he wants to be made an *officer* of he of course does not wish *to stay in* the Blues. And if a man cannot learn to be an officer pray where does the fault lie?—in the head. Let *her* find out the head of what ——

Now for the second part, I am very sorry that you and my father had any uneasiness, occasioned by me, although I am at the same time very glad no fault of mine occasioned it, I am very much obliged to the Duke of Richmond and I shall certainly write to him the letter you told me whenever I receive an answer to my first letter, George wrote me word yesterday I would be in the *Gazzette* of today, I am very much obligded to General Moore for his kindness, Lord Frederick expects to get the Lieut-Colonelcy of the 52nd emidiately and George to get his Company but neither of them are certain.

Field Marshals being ignorant is not so odd, because I think they only make them so by way of putting them on the shelf without affronting them, and when once they are on the shelf of course they are moth eaten and their *Larning's* rub'd out. Mrs. Johnston has written me a letter in which she says George is a damned rascal for not writing her word I was ill at the beginning that she might have come down to nurse me and have written her word I am very much oblidged to *her* but very glad George did not write as I would always be called the man with the Aunt like the man of the face in *R. Cœur de Lion*. Charles is a lazy theif, I wrote to him a week ago to send or come himself with my 10 guineas and has neither sent it nor answered me the unatural villain; I am gaining strength every day give my love to everybody, and tell Richard to trudge to Mr. Boyce the bookseller and buy a Davis'es Grammer for me which must be sent along with my case of instruments when you send me the paper as I have stopped my french translations in order that I may have enough of this long paper to write letters to you, for (except a few sheets which must be kept for Lords and Dukes) other I have none neither can I get it here.[4]

    I am &c.
      W. Napier.

TO HIS FATHER.

My Dear Father,   Canterbury, Dec. 28, 1803.
I received your letter and the draft on the 26th; and if I can thank you by attention to my duty in the 52nd, I certainly will do everything I can to show you how much I am obliged to you. I think too that were I inclined to go wrong I could not in such a good regiment and along with George.

  Believe me, my dearest Father,
    Your affectionate Son,
      W. Napier.

TO HIS MOTHER.

[*Lieutenant in the 52nd.*]

      Folkstone, 21st March, 1804.
General Moore spoke to me yesterday about a letter Colonel Leith had written to him, in which he says he thinks I will be of use to him, from being in the 52nd, to help to form his battalion, and begs him to say so to the Duke of York. General Moore says I must know that from the little time I have been in the 52nd I cannot be of much use in forming a regiment, and therefore he will not say so to the Duke of York; but that, from

---

4. The imperfect spelling of the letters, which rapidly diminished although it never wholly disappeared, is henceforth corrected for the convenience of the reader.

what he has seen, and from Colonel MacKenzie's report of me, he thinks that I would be if I stayed five or six months longer in the regiment However, as a Company is not to be had every day, he will write everything to the Duke that he thinks will make him give it me. Thus you see that it is only from want of time, and not for want either of capacity or attention to my duty, that he does not do as Colonel Leith wants him.

Sir John Moore to Lady Sarah Napier.

Madam,   Sandgate, 12th May, 1804.
I am honoured with your ladyship's letter, which I should have acknowledged sooner, but the same reason which has led me to defer answering Colonel Napier's letter has induced me to delay to write to you. I mean the hope of being able to congratulate you on my young friend William's appointment to the Company in Colonel Leith's Reserve. I am however mortified to find that another person has been gazetted for the Company which Colonel Clinton in his letter promised should be given to your son. I cannot account for this seeming contradiction; but as I cannot think that either the Duke of York or Colonel Clinton are men to break their word, I conclude either that what we have seen in the *Gazette* is a mistake, or that the person appointed is so for the moment only, will speedily be removed, and William named in his stead. Under this impression I shall defer for some days to write to Colonel Clinton; in the meantime I should hope that Colonel Leith will notice it.

Your ladyship as well as Colonel Napier are kind enough to express your thanks to me much beyond what I am entitled to. There is little merit in wishing well to two such young men as your two sons, and if ever I have it in my power I shall be happy to serve them. I communicated to Colonel Mackenzie what you desired, and his answer was, he had never shown either of the Napiers any attention they did not merit: in short, there is but one sentiment about them; and if your ladyship had a dozen sons, you could not do Colonel Mackenzie or me a greater kindness than by sending them to the 52nd. I am much grieved to find the Colonel is so unwell. I beg to be kindly remembered to him.   I have the honour to remain

    Your ladyship's very faithful, obedient servant,
                                        John Moore.

To his Mother.

Folkstone, October 9. 1804.

I cannot say to you anything more about my father[5] than you know already, for I feel many things that I cannot express. I can only offer up my prayers to Heaven, and put my trust in that Being he has so often told me never deceives. To Him I now look up more than ever, for I find myself almost alone; when I leave this brigade
I shall probably be quite so. How I envy George! he looks round him and sees every officer truly a brother. He knows their friendship is worth having, and he knows he deserves it: I look,[6] and see hardly three men whom I would wish to call acquaintances, and they only because their manners are those of gentlemen, as I know too little of them to judge of anything else; in the others I see a set of mean shopboys, who are cunning fools, always busy, never doing anything of use, always on the watch to find out something in their brother officers that they may report and get them into scrapes, and thus show off their own zeal; narrow-minded people who do not consider that true greatness is to be marked from their own *good* conduct, not from comparison with the *bad* of their neighbours.
They are jealous of the 52nd, hate General Moore, abuse them behind their backs, yet toad-eat them to their faces. The greatest pleasure I have had since I came was, when General Moore was made a knight, to make them drink his health: my fingers itched to throw the bottles at their heads when they seemed to make difficulties about it; had they refused I would have by myself drank a bumper, broken the glass on the table, and left the mess immediately. My company was £30 in debt and wanted £16 worth of necessaries. I have paid their debt and given them the necessaries. This looks alarming, but the pay-master gave me the money, and I shall not (except by deaths or desertions) lose anything, as my father will explain to you.

The reader may find already in the foregoing pages proof of the warm—it may be said passionate admiration with which William Napier regarded Sir John Moore. He appears to have early distinguished

---

5. His father was in a dying state.
6. He means in his own regiment, the 43rd, which was, when he first joined it, in a very bad state of discipline.

the three Napier brothers from the crowd by which he was surrounded, attracted by their personal merits, for his acquaintance with their family was slight. Charles Napier was one of "*my majors*"—Stanhope being the other—to whom Sir J. Moore addressed the encouragement, "Well done, my majors," at Corunna: George Napier was his *aide-de-camp*; and his opinion of William has been given in his own words. His influence had a signal effect in forming and maturing their characters; and it is no small glory to have been the hero of these three men, while his early discovery of their mental and moral qualities is a proof of Moore's penetration and judgment of character.

The lofty disinterestedness and parity of his public conduct especially captivated the imagination of these young and ardent officers; and ample proof is afforded by the story of their lives that in this particular they emulated the model which they pre-eminently proposed to themselves for imitation.

Moore appears to have been not less remarkable for the imposing dignity of his outward presence and demeanour than for that of his invisible nature. "Where shall we find such a king?" are W. Napier's words in a letter to his mother some years later when speaking of the little Court by which Moore, like other generals, was surrounded. And the historian of the Peninsular War has cited one instance of the calm dignity with which Moore repelled a threat addressed to him by Lord Castlereagh of deprival of his command. Another instance equally forcible is given by the same writer in a notice of Sir John Moore's Life, published in the *Edinburgh Review*, where Moore, only a colonel in temporary command of the troops in Corsica, at the great risk of his professional advancement, withstood the naval commander-in-chief, a man of hasty overbearing temper and powerful influence, in his attempt to engage the land forces in an injudicious enterprise. Again, the influence which he obtained in the Councils of Palermo over the Royal family and Government, who were at first violently predisposed against him, is one among many examples of the power over men's minds with which he was gifted by nature.

Moore's character appears to have been a singular mixture of softness and severity. Attractive as few men could be towards those whom he distinguished by his regard, he so favoured only the good; for he was uncompromising in his open reprobation of all that was base, as well as in contempt of what was merely little. "The honest loved him, the dishonest feared him," as his youthful admirer wrote when he became his discriminating but always admiring historian.

And here let it be recorded that to Napier's affection for Sir John Moore the world is mainly indebted for the *History of the Peninsular War*; for, doubting seriously of his ability worthily to accomplish such a work, when strongly urged by his friend the late Lord Langdale to undertake it, he remained long in hesitation, and his scruples were finally overcome only by his burning desire to vindicate the memory of his beloved chieftain from the unjust aspersions with which it had been assailed. This fact was communicated to the author by Lady Napier after her husband's death, and the historian has besides left the record in his own handwriting, that when he, at length, determined to attempt the task, he limited his intentions to the narration of those operations which terminated at Corunna, and was only induced to proceed by the encouragement he derived from the success of the first volume.

The following letters from officers of the 43rd may serve to convey some idea of what William Napier was at this period.

EXTRACT OF LETTER FROM MAJOR HOPKINS.

At the period when I joined the 43rd as an ensign, Sir W. Napier was a captain in the regiment; and although I was not on terms of great intimacy with him, yet I could not be otherwise than flattered by such attentions from him as led me to suppose that his opinion of me was favourable; for in that day, under the system of Sir John Moore, the rank of captain was looked upon by the junior officers of the regiment as one of superiority and consequence; and the naturally polished, pleasing, gay manners of Captain Napier, his fine noble figure, beautiful features, and intelligent countenance, gave me the idea of one far superior to any person I had ever seen or imagined.

He was ever eager to excel in all feats of activity, joining and competing with the soldiers in all their sports—leaping, running, swimming, &c.,—delighted when victor. He was very fond of drawing, particularly the human figure, taking for his models the soldiers most remarkable for their strength and muscular figures. He read much at this time, surprising every one by the accuracy of his wonderful memory, particularly in what related to ancient history, military achievements, and the chivalry of romance and poetry,—entirely from English writers. His admiration for Napoleon and his campaigns was very great, studying them with his friend Lloyd by the best plans and maps.

He was often with Sir John Moore, with whom he appeared to be a great favourite. He felt pride in being considered an Irishman, was extremely partial to the country, but strongly prejudiced against Lord Castlereagh for his treatment of Ireland.

Herein is manifested the influence of the Celbridge training; and it will be remarked throughout the story of his life that his "prejudices," if they are to be called such, and his strongest feelings, were always ranged on the side of the weak against the strong.

Here follows a letter from another old 43rd officer. General Shaw Kennedy, one of the ablest and most distinguished of the officers who received their training in the schools of Moore and Wellington. The writer is the same Lieutenant Shaw whose remarkable coolness and daring at the storming of Badajos Napier has commemorated in his *History*.

Extracts of Letters from General Sir James Shaw Kennedy, K.C.B.

My acquaintance with Napier began at Hythe and Shorncliffe in 1805; and as I have been on terms of intimacy with him ever since, and seen him tried in situations of the greatest difficulty in war, in politics, in literature, and all the ordinary occurrences of life between man and man, I think I have grounds for forming an opinion of him. I assert without any qualification whatever, that I consider William Napier to have been the man of the greatest genius that I have ever known or communicated with personally; yet I have communicated and done business with many men of the highest reputation of their time that this country has produced. I once expressed this sentiment to Chantrey, who said that his genius and *perseverance* had quite astonished him.

Again:

His immensely high animal spirits when young seemed to render him quite wild, but this was only in appearance, for he had so completely the control over himself that I must quote him as about the purest character I have ever known: in my 55 years' acquaintance with him I have never known of him anything but purity, and the most high-minded and honourable bearing in all that he has said or done.

Again:

> When a young man, his manner and appearance would give a superficial observer the impression that he would have been ruled by his impulses. So far from this being the case, he was ruled, not only by the deepest sense of honour, but of the greatest purity. Nor from superficial observers did he by any means get credit for even a tithe of the talent he possessed, as the great buoyancy of his spirits was misconstrued.

> As an instance of his wonderful memory at this time, General Kennedy assured the writer that he has frequently known Napier take up the newspaper on its being brought into the mess-room, where he had been up to that moment joking and "larking" with the other officers, and, abstracting himself for half an hour, he would seem to devour its contents; and when he laid it down, he would not only be able to give the substance of the greatest part of the matter, but would actually repeat many long passages by heart He knew and could repeat the whole of Pope's translation of the *Iliad* and *Odyssey* word for word, with many other poems.

> In after years, when he was commencing his *History*, he frequently met, at General Kennedy's house in London, two of the ablest reviewers of the day, with whom he was accustomed to argue on the system and writings of the English philosophers; and, in support of his arguments, he would sometimes repeat long passages from their writings, with all of which he appeared thoroughly familiar, from Lord Bacon down to Adam Smith and Dugald Stewart His opponents afterwards told General Kennedy that they were amazed by the extent of his knowledge, and particularly by his wonderful memory.

> He appears indeed to have excelled in all he attempted. Among his other acquirements, he was a first-rate billiard-player and very fond of the game; but he gave it up entirely from the fear that it might become too engrossing.

> Here let us pause a while to reproduce the outward image of the man as he appeared to the eyes of his fellow men in the old 43rd days, when he was between eighteen and twenty years of age, and before he knew those terrible realities which are signified by the words disease and pain, which during the rest of his life so fearfully dominated his body, though they never had any power over his spirits

> In appearance William Napier was one of the handsomest men of his time. Six feet high, formed in the most powerful mould it is pos-

sible to conceive as compatible with extraordinary grace and activity. He was able to jump six feet in height. The head of an Antinous covered with short clustering black curls—the square brow, both wide and high—the aquiline nose—the firm mouth and the square massive jaw, indicating indomitable firmness and resolution—the eye of that remarkable bluish grey, so terrible in anger, so melting in tenderness, so sparkling in fun. In his youth his head and face might have served for a portrait of the war god. In his latest years, with milk-white hair and beard, his appearance was that of a Jupiter.

Here was his visible image. Now for his demeanour.

Quite wild with animal spirits and strong health; brimming over with fun; joking with his comrades; racing, jumping, swimming with his men; studying Napoleon's campaigns with his friend Lloyd; poring over the lives of real and fictitious heroes, and the writings of ancient and modern philosophers, and astonishing all by his wonderful memory; raging like a lion at any story of oppression; melting in pity over any tale of misfortune; with a fondness for animals amounting almost to a passion, and delighting to observe individualities of character even in a bird or a kitten;—this strong, tender, beautiful, and gifted man, surrounded by so many temptations, passionately admiring beauty in women, and with every attribute of success, was yet never known to have been otherwise than pure in thought and deed by comrades who lived with him in all the intimacy of a barrack life; and this, too, at a time when society was far more indulgent to certain transgressions than it now is. It is a beautiful and noble picture.

It was at this period of his life that William Napier made the acquaintance of Mr. Pitt, then prime minister; and he has left the following graphic and interesting account of his intercourse with the great statesman:—

In 1804, being then near nineteen, and having been a brother officer of Charles Stanhope Mr. Pitt's nephew, I was through him invited to pass some, time at Putney, in Mr. Pitt's house. Arriving rather late, the great man was at dinner when I entered the room; he immediately rose, and giving me both hands, welcomed me with such a gentle good nature, that I instantly felt—not at ease, for I was not at that time much troubled with what is called *mauvaise honte*, but—that I had a friend before me with whom I might instantly become familiar to any extent within the bounds of good breeding. Lady Hester Stanhope also treated me with the most winning kindness.

All this produced a strange sensation; for I came determined to hold fast by my patriotism though in presence of a wicked minister, however polite or condescending he might be found. Brought up amidst Whigs, and used to hear Mr. Pitt abused with all the virulence of Whigs, I looked upon him as an enemy of all good government; and my father, though not a Whig, had always condemned his war with France as an iniquitous and pernicious measure. Thus primed with fierce recollections and patriotic resolves, I endeavoured to sustain my mind's hatred against the minister, but in vain; all feelings sunk, except those of surprise and gratification, at finding such a gentle, good-natured, agreeable, and entertaining companion. I say companion deliberately, and with a right, as will be seen from what follows.

Lady Hester moreover was very attractive; so rapid and decided was her conversation, so full of humour and keen observation, and withal so friendly and instructive, that it was quite impossible not to fall at once into her direction and become her slave, whether for laughter or seriousness. She was not certainly beautiful, but her tall commanding figure, her large dark eyes, and variety of expression, changing as rapidly as her conversation, and equally vehement, kept the mind in continual admiration. She had not much respect for the political coadjutors of Mr. Pitt Lord Castlereagh she always called 'His monotonous lordship,' and Lord Liverpool was a constant theme of ridicule. Thus, speaking of a design at that time entertained of conferring military decorations, she told me that it had been agreed to by Mr. Pitt, but was stopped by the meddling of Lord Liverpool, who insisted on being a co-partner with her in choosing the colour and texture of the ribbons. *That*, she said, she thought, as a young woman, she might have been allowed to settle; but Lord Liverpool, being an old woman, was jealous, and sent her four thousand yards—she positively affirmed that—four thousand yards of different ribbons at the expense of the public, which he proposed to examine in conjunction with her for the purpose of fixing on the most suitable. She sent them back with her compliments, saying she declined the concert, and could see no use whatever for the ribbons, except to make braces for supporting his lordship's culottes, which she had observed were always weighed down by the heavy official papers in his pockets. This stopped all further progress in the plan for military decorations.

Of Sir John Moore she always spoke with admiration, and said Mr. Pitt had a like admiration for him; that he never received even a common note from him at Deal without showing it to his company and pointing out the grace and felicity of the expressions.

Mr. Pitt used to come home to dinner rather exhausted, and seemed to require wine, port, of which he generally drank a bottle, or nearly so, in a rapid succession of glasses; but when he recovered his strength from this stimulant he ceased to drink. His conversation with us was always gay, good-natured, and humorous, telling all sorts of amusing stories; some of them about the colonel of the —— regiment, General ——, who was certainly a very comical character, of which two of Mr. Pitt's stories will give ample proof. The first was that, in the midst of the fears of a French invasion. General —— sent an extraordinary express with a parcel supposed to contain important news, but which turned out to be the night-cap of a member of the Government, who had left it behind when on a visit to the General The second was also an express story; being a despatch from ——, when he commanded on the south coast, telling Mr. Pitt that '*two* French ships were actually then landing troops in *three* places.'

Mr. Pitt liked practical fun, and used to riot in it with Lady Hester, Charles and James Stanhope, and myself; and one instance is worth noticing. We were resolved to blacken his face with burnt cork, which he most strenuously resisted, but at the beginning of the fray a servant announced that Lords Castlereagh and Liverpool desired to see him on business. 'Let them wait in the other room,' was the answer; and the great minister instantly turned to the battle, catching up a cushion and belabouring us with it in glorious fun.

We were however too many and strong for him, and, after at least a ten minutes' fight, got him down and were actually daubing his face, when with a look of pretended confidence in his prowess he said, 'Stop, this will do; I could easily beat you all, but we must not keep those grandees waiting any longer.' His defeat was however palpable, and we were obliged to get a towel and basin of water to wash him clean before he could receive the *grandees*. Being thus put in order, the basin was hid behind the sofa, and the two lords were ushered in. Then a new phase of Mr. Pitt's manner appeared, to my great surprise and admiration. Lord Liverpool's look and manner are well known—melancholy, bending, nervous.

Lord Castlereagh I had known from my childhood, had often been engaged with him in athletic sports, pitching the stone or bar, and looked upon him as what indeed he was, a model of quiet grace and strength combined. What was my surprise to see both him and Lord Liverpool bending like spaniels on approaching the man we had just been maltreating with such successful, insolence of fun I but instantly Mr. Pitt's change of manner and look entirely fixed my attention. His tall, ungainly, bony figure seemed to grow to the ceiling, his head was thrown back, his eyes fixed immovably in one position, as if reading the heavens, and totally regardless of the bending figures near him. For some time they spoke; he made now and then some short observation, and finally, with an abrupt stiff inclination of the body, but without casting his eyes down, dismissed them. Then, turning to us with a laugh, caught up his cushions and renewed our fight

Another phase of his countenance I had yet to learn. Sometime after my visit, which was twice renewed at Putney, I was walking across the parade-ground of the Horse Guards, where I saw Mr. Pitt talking to several gentlemen evidently upon business which interested him. I caught his eye while some forty yards from him; he gave a smile and nod of recognition, and I was advancing to greet him: instantly his countenance changed with a commanding fierceness of expression difficult to describe, but it emphatically spoke, even at that distance: 'Pass on, this is no place for fooling,' was the meaning, and not to be mistaken.

I had often been in Mr. Fox's company, not only when he was on a visit at my father's house in Clifton, but afterwards at his own house, or rather the Duke of York's house, then standing on the present site of Stafford House. His manners were totally different from Mr. Pitt's, always agreeable, gentle, kind, and good-natured, but not attractive to young people, inasmuch as he did not seem to take much interest in them, and rather to bear with than to like them; at least, such was the impression he made on me. Whereas Mr. Pitt's manner was that of joyous hilarity and delight at being able to unbend his mind, as it were, when he could do it safely: he was very attractive.

The affectionate regard for Lady Hester Stanhope which William Napier contracted in those early years, he preserved throughout the life of that remarkable woman, as he proved by coming forward warmly in her defence when, many years later, she was coarsely assailed and misrepresented in the newspapers.

CHAPTER 3

The Peninsula

When the great volunteering from the militia to the line took place, William Napier was selected to procure volunteers from regiments in Ireland; and this duty was at that time not unattended either with danger or expense. For the travelling allowance was insufficient to cover the charges; and as he had nothing beyond his pay, he was thrown into difficulties and forced to borrow money, the repayment of which cost him many privations. The danger consisted in this, that there was a great race for appointments to the regular army among the militia officers, who were promised commissions if they brought with them a certain number of volunteers for the line. Those officers naturally regarded anyone who deprived them of men as an opponent, and indeed in many cases as a personal enemy; and as many of them were very illiterate and vulgar men, it was difficult to avoid duels.

Napier had serious official disputes, too, with a few of the superior officers, but the most difficult matter was to avoid duels with the subalterns. And this was not the only danger incurred in the performance of this invidious duty; for knowing how much soldiers are taken by the display of feats of strength and activity, and being remarkably strong and active, he was constantly engaging in such feats, and in one of these he broke two of his ribs. On one of these occasions he jumped clear over two cows, placed side by side, in the street of Ballina, having been dared to perform the feat by Kitty ———, a famous beauty of the neighbourhood.

The story was told his son-in-law by Colonel Knox Gore, who had it from an eyewitness. He extricated himself, however, adroitly from his recruiting troubles, and with remarkable success in obtaining recruits; and notwithstanding that the official differences with some of the superior officers referred to were pushed to his disadvantage, his zeal and activity gained the approval and support of the different general officers who commanded in the garrisons, three of whom he has recorded gratefully by name; *viz.* General Dunne, General John Mitchell, and General Payne of the cavalry.

In 1807 he served with his regiment in that operation of most deplorable expediency, the Copenhagen expedition; was present at the siege of that capital; and afterwards marched under Sir Arthur Wellesley to attack the Danish levies assembled in the rear of the besieging force. He was detached under command of the German general ——, was engaged with his part of the troops at the Battle of Kioge, and followed that general in his pursuit of the beaten enemy. He has left some curious records of German habits on this occasion.

"The general," he writes, "asked an old grey-haired peasant which way his countrymen had fled. The old man proudly answered he would not tell; and —— immediately made his orderly shoot him dead. His brigade-major had in my hearing two days before ordered Major McLeod to shoot all the peasants he met with; but he pronounced it pheasants, and McLeod laughingly promised that he would certainly obey that order. I saw General —— in his uniform groping in a common sewer for money, and I ordered a soldier of my own, named Peter Hayes, whom the general had called to aid him, to quit such an infamous work and behave like a soldier.

"The general afterwards performed a very indecent and cruel act, and finished by rearing in person a ladder against the church to enable his men to rob the place. It was then that, unable to bear the disgrace any longer, and my company being then the only British force with General ——, I desired to be allowed to join my regiment. This was granted; but eight waggons loaded with captured arms, and two loaded in the most unsafe manner with powder in open barrels loosely covered with straw, were, together with nearly 400 prisoners, placed under my escort to convey to the army.

"I received no route, no instructions; I was not even informed that two of these waggons contained these barrels of loose powder; no rations were given to the men, and no authority was given me to draw them from the country. And I was to find my way through the disturbed districts without knowing where Sir A. Wellesley was. Guiding my movements by the steeples, I made a march of three days, lodging my prisoners at night in the churches, and keeping under arms with my whole company in the churchyards. I obtained rations for the prisoners by requisition on the villages, and in this manner I reached the army without the loss of a prisoner, if I except some women, who had been taken, I fear, for a shameful purpose, but delivered to me as prisoners of war! I thought it scandalous to carry them through the country and to shut them up at night with the men, and therefore left them in the first village I halted at.

"During this march and previous to it, my company never took so much as a cherry from a bough, though the country was covered with that fruit-tree, and not a man plundered or misbehaved, although General —— called upon them to join his Germans in the disgraceful scenes that were enacted. I mention these facts, the truth of which I vouch upon my honour as a gentleman, with the less repugnance now, because at the time I did, at the risk of my commission, tell General —— my opinion of his conduct when he was encouraging my men to plunder; and because the 43rd Regiment was falsely and injuriously reported by him to have committed the outrages which his own Germans perpetrated under his eyes and with his approbation; nay, more, with his personal assistance."

The following extract from a letter written by Major Hopkins has reference to this expedition:—

> During our march through Zealand to meet the Danish troops assembled at Kioge, I remember Napier's extreme anxiety to preserve the strictest discipline amongst our men, and to prevent the ill usage and plundering of the inhabitants. He broke out in great indignation on witnessing the conduct of the officers of a German regiment, who were helping themselves most freely to the property in a house which they had entered during a halt in our march. His humanity was continually exerted, not only in favour of our own wounded, but also for those of the Danes. The Danish general had very foolishly placed many of his advanced skirmishers on the high branches of trees in a wood through which we had to advance to attack the main body of the Danes. In their position in the trees they only served as a mark for our soldiers to wound and bring them down, but Napier, pitying their helpless and cruel situation, would not allow his men to fire upon them.
>
> On the return of the 43rd from Denmark the regiment was quartered at Maldon, where the young captain became a great favourite among the neighbouring gentry, and where he was foremost in schemes of fun and mischief. Being on the committee of manage-

ment of a ball given to the inhabitants, he undertook to adorn the floor of the dancing-room, which he executed in beautiful devices of coloured chalks of Cupids on rosebuds, designed by himself and surrounded with borders *à la Grecque*, These were much admired by the company until the dancing commenced, but then, the artist having been ignorant of the necessity of mixing *size* with the chalks, such clouds of coloured dust filled the air that the room was obliged to be cleared of the dancers, in order that the offending Cupids might be swept away.

Young Napier was also the leader in a freak which at one time threatened serious consequences. He and some of his brother officers entered a lecture-room at Maldon masked and disguised. The lecturer had given offence to some of them by, as it was supposed, purposely sprinkling them with water at a previous lecture; and he now excited the audience to attack the intruders. A disturbance ensued, and the town was divided into two parties, one favourable, the other hostile, to the military.

The hostile party, the lecturer at its head, endeavoured to procure the committal of the offenders under the 'Black Act;'[1] it was ultimately accommodated, and the officers were quit at the expense of their pockets, and in Napier's case at the additional cost of the severely expressed displeasure of Sir John Moore, who was very angry. He spoke only as a private friend, not having any official authority in the matter.

The following letters to his mother refer to the foregoing period.

My Dearest Mother,   Hythe, July 6, 1805.
I have been very busy about my accounts and company, otherwise I would have answered your letter before; besides, until I knew more about my accounts I could not answer your questions properly—now I can.
In the first place, I cannot help laughing at the way you first accused, then tried, at last condemned me for a crime I never committed nor had the least intention to commit I stayed in London to wait for George, in order that, as you told me he wanted to remain there, I might take charge of his party[2] for him (by my going to Holyhead I missed him completely); he

---

1. The "Black Act" was an Act of Parliament which was in force at the time, directed against highwaymen.
2. They were both returning from raising recruits in Ireland.

came not, so I went to Hythe, told General Moore what I had done; he said all was perfectly right. When I was in London I had more invitations than I could accept if I had stayed twice as long, therefore I had only to pay for my lodgings: thus you see I was neither extravagant nor stayed from my regiment when I ought not; besides, had I wanted to be extravagant, where was the money to be got? I cannot tell.

When I came first here my accounts frightened me; I thought I should not be able to clear myself for less than three hundred pounds. I have been used infamously by the (*illegible*), more as if they wished to ruin me at any rate than anything else. However, I have on examining more closely and by Government allowing us our expenses found that 60*l*. will make me free of the world and its inhabitants, 37*l*. of this being paid by the Company, being the amount of their debt to me. God bless you, my dear mother.

     W. Napier.

           Hythe, January 1807.

I had intended to answer your letter in person, but I have unfortunately had my room robbed of my jacket and three guineas, the sum I had intended for my passage. I think there is no chance of an expedition, from the accounts we have received of the Russians being totally defeated by the French. There is a subaltern of mine whom I wish to serve if I could, and his brother, who is now an officer in the York militia, wishes to get an ensigncy in this: if you could by any means get one in this regiment, or point out the way, I would be very glad of it, for to tell the truth I do not see how I can do without you show me the way.

Some of your friends might perhaps be able, particularly as Lord Dundas will recommend him as an excellent young man. His brother would have applied to him to get one for him, but he has no other dependence in the world for himself, and he is afraid of asking too much; this is fair because he is an elderly man(!), and therefore has less chance of getting on without interest than his brother of the militia, who is a boy of 18. In case you could not get one in the 43rd, you might in the 35th, as the Duke would probably be glad of a young man of good character. &c. &c.

Hythe. One o'clock in the morning.
I have these three days back expected the route to embark, but have been so often disappointed I did not like to flurry you with the news, but the Wolf is come at last, this moment arrived, to march in four hours; where I have not heard yet, but it must be Deal I think I can do without drawing on you,—at any rate I shall only want ten pounds if I do draw. God bless you, my dearest mother. &c. &c.

Ramsgate, Tuesday.
We this moment embark. You will, I know, excuse my brevity when I tell you that our Colonels seem to vie with the transport masters and ministers who can make most confusion, even on our own shores: some of the men faint for want of food, my last sixpence is gone to them; and the second Colonel took both my bugles to make a band on board the headquarter ship. Heaven bless their bodies, their heads can't be hurt. &c. &c. Postscript (overleaf).
I think the other side is not as it ought to be, my dear mother, but I have only time to tell you that I love you dearly, and always will be your
Affectionate son,
W. Napier.

At sea near Lisbon, June 25, 1807.
We have just been spoke by the frigate to tell us that we might send letters tomorrow, so that I can tell you I am well; so is George, for I just hailed him this instant. We have had an excellent passage. Tell Charles that I got his letter at Yarmouth in the Isle of Wight, and could not answer it. I did not nor will I propose a subscription about the plate; for although there are many excellent good men in our regiment who would willingly do it, yet by what I saw when I sounded them there would be an opposition to it; and as I conceive it would be a mark of honour granted to them to be allowed to subscribe, I would not subject anything connected with him[3] to a refusal, or allow the propriety of it to be discussed by a parcel of interested gamblers or extravagant ensigns. For my own part, if Colonel —— proposes it, his rank may carry it, and I of course shall subscribe, otherwise I shall apply to the 52nd to let my name go in with

---

3. Probably Sir John Moore.

their regiment.

We left the Isle of Wight the day before Lord Grantham was to have come down. I was sorry not to have seen him, I like him much. George of course will tell you the news, and as it is of little interest I shall not tell it you, but I must have long details of the battles[4] in Germany after the bridges were rebuilt God bless you, my dear mother. &c. &c.

Uteralaugh, August 19, 1807.

We are now before Copenhagen, at the distance of one mile and a half, where we arrived without opposition; we have been here three days. We have had some trifling skirmishing on the outposts, taken some prisoners, and killed about 50 I believe, with the loss of an officer of artillery and no men. Tonight we begin to dig the approaches, as it is intended to be a regular siege. Henry[5] I saw at Elsineur roads. Some of our Generals have dreadful thick skulls, for I never saw any fair in Ireland so confused as the landing: had they opposed us, the *remains* of the army would have been on their way to England.

The country people are like the Irish—give the soldiers everything they want, and in return are plundered and abused, for which we hang and flog the soldiers every day. British soldiers fight well, but are the greatest scoundrels possible. I shall write again soon, but I have not been in bed or off my legs for four days and nights, and my eyes are so heavy I can hardly see to write. We are now in cantonments (at first we lay in the fields), but there is an alarm every hour, which murders sleep, besides the out pickets, which last twenty-four hours at a time. I do not know how you can direct to me. Neither the King or Crown Prince are at Copenhagen, and the Danes have few troops, and those bad. &c. &c.

To Major Charles Napier.

My Dear Charles, Roeskilde, Sept 2, 1807.

The account of our operations is short, being a compound of stupidity, vanity, and villainy. We stayed eight days off Elsineur without landing; at last landed at Webek in the greatest confusion; marched in two days to Copenhagen, at which time we might have gone straight into the town, they having only 3000

---

4. Battles of Eylau and Friedland.
5. His brother, a midshipman.

regulars in the town or in the island; remained in villages ten days, in which time we erected one battery that on trial was found not to answer, being too great a range; on the eleventh day a sortie was made by the garrison, when the Germans, Rifles, and ours drove them in in about five minutes—they are the greatest cowards I ever beheld. On the twelfth day 6000 troops were sent under the command of Sir Arthur Wellesley in two divisions, five companies of ours with each.

The German General L—— went with the second to disperse the levy *en masse* collected near Roeskilde, and commanded by regular officers. We hunted them for four days; on the 5th Sir A. Wellesley fell in with them to the amount of 9000 near Kioge; fired one volley; the 92nd charged and they ran in every direction. Our five companies were upon the right flank, and were not within shot; the other division, with which I was, ought to have been in their rear and made the whole prisoners, but by General L—— halting where he had no business we were too late, and merely had what they call a gallant action, but which I call a murder of some poor runaways who did not intend to resist

The number of prisoners and the killed are correct, but all the nonsense that you will see in the *Gazette* is no more than what I tell you. You may probably see my company put down as missing; everything was in such concision that the other four companies lost their way and joined Sir Arthur's division and returned me missing. I stayed with my own General, and did the same by them. They have now, I understand, collected 5000 or 6000 more, and we are to have another hunt after them in a day or two. It is damned easy to be a General—no disparagement to the big wigs. I understand they have now erected 63 mortars with which they are bombarding the town, in which case they will have it in three or four days, and then all is over. I fancy plunder is the order of the day, and the Germans add murder to it.

To his Mother.

Roeskilde, October 1.

I received your two letters, but you must not be surprised that do not write often, as we are in the interior and not always able to procure paper. You will have seen by the letter I wrote to

Charles that I did fight a battle, such as it was. People say here we are to winter in the island. Reports fly as thick as the Generals' skulls. Copenhagen is extremely like Cork, which you know as much about as you do of Pekin; however, there is a very fine collection of pictures in it, and *seven millions worth of French property*, which our clever Generals contrived to have put down as private property in the capitulation, and great quantities of prize money, which I don't believe we shall get. Henry was gone to England before your letter came. Tell the Duke of Cumberland that we are the *reserve*; that is, men reserved for the most dangerous service.

I saw General Spencer, and gave him the Duke's letter, and I never met with so much real civility in so short a time from anybody. &c. &c.

Gravesend, 9th Nov. 1807.

As I did not know exactly when I landed whether you were at Goodwood or London, nor do I know now, I wrote to Charles desiring him to write to you of my arrival; but neither seeing him or hearing from him in answer, made me imagine that the letters must have failed. I write to you at hazard of its reaching you. We are now on our march to Ipswich barrack, being in number, two companies parted from the regiment in a gale of wind off Yarmouth.

I expect three hundred pounds prize money; people tell me I shall get six hundred; I am not sanguine myself.

When I arrive at Ipswich I intend to write a journal of my warfare, interspersed with witty anecdotes, sound remarks, and severe military criticisms, interspersed with moral and political reflections, to be dedicated to the Right Honourable Lady Sarah Napier. &c. &c.

Ipswich. Nov. 15. 1807.

I am extremely surprised at your account of our marauding, but what puzzles me most is that you seem to have heard something particular about my company, and talk as if some of them had been hanged. All I can say is, that our regiment did plunder now and then, particularly at the beginning, but certainly less than most; but unfortunately the 43rd officers considered it their duty to punish the men that did it, and the other regiments passed it over in silence, by which means all the mischief they did was placed to our account also. The Germans, being foreigners, and therefore incapable of plundering, were taken under Lord Cathcart's particular protection, and extolled at the expense of the British; but I can assure you, from sad experience, that from the General L —— of the Germans down to the smallest drumboy in the Legion, the earth never groaned with such a set of infamous murdering villains, and that being highly *laudable*, Lord Cathcart returned them thanks for their conduct .... &c.

(No date.)

The post not going out on Saturday, and a review the next day, prevented me from acknowledging your letter with the 5*l*. note, for which I am much obliged to you. Charles says true when he says I got large allowances, and I am in excellent circumstances, as I have near 20*l*. in circulation among the officers, who will pay me when they come from leave; this I lent to them at Zealand. *Your letters are burnt*, I think I shall get leave on the 24th. &c. &c.

Maldon, Dec. 18, 1807.

I wrote to you some days ago, and directed it to Midhurst, where it probably is. Henry I believe is wrong, as we expect six or seven hundred pounds, but nobody can tell what it will be; indeed, some people say they intend not to give anything. This I think they would be afraid to try, because it would not be very safe to discontent 30,000 soldiers and twenty-six sail of the line.

I should like to go to High Wycombe[6] very much, for the sake of the French, drawing, and German masters, and also because all the Quartermaster-Generals, &c., are taken from High Wycombe, and there are so many of them that very few are of use on an expedition, and by these means get leave to gallop about where they choose; and I have seen enough service to know that is the best way of acquiring knowledge. Also you learn how to write a despatch, which is the grand *arcana* of a general, fighting having little to do with it. But I would like to know three things first before I went there, *viz.*—

1st If it will prevent me from going with my regiment on an expedition if it is ordered.

---

6. The staff school of the day.

2nd. If I may leave it when I choose (if I find it does not answer the intended purpose of instruction) without incurring the displeasure of the Commander-in-Chief.

And 3rd. If I have to procure a whole kit of new uniform. &c. &c.

Maldon, June 1808.

I have not answered you before in hopes of being able to get leave, but the answer I received on applying was that no officer could get leave without assigning a reason, which reason must be given in writing to the War Office, and consequently I could not get it, as my reason, besides its being improper to give in at that place, would not be considered sufficient; but, however, it is not of so much consequence as you might think (although I know it is a loss not to have Mr. Arnold's advice upon any subject, and I am particularly obliged to him for his very kind offer), because I have placed the management of the business in a Mr. Hall's hands at his own request

Now Mr. Hall is a gentleman of large property, who has been a magistrate in the county for ten years, very much respected, very clever, and the reason of his taking so much interest in the business is that his son and nephew are both in our regiment, and for some reason or other he considers that I had obliged his son particularly, so that be adds to his natural eagerness, which is very great on every subject which he enters into, an interest in the officers of his son's regiment. I believe Mr. Arnold is mistaken about its being tried in Westminster Hall, for although I know it is removed into the King's Bench, yet I am pretty certain that it will be tried at the County Assizes in August next, particularly as the indictment is for a *riot*, and not an assault I have retained Garrow, Pooley, and Trower for my defence, and Garrow alone for my action which I am going to bring against the opposite party in conjunction with the other officers who are engaged with me.

The circumstances of the case I cannot detail to you on paper well, but the heads of it are as follows. I was asked by some ladies and gentlemen of Maldon at a party to engage in a plan to amuse them, to which I consented on hearing that it was only to dress myself in an odd manner, and to attend a lecture of a foolish, pert, prating animal who had come down to this town as a lecturer. I had never been to these lectures, and therefore did not know who went there, nor what kind of meeting it was; but I thought, as I was told, that many of the townspeople would be in the same dresses, and that we were only to look grave and not to engage in any disturbance; indeed that was entirely out of all our minds.

Our dresses were that of *Dr. Pangloss,* an *hostler,* a *countryman,* and a *Quaker.* However, we had no sooner arrived, and actually before more than two of us had got into the room, before we had spoken a word, above 20 people attacked us with sticks, gave me so violent a blow with a stick that it stunned me and made the blood run from my nose and ears, and knocked down and beat my companions; by (I believe) the interference of some gentlemen in the room, they stopped for some moments beating us, at which time I recovered my senses, and, seeing a man in the crowd whose figure I thought was that of the man who had struck me, I went up to him and asked if he was the person: he answered with a sneer that he *believed* it was him, upon which I knocked him down, and the rest of the crowd attacked us again, and threw us downstairs.

At the bottom of the stairs we found, after we had recovered ourselves, five or six officers who had come there hearing the noise, and with their assistance, and that of three sergeants who had come by at the time, we beat these people out of the room where they were assembled; but you must know that we did not attack them without further provocation the second time; for we merely went into the room, and they a second time began the affray by telling an officer who was in his uniform, and not engaged in the first row nor even present, that they would throw him over a table which was in the room, without any provocation on his part, whereupon he knocked the first man down who said so to him.

Two days after this we were all arrested for a felony under the Black Act; and although we offered unexceptionable bail, it was refused, and we were kept in custody from Saturday until Monday, when on a meeting of magistrates we were released on giving bail and being bound over to the Sessions. 'The clergyman of the parish is one of my bail, and all the magistrates of the county, *except* those who committed us, are indignant at the way we have been treated. The opposite party have twice endeavoured to compromise the business, but as they were not sufficiently humble I refused to have anything to say to them, and I would rather be imprisoned than give way to them after the way they have treated us. Besides, we have not only numbers but respectability in our favour, and party runs so high that our side have written to one of the *members* that if he took any part against us he would lose his election the next time he set up. I confess to you that it is better it had not happened, but it has been carried tod far by the opposite party, and if I can make them smart for it I will do it &c. &c.

To Lady Louisa Conolly.

My Dear Aunt,   Colchester, June 17, 1808.
I am extremely obliged to you for your letter, although I cannot let the affair drop in the manner which that person proposes to you, and indeed, if I was willing to do so, the other officers would not be so. My reasons for this are as follows. In the first place, their conduct to us was infamous and public, and were we to drop it in that equal manner we should be supposed guilty of shameful conduct, more particularly as they published their account of it in the papers; in the next place, the people of Maldon, who have espoused our cause, have pledged themselves so far that we should quarrel with them were we to draw back; and thirdly, I think that having a good cause it is an opportunity that should not be lost of proving to the people of England (what they are not at all convinced of at present) that officers have means of redress (when they are injured) by having recourse to law; besides which, my dear aunt, I (believe you do not know that they kept us in custody under the care of constables for three days under a warrant for felony, which if they could have proved would have hanged every one of us, and that they boasted publicly that we would be hung. Finding however that could not be proved, they changed it into a riot, and now, being frightened, they want to make it up on even terms, for this is the third proposition they have made to us, every time coming down in their demands.

I am very much distressed to hear the bad account of Cecilia, and I do not know what to say to my mother when I write to her, for as I do not know in what state she is I cannot say anything to comfort her, and I am afraid of saying anything to the contrary. But I hope that the good advice that she has will cause an amendment in a little time; indeed I can hardly bring myself to suppose that she is dangerously ill, for I feel that I should be so miserable, both from the loss of her whom I love so much and the misery it would cause my mother and every one of us, that I am afraid to think of its being possible.

your very affectionate nephew,
W. Napier.

My dear Mother,   Colchester. July 1808.
I have not heard a word from you about Cecilia since I came here. I hope you got my last letter, and that she is so much better that you do not think it necessary to write.

I cannot tell yet whether we are to embark or not, as we have been countermanded for some time, I *suppose* to belong to Lord Chatham's division, or some other man who delights in having handsome showy *guards* for himself, and to take the credit of making the regiment to himself, and consequently ask for all the promotion that ought to go in it for *his* friends. We have now been for five years considered as the *best* regiment in England, and the reward is to put everybody they could think of over the heads of our officers, and to finish it all they are now going to give a Lieut-Colonelcy in the regiment to some friend of Colonel ——, whose neck may the Lord break! and in order to make room for him they send the Major, whose claims they could not get over, into another regiment, notwithstanding he is an excellent officer, and has been 20 years in this regiment, by which you will perceive, my dear mother, that the worst regiment I could possibly have got into is the 43rd, and that I never can have any chance of promotion or real service in it &c &c.

In 1808 Captain Napier went with his regiment to Spain, and bore more than his share of the hardships of Sir John Moore's retreat. Some of the incidents are related in his own words:—

Two days and nights my company and Captain Lloyd's were employed, without relief, at the bridge of Castro Gonzalo, on the Esla River, having been engaged half of them working to destroy the bridge,[7] half to protect the workmen from the en-

---

7. These two companies were left behind the army as a sort of rearguard to delay the pursuit of the French by destroying the bridge over the Esla.

emy's cavalry. My sentinels were cut down, but my picquet was not surprised, and we were twice slightly engaged. After this hard duty, during the whole of which we were mid-leg in clay and in snow, which fell mingled with sleet and rain, we retired to Benevente, and thence, to regain the army, made a forced march of thirty miles without being disorganised or leaving more than a few stragglers behind.

During this march from Castro Gonzalo, having stopped half a mile from my company to aid an exhausted soldier, I was attacked by some marauders of the 3rd German Hussars, and forced to defend myself with the musket and bayonet of the soldier; nor should I have escaped with life had not a rifleman started up from behind a wall and aided me. The cause of this attack was my having stopped a spring cart with two strong horses which these fellows had filled with plunder, and my insisting on their taking up my exhausted soldier. This they resisted with violence, endeavouring to ride over me, but I finally made one of them a prisoner, and brought him up to the column, where Colonel William Campbell, A. D. C, took charge of him, and delivered him to the general provost guard.

During the subsequent retreat to Vigo I was charged with the care of a large convoy of sick and wounded men and stores, with which I crossed the great mountain between Orense and Vigo, without leaving any person or a cart behind; but the hardships suffered on this occasion and at Castro Gonzalo threw me into a fever, from which I hardly escaped with life, and which weakened my constitution. I had marched for several days with bare feet, and with only a jacket and a pair of linen trowsers for clothes; my feet were swelled, and bled at every step in such a manner that General Craufurd, who saw me in that state, turned his head away, and I must have perished if McLeod, hearing of my state, had not lent me his spare horse.

But William Napier was not one of those whose zeal and spirit were damped by the hardships of that retreat; for while at Vigo, being on board the *Hindostan* 50-gun ship, hearing of a secret enterprise being prepared to cut out a Russian frigate which was moored in the harbour, with boarding nettings and all things ready to meet an attack, he borrowed a sailor's dress and a ship's cutlass, and was with the seamen in the boats when the Commodore of the squadron relinquished the attack as too desperate.

In 1809 Captain Napier became *aide-de-camp* to his uncle, the Duke of Richmond, Lord Lieutenant of Ireland, but gave up the appointment to accompany his regiment to Portugal. On the march to Talavera he was attacked with violent pleurisy, and carried to Placentia, where he was bled four times in two days; but hearing the army had been defeated, and that the French, under Soult, were close upon Placentia, he got out of bed, walked forty-eight miles to Oropesa, and there getting post-horses he rode to Talavera to join the army, which he supposed to be in a dangerous position.

The exertion coming so soon after his recent bleeding was too much for him, so that he fell from his horse at the gate of Talavera, and some Spanish soldiers, seeing him in a blue great-coat, thought he was a French officer and were going to kill him, when he was saved by an officer of the 45th regiment, who was fortunately passing at the time. His brother George, hearing of his state, soon arrived with a mule and carried him to the light division at the outposts of the army. He was afterwards in the quarters of Campo Mayor, where he tells us that his regiment lost 150 men by the Guadiana fever in six weeks.

At the fight on the Coa, where Craufurd with 5000 men and six guns stood to receive the attack of 30,000 French, having a steep ravine and river in his rear over which there existed but one narrow bridge for retreat, Captain Napier received on the field the thanks of Lieutenant-Colonel McLeod, his commanding officer, for rallying his company under a heavy fire, and thereby giving time to gather a few hundred men and to cover the passage of the broken troops over the long narrow bridge. He was also thanked by General Craufurd himself.

> He (*Craufurd*) came upon me in the road, and seemed overwhelmed with anguish at his own rashness in fighting on that side of the river. I have always thought he was going to ride in amongst the enemy, who were close to us, but that, finding me with a considerable body of men in hand whom he had given up for lost, he changed his design; at all events he was confused and agitated, and very wild in his appearance and manner.

In that "bitter fight" Captain Napier's company lost one ensign killed and thirty-five men killed and wounded The hard fighting of this company may be inferred from the fact that the loss of the whole division, about 5200 strong, was not quite 300; whereas the proportion of Napier's loss, if extended to the whole force, would have made it more than 2000. Captain Napier was shot through the left hip towards the end of the action, but fortunately the bone, though injured, was not broken, and, although suffering considerably, he continued with his regiment until the battle of Busaco, where his brothers Charles and George were both wounded, Charles desperately in the face; and where another member of the family, his cousin Charles[8] Napier, was shot in the knee.

At the combat of Cazal Noval, during Massena's retreat, the 52nd regiment had been rashly pushed forward during a fog into the midst of Ney's corps. The fog suddenly lifting, the 52nd were discovered fighting in a very perilous position, appearing "like a red pimple on the face of the country, which was black with the French masses;" and Captain Napier was detached with six companies 43rd to support the left of the 52nd. The incident is here related in his own words:—

> When I arrived at a certain round hill under fire, which I judged a good point of support, I halted four companies to watch our flanks, and with the two others hastily descended a deep ravine on my right to join the left of the 52nd, whose charging shout I had just heard on that side, though an intervening ridge prevented my seeing them. Unfortunately for me, this charge was partial; a momentary effort to extricate the regiment from a dangerous crisis. Thus with two companies I suddenly found myself in the midst of the enemy, but I arrived just in time to save Captain Dobbs, 52nd, and two men who were cut off from their regiment. The French were gathering fast about us, we could scarcely retreat, and Dobbs agreed with me that boldness would be our best chance; so we called upon the men to follow, and, jumping over a wall which had given us cover, charged the enemy with a shout which sent the nearest back. But then occurred the most painful event that ever happened to me.
>
> Only the two men of the 52nd followed us, and we four arrived unsupported at a second wall, close to a considerable body of French, who rallied and began to close upon us. Their fire was very violent, but the wall gave cover. I was, however, stung by the backwardness of my men, and told Dobbs I would save him or lose my life by bringing up the two companies; he entreated me not, saying I could not make two paces from the wall and

---

8. Afterwards Admiral Sir Charles Napier, K.C.B.

live. Yet I did go back to the first wall, escaped the fire, and, reproaching the men, gave them the word again, and returned to Dobbs, who was now upon the point of being taken; but again I returned alone! The soldiers had indeed crossed the wall in their front, but kept edging away to the right to avoid the heavy fire.

Being now maddened by this second failure, I made another attempt, but I had not made ten paces when a shot struck my spine, and the enemy very ungenerously continued to fire at me when I was down. I escaped death by dragging myself by my hands—for my lower extremities were paralyzed—towards a small heap of stones which was in the midst of the field, and thus covering my head and shoulders. Not less than twenty shots struck this heap. However, Captain Lloyd and my own company, and some of the 52nd, came up at that moment, and the French were driven away.

The excuses for the soldiers were—1st. That I had not made allowance for their exertions in climbing from the ravine up the hillside with their heavy packs, and they were very much blown. 2nd. Their own captains had not been with them for a long time, and they were commanded by two lieutenants, remarkable for their harsh, vulgar, tyrannical dispositions, and very dull bad officers withal; and one of them exhibited on this occasion such miserable cowardice as would be incredible if I had not witnessed it. I am sure he ordered the men not to advance, and I saw him leading them the second time to the right.

This man was lying down with his face on the ground; I called to him, reproached him, bade him remember his uniform; nothing would stir him; until losing all patience I threw a large stone at his head. This made him get up, but when he got over the wall he was wild, his eyes staring, and his hands spread out He was a duellist, and had wounded one of the officers some time before. I would have broke him, but before I recovered my wound sufficiently to join, he had received a cannon-shot in the leg, and died at the old, desolate, melancholy mill below Sabugal. Everything combined to render death appalling, yet he showed no weakness. Such is human nature, and so hard it is to form correct opinions of character!

In this same fight his brother George had his arm broken by a bullet, while carrying his mortally wounded subaltern off the field, under a heavy fire. And it was after this fight that his brother Charles, in hastening up with his dreadful Busaco wound unhealed to the front of the army, met the two litters carrying his brothers, of whom he was informed that William was wounded mortally. The circumstance is related in the *Life of Sir Charles Napier*, by that brother whom he supposed he was then beholding for the last time.

> Combat followed combat, the light division led in pursuit, and Charles Napier, with his wound still bandaged, rode above ninety miles on one horse, and in one course, to reach the army. His regiment being with the main body, he heard each morning the ever-recurring sound of the light division's combats in front, and had hourly to ask of wounded men if his brothers were living? Thus advancing, on the 14th of March he met a litter of branches, borne by soldiers and covered with a blanket. What wounded officer is that? Captain Napier of the 52nd, a broken limb. Another litter followed. Who is that? Captain Napier, 43rd, mortally wounded:—it was thought so then. Charles Napier looked at them and passed on to the fight in front!

This engagement of Cazal Noval is related by Napier in his work in two pages of letterpress. So it is that a few pages of history, which flows so smoothly and grandly along, cover a multitude of actions, heroic or shameful, in which every human passion has played its part. The stream of history closes over them all with its fair smooth surface, like a grand and rolling river, beneath whose waves navies have been engulfed, bearing no trace of the smaller vessels, and with only here and there a mast to reveal the resting-place of some "huge Ammiral."

We may estimate the peculiar fitness of Sir William Napier for his work, when we find him acting a personal part, as in the present instance, which would embellish the pages of *Amadis of Gaul*; yet taking the grand unimpassioned view of the historian, and so little egotistical, that his very regiment, much less himself, is not once mentioned.

The following letter from Colonel Sir John Morillyon Wilson, addressed to the author, will be read with interest in connection with the above account:—

> My first interview with my dear departed friend Sir William Napier was on the battlefield of Cazal Noval. I was then captain of the grenadier company of the Royal Scots. We were advanc-

ing towards the enemy, when I saw an officer at the distance of about eighty yards stretched on the ground beneath an olive-tree, to the right of my company. Believing him to be either dead or badly wounded, I ran towards him and said, 'I hope you are not dangerously wounded,' at which he shook his head. 'Have you been attended to by a surgeon?' He nodded assent 'Can I be of any service to you?' I said; and he again shook his head, but did not utter a word.

He looked deadly pale, and I was deeply impressed with the classical outline and beautiful expression of his handsome countenance! I told him I had some cold tea and brandy in my flask, and asked if I should give him a little of it; at which he raised his head, a sudden beam of pleasure sparkled in his eyes,—he stretched out his hand, and I gave him a tumbler-full, which he drank with a most interesting expression of unexpected enjoyment—so much so, that I gave him a second dose; and when he had finished, he seized my hand and grasped it several times, as much as to say, 'I don't know who you are, my good fellow, but I feel most gratefully thankful for your kindness.'

I then said, 'Heaven protect you!' and ran off to join my company. I had not the slightest knowledge who he was, and amidst the firing and excitement of the moment I did not notice his uniform. In after life I often spoke of this wounded officer as the handsomest man I had ever beheld. I never met him again in my wanderings through the various thoroughfares of military life, until about sixteen years afterwards, when he resided at Freshford near Bath. I was then on a visit to Lady Wilson's father, when dear 'William' dined there, and after dinner when we were just about to join the ladies, and while I was standing near the fireplace with my arm resting on the mantelpiece, the gentlemen were speaking about 'handsome men,' and I said, of all the handsome men I had ever seen in the various parts of the world where I had been, there was none to be at all compared with *the one* whom I then described to them as above written. Napier sprang from his chair, put his arms round me, and exclaimed, '*My dear Wilson, was that you? that glass of tea and brandy saved my life!*' And a few tears trickled from his bright and animated eyes, expressive of his grateful recollection of the good service I had rendered him in that hour of his need and painful suffering,

As a reward for their zeal and courage during the operations above referred to, William and George Napier were two out of eleven captains who were at this time selected out of the whole army by Lord Wellington, for the brevet rank of major. Verily since those days, if we have not improved on Lord Wellington's generalship or the splendour of his victories, we have become rather more liberal in the matter of honours and rewards.

Major William Napier was, on rejoining the army with his wound still open and with a musket-bullet never extracted lodged near his spine, appointed brigade-major to the Portuguese brigade of the light division; he was present in that capacity at the battle of Fuentes Onoro, and until, after the raising of the second siege of Badajos, a fever he had caught in the Caya River attacked him, and terminated after a hard struggle for life in ague, from which he suffered at intervals during the remainder of his days. Ill as he was, he would not quit the army until Lord Wellington specially ordered him to do so, and sent his brother to carry him down to Lisbon, lending a headquarter *calèche* for the purpose.

From Lisbon he was sent to England in the autumn of 1811; and in the spring of the following year he married Caroline Amelia, daughter of General the Honourable Henry Fox, and niece to the great statesman, a lady as remarkable for intellectual vigour as her husband, and admirable in every relation of life.

It is interesting to learn, on unquestionable authority, that she had, while in Sicily, where her father commanded the English force, touched the heart of him who was so loved and admired by her future husband.

> General Anderson, his bosom friend, assured the writer of this biography, that the only person Sir John Moore thought of marrying was Mr. Fox's niece, Miss Caroline Fox—a lady who has since displayed a power of mind and enduring fortitude in terrible trials that surpass even the creations of fiction. To her, when in Sicily with her father, Sir John Moore did at one time design to offer marriage; but she was then not eighteen, and after a hard struggle he suppressed his passion with a nobility of sentiment few men can attain to. 'She is,' he said to General Anderson, 'so young, that her judgment may be overpowered. The disparity of age is not at present very apparent, and my high position here, my reputation as a soldier of service, and

my intimacy with her father'—he might have added his great comeliness and winning manners—may influence her to an irretrievable error for her own future contentment; my present feelings must therefore be suppressed, that she may not have to suppress hers hereafter with loss of happiness.' Corunna would have ended that union in blood and misery.[9]

The following letters were written during the period between 1808 and 1811.

My Dear Mother,   Colchester, September 11th.
We are still vexed by the ministry: instead of marching on Monday, here we are on Friday, and no chance of our going *at all* that I can perceive. The first order was that we should embark the moment the transports had arrived; they have been there a week, and we have not even got orders to march, and yet the first order was so peremptory that we broke up our mess, and have been living ever since on pounds of raw meat per day for those who have not got money or gridirons of their own. It certainly is the most plaguy disagreeable Government in the world: they give orders to a number of troops they never intend to employ, break up their messes and half ruin the officers, and then congratulate themselves on their vigour and foresight. Precious rascals!
In short, my dear mother, you may damn the ministry, but believe me your affectionate son,
                                        W. Napier.

                                        Sunday, 13th.
The post did not go on Saturday, so that I have opened the letter to tell you that we have at last received the final order for sailing. We do really march this night at 12 o'clock for Harwich: the north of Spain is I believe our destination, as we are victualled for six weeks only. &c. &c.
                                        W.N.

                        Deal (in the Downs), 22nd Sept.
After being windbound for a week at Harwich we have arrived here, where we shall stay about two days, and then sail for Falmouth. I think Sir Arthur's laurels and talents for war are eclipsed by his talents for negotiation: they will now be

---
9. *Life of Sir C. Napier,* vol. 1.

called Portugal laurels by way of eminence, and the convention of Dalrymple and Wellesley. I am perfectly well; I need not ask how you are, because I can't hear unless you wrote to Falmouth; pray get it franked, for I have not a penny to release it otherwise, *nor do I want one* except to get a letter out of the post. The boat is waking. &c. &c.

Falmouth, 1st October.

I received both your letters, but I could not answer them before, although I have been here four days, and we are likely to wait a fortnight longer. Sir David Baird arrived here on Tuesday last, but we are to wait for cavalry. The 95th Rifle Corps, and the 1st Battalion 43rd, are to be in one brigade under Craufurd, who has the rank of Brigadier. I am very glad Charles has got two steps. I must conceive that General Moore's approbation of Sir Arthur Wellesley was given before the convention was made, as he never could have praised a man who signed his name to the first agreement, which is worse than the final one; in short, my dear mother, somebody must be *hanged*. I have not the least idea where we are going to; the Spaniards I think will not allow us to go to them, as they must be afraid we should endeavour to force them to give up their prisoners not taken in war, according to the promise of Sir Scoundrel Dalrymple in the convention. &c. &c.

NOTE BY SIR WILLIAM NAPIER.

[No date.]

We were all deceived by the false reports propagated by the Bishop[10] and the English ministers, and hence we talked nonsense. It is curious that I have since been the means of exonerating Dalrymple from all blame before the whole world. I had then an exalted opinion of the honour and high feeling of the English Government about the prisoners, which experience did not justify at all.

W. Napier.

Falmouth, October 3rd.

Since writing to my dear mother we have received an order to sail tomorrow or next day, for Corunna it is thought. I have not heard anything worth writing since the last, except that Sir

---

10. Of Oporto.

Harry Burrard remains in Portugal and General Moore goes to Spain, where it is probable we shall be under him, as Sir David is a younger officer—I hope so with all my heart This is a detestable place, the sooner I get out of it the better. I am quite well, and well stocked with provisions and a stomach. &c. &c.

Corunnia, 14th October.

We arrived at this place yesterday after an uncommonly fine passage of four days: we are to stay here for some time, as there are couriers sent to Madrid about us, the answer to which can't arrive under ten days. The French have got possession of Bilbao again, but are surrounded and can't escape. The Sp*a*ns here are like *Connaught* men, as like as sixpence is to a shilling. I believe all the leviathans in the ocean held their jubilee in the Bay of Biscay, for such a confounded kick up as there was I never saw before. People say we are to be encamped here until Sir John Moore arrives, but nothing is known certainly as yet.

Pray tell Richard that the gentleman scholar who wrote the character of Professor Person might as well have given the *deceased memory* of the immortal Lord Nelson as a toast, as have said that to the *departed* names of Bentley and some others we might add that of Person.

This letter goes by a man of war, so that I cannot write as much as I otherwise would, because those gentry are not of a patient nature. You need not be in a fright for fear the French should eat me, as they are too much of epicures to do it until I *am well done*, and that, as I am tough, will take two months in Spain at least, as it is not very hot: indeed I do not think that under that time any operations will take place.

I do not think I am likely to see Charles, but George I think I shall.

Corunna, 23rd October, 1808.

We have just received orders to land tomorrow and march to Lugo, a town about 40 miles from here, where we are to be cantoned until the arrival of General Moore, who takes the chief command, bringing with him an army from Lisbon: we shall then commence active operations. I think that both Charles and George will be with him, George certainly. The people are very good-natured to us: I have been several times at the play, was introduced to several ladies, and been every night at balls, where I danced the waltz, which is their chief dance. It is a mistake to say Spaniards are jealous; so far from it that the women are extremely attentive to us, endeavouring to teach us the language, which is very easy, and also delighted if we dance with them, and the men equally so: in short, we are on very near the footing with them that we should be with old friends in England,—that is some of us, for some of the Guards and others are very impertinent and not liked.

The men are poor frippery little apprentice-looking people, but the women have all beautiful black eyes and generally very good figures. Do not be afraid of stilettoes, for they only use them when people behave ill, which I have no inclination to do; some however have, as two officers have been already stabbed, but both have recovered. The peasants who are training here are extremely well drilled to the use of the firelock, and if they have the courage to fight they are as good troops as our militia, that is in discipline, for they are of a very inferior race of men to the English in point of personal appearance, except the carmen, who are the strongest-looking men I ever saw.

As I have a good deal to do, I must conclude, and I think it very probable I shall not be able to write again for a long time, as the orders about baggage are very strict, and I shall not be able to carry my writing desk, besides which, the posts will not be regular when we go nearer to the enemy, who are however not nearer than 300 miles. If you could get me some letters from Lord Holland they would be of use to introduce me to good company, by which I shall learn the language better than any other way. I forgot to say that the religious processions are magnificent and beautiful, and the nuns *old, ugly*, and *loquacious* to a great degree. We go to the convents often, and talk to nuns and monks, who are handsome, dirty, good-natured men.

LETTER FROM HIS MOTHER.

14th November.
Your charming letter from Corunna, my dearest William, delighted me, and I hope you will find means of writing to me from Lugo. Mr. F. Moore tells me he thinks his brother will not complete his march till near Christmas, but I think he who wields the sword is more alert than he who holds the pen; however, I suspect you will have time to have a fight of your own

before Sir John comes. Sir David can dash as well as Sir Arthur, and with more success in the end I hope. I have kept this letter a long time, for I have not the pen of a ready writer,[11] though by a most delightful invention of your aunt's and Richard's I am enabled to write this with my own hand upon carbonic paper, invented by Wedgwood for taking copies, but which will suit me to perfection if you find it, my writing, legible; so pray report to me the success of this my first carbonic to you.

I have by this date (14th) written to your brothers each a carbonic, to congratulate them on being as happy as a sensible human being can be, whose ardent wishes to distinguish themselves are on the hot anvil under the piercing eye of a general they love and admire. An *aide-de-camp* on service and the command of the 50th in a long march are no joke, and if not executed in a superior manner the Napier heart will not be satisfied with itself. I leave you, who so well know what ought to be the feelings of the widow of such a person as your father—to you, I say, I leave it to form a judgment on mine at a crisis so important as will probably be the close of this year.

I hourly expect news from Spain, for we have as yet nothing of later date than yours. I will write to Lord Holland to send you letters of introduction to such as they know who may be in your line of march; but, in the meantime, write to Charles Doyle for some, and try to see General Leith, who I have just heard is gone to Spain.

   Your affectionate mother,
     Sarah Napier.

TO HIS MOTHER.

       Villafranca, 10th November.
I take the opportunity of an express going to Corunna to write to you. We marched in here yesterday after a very fatiguing one of 120 miles, raining the whole way, and our quarters are worse than anything you can conceive from the worst description of the worst inns in the very worst part of Spain. The march however was pleasant, because the romantic scenery of the mountains of Gallicia and Leon is beautiful. I am perfectly well, and having made acquaintance at Corunna with some families, they gave letters to Lloyd and me of recommendation to the next

---

11. She was almost blind.

town, which was four days' march, called Lugo; there we met with more attention and pleasant parties than I ever saw before in anybody to strangers.

The girls teach me the language fast, and we were such favourites that they gave us more letters to this place, where we meet with the same kindness; *à propos*, the only way I can repay them is to give them some toothbrushes and powder, as they complain they have no method of cleansing their teeth, to their sorrow.

Whenever you have an opportunity, pray send me a large assortment of the above articles. The women and the upper class of men are as far as I can see *good*, the men proud and *dirty*; the lower class *cruel, dirty, cheating, proud*, and *crafty*; they ought to be exterminated for their treatment of animals, and flogged for their laziness.

We have just heard of a proposition from Bonaparte and Russia for a general peace; this has put us in a fright, because we have 300 miles more to march, and we are afraid of coming back without fighting—the only consolation we have for our long marches, because then we punish those who caused them: I think however that Napoleon will conquer Spain, because I observe that all the prisoners that I have seen are Germans, the troops that he has from the Rhenish confederation, and not one good soldier among them; thus the Spaniards will imagine that they can beat French soldiers, and when Bonaparte comes himself with his good troops they will be woefully mistaken.

I hope I am no prophet; but if the British troops don't save Spain, I think the Spaniards can't, for so vain are they that already they talk of invading France, forgetting that the best general and 300,000 of the second best troops in the world are to be conquered first They all seem to be well inclined to throw off the yoke of the priesthood; and as they are up to any kind of villainy, I should not be surprised if they murdered the monks and destroyed the convents.

By the bye, the aforesaid monks are the fattest people in Spain, and there are 200,000 of them, and their bishops very impudent, refusing to allow British officers into their houses although they were regularly *billeted*, for which the Spanish officers who accompanied us called them damned cooks and wig-makers to their faces; the analogy between a barber and a bishop I leave

you to find out, and only beg you will believe me, &c. &c.
I like our General Craufurd much; he is very attentive to the men.

The following was written on his return to England after the battle of Corunna, where it was supposed his brother Charles had been killed.

My dearest Mother,   Plymouth, February 1809,
You have before now heard I hope from George himself of the misfortune that has again befallen us all by the death of Charles, but it must be some comfort to you to know that he fell like a soldier fighting for his country, that his regiment distinguished themselves, and more than all that he fell with Moore, the best and bravest soldier that England had; these thoughts, my dearest mother, although they may be lost in the first moments of affliction, will in time have their effect, and you cannot therefore bring them too often to your recollection; they must mitigate your grief, and will, I hope.

For me, my dear mother, my unlucky fate has still followed me; having been sent to Vigo, I have returned without having an opportunity either of dying like my darling Charles, or of contributing to revenge his and Moore's death. We go round to Portsmouth today, from whence I have got leave to go to London to see you. I long much to do so, for sorrow draws the chords of affection close, and our sorrow is great, and with reason, for we have lost the best friend and best brother and son that God ever made. God Almighty bless you, my dear mother! I hope to be with you as soon as this letter.

TO THE SAME,

Colchester, 6th May 1809.
. . . . .I have not altered my intentions undoubtedly with regard to the Duke[12] (as if he had felt himself annoyed by anything I had written to him I would not have accepted the situation), knowing as I do that I paid him every attention and gave him all the thanks that were due, and further I will give to no man.
I hope you will cause my things to be sent down as quick as

---

12. His uncle, the Duke of Richmond, then Lord Lieutenant of Ireland. William Napier accepted the poet of A.D.C., but gave it up to go to Spain with his regiment.

possible, because we are *ordered to embark* on the 24th of this month. In addition to what I already have I shall want another pair of walking shoes from Mr. Burrows, and I beg particular care may be taken that every pair of pantaloons may be sent of whatever colour, also all my jackets and epaulettes; they cannot come too soon, as I am under the evil eye of the Commanding Officer for being in coloured clothes, &c.

Deal, May 26.

I have received by Tom Lloyd all the things you sent me, and am much obliged to you for them. The ship that George is in got a little damaged and is gone round to Portsmouth to refit; I have not seen him. When I ordered the pictures of General Moore, one was for Emily, and I did not pay because I was to see the likeness first so that if they are bad I am not obliged to take them.

If we go to Falmouth I shall write again, but the boats are awaiting, and I can write no more now. &c. &c.

LORD WELLINGTON TO LADY SARAH NAPIER.
(*Immediate.*)

My dear Madam,   Coimbra. Sept 30, 1810.
I am concerned to be again the channel of conveying to you intelligence of a distressing nature; but you received the last which I communicated to you in a manner so becoming yourself that I have less reluctance in writing to you than I had on the former occasion, although the cause is more disastrous. The army was engaged with the enemy on the 27th, and your sons Charles and George were wounded.

I saw the former after he was wounded, and he was well and in good spirits, although he had a severe but not a dangerous wound in the jaw. George is wounded in the hip, but very slightly, and both are doing well. You will see the account of the action in which the troops were engaged, and I hope it will be some consolation to you to reflect that your sons received their wounds on an occasion in which the British troops behaved so well. Ever, my dear Madam, your most faithful and obedient humble servant,

Wellington.

My Dear Mother, Quinta de Fonte Voa, Jan. 1811.
Your long letter I have received, and it certainly did not tire me, much the contrary. I am glad that George's letter answered the business part, as the first part of it totally unfitted me from giving you a regular answer. If I could write anything that would drive away melancholy ideas from your mind, I would be very happy, but I feel that what you complain of must be in spite of reason or writing—nevertheless I think I can put your thoughts (upon some of the unhappy subjects that engage their attention) in a train that will alleviate them at least You complain of the weakness of your mind in giving way to every thought that pictures a new misfortune: it is the common attendant of nervous people, young or old,—a disease of the body and not of the mind; and strong indeed would you be if with the pressure of real and heavy misfortune, aged and deprived of sight, you should be able to resist such sensations.

You may rest assured, my dear mother, that you have an energy of mind that few can boast of, and it has its consequent good effects. The sentiments that caused you to undergo the pain of that dreadful operation on your eye are the original causes also that give to Charles his intrepidity and his ambition of honourable fame, to George his impetuosity and supreme contempt for everything that is not noble and belonging to the character of a soldier.

You may smile at my saying George is impetuous, but your smile will cease when I tell you that at Busaco he attempted to break the head of the French column with his own hand, and when *shot* in the attempt continued on the ground to wave his sword and shout to his men to go on.

You feel rejoiced that people of acknowledged merit take notice of your sons, and you attribute it to their own merit; you yourself are the original cause of that friendship. Many officers are as brave and have more talents than us without meeting with the same attention: few people do things in this world without an interested motive; and as most of our friends know you, and the firmness with which you support your misfortunes, they naturally expect that your sons have derived from you the same spring of mind and the shame of doing anything inferior in constancy of mind or courage to yourself; and as naturally wish to attach us to their persons or fortunes: I speak of military men, who are all fond of having a court, I may call it, belonging particularly to them: such had General Moore,—where shall we find such a *King?*

In any religious point of view I cannot advise you. I think you feel it strongly and rightly; if you did not it would be strange with such a friend and help as my aunt,[13] whom I should esteem if she were my deadly enemy. I can feel her excellence more strongly here, where murder is sport for great men. I do not think there will be much fighting here, rather that we shall be obliged to leave the country from want of provisions ourselves, strange as it may appear.

There will be one grand cause of nervous sensations taken away, and if we die, perhaps the loss of one of us might not be so great a misfortune. I speak from reason, not from low spirits. If I prove that death to me would be rather a gain in point of sensation, you must allow that it ought not to affect you immoderately, more particularly as you feel yourself you are on the verge of the grave, and that it would be the means of our meeting the sooner, *happily* if we meet at all, for hell cannot be where friends meet.

You see I do not consider your mind weakened, or I would not write upon a subject that requires the full exercise of reason to divest it of the effect of passions and give it a fair investigation. I am a soldier unfitted for any other profession, and yet I took up my present one lightly and without consideration. I detest it; we are but licensed murderers, and the most brutal ferocious sentiments are constantly expressed, and actions of the same stamp as constantly committed, by us and our allies. This I cannot prevent, nor can I leave the place or people where and by whom they are committed; the very circumstance of their being committed makes it the more incumbent on me to serve my country in that profession I am most capable of serving her in, to prevent the same scenes from taking place at home.

The nature of war is misery. Thus I am condemned to a profession I dislike by religion, honour, and necessity. At the same time I, who can feel well the happiness of a domestic life, am nearly cut off from every chance of being so fortunate. I had two friends who could well have supplied me with sentiments of pleasure to reconcile me to my situation, but Lloyd has left

---
13. Lady Louisa Conolly.

the regiment, and Macleod, whom I love as my friend and admire as the facsimile of General Moore's character, is gone home—I am afraid merely to give his poor father the task of putting him in the grave. With these considerations and with the thought that if I fall I do it with honour for my country, that I fall the way my father would have wished and like Moore, that my name will be respected,—will you not allow that I have reason to say death may be a gain? Do not imagine from this that I will expose myself more than my duty requires; notwithstanding reason is on my side, I feel the command of God to live as strong as ever, and I tremble in danger as well as my neighbours, but I feel I cannot lose much by the change into the other world.

John Ash is in the 95th; I have seen him before; he sends two guineas to his father and mother: pray give it to them out of my money, he has given it to me.

I need hardly tell you to desire the person who reads this to you not to talk; what I say might do me mischief and cannot do me good. I tell my thoughts to you because I feel them, but I put a different face upon it here and am very gay.

I am, my dear mother, &c &c.
W. Napier.

P.S. On reading over my letter it strikes me that you will think I am unhappy, and torment yourself about it I am not, I can reason and yet take amusement; it only prevents a great deal of folly and gives me a turn of the serious.

LORD WELLINGTON TO LADY SARAH NAPIER.

My dear Madam,   March 16, 1811.

I am sorry to have to inform you that your two sons were again wounded in an action with the enemy the day before yesterday, but neither of them, I hope, seriously. William is wounded in the back, and this is supposed to be only a flesh-wound;[14] George in the right arm, which is broken. Both are doing well, and will I hope soon recover to return to their duty. Your Ladyship has so often received accounts of the same description with that which I am now writing to you, and your feelings on the subject are so just and proper, that it is needless to trouble

---

14. A mistake. A bullet lodged itself near the backbone and was never removed. The bone was seriously injured.

you farther. Your sons are brave fellows and an honour to the army; and I hope that God will preserve them to you and their country. Ever, my dear Madam, your most faithful humble servant,

    Wellington.

Here is a sketch of William Napier as he appeared to Mrs. Opie in 1811. Major Napier was on leave in England after his severe wound.

When most of the company was gone. Lady C. took the seat vacated by Lady Mornington, that mother of great men, and it was next a venerable-looking blind woman, whom Lord C. had previously pointed out to me as the once celebrated beauty Lady Sarah Lennox.[15] She is now grey, blind, and seems both by her voice and manner to be bowed by various cares, but perhaps I fancied this. . . . . By Lady Sarah was one of her sons, who with his brother was wounded in every engagement abroad, and one of them taken up for dead. I never saw a handsomer man! I could not help looking at him. He is very black, with black *moustachios*, that make him look like a picture of some young Venetian by Titian, and his manner was so pleasing. He had his mother's outline enlarged into manly beauty, and he has such fine dark eyes.

---

15. Lady Sarah Napier.

CHAPTER 4

Storming of Ciudad Rodrigo

On the 19th January, 1812, while Major Napier was in England, Ciudad Rodrigo was stormed, and Major George Napier, who commanded the storming party of the light division, lost his arm on that occasion.

The two letters following were written to William Napier by his friend Colonel Macleod:—

LIEUTENANT-COLONEL MACLEOD TO MAJOR WILLIAM NAPIER.

My Dear Bill,   La Encina, January 21st, 1812.
I have just been over to see your brother; he was asleep, and therefore I did not go into his room. Bob and all the surgeons who have attended him say that he is going on well, and that altogether he has supported himself better than anybody they ever saw in the same situation. I was with him yesterday for some time; he talked very composedly, and seemed to have made up his mind to his misfortune. I am truly sorry for him, which I need not tell you, but, taking into consideration the service he was employed upon, one could hardly expect him to come off with whole bones. He has covered himself with glory, will be made a lieutenant-colonel, and be as well as ever he was for health and society; the pain he will suffer in the interim is the greatest part of the ill; he is in a comfortable quarter in the suburbs of Ciudad, and will not be removed until he is much recovered from the effects of the operation.
I am writing this as if you had accounts of him before, knowing that much had been written to you by the officer who carried the despatches, but find I have left you to guess what the wound is after all. He was hit by a grape-shot in the arm, the same as

he was hit in the *time before* the two last times he was wounded, and the bone so shattered that the surgeons were all of opinion that it was impossible to save it, and George determined at once to have it amputated, which was done the same evening by Dr. Guthrie who is a clever man, and I have no doubt has performed the operation in a way that will prevent his feeling any inconvenience hereafter.

Poor Colborne's[1] wound was at first thought to be slight, but today the surgeons say that they fear it will be very troublesome: the ball entered his shoulder and was lodged deep in, and they are afraid to try to extract it. Craufurd is very bad, his life is almost despaired of. The ball passed through his arm into his body, and has either lodged in his lungs which is inevitable death, or has passed through and settled in some less vital part; but at all events his lungs are injured, and the best that can be said is that there is a *chance* of his recovery.

All our own are likely to do well; Brummel is the only one there is any doubt about; his wound is near the femoral artery. Ferguson behaved beautifully; he is turning out one of the best soldiers extant.[2] I am glad to find by your last letter that you are doing well; we were under great anxiety about you for some time. The siege of Ciudad was certainly carried on with great good management, and achieved in good style; it was well begun and well finished. The governor ought to have been killed if he had not *preferred his life to his honour*. I do not believe he was near the breach, although he says the contrary; he would have surrendered the next day they say. I am in ill humour, and perfectly knocked up,

Yours very affectionately,
Charles Macleod.

FROM THE SAME.

My Dear Bill,   El Bodem, Feb. 4th. 1812.
When I wrote last I was in so great a hurry that I am afraid I gave you a very wild and unsatisfactory account of your extraordinary and inimitable brother; he beats you all out and out, to use Dalyel's distinguishing appellation for the family, in *Tan-*

---

1. Lieutenant-Colonel Colborne, commanding 52nd Regiment, afterwards Field-Marshal Lord Seaton.
2. General Sir James Ferguson.

dyism. When I saw him last, three or four days ago, at Gallegos, which is a distance from hence that prevents my seeing him so often as I wish, he had just finished a letter to Lady Sarah with his left hand, which I directed and sealed &c. for him, in order to give him an opportunity of eating his soup which he was very impatient for, and which he devoured with an appropriate quantity of toast with a most excellent appetite.

He was perfectly free from all fever, slept very tolerably, and in as good spirits as I ever saw him, talking upon all sorts of subjects and admitting as many people as the surgeons would allow, which very probably are not near as many as he wished. I believe he will not remove from Gallegos for some time, until he is quite able to bear the journey without pain. Colborne's wound is still giving him a great deal of pain, but I hope from what I heard is going on as favourably as can be expected; the ball had worked its way towards his elbow from the shoulder, and they have by this time, I dare say, extracted it; when this occurs his case will be easy.

Ferguson and Patterson are both going on well; the latter was made a terrible figure of by the explosion of some gunpowder, whether placed there purposely or not is not easy to determine, but it was certainly a large quantity to have been left there accidentally. This scorched his face and one hand very badly, and he had scarcely recovered his astonishment at this summerset over the wall, when he received a pretty deep graze from the splinter of a shell or a ball in his *counterpart*, but he is likely to recover completely, and be as beautiful as ever.

Poor Jim Ferguson is wounded nearly where you were, by a musket-ball, as near as it could be with any safety to the backbone, and it is uncertain whether the ball is in or out, but the surgeons say it is of little importance which; he is recovering, which I am truly glad of, very fast. Poor Brummel died of his wounds about a week ago. With the exception of Uniacke, who also died of his wounds, all the officers of the light division are doing well. Having now given you an account of all your maimed friends and acquaintances, I suppose I must make some remarks upon the siege for your amusement.

It is reckoned a brilliant operation. It was certainly unexpected by the French, and the place is of importance to them in their future designs upon this ill-fated country, as commanding the great road and the only good bridge of the Agueda; they must therefore retake it with a loss of time and men before they can invade by this route again. In short, they are now evidently worse in this quarter than they have yet been, and we know that they threw away 80,000 men before, in similar circumstances, without effecting their ultimate objects. How it will end admits of a doubt, but let it end either way it may, the defence of the town as far as it has gone does infinite credit to the military skill and talents of Viscount, and Baron, and Knight, and Condé. They talk of taking Badajoz, but that preparations cannot be made to begin sooner than April.

Stewart, I am told, is going to send me back your horse, which I am sorry for, because I do not think you will find him to answer. I want horses very much and mean to write to my father to send me out one or two; my own are all dying. We are in bad quarters, particularly for the men, who are obliged to go leagues to cut wood and bring it home on their shoulders in the worst weather; and if Dr. Pangloss was here, and was to tell me that all was for the best, I should infallibly knock him down. *Adieu*, my dear Bill. I hope you are getting well, but sick enough to keep you quiet for some time.

C. M.

In connection with the storming of Ciudad Rodrigo the following curious circumstances have been communicated to the author by Colonel Angelo, formerly of the 43rd Regiment, and a personal friend of both Napier and Gurwood,[3] who was at that time a lieutenant in the 52nd Regiment. They furnish one instance of the great difficulties which a contemporaneous historian has to encounter in relating such exciting events as battles or assaults; where those engaged in them, though men of unimpeachable honour and veracity, are often found afterwards to give such contradictory accounts. Lieutenant Gurwood led the forlorn hope of the light division to the assault of the lesser breach of Ciudad Rodrigo, and behaved with the most conspicuous gallantry.

In writing his account of that affair in the *History*, Napier related that, in consequence of the "forlorn hope" having taken a wrong direction for a time, that body reached the foot of the breach simultaneously with the stormers under Major George Napier, and that, then,

[3] Afterwards Colonel Gurwood, the distinguished editor of the *Wellington Despatches*.

these two parties intermingled rushed up the breach together. On the other hand, Colonel Gurwood claimed to have twice ascended, and to have been twice forced back down the breach, before the arrival of the storming party at its foot; and he published a very curious and interesting pamphlet in support of his statement in 1848.

In that pamphlet Gurwood stated that, having got with his party (forlorn hope) into the ditch at the angle to the left of the breach, and seeing that the attention of the enemy within the *fausse braie*[4] and on the ramparts was directed to the breach in the *fausse braie*, he placed the ladders, "with which Sergeant M'Currie had joined him," still further to the left, on the other face of the salient angle of the *fausse braie*, so as not to be visible from the breach, which was in the re-entering angle; and having, unobserved, mounted with all his party by means of scaling ladders, gained the *terre pleine* of the *fausse braie*, and thereby turned the breach of that work, which was then abandoned by the enemy, who ran up the breach of the wall of the town—that Gurwood then followed with his party to the top of the breach, whence he was toppled over by a round shot or stone flung at him, and found himself and party again at the bottom—that, seeing it impossible to carry the breach with the bayonet, he directed his men to load, and posted them on both sides of the breach to fire at the top—that the storming party then arrived at the foot of the breach—that he himself again ascended the centre of the breach, and was a second time hurled down, wounded in the head.

In support of this statement Gurwood published a letter from Sergeant M'Currie, named above, in which he says,—"I perfectly recollect and am positive that Lieutenant Gurwood *carried the breach*. I myself went up the *scaling-ladder to the left of the gun*, and Lieutenant Gurwood was the first man I saw on the ramparts." Here however there appears some confusion, as the inference to be drawn from Gurwood's own account is, that *scaling-ladders* were not used at all at the breach, which he declares to have been quite practicable, and which he scrambled up after the retreating French.

On the other hand, the testimony of Major George Napier, who commanded the stormers, and of Captain Ferguson, one of the captains of the party, is opposed to Gurwood's statement. Both declared that some of the storming party arrived at the foot of the breach be-

---

4. The *fausse braie* is a sort of lower rampart, in front of, and connected with, the main rampart. In the present case there was a breach in the *fausse braie* as well as in the main rampart, or, as it is here called, the wall of the town.

fore the forlorn hope. Captain Ferguson says,—"When about 30 or 40 men were collected together at the foot of the breach, a simultaneous rush was made, both by officers and men, scarcely allowing any man to claim being the first to enter, having no forlorn hope to lead them;" and he adds—"I do not dispute that Gurwood and some of his party were amongst the number; but as to his having twice mounted the breach *before us,* I cannot understand it, and Steele[5] always denied it"

Captain Ferguson also stated that, when the storming party were descending into the ditch, they observed the forlorn hope placing the ladders against the wall of the *fausse braie* considerably to the left, and were turning in that direction, when the engineer officer appointed to guide them called out that they were going wrong, and led them to the proper point of attack. Captain Ferguson was never able to recall the name of that engineer officer, and, in connection with that officer, now comes the curious part of the story.

Many years after, Colonel Angelo met at the United Service Club the late Lieutenant-Colonel Theodore Elliot, who had been employed as a young officer of Engineers at the siege of Ciudad Rodrigo. The conversation turned on the sieges in Spain, and Elliot spoke of his having led the storming party of the light division at Ciudad Rodrigo. It then transpired that he knew nothing of the controversy between Napier and Gurwood, having lately returned from Madras, where he had been employed on his father's staff for several years. Curiosity led these two officers to refer to the respective statements concerning the disputed points, which were in the club library; and on reading Ferguson's statement, Elliot corroborated it in every particular, declaring he had used the very words imputed to him by, Ferguson at the time when the storming party, misled by seeing Gurwood's men planting scaling-ladders against the *fausse braie,* was about to follow the forlorn hope. He further declared positively, "that no forlorn hope led us up the breach, and that it was a general rush of such of the storming party as were first collected together."

In explanation of the fact that Elliot guided the storming party on the occasion, he not having been detailed in orders for that duty, and of Ferguson's inability to remember who the engineer officer was, whose words he distinctly remembered, but with whose person he was unacquainted, the following very curious statement was then made by Elliot

---

5. One of the lieutenants of the storming party.

On the evening of the 19th January, 1812, Elliot and Rice Jones, both belonging to the Engineers and to the same brigade, had returned to their quarters (having been on duty the whole of the day), and, hearing that the assault was ordered for that night, they agreed to go down together to the trenches to see the attack, and they reached the convent of San Francisco only a short time previous to its taking place. Whilst standing near the troops already formed, Major —— of the Engineers came suddenly up to them, desiring Jones to join the storming party of the 3rd Division, and Elliot to lead that of the light division. Elliot had been employed at a different part of the works, knowing nothing at all about the localities of the breach, and said as much; but he was desired *to do the best he could*, and to employ the few minutes which remained before the time fixed upon for the assault in making himself acquainted with the localities.

In this state of uncertainty he had barely time to go towards the ditch and find out where the breach was, when, the troops having come up, and the firing commencing from the walls of the town, the flash of a gun showed him the breach at the moment when they were about to descend into the ditch: he at the same time observed some men (the forlorn hope) going away to the left with some ladders, upon which he called out, "*You are going wrong, there is the breach,*" pointing towards it, and with the foremost men of the storming party passing up by the breach in the *fausse braie,* and so arriving at the bottom of the breach in the wall of the town.

After waiting some time until more men gradually came up, a general rush was made, and although he believed he got to the top (passing over a gun that was laid across it) nearly as soon as any other person, he always considered that no one could claim having led the attack, as it was a simultaneous movement from the bottom of the breach, and he saw no distinction at that point between a forlorn hope and a storming party.

On the breach being carried, and the troops moving along the ramparts, he immediately returned to make his report to his commanding officer, Colonel Fletcher, when to his great surprise Fletcher said, "What are you talking about, sir? *you* did not lead the attack—you were not the engineer officer attached to it;"—and on Elliot repeating that he was the only engineer officer with the storming party of the light division, Fletcher became still more angry, and desired him to go away. Major —— was present, and *heard all this without making any remark,* but he followed Elliot and told him to say nothing farther on the subject, as it might reflect upon the corps, the officers *named* for the storming parties not having been present.

Elliot, a very young officer at that time, conformed strictly to Major ——'s somewhat dictatorial advice, and avoided as much as possible any conversation upon the assault of the lesser breach, and ultimately quitted the engineer service to enter into the line.

CHAPTER 5

Letters to His Wife

In March, 1812, hearing that Badajoz was besieged, William Napier, though far from being recovered and only three weeks married, sailed again for Portugal. On reaching Lisbon he heard of the bloody assault and capture of Badajoz, and learnt that his dearest friend, Lieutenant-Colonel Charles Macleod of the 43rd Regiment, had been killed in the breach. Napier was terribly affected by the loss of his friend, and the first letter he wrote to his young wife betrays the storm of passionate sorrow which swept through his soul.

LETTER TO HIS WIFE.

Lisbon, 17th April, 1812.

Macleod is dead, and I am grovelling in misery and wretchedness—my temples ache with the painful images that are passing before me. He was the best and will be the last of my friends, for I cannot endure the torture that I feel again, and where can I find another like him? You must be my friend and wife and everything. When I lose you there is still another world to find you in. I had buoyed myself up with the hope of meeting him, and now I must weep over his grave. Farewell my dearest Caroline. George sailed two days ago,—take care of him. I cannot write more now, but I could roll in the dust if it were not for shame.

This beloved friend Napier has commemorated in his narrative of the storming of Badajoz, in the following words:—

Officers of all ranks, followed more or less numerously by the men, were seen to start out as if struck by sudden madness and rush into the breach, which, yawning and glittering with steel, seemed like the mouth of a huge dragon belching forth smoke and flame. In one of these attempts Colonel Macleod of the 43rd, a young man whose feeble body would have been quite unfit for war if it had not been sustained by an unconquerable spirit, was killed. Wherever his voice was heard his soldiers had gathered, and with such a strong resolution did he lead them up the fatal ruins, that, when one behind him in falling plunged a bayonet into his back, he complained not, but continuing his course was shot dead within a yard of the sword-blades.[1]

His letters to his wife continue to show how deeply he felt the loss of his friend.

Sabugal, 23rd April, 1812.

I wrote by the *Latona* frigate from Lisbon, and as I was in great agony of mind at the time, you must not let anybody see my letter nor allow it to hurt your own spirits. I arrived here late last night where I found headquarters. I am exceedingly tired from riding 200 miles post on the country saddles without a stop, and am therefore going to remain this day with Lord March,[2] who has been as usual as good-natured as it is possible to be. My regiment is only four leagues from here. I shall take the command of it tomorrow, as the only field officer not killed or wounded is gone home sick of fever. Everybody says I am the most fortunate of men to have command of such a regiment; for my part, I only find that the recollection of Macleod comes with more bitterness to my mind.

What comfort or pleasure can I have in filling the place that belonged to him! The greatest pride I had was to hear him praised and see him admired as he deserved; and now I must be content to recollect that he was everything that is noble and kind, and convince myself that I shall never see him again. I cannot give myself up to the sorrow I feel pressing so heavy upon me, and yet every occupation I have tends directly to place him in the point of view in which he was most to be admired. My poor Charles! if I could have seen him once before he was killed, or have been with him when he fell!—but there is little use in talking about him: some time or other I hope to see him again.

---

1. *Peninsular War*, book 16, chap. 5.
2. His cousin, afterwards the late Duke of Richmond.

Take care of yourself, my dearest Caroline, and don't let me have any additional cause to grieve about you.

TO THE SAME.

La Encina, April 29th, 1812.

Yesterday both your letters arrived by the same post It pains me, my love, to find your spirits so low; I also am in very bad spirits; how indeed can I be otherwise under so great a loss as I have sustained in the death of that gallant noble-minded man Macleod? and it is vain to look for consolation here, where everybody feels his loss as much as I do. But I must not repine; I have always observed that good and bad fortune have run like a tide with me, sometimes one, sometimes the other; the latter seems now in full force; when it will stop God only knows; if short of you I will be content. You will have seen by the despatch how highly Lord Wellington thought of Macleod's courage and abilities, and yet he only knew half his worth.

The storm was dreadful; for three hours and a half the light division were in the ditch and on the breach in close order, exposed to the fire of 4000 men at 20 yards from them, while artillery from the flanks, and shells, stones, fireballs, and beams, were poured upon them incessantly, and yet not one man left his post, or for a moment gave up efforts to tear away the obstacles that were laid across the breach; every officer and man has received two or three wounds each; those that are returned are amputations or body wounds.

My poor friend was struck down from the breach twice before he was killed, once with a stone, once with a bayonet wound in the head; nevertheless he persevered in his attempts till a shot went through his right breast and finished his career in the only manner that was worthy of his life, I have 520 or more men left in the regiment, but the plundering after the town was taken, and the death or wounds of almost all their officers (only seven being with the regiment fit for duty), has so disorganized them for a time, that I have been forced the two first days of my command to punish three of them by that most infamous manner of flogging, which is now doubly so from the gallantry of their conduct at the storm; but robbery and insolence to their officers are crimes not possible to be forgiven.

Cheer up your own spirits, my Caroline, and write to me much about yourself; it will go further than anything to dispel the gloomy prospects and thoughts that torment me just now."

La Encina, May 4th, 1812.

I have been so occupied by the misery of losing Macleod, that I have not attended sufficiently I fear to the lowness of spirits which you described to me in your letter, nor have I expressed myself as I feel for the tenderness you display in your expressions of love for me; but be assured, my Caroline, that they are not lost upon me; and although they add more sorrow from their being written instead of spoken to me, still it is of a softer and more pleasing kind than that which occupies my mind when I think of the valuable friend that I have lost It is indeed a source of the utmost pleasure to me to know without the most distant doubt that you love me with all your soul, and I pray sincerely to God that our separation may not last long.

The business of the regiment is of such an imperious nature that in spite of my disinclination I am obliged to give my mind to it for some hours of the day, and this has in some measure calmed my spirits. The officers have a mind to erect a monument in Westminster Abbey to Macleod, but are not aware of the expense being within their means: pray ask Bunbury what it might be done for. If it can be done, how dear to me will be the place! doubly dear from the ties of sorrow and of joy. My voyage was a very unpleasant one, full of bad management and accidents of a shocking description. The Commodore kept us so close to the land, that we were on the third day embayed in the Groyn near Corunna, and remained there beating about for six days while a fair wind blew out at sea.

During the gale we lost all our topgallant masts at one crash, and one man fell from the main topgallant mast-head on to the deck, crushing a soldier under him, and I fear that they both died soon after I left the ship. We had also a man overboard, who was picked up with some difficulty and at the nick of time. My horse Tamerlane was sold for 67*l*., and was very near dying; poor beast! I did not know him. My own mare I found at Lisbon completely done up, and my servant (not Feagan, who by the bye has not arrived with my baggage) burnt my dressing-case the first day I arrived at the regiment. It is not rendered useless however.

You perceive by this, my dear Caroline, that I have been crossed by minor accidents as well as grieved by misfortune. I date the beginning from the time I left you. How little did I think that happy night we passed at Portsmouth when I returned from on board the ship was that which finished my dearest friend's admirable existence! how dreadful it is to find in one half-year that I am deprived of so many friends as I have been! I left the regiment so full of officers and men, and now I stand almost alone; but one officer whom I know is left. Both the young boys that I had in my company are desperately wounded. I was very proud of them, and they have not disgraced their captain. Poor little fellows! their courage and fortitude surpassed that of much older men; but I am sick of the wretchedness that every report brings in. The poor fellows are dying fast of their wounds, both officers and men, and I fear we have not yet heard the worst.

5th.—I was interrupted yesterday in a train of melancholy ideas which I might better have spared to you I believe, and yet I think there is a pleasure in being unhappy with people we love, as well as merry: I feel it so with regard to you, and hope when you are low you will not let it prevent you writing to me. In short, I think you have in a great measure overcome that aversion to letters that I had; at least, I look very anxiously for the post now, and find more time for being alone than I used to do. These are suspicious symptoms; if they will last they may be termed curious; but remember, that they are never to argue for or against my affection for you, which is in my heart and not my fingers.

La Encina, May 13th, 1812.

Your letters are the comfort of my life, and I look as anxiously for them as I used formerly to avoid the post and everything that had a connexion with it. It is so new a sensation with me to have a person who makes my happiness the first consideration of their mind, and who knows how to mix with that consideration a tenderness that only women can express, and even few of them can feel. Do not then spare your letters, or let anything check the current of your feelings when you write to me. If they should be nonsense it is no matter, for I am a stern animal as a commanding officer (although, I trust, not an inhuman one); and the pleasure of unbending from my dignity to talk nonsense with you, greater than you can imagine.

I had sent you the music of four *boleros* before I got your letters about them, and I expect that you will dance much with George, who is I suppose now with you; it will be a good recommendation for him to Lady M—— C—— if he succeeds so well as a dancer. When I desired you to ask Bunbury about the expense of a monument at Westminster, I meant the fees of the place; but if you could find out what a figure in marble about 3 feet high would cost by a good sculptor, I wish you very much to do so.

La Encina, May 19th, 1812.

The post was so much sooner than I expected the last time I wrote to you, that I think you must have imagined I felt tired of corresponding with you, but you must forgive me if sometimes you get short letters from me, and you must believe that the short letters are not proofs of want of affection, but the little wanderings of a genius but newly broke in to write at all. You express a wish to know about my staff employment: I have none; having given it up in order to assume the command of the regiment; when I am superseded in that command I will go upon the Staff if they will put me with the light division, otherwise I will go home to you.

The wish to learn my profession, and to make myself worthy of you, were the reasons why I left you before, and most certainly when they cease (which they would do away from the light division) I have no inclination strong enough to keep me away from you; but that it was necessary yon will allow when you know that five junior officers have obtained rank above me for their services even in the short time that I was away; and yet I do not think that they were more capable, at least they did not prove so when I was present; but a soldier's life is one of hard striving; if your foot slips you will fall inevitably. I have just got an order to enlist 100 men from the Spaniards into the regiment

This I think is the fairest prospect we have yet had of succeeding in the Peninsula, that is, if it is followed up on a great scale. They have given us the inch, and we ought to take the ell by all means in our power, but the French have still 200,000 men in the field besides their garrisons; Bunbury won't believe this, but I had it from Lord Wellington's mouth. Tell George that the mutiny at Ciudad stopped of itself, and I believe they were paid. I have been offered my old horse Tamerlane again: if the man will get him to England for me, you may perhaps see him and make a pet of him for me; he certainly is the most beautiful of horses even now in his bad condition.

I cannot give you any news of what we are likely to do. The bridge of Alcantara is repaired, but that speaks two ways, and this recruiting of Spaniards may alter the designs Lord Wellington had before. I think it very likely that he may advance to cripple Marmont in the north, so. as to prevent him from undertaking anything against Ciudad Rodrigo while we find it necessary to move southward; but everything must be conjecture, as the present movements are evidently with an intention to deceive the enemy as to the real object I am weary of conjecture and of writing. . . . .

I had a bad fit of ague, but by dint of bark I have chased it away.

La Encina, May 26th, 1812.

Since I last wrote to you we have made no move of any kind. You have of course heard before this of General Hill's business at Almaraz. The post has been uncommonly long this time in its passage from England, and I am very impatient for the time when you will be enabled to tell me certainly how you are. Major D—— will give you the trinkets. The lieut.-colonel of the 3rd Caçadores having been reported dead, the officer who commanded them paid me a visit with the next eldest officer to request I would apply to enter the Portuguese service and ask for this regiment

This was very flattering to me, but I declined it without any hesitation for many reasons, the most prominent of which was that it left me a most indeterminate time to look forward to seeing you, and, if that was not the case, I cannot reconcile to myself perfectly the idea of fighting for any country but my own; besides which, I am perfectly dead to all the feelings of glory that I used to have; and so little pleasure do I find in command of troops, that if the Duke would allow me to sell my commission I should go. This was my home; I knew no difference hardly between it and my mother's house; it is now a desolate deserted dwelling, and the grave of my friend is always present to me.

Where can I or how can I find a pleasure in that pursuit of fame which formerly pleased me? and without aspiring of a very strong nature it is impossible not to be disgusted with war. You will easily understand this when I tell you that the barbarity of our soldiers extended to that pitch that they would not for two days carry off the wounded men at the foot of the walls—our own men!!! They also stripped them naked, the officers as well as the men who were wounded; I do not mean our regiment in particular, the —— were the worst The town was dreadfully plundered, and the inhabitants murdered of all ages and sexes. The French were the only people to whom they gave quarter, out of a spirit of honour, not humanity. They even killed one another. Such is war, and such the inducements I have to remain.

La Encina, June 3rd, 1812.

Your letter of the 6th is the last which I have got from you, although the packet was up to the 13th; I find I must have patience. The news of Perceval's assassination has reached us; it is a horrible unmanly deed in itself, but there is a kind of retribution in it; he first began the cry of intolerance in England; he refused to let bark be sent to France for the sick; and his party first broached those horrid principles of giving no quarter to Frenchmen,[3] and of the propriety of assassinating Buonaparte. He has become the victim of his own doctrines. What effect will it have on the war here? it ought to have none, but I suppose it *will*.

The plan of enlisting Spaniards I think fails, at least hereabouts; the young men have already been swept away, and the people who do offer are very few and for the most part unfit. It becomes a very painful business: if we refuse them, their answer is that they must go and die, for that they had but strength sufficient to carry them to us, many not having eaten for several days before: their appearance fully justifies their words. We are too nice in our choice, and we want men taller than they grow

---

3. *Did* his party ever broach those horrid principles? certainly Perceval did not Bonaparte made a similar accusation against Pitt. We all know that imputation to have been utterly unfounded.

in the country; for my part, I would take women sooner than none, as I think the time is too short to admit of being fastidious. I see in the papers that a translation of the Napoleons Code is published by a lawyer of the Inns: if it is not very large send it to me. I have been drawing lately, and Louisa's present is excellent Give my love to her, and everybody else.—If you can read this I give you credit.—I am fast asleep and can't see, having been up early.

La Encina, June 8th, 1812.

I am exceedingly shocked by the death of Mrs. Staples's[4] son William, whom I knew when a little boy and was exceedingly fond of; but his death is not the occasion of grief farther than what everybody feels at the loss of a little engaging playfellow; but his poor mother, who is the most amiable, excellent, and interesting creature that it is possible to meet with—her whole soul was wound up in the life of that boy; she had educated him herself; and as her talents and judgment are more than those of any person I know, he must have fully answered her expectations; certainly nobody is to be pitied more than she, nobody more deserving of the attention and sorrow of her friends besides, for nobody ever felt a friend's sorrow with keener anguish, or strove to allay it with more tenderness and assiduity. When so excellent a creature is thus at once deprived of happiness, and that happiness dependent on a single thread, it makes me tremble for him, who certainly
cannot claim the protection of Heaven when it is denied to so infinitely a better being than myself.—I hate this life, which keeps me from you and prevents us from enjoying the few short days of happiness that may be allowed us.—Emily[5] probably will be with you when this arrives, or I would beg you to watch her with the greatest care, and soothe her mind; for she fully knows and as strongly feels the worth and the affliction of her friend. I need not however say this to you, as I know your tender affectionate soul need never be reminded to take an interest in any of your friends' feelings, much less in Emily's or *mine*, who I think you look upon as your best friend.

I was once glad that I was born in these times, when great minds are at work, and the whole world in arms; now I regret

---

4. Afterwards became Mrs. Richard Napier, having married his brother.
5. His sister.

it, and sigh for the quiet of peace, when I could without loss of credit live in retirement, and only look to you for my reward in this life. I think that Bunbury need not have been so modest about his abilities, when D—— has carried on the office since M—— left the army, and when Colonel G—— is to carry it on. We expect to move in a day or two, as the whole army is concentrating about this place, and the stores have been moved to a great extent. I think that Marmont had certainly better look about him, or we shall be disagreeable. It will be curious if Lord W. should make the same manoeuvre that General Moore did three years ago upon the line of French communication on the North.

CHAPTER 6

Offer of Employment in the Portuguese Army

On his arrival in Portugal in April, 1812, Major William Napier took the command of the 43rd Regiment, in which he had now become Regimental Major. Soon afterwards the officers of the 3rd Caçadores (Portuguese) waited on him to say that their colonel was going to leave them, and to urge him to enter the Portuguese service, and accept the command of their regiment, stating that they had sufficient influence to obtain it for him. This solicitation on their part was very flattering, as he was not acquainted with any of them personally, and had gained their good opinion simply by his conduct as a captain in action, and by the manner of his discharge of the duties of brigade-major to their brigade. He refused their offer, however, from the belief that he had a better chance of distinction at the head of the 43rd. Major Napier assumed the command of that regiment at a time when, by the frightful licence of the storming of Badajoz and the removal by death or wounds of most of the old officers, habits of violence and insubordination had been formed which required both tact and firmness to eradicate.

On the heights of San Christoval at Salamanca Major Napier was obliged to flog four of his men within reach of the enemy's guns, and while some skirmishing was actually going on. They were the ringleaders of two hundred who had absolutely mutinied, inasmuch as they refused, when detached, to obey their officer. The Duke of Wellington was close by during the infliction of the punishment, and the men called to him, but he took no notice of them. The pain with which Napier felt himself compelled to adopt this mode of punishment towards men who had so recently behaved with such desperate valour in the fatal breach of Badajoz, is expressed in one of the foregoing letters.

From Major Hopkins to the Author.

After the fall of Badajoz, the men of the 43rd, having lost their beloved commander and most of their officers killed or wounded—*proud* from their feelings of having behaved well in the fight—full of *plunder*, which was permitted instead of being restrained—had lost their discipline when Major Napier assumed the command; indeed, they were actually mutinous; but his energy, strictness, and constant attention, not only restored their discipline, but made them superior to what they had ever been; for at the Battle of Salamanca I never witnessed such order and obedience as when they marched coolly forward with sloped arms against the enemy, who were bringing them down; and their spirit was so great, that I had the greatest trouble to get any man in the midst of the fight to fall out and assist the wounded; the reply was always, 'No, sir, I would rather go on with the company.' They never lost their high discipline, and fully evinced it by their conduct at Vittoria, as we actually walked over the richest articles of dress, furniture, &c., without a man picking up the most trifling article during the fight.

In the Battle of Salamanca the 43rd led the heavy column employed to drive back Foy's division and seize the ford of Huerta; and on that occasion the regiment made a very extraordinary advance in line for a distance of three miles, under a cannonade which, though not heavy, was constant, with as clean and firm a line as at a review. What renders this march more remarkable is that it was made after dark; the regiment kept its line simply by the touch to the centre; and the present General Shaw Kennedy, who commanded the left centre company on that occasion, has assured the writer that the line was so well kept as to have been able at any moment to fire a volley and charge with the bayonet Major Napier rode during the whole time in front of the left centre company, and from time to time joked with Captain Shaw on the safety of the humble pedestrian compared with the lot of a mounted officer, as the round shot all flew over the heads of the men on foot

A sketch of the battle of Salamanca, by an eyewitness, which appeared in the *United Service Journal* for March, 1829, has the following paragraph:—

Our skirmishers were obliged to give ground to the obstinacy of the enemy. The line of the 43rd was one of the finest specimens of discipline I ever saw, as steady as a rock, with Major William Napier twenty yards in front of the corps, alone; he was the point of direction. Our skirmishers ceased firing, and the line marched over them, dead and alive. I expected to see our chief unhorsed, and carried away in a blanket

The following account of the Duke of Wellington having been slightly wounded at Salamanca is related by Napier himself, who witnessed it:—

After dusk, at the battle of Salamanca, the Duke rode up *alone* behind my regiment, and I joined him; he was giving me some orders when a ball passed through his left holster, and struck his thigh; he put his hand to the place, and his countenance changed for an instant, but only for an instant; and to my eager inquiry if he was hurt, he replied, sharply, 'No!' and went on with his orders. Whether his flesh was torn or only bruised I know not.

Here follow some letters to his wife.

4 miles in front of Salamanca, June 18, 1812. We have been on the advance for the last seven days: what we are going to do I cannot tell; some say going to Paris, some to Madrid; I think, as far as we can, and then we shall come back again. Tell George we had a slight skirmish of cavalry six miles from Salamanca. The French evacuated the town, save about eight hundred who are in very strong forts near the bridge. The ground was broke before them last night, I believe with trifling loss. The 6th division carry on the operations; I think three days will finish them. I hear that a general combination of Sicilians, Spaniards, and English, are the means we are to use for the expulsion of the French, which nevertheless will not take place,—at least I think not I have been very well since we marched, which I was not before by any means.
Pray tell Major D—— when you see him that the butchers shot poor 'Jim,' the horse I bought from him: he however is not dead; the farrier says he will die, I say not. I am sorry for him, as he was long the property of poor Charles Macleod, which gave him an interest with me, besides being an excellent horse.......

Take care of yourself and some of these fine mornings you may chance to be a colonel's lady.

Parada Rubelias, June 29th, 1812.

There was no post after the army last week, which I will satisfy you about the lapse in the dates of my letters. Since I wrote last we have been constantly in position within cannon-shot of the French army under Marmont. There have been several skirmishing affairs along the line, and some manoeuvring. The forts in Salamanca have taken eleven days, and one unsuccessful assault by the 6th division, in which General Bowes behaved most gallantly and was killed. The loss has been severe, I believe, for the extent of the operation. I think Marmont had about 35,000 infantry, for which I am laughed at by most people, who say he had only 20,000; I believe Lord Wellington thought as I did, as he did not attack him, which he might have done.

Marmont crossed the River Tormes with nine or ten thousand men and threatened our communications, but was stopped by two divisions sent for that purpose; his view appeared to be to induce Lord Wellington to pass the river with his whole army, in which case Marmont would have taken up the line of the Tormes, which is very strong. Lord W. was not a young bird. After the forts fell the French retired, and we have made a march of four leagues after them.

The news of their retreat is various: some say they have divided,—part for Madrid, part for Toro; but George, for whom this is intended, will see best and most from the despatch. Should Buonaparte beat the Russians, as is most probable, I think the game will be up in the Peninsula, as we certainly cannot drive them out this summer, although I have no doubt we shall distress them a good deal I am sorry to say you are not yet the colonel's lady, but all in good time. By the bye the abuse of the French is all nonsense: they are certainly great scoundrels, as certainly as that the English are as great. General Moore was the only general who knew how to make good men and good soldiers. I could write a great deal and very seriously to you now if I liked, but I won't.......

P.S. Your watch-chains were good, but I have not lost the first one you gave me yet. Tell George I am second in command of the brigade and likely to continue so.

Rueda, July 7th, 1812.

You are a good little girl for taking so much trouble about the monumeut, and a clever little one too. Thank aunt Fanny for me, as many times as you wish yourself to be thanked. I know Westmacott's brother in the Staff Corps very well, and I am obliged to him for the interest he takes in it. George's sword is one of 5000 presents he has made me—so much for his veracity. With respect to us, General G—— is going home with sore eyes, and I believe old age. Lord W. has astonished everybody, and most people here abuse him; I confess it appears to me not only without reason, but contrary to reason, to do so. He has had several opportunities of figting with great advantage, which he has declined, and has not even pressed the enemy in his retreat.

I think his object is to force the enemy to cede territory to him, in which he succeeds, and also to inspire the Spaniards with confidence in the strength of his army and the greatness of his means. Were he once to fight, this would all vanish, because the French army, by acting on less extensive lines than they do at present, would again be able to show a force superior in number to himself, and he would have to retreat as usual after a victory; besides which, any movements from Madrid upon the road leading through Placentia or Avila would threaten his communications and oblige him to return much quicker than would be convenient with the train of wounded &c. which he would have after a battle. The proclamation is a forgery I am certain. I am not at all well, but cannot tell what's the matter with me. I believe a year's rest would be the best cure, but that cannot be.

Rueda, July 9. 1812.

I had hardly sent my last letters to the post when two packets containing letters from you arrived. This was a cause of much pleasure to me, feeling as I do such an earnest wish to get letters from you. They are a food to my mind that relieves it from sickly longings to which it has been subject ever since I left you; nevertheless it only relieves it for the moment, and they return with more force when I get to the end. Beading them over again does not do; I want something new about you every moment Major Bury, Lord Wellington's A. D. C, puts this letter up with the despatches which go off this night, although not the regular post-day for the army—he is a good fellow for his pains.

I am very sorry to hear that Lady Louisa[1] has not recovered quite from her fall. The widespread sorrow and gloom that any misfortune happening to her would cause is matter of much reflection, and makes one doubt whether it is a real good to be liked and loved as much as she is; it surely is enough to make persons so loved very selfish and careful of themselves when they consider the load of misery that hangs upon their existence.

Most earnestly do I hope that Charles will get Gifford to exchange with him; for my own part, I would almost sooner quit the army than go to garrison the Bermudas; not from fear of the climate, but from the knowledge that you are among people whose whole soul is given up to their luxurious appetites, whose enjoyments are founded on cruelty, and whose principles will every moment shock the feelings of a man of honour, while any abhorrence he expresses of them will engage him in quarrels or expose him to derision. Do not think this a picture at all exaggerated; our regiment was many years in the West Indies, and I know the amusements, the principles, the feelings that belong to them:—Enough of them.

Go more into company than you do; George was right to scold, and wrong to applaud you. Aunt Johnstone, to whom I send my love, has a good house in summer, but, if I guess right, it floats in winter—besides which I don't like the situation; nor shall we want a house if I stay in the army after this campaign. You have not sent me the drawing Westmacott promised you. Remember me kindly to Bunbury, from whom I received a letter this day; tell him Lord Wellington does not appear to be anxious to shake Marmont; the latter has been these last six days in front of us at Tordesillas, entrenched behind the Duero, seeming to care very little about us.

Florres de Avila, 25th July.

As I am sure you wished much to hear of a bloody battle, and that I should be at least wounded if not killed, this is to let you know that in the latter part you have met with a disap-

---

1. Lady L. Conolly.

pointment Our division had little to do; the regiment has only had 18 men wounded and two officers, of whom I am not one. Lord Wellington has beaten Marmont with the loss of near 5000 men prisoners, 4000 killed and wounded, and 16 pieces of cannon, and this is the second day's march in pursuit. Marmont has lost an arm, and is otherwise wounded.

We have lost one general killed and six wounded, with 4000 killed and wounded of the men; 2 eagles are taken. I am sorry to say that Cole has been wounded in the arm; Smith has lost an arm. Tom Lloyd commanded the 94th, and I have not heard of his being wounded. I have not had a letter from you later than the 25th of June. Although we had not as much as we wished of the battle, yet I am much pleased with the conduct of the regiment, which marched in line near three miles under a disagreeable fire from the French, with a degree of correctness that I never could persuade them to do on a field-day.

We should have lost a good many men was it not for the dusk, which prevented them from seeing correctly; great part of the battle was fought after dark. General Pakenham has particularly distinguished himself For George's information I give you an abstract of our movements, which will be better than bothering you with military affairs; to say the truth they bother me as much. I am really tired of seeing people butchered in a skilful way, and the more so as I do not perceive how we are to be ultimately successful, but that must be a secret. How much pleasanter it would be my Caroline to live with you in quiet and peace!

I might perhaps do as much good to my country there as here, and I really do not think that my wonderful military genius would be much missed in the army; besides, I should be retiring with wounds, honour, and a medal, and live to a green old age in comfort, with the power of saying, 'It was a pity I retired, as from my early promise I must have been a good general if I had persevered;' and farther, I could point out in the Army list the place I would have been at had I not left the profession. In short, I could be a much greater general than I ever will be by staying. 'Bleth my thoul, mama!' how the Club would stare when I told my stories! and the children would say, '*La, papa!* did you see Buonaparte? hath he got *mustachios?*' Instead of which I am obliged to flog men for being tired of marching 20 miles with 60 pounds weight on their shoulders and nothing to eat, and I am every day getting to be more and more of a savage in body and mind,—in short, very like the dragon when he swallowed the steeple clock.

Write to me, Caro, all the news, true or false, which you hear; flatter me up to the skies, it is very pleasant; never contradict me, and make your letter as long as possible, and tell me that a lieutenant-colonelcy is not worth having; that a man of spirit is, and that it is more meritorious to be, poor, miserable, and discontented, than rich, happy, and quiet; and that to be at home with one's wife is of all others the thing a man ought most to avoid.

A propos, get your picture painted; I want it to put in my baggage; and then if it is taken I shall have a fine paragraph in the *Moniteur* about my connubial love and your beauty, and your letters will be printed with the comments of the editor, and the ladies of Paris will be full of '*la belle* Caroline.' Should you want anything from Paris let me know, as we are going there directly; at least the Staff say so, and I suppose it is true. Of course you have had a rebellion in England before now. I hope you have not taken the benefit of the times and divorced me, as I really am not tired of you yet, although I am tired of writing.

Aldea Mayor, August 3rd, 1812.

I have been waiting with the greatest impatience to get letters from you, but no such thing appears: the 23rd of June is still the latest date, and I fear the mail is lost, which would be very unfortunate for me, because your letters are now more agreeable to me than they would be at any other time, we having no sort of rest or amusement, long marches, camps without water or wood, and the pleasant sight of murdered French, sick and stragglers, and the still more agreeable occupation of proving the truth of Vitellius's observation that *dead enemies are pleasant perfumes*.

I cannot be pleased with my luck, which by preventing me from having any considerable share in the battle has deprived me of the chance of getting the brevet rank of lieutenant-colonel. It certainly was not my fault, nor should I have failed in gaining it if we had been engaged, as the regiment was in such a state as to make Lord W. mention them several times since in public conversation; at all events, I shall have a medal tied to the fourth button of the right side with a blue and red riband of full three inches long. Lloyd is to get a lieutenant-colonelcy, whereat I am glad, but then Hearn is arrived at Lisbon to take the command from me, whereat I am sorry. Our loss has been greater than was at first supposed—5300.

Tell George poor General Terney, who fought the light division at Barba de Púerco, at the Coa, and at Busaco, died of his wounds at Olmedo; and the fine-spirited Spaniards dug up his body and bruised his head with stones. For the honour of the light division I have buried him again in spite of them. Marmont lost his arm and had two or three wounds. The people of Tudela say he died three days ago. He was a brave fellow and a good officer, and had the best of the business until the 22nd. when he extended his left wing too much, and Lord Wellington seized the opportunity like a hawk.

We have so little communication at present that I really cannot give you any idea what we are going to do; Soult may however insist on our fighting him. When you see Mark, tell him to let you know where Lopez' grand map of Spain, in sheets of provinces, is to be found in London, and then if you can get it for that sum give 20 guineas for it; if for less, so much the better; but remember it must be Lopez', his own and not Tadius. . .

I hope most earnestly that Charles is not gone to the West Indies.

After the Battle of Salamanca Wellington with his victorious army entered Madrid; and here Napier remained with his regiment, while the lives of so many gallant men were being vainly sacrificed before Burgos through the negligence of the English ministry to supply Lord Wellington with a proper battering train. After the raising of the siege of Burgos the 43rd joined the army on its retreat into Portugal; and the following graphic narrative of an incident during that retreat is from a private memoir of Sir William Napier.

On the retreat from Salamanca in the winter of 1812 I was the person who first discovered the approach of the French cavalry, to the number of 6000, when they were within a mile of our bivouac. The front of the division had been without any notice uncovered by our cavalry, and that great mass of French horsemen would in a short time have tumbled unexpectedly into our bivouac before we had got under arms, if I had not discovered them and given the alarm. Some of their light parties had already passed our flanks, and were in our rear; and these were the people who took the baggage and made Sir Edward Paget prisoner.

The main body lost time, because Colonel Alex. MacDonald, myself, and another officer (I think it was Sir John Tylden), drove back some of their scouts; and having thus got a perfect view of their main body, we were enabled to give information to Julian Sanchez' guerrillas, and to a squadron of the 14th Dragoons (Townsend's squadron I think), who favoured by the woods kept them for a while in check, and gave time for the division to commence its march without being seriously engaged; but the light horsemen infested our flanks at a few hundred yards' distance the whole way to the Huebra.

When we arrived at that river Lord Wellington rode up, and finding the division, strangely enough, formed in squares while the French infantry skirmishers were actually infesting our flank and rear, he appeared much displeased, gave the word himself to retreat across the Huebra, and directed me to take four companies, two of the Rifles and two of the 43rd, and cover the retrograde movement.

He was very angry, and reprimanded Alten who was near by his mode of addressing me: 'What the devil are you about here with your squares?' 'They are not my squares, they are General Alten's' 'Get into column, and retreat with the division.' 'There is General Alten, sir.' 'Don't reply—order the division to retreat,—and—do you hear, sir?—cover it with four companies of the 43rd and Riflemen.' I took the hint, and carried the order to Alten to retreat

We were then on the woody brow of a hill overlooking the river, but with an open and smooth though steep descent of about half a mile to the nearest ford. There was rain and a mist, which prevented the French from discovering our numbers and true position, and we kept the edge of the wood above, until not only the division, but many stragglers and some wounded cavalry men, had passed the fords. By that time thirty-six pieces of French artillery were playing upon the division from a projecting brow farther to our left, but not so near nor so favourably situated for annoying the columns.

Their infantry also had descended still further to our left, and were engaged with the 52nd, who were defending a ford a good cannon-shot higher up the stream, and actually in our rear, while the French cavalry were close behind their skirmishers in our front, waiting to charge us when we should retreat down the open descent. Nevertheless, by giving a quick and well-sustained fire and then running down before the smoke cleared away, we gained the fords in safety. Ross's guns fired shrapnel shells over our heads as we descended, and thus kept the enemy in check.

General Alten was present during this operation, but he gave no orders and did not in any manner interfere with me except at the moment we were descending the hill, when he ordered me to halt half-way down and form a line, but I convinced him that as there was nothing to wait for we should only lose men without an object My clothes were twice shot through on this occasion, and my horse was grazed. Charles Beckwith also joined in remonstrating with him on the inutility of stopping, for he was a very obstinate man in fire, his remarkable courage overwhelming every other faculty.

During this retreat, which so severely tried the discipline of the army generally, the 43rd committed no disorders and left no stragglers behind, which Napier generously attributed as much to the exertions of Major Ferguson as to his own. Of this officer he always entertained the highest opinion; and in after years, when Napier memorialized the commander-in-chief to obtain what he felt to be his due, he thus expressed himself:—

> Your lordship [2] is aware how earnestly I urged Ferguson's claims to notice; and I can never forget how you persevered until you obtained promotion for him. He has long since received the regimental rank of lieutenant-colonel, while I remain a major; but far from complaining of his success, I rejoice at it; and if he had been selected for any honour before me I would never repine; a braver and more zealous officer never entered the field, and I hold his services before my own. I mention him merely to show that I have no mean jealousy of others' merits.

When the army terminated the retreat above referred to at Ciudad

---

2. Addressed to Lord Fitzroy Somerset, Military Secretary to the Commander-in-Chief.

Rodrigo, the 43rd were quartered in the suburbs of that town; and one of them was brutally stabbed by a Spanish artilleryman. Major Napier got an order to have the artillerymen paraded for the purpose of identifying the assassin; but the commander paraded them in the evening, and dismissed them a quarter of an hour before Napier arrived with his witness. Captain Carrol, *aide-de-camp* to General Carrol, from whom the order for inspecting the regiment was obtained, was also with him. This trick, for they had arrived ten minutes before the appointed time, was followed up with a great deal of blustering insolence in the barrack-yard, and when the parading of the regiment again was peremptorily demanded, the Spanish officer would only do it in the barrack-rooms, and would not then allow Napier's witness to enter with him.

Night was setting in, the rooms were low and dark, and the officer spoke so insolently and was so evidently encouraging his men to tumult, that Captain Carrol begged Napier to retire, as he feared an outrage would be perpetrated. This Napier would not do; and in going down the ranks he observed one man rather uneasy, and remarked that he wore a cleaner shirt than his comrades. Napier immediately seized this man and demanded to see his knapsack. The officer refused and actually encouraged his men to violence; but there were amongst them some of soldierlike feeling who kept back the more turbulent, and a sergeant pointed out the man's pack, which Napier opened, and from which he pulled out a shirt covered with blood on the right sleeve.

The man's guilt was now evident, and Napier attempted to make him a prisoner, but it was getting quite dark, and he was hustled in such a manner that the man escaped from his grasp; and although afterwards, by application to the governor and complaint to Lord Wellington, the assassin was arrested, and several witnesses to his crime were obtained who identified him in prison, Napier never could succeed in getting him tried.

Soon after this affair Major Napier obtained leave to go to England, because he properly belonged to the 2nd battalion of his regiment, and because he was superseded in the command of the 1st by the arrival of the lieutenant-colonel. He was at this time suffering severely from what was then considered to be a nephritic complaint, but which was in reality the commencement of neuralgic pains, caused by the bullet which had passed round his spine, fracturing one of the processes in its course, and which continued to lie near it during the remainder of his life, creating at times intolerable anguish.

The following letters to his wife were written between the battle of Salamanca and his return to England.

Getaffa, near Madrid, August 13th, 1812.

I have received your letter of the 29th. Don't send me any more papers, as we get them regularly. I had written a long letter to you which was to have gone by Major Bury, but charming Mr. Feagan lost my fine writing-desk and your letter in it, together with my drawings and several curiosities which I had collected for you, a Legion of Honour, &c. &c. The worst of it is that it has put me to much inconvenience about writing, and I fear you will suffer in these points. In the letter there was a description of the palace of St. Ildefonso, of the Escurial, and Madrid, which I must defer until I see you, save that Madrid is an enchanting and enchanted town, and the palace is the most superb, the most chaste, and the richest thing both inside and out, that ever was reared by the hands of man. How it came to be in Spain God only knows....

Have you ever called upon Mrs. James Moore since I left England? are they angry at my neglect, which I acknowledge? and will you give her a Lisbon chain with a fine speech from me? that is, if it is a curiosity; if not, I will send you a beetle-leg for her the first opportunity...... I feared that Westmacott would not do at first, as I have seen several of his which I think bad. Bacon would be better; at all events get somebody, as a battle would deprive me of half my subscriptions, and the affair drop to the ground Feagan has lost also my cocked-up hat and a few other trifles, and my best horse is dying; but I am a philosopher. &c. &c.

Madrid, August 25th, 1812.

I have been the whole night at a ball at the palace, and notwithstanding that it is now only two I am already up and sufficiently awake to write you a long letter...... We have and are likely to be very quiet for some time; the army seem to be lost in the delights of Capua. The scene is very amusing here: all the *heroes* of Spain in the form of guerrilla chiefs are here, mixed with old marquises, young counts, English generals, and amateurs, all as gay and confident as if there was not a Frenchman in the country. Tell Bunbury that the picture in his office of the *Em-*

pecinado[3] is not at all like him. . . .

Adieu, my best friend. &c. &c.

Madrid, 30th Aug. 1812.

I am much surprised at your saying I missed a packet about the latter end of June; I not only wrote every time the mail went, but once out of the regular post I have since that, in the first part of this month, failed in one, in consequence of not knowing in time when the letters were to be put into the bag I perceive upon looking over your letter that it is Bermuda, and not as I supposed Barbadoes, where Charles is gone: there is much difference in the climate, although I suppose he will go on to Halifax or Canada. I think Bunbury very wild about his *must* succeed with the Russians and French: as yet it appears to me that Buonaparte has beat them to a good tune without fighting, and certainly I see nothing to augur good from in the destruction of magazines, and the loss of a nation of seven millions of good warlike people. Their armies appear to be badly managed into the bargain; and I think on the whole they appear to have the worst of it. &c. &c.

Madrid, Sept 5th, 1812.

Since I last wrote to you we have been quiet, if dancing and other sports can be called quiet Lord W. left this three days ago with a division to oppose Marmont's army at Valladolid, which is again in force, I believe 28,000 men. The 3rd and light divisions have been left here, and it seems to be the object now to let the latter have nothing to do: it is rather hard that the only period in which this has happened should be the time I command a regiment I have seen a bull-fight, which is really too horrid, although the dexterity of the men who fight is so great as to leave you in doubt whether it was in earnest or not, and yet three horses were killed and nine bulls; it is much more cruel than bull-baiting.

Since my last letter there has been a great change in the household; the senior Feagan has been turned away, and William near dead; he is however now quite well, but rather weak. I have got in place of Feagan a very handsome young gentleman whom I hope Mrs. Holm will not think so very *outré* as Feagan. The siege of Cadiz they say is raised, and there seems to be some

---

3. Juan Martin, the Guerrilla chief.

ground to believe that the French mean to pass the Ebro, but nothing certain. M—— has landed at Alicant, the worst place he could; and since he has landed he acts like a blockhead. This is a great pity; I am afraid he will get a beatings although he is cautious enough, as he made a forced march of seven leagues to avoid a French army who were only 150 miles from him. Tell Louisa Bunbury that I know of but one way of getting out of the red hair that Ned is afflicted with, and that is by cutting off the head itself. &c. &c

Madrid. Sept. 20th.

I am very much distressed at the accounts I get (both from yourself and other people) of the extreme lowness of spirits and anxiety that you have undergone. You say that you have not spoilt a good soldier, but if you have not you very soon will at this rate, for I cannot consent to let you kill yourself with fretting because Sir Home Popham is on the north coast of Spain. "We have been now a month without a post starting from here, which will account to you for the long time you must have been without a letter from me. *A propos*, there is a mail every fortnight by the way of Coruna, which you may as well write by *also*, as I believe it will bring the news to a later date than the Lisbon mail. . . . . If Patrickson comes out I will go home, provided that Hearn does not fall sick. &c. &c.

Madrid. Sept 27. 1812.

We are still at rest here while the divisions under Lord Wellington are besieging the castle of Burgos; it is very strong, and we have lost 420 men in storming *one* of the outworks, but it will probably fall soon. Always please yourself about living in any place or how you like, and then you will please me. 'Nowney'[4] is an excellent good thing for taking care of you so well.

I am not at all of Bunbury's side about Russia; so far from thinking Napoleon in a scrape, I think he has placed the Emperor Alexander in one of a very serious description. Take a large map and look for Witepsk on the Dwina,—that is the headquarters of the French; then look at Moghilev, Orcha, and the mouth of the Beresina where it joins the Dnieper,—that marks the right wing of the French; then look back to the Dwina at Polotsk, Drissa, and Dinaburg,—that marks the left

---

4. His wife's former governess and lasting friend, Miss Townsend.

wing of the French. Smolensko is the headquarters of the Russians. *Now* observe that *Nap* is between Smolensko and Riga, which is at the mouth of the Dwina; observe also that he has two corps, about 70,000 men, before Riga.

Having seen this, you will know that Buonaparte's army is in a very strong position, having the Dwina on the left flank and the Dnieper on the rights while his front is very short between these rivers, and he has the whole of Poland full of corn in his rear. It is evident that if he can force Alexander to fight without going out of that position, it will be much to his advantage. To do this he has only to take possession of Courland, Livonia, and Esthonia, which include Petersburg, Bevel, and Riga, the best towns of Russia; he may at the same time declare Livonia, &c., separated for ever from Russia, and he has *ruined* Russia as an empire. To get it back she must fight him where he is now, as I said before.

If he does not fight, he will have time to organize these provinces into a kingdom, which will have the Narva and a great lake to cover its front to the north-east; while the Dwina with its strongholds will defend it on the south, and the kingdom of Poland will flank any army marching against it. The first step towards this object will be the siege of Riga; the next will be manifestos against Peter I. for his injustice in annexing the Livonians to Russia; the third will be the siege of Bevel; and the fourth, taking possession of St Petersburg. If Alexander beats him in a battle, all this will not take place. If it does take place, say I am a general; if not, hold your tongue.

It is by no means improbable that the programme thus sketched out for Napoleon might have been carried out almost to the letter, if the French emperor had not relinquished the secure and commanding position he then held to advance on Moscow.

Letters to his Wife continued.

Madrid, October 12, 1812.

Your letters come to me constantly and always with the greatest welcome and joy. I have also received your painting-box, but your friend —— lost all his parcels; and Stanhope, thinking I should not want paper at Madrid, left his parcels behind. How dare you talk of sorrow for my absence, when I am at this moment preparing to hand over the command of the regiment to Daniel Hearn, resigning my glory and my dearer promotion into his hands? and yet I live and am merry, very merry. Have you seen Marmont's despatch? it is scientific, modest, and true to the utmost extent; and is, methinks, a hard hit upon the French despatches in general. Burgos goes on ill, very ill, and doubts are entertained if it will ever fall.

Alcala, October 25, 1812.

I believe I told you Stanhope left all the writing-paper in Lisbon; and as they have not given us any money for three months I could not buy any in Madrid,—what a long excuse for such short paper! I believe I am rather afraid of you. I don't understand the cause of your growing so thin and pale. Are you sure that you take good care of yourself? My Caro, you must not fail to grow better, if you wish me to be at all easy about you. If it is only anxiety I am in hopes you will soon find the end of your uneasiness, as Hearn[5] is at last arrived, and I believe that Patrickson[5] is at Corunna, in which case I have no doubt that I shall be ordered home when the latter arrives at the regiment Soult has been making some demonstrations near us, which is the cause of the present move.

Burgos has cost us 3000 men, and I am afraid there is little chance of its falling at all, certainly not without a farther loss of at least 2000 more; all the assaults latterly have failed; it is now a sort of blockade under Pack. Lord Wellington has moved forward under the idea of fighting Masséna, who is said to command Marmont's army now. In the meantime the Spaniards do nothing in the way of exerting themselves; they voted three months back 50,000 men, and they have not at this day taken the census of the villages from whence the men are to be drawn.

The government is abhorred, and with great reason; each night from twenty to thirty poor people are taken up in Madrid and put into the Retiro. No trial takes place, nobody knows what becomes of them; their estates are confiscated, and their families driven to die of famine in the streets. Nothing but the presence of the British army prevents an insurrection, and I am certain that if we were to set up for ourselves the people would will-

---

5. The two senior field officers, 43rd.

ingly and instantly join us and declare Lord Wellington king of Spain. They have even felt the pulse of the English by expressions of that nature in the theatres. If we do not interfere, I am convinced that the French will be welcomed back again, although at present they do not like them. It is an unfortunate country, cursed with a thousand ills, and of all the thousand there is none so bad or so cursed as the guerrillas that are so much admired in England,—happy, stupid, credulous England! I cannot describe to you the grief of the people when the English left Madrid. We had fed numbers of them by subscription, and they said, 'Now we shall starve, and worse than starving, we shall have the dreadful guerrillas again.'

This was the language not of the poor alone but of every class of people. I have seen the eighteenth bulletin; I suppose Bunbury does not think that the Russians *must succeed* now, unless he can see a victory on the side of the latter at Mojaisk,[6] which I have seen some people here do. Your friend Maitland has been superseded in the command, and his army has done nothing. This seems to be a melancholy prospect in the political way, yet Lord Wellington has a great force under him, a month of fine weather, and a head that I believe is not overmarked by any Cabeça in the Peninsula.

His next letter is dated from Ciudad Rodrigo after the retreat from Burgos.

            Caridad Convent, Ciudad Rodrigo, 20th Nov. 1812.
I have very little time to write, but I am in much fear of your hearing bad news of me, a report having spread that I was slain. I am not wounded or sick. We have had a retreat of 68 leagues, bad roads, rainy weather, no provisions, and constantly lying out at nights. The retreat to say the truth was badly managed, the loss immense . . .

From Salamanca the number of stragglers amounts to at least 5000 men. We had on the 17th marched some hours through woods when we found the French cavalry had cut us off from the other divisions, taking baggage, sick, and Sir Edward Paget We were attacked, formed squares, and then found that their infantry were upon us; retreated, leaving four companies under my command to skirmish and cover the retreat over a deep

---

6. The Battle of Borodino.

narrow river, under a hill[7] within musket-shot. This we did, losing 27 men. I had a shot through my clothes, nothing more on my honour my dear, and I *beant* a hero, for Barnard and General Alten were both there directing, although I had the command. We were afterwards cannonaded severely and lost an officer wounded and some men; Rideout had his leg off. This is for George, who I am glad to hear is married. Tell him so—and also that Dawson is killed, poor fellow! and Fuller badly wounded. Hearn is very ill and I have the command.

Gallegos, Dec. 1, 1812.

We are settled in winter-quarters, and you are a good girl for writing as you do. Your present letters, just received, are full of fun and uncommonly diverting. I never got your letter about your brother's intentions of getting into Parliament When he next sets up for Maldon, don't let him divulge that I am his brother-in-law, or else the whole of the Low Church party, who I suppose are his friends, will be against him; I having personally annoyed them even to the *marrow*.[8]

The sketch you sent me by Bacon is good, and I think will be adopted, that is, without the little genius at top, which is perfectly absurd; the inscription is to be in Lord Wellington's words about him[9] in the despatch. I am doing a copy for the officers to decide upon which they like best; mine is without the boy, which I think will, by being taken away, allow the artist to give more relief and execution to the figure. It must not cost more than £300, although I would pay myself a few more guineas, if it were necessary to do it without the officers knowing anything of it In my next I will let you know more about it I am in command again.

Hearn is sick, but I hope he will not go home, as that would put an end to my hopes when Patrickson appeared. I am with other officers suffering very severely in my feet from a fever in them. We are the funniest cripples you ever saw, in uncommon pain, our toes feeling as if they were always out of bed of a cold winter night, and the foot has all sorts of *aitches* in it There are no marks, and we hobble along like Grimaldi, everybody laugh-

---

7. This hill was on the enemy's side of the river, and in possession of the enemy, who thus were able to fire on the British troops while crossing.
8. Refers to an early escapade, when a young man, quartered at Maldon.
9. Colonel Macleod.

ing; for my part I think it a bad joke. Poor Rideout, who was so badly wounded, is dead. He bore the amputation with the most admirable serenity and fortitude, and two days after died of a gangrene in the *well* foot from cold. We regret him much; he was so inoffensive, so hardy, and so willing to do everybody service, that if he did riot make very attached particular friends he certainly left no enemies of any kind. It was astonishing how the recollection of his unoffending manners seized upon everybody during his funeral, and people who seldom thought of him before actually wept then. I always liked him much, poor fellow!

Gallegos, 15th December, 1812.
I received your letter and parcels. The book[10] is delightful; certainly the best of the kind that has appeared for many years, and not till it was wanted. Wordsworth is the best, and I am particularly obliged to them for it Cobbett's I don't think good, but all things of that kind must be in verse or but indifferent. Doctor Johnson's excepted, which is a peculiar style. Scott is the truth, the whole truth, and nothing but the truth: I always thought that his poetry contained more words than wit, more sound than sense. *The Morning Post* is excellent, and not a bit overdone, and is an epitome of 'the always to be blamed and never enough to be sufficiently censured and bedamned ministry now guiding the helm of affairs.' The muffetees you sent are very useful, as I exchange them for worsted stockings, with which I make racket-balls.

The Peer Wellington has just issued what he calls a circular to the army, in which he obligingly informs them that they are a parcel of the greatest knaves and the worst soldiers that he not only ever had to deal with, but worse than any army he ever *read* of. He was good enough to say that he excepted the Light Division and the Guards, but he makes no exceptions in writing . . . . King Joseph is an excellent man, as I can prove in a thousand instances of his merit and good nature told me by a prisoner who benefited by his disposition . . . . How much I admire Mr. Brougham! ardent, zealous in the just cause, daring, enterprising, and eloquent to the greatest possible pitch.

If any man is gifted sufficiently to pierce the thick skulls of

---
10. *Rejected Addresses.*

the English, to prevent them from deliberately walking over a precipice, it is Mr. Brougham. How Canning could be chosen instead of him is astonishing. . . . . The papers are uncommonly diverting about our movements. Wise people! how much they flatter themselves they know about it! Lord Wellington gone to Cadiz with Lord Fitzroy Somerset only attending him. *Apropos*, the last is as good as he is clever, and nearly as clever as Lord Wellington himself; he will one day be a great man if he lives. As soon as Junius is known in England send me an express. &c. &c. &c.

CHAPTER 7

The Petite Rhune

Major Napier went to England in January 1813. He remained at home till the following August, when, being again posted to the 1st battalion, he returned to the Peninsula. The advance of the British army to Vittoria had enabled Wellington to sever his communication with Portugal, and to adopt the northern Spanish seaports as his ports of supply, and Napier accordingly landed at Passages on the 19th August, and proceeded to join his regiment at the camp above Vera, in the Pyrenees. Part of the army under Graham was employed in the siege of San Sebastian, and the breaches and trenches of that place had been vainly saturated with British blood in the assault of the 24th July. Always eager for distinction, when Lord Wellington issued his well-known order calling for volunteers from the 1st, 4th, and light divisions, "men who could show other troops how to mount a breach," Major Napier volunteered to lead the light division stormers. He was accepted, and even put in orders for that service.

Many officers and men who had before been engaged in affairs of the same kind offered themselves expressly to give him support, and, following the order of the day, these officers and men found their way to the market-place of Lesaca, where they were to parade. But when he arrived there to take the command, he was suddenly informed that Lieutenant-Colonel Hunt of the 52nd was to lead them, and that his services would not be required. Much mortified, he remonstrated with General Alten, but without avail, on the injustice done him. He then went to Colonel Hunt and urged him to forego his claim. Hunt then told him, that having gained his rank and having been on several storming parties, he had had no intention of offering himself and did not know Napier had volunteered.

He had heard a Major —— was the man, and not thinking him

of sufficient capacity to do the division justice he had come forward; feeling now how hard it was upon Napier, he consented to forego his claim if the other could procure an order from Lord Wellington to that effect to save Hunt's honour, but not otherwise.

He did apply to Lord Wellington, who would not listen to him, saying, he did not approve of volunteering, although obliged to resort to it sometimes, as he lost his best officers in that way. Napier was so chagrined that he was resolved to take a musket and march with the men who had come forward at his call, since he could not command them; but General Alten, getting some inkling of his design, ordered him forthwith to join his regiment. Of Hunt he thus speaks in the *History*:—

> Lieutenant-Colonel Hunt, a daring officer, who had already won his promotion at former assaults, was at the head of the fierce, rugged veterans of the light division.

The following account of the storming of one of the strongest mountain positions on record, *viz.* of the hog's-back ridge of the Petite Rhune Mountain in the Pyrenees, is transcribed from Sir William's private memoir, both for its intrinsic interest and for the lesson it affords to the military student

> On the 10th November (1813), Colonel Hearn having resigned to me the command of the 43rd, I was charged to storm the hog's-back ridge of the Petite Rhune mountain, which had been entrenched by six weeks' continuous labour on the part of the enemy. I have given an accurate description of it and of the action in my *History*, and the strength of the rocks may be in some measure understood from Heaphy's picture of the British Generals, of which they form the background. But there are some passages which were not fitting for a history as only regarding myself, which I will now relate.
> The plan of attack was entirely my own, for General Kempt wished me to attack the rocks with my whole battalion, and it was with difficulty I obtained his leave to detach Captain Murchison with two companies to try the marsh on our left, and to keep down if possible the enemy's fire. A rifle sergeant sent to sound the marsh had assured the general it was impassable, but I was convinced it was not; and so it proved, for Murchison passed it, and contributed by his judgment and gallantry very much to the success of the attack: he was mortally wounded at

the very moment of victory.

I had a great distance to march on a front line towards the rocks and under fire, before I could gain the narrow entrance between the lower part and the marsh, where only the enemy could be attacked, for in other parts the rocks were 200 feet high. There were two things to be principally looked to: first, not to blow the men by running too soon, and thus coming breathless upon the stone castles which had been built up by the enemy, and would require great exertions of bodily strength as well as courage to face—this my experience at Cazal Nova made me very anxious about; secondly, as the men were sure to be so broken and dispersed by fighting among the rocks, and as they would be liable to disasters when they had carried them—for we knew nothing of the nature of the ground nor of the enemy's reserves behind the ridge—it was essential to have our reserves well in hand.

In this view I placed four companies under Major Duffy at the distance of 300 yards, and with the four remaining companies advanced in person to storm the rocks. I had not however proceeded above half the distance when the fire became very heavy, and at this moment when I had the greatest difficulty to keep the men from breaking into the charge, the Hon. Captain Gore, A. D. C. to General Kempt, who looking down upon us from the heights behind could not see how rugged the ground was, nor judge of our distance, thinking us slow—with the impetuosity of a young staff officer rode down at full speed and galloped up behind my line, waving his hat and shouting out to charge.

The men instantly cheered and ran forward. It was in vain to try, and would have been dangerous, to stop them, and I could only make the best of the matter. I was the first man but one who reached and jumped into the rocks, and I was only second because my strength and speed were unequal to contend with the giant who got before me. He was the tallest and most active man in the regiment, and the day before, being sentenced to corporal punishment, I had pardoned him on the occasion of an approaching action. He now repaid me by striving always to place himself between me and the fire of the enemy. His name was Eccles, an Irishman; he died afterwards a sergeant and pensioner on the Irish establishment.

The mischief I had foreseen now arrived; the men were quite blown, and fell down in the rocks within a few yards of the first castle, from whence the enemy plied them with a heavy musketry. When they had recovered wind I advanced against the first castle, leading the way with one man: the enemy fled, with the exception of an officer and two of his men; but, aided by my own man I scaled the wall. We put the two men to flight, and wounded and took the officer, for he fought to the last, standing on the wall and throwing heavy stones at me. One I parried with my sword, but I received a contusion in the thigh from another.

The regiment then carried several castles in succession, the enemy fighting us muzzle to muzzle the whole way, so that many of the men's clothes were scorched all over the front with the fire. This fact Lord Seaton knows, for I showed him my own clothes thus scorched. When I got to their principal place of arms, and had only one remaining castle called the Donjon to carry, I saw that a breastwork entrenchment and fort below the ridge were still defended by the French and that they were very numerous. I therefore endeavoured to rally my companies, both to make a vigorous assault on the Donjon and to have a body of men in hand to attack the rear of those defending the entrenchment below.

At this moment Sir Andrew Barnard came up to me alone, and I explained my intentions to him. While thus employed, Lieutenant Steele, a very quick and brave officer, called out that they were wavering in the Donjon; and as it was very strong and covered by a cleft in the rock fifteen feet deep, and only to be turned by one narrow path winding round a rock on the right, I gave up the notion of rallying the broken men, and, rushing forward with what I had, carried the Donjon. I now saw the French flying from the entrenchment below also, and had an opportunity of cutting them off or driving the greatest part into the hands of the 52nd, who were in the ravines beyond the table-land upon which the French were retreating. I looked for my reserve under Major Duffy, but I was told it was dispersed; I could therefore do no more. How or why my reserve was dispersed, so contrary to my orders, and without any apparent necessity, I never could learn.

Nevertheless I had with six companies (my own four and the

two under Captain Murchison) stormed the rocks in twenty minutes from the time I first jumped into the lower part; I took about 100 prisoners, and the violence of the action may be judged by the loss; 67 men and 11 officers of the 43rd having been killed or wounded, and, of the 11 officers, four were killed on the spot or died next day of their wounds, and two others were so desperately wounded as to be reported killed. I do think, if Lord Wellington had witnessed the action, he would have mentioned it in the despatches.

The storming of the Petite Rhune Mountain, although it contributed powerfully to the general successful result, was yet only one part of an operation covering a great extent of ground; and in mountain warfare it is impossible for the commander to see what is going on all along his front. Unfortunately for Napier, the exploit did not fall under Wellington's personal observation. Had it done so, his name would certainly have been prominently mentioned in the despatch. Such a lottery is military life! Here was one of the most brilliant exploits of the whole war, in which was combined the fiery courage of the Sabreur with the calm observant sagacity of the skilful leader, unknown to and unnoticed by the Commander who was so deeply indebted to it for his success.

The following extracts from letters written by Sir Andrew Barnard, who commanded the Rifle Brigade in this action, refer to the above account

SIR ANDREW BARNARD TO COLONEL W. NAPIER.

Jan. 3. 1841.

I feel proud in having it in my power to record that moment, which I had the good fortune to witness, when the fire from an enemy's musket had severely scorched your pantaloons, bearing a proof of how closely you had been engaged with the enemy; at the same time I cannot forget how judicious were your intentions, which you explained to me, regarding the future operations of the 43rd Regiment in the midst of the excitement of the storm which was then taking place. Had any report of the action been made to the Duke, your name deserved a most prominent place; but, if you recollect, in the hurry of his writing his despatch he forgot to mention the division at all, and made the *amende* in strong general terms in a subsequent letter.

Again:—

> I am convinced that if any officer of superior rank had had the opportunity of observing your conduct on the occasion of the storming of the '*Petite Rhune*,' it would have been the subject of a particular report. I am sure Kempt will bear me out in this, as he witnessed the style in which the 43rd carried the stronghold of the enemy's position.

The events above referred to in connection with the storming of the "Petite Rhune" were comprised in the Battle of the Nivelle, and are related in the *History* under the head of that battle; but although Napier acted so distinguished a part, a part which if played by any other officer would have drawn from him especial praise, he does not once mention his own name. In this Battle of the Nivelle was killed Napier's old and dear friend Lloyd, he being at the time lieutenant-colonel commanding the 94th Regiment

The character of Lieutenant-Colonel Lloyd, and of Lieutenant Freer of the 43rd, who was also killed at the battle of the Nivelle, are described in the *History* as follows:—

> The first, low in rank, for he was but a lieutenant; rich in honour, for he bore many scars; was young of days—he was only nineteen, and had seen more combats and sieges than he could count years. So slight in person and of such surpassing and delicate beauty that the Spaniards often thought him a girl disguised in man's clothing, he was yet so vigorous, so active, so brave, that the most daring and experienced veterans watched his looks on the field of battle, and, implicitly following where he led, would like children obey his slightest sign in the most difficult situations.
>
> His education was incomplete, yet were his natural powers so happy that the keenest and best furnished intellects shrunk from an encounter of wit; and every thought and aspiration was proud and noble, indicating future greatness if destiny had so willed it. Such was Edward Freer of the 43rd. The night before the battle he had that strange anticipation of coming death so often felt by military men; he was struck with three balls at the first storming of the Rhune rocks, and the sternest soldiers wept, even in the middle of the fight, when they saw him fall. On the same day, and at the same hour, was killed Colonel Thomas Lloyd. He likewise had been a long time in the 43rd.

Under him Freer had learned the rudiments of his profession; but in the course of the war, promotion placed Lloyd at the head of the 94th, and it was leading that regiment he fell. In him also were combined mental and bodily powers of no ordinary kind.

Graceful symmetry, herculean strength, and a countenance frank and majestic, gave the true index of his nature; for his capacity was great and commanding, and his military knowledge extensive both from experience and study. Of his mirth and wit, well known in the army, it only need be said that he used the latter without offence, yet so as to increase the ascendency over those with whom he held intercourse; for though gentle, he was ambitious, valiant, and conscious of fitness for great exploits. And he, like Freer, was prescient of, and predicted his own fall, but with no abatement of courage; for when he received the mortal wound, a most painful one, he would not suffer himself to be moved; and remained to watch the battle, making observations upon its changes until death came.

It was thus at the age of thirty, that the good, the brave, the generous Lloyd died. Tributes to his memory have been published by Wellington, and by one of his own poor soldiers; by the highest and by the lowest To their testimony I add mine: let those who served on equal terms with him say whether in aught it has exaggerated his deserts.

The following extract from a letter written to the author of the *Peninsular War* in 1840, by Captain Thornton, formerly of the 42nd Regiment, bears interesting testimony to the affection Napier felt for his comrade.

I have received a letter from a brother officer who is brigade-major at Barbadoes. He says, 'The packet before last brought us out the sixth volume of Napier's *History*: he has kept his promise to you about *his* and our ever-to-be-lamented friend Lloyd; well may his family and friends be proud of his fame. Two officers are now in this garrison, Jones the barrack-master, and Captain Hill of the 81st Regiment) who were in the 43rd at the Nivelle. When the news arrived of the death of Lloyd they both declared that Napier threw himself on the ground and cried like a child. This trait in Napier's character raises him more in my estimation than even his splendid and eloquent

History; it stamps the feeling, the enthusiasm of the historian for his profession, and his grief at Lloyd's glorious professional career being thus so soon brought to a close, increased by his sincere friendship founded indeed on admiration, was more than the surviving *real soldier* could bear with his usual fortitude.

The presentiment felt by Freer of his approaching end, which the historian has recorded in the character of that officer above given, became known to his friend and commanding officer in the following manner.

The night before the Battle of the Nivelle, Major Napier was stretched on the ground under a large cloak, when young Freer came to him and crept under the cover of his cloak, sobbing as if his heart would break. In his endeavours to soothe and comfort the boy, Napier learnt from him that he was firmly persuaded he should lose his life in the approaching battle, and his distress was caused by thinking of his mother and sisters in England.

The nature of the man must have been tender and loveable which could draw the boy to his side at such a time with such touching confidence in his sympathy, and induce him to confide all his trouble to his commander rather than to some friend among his brother subalterns more nearly his own age. And the contrast which this incident reveals, of Napier's tenderness of nature, with his heroism in the field, and with the fierceness of his attacks upon any wrong perpetrated on the weak, is very interesting.

The following letters to his wife relate to the period which intervened between his quitting England on the 23rd July, 1813, and the Battle of the Nivelle.

Weymouth, July 31st, 1813.

We have again been brought up here with a contrary wind, and you see that I am as good as my promise, losing no opportunity of writing to you.[1] I am very anxious to get to Plymouth, as I expect a letter from you at that place, telling me how you are. How did Dick get back? he was not much the better I thought for the journey down. I hope you sent him the wine. How curious it is that when I want to say most to you I can say least! my mind is full of you at this moment, and the result is only a short note and brief sentences.

---

1. He had written on the 23rd and 27th.

                              Plymouth, 4th Aug. 1813.
I found your letter and enclosure here this morning. You have
made me very happy about your health, but I shall not be quite
at ease until I hear that Emily has arrived to take care of you.
Continue your letters to this place, as I do not think we shall
leave it these eight or nine days. I was not very well yesterday,
my side was very painful, and I do not find that Baily's medicine
has been of permanent service to me; there are warm sea-baths
here, and I intend to try them, although I do not expect any
benefit from them or anything else until I can go to a sea-
bathing place for a year or more.
Don't be alarmed at what I tell you, as I am not worse than
I was when with you. I did not see the Catholic address, or
rather the Speaker's address, but if you get it send it out to me.
I perceive Soult is come again, and I do not doubt but Ciudad
Rodrigo will also come again.[2] I am delighted that Canning
has played his friends a trick; it is perfectly consistent so to do.
*Let everyone take care of himself, as the donkey said when he danced
among the chickens.* I suppose Sidney Smith will be down upon
him in the next *Review,* '*as the extinguisher said to the rushlight.*'
Mrs. Lock is excellent upon Murray, who is I suppose '*in a
devil of a sweat, as the mutton chop said to the gridiron.*' I am more
inclined to be sad than merry, notwithstanding my nonsense.
Why do you thank me for my kindness to you, when I have
been as cross as a devil half the time we have been together?
Have you not been my little *helot,* and performed everything
you were desired, like a good little slave, never cross and always
kind? and are you not now thanking me for being only half
good to you? Besides which, you say that you won't plague me
with your complaints; but *I* tell *you* that it is no plague to me
to hear that you love me dearly and that you are sorry for my
absence.

                              Plymouth, August 8, 1813.
I am very much afraid you have concluded that I should not
stay above one day in Plymouth; but one letter since I left you
is not after your promise of plaguing me with them. I do not
know when we shall sail, and I feel very forlorn when the post-
man answers 'No letters for you.' If I do not get one soon I

---

2. Meaning that Soult would retake it.

shall be rather anxious about your health, as I think you would otherwise have written when you got my first letter from here. This may seem unusual with me, but I do feel all the anxiety the greatest letter-writer in the world could feel both to write and to be answered; in short, I love you, and write to you; I do not care much about other people, and I do not write to them.

The Archbishop of Canterbury has afforded the world a new specimen of prayer. 'Thanks to the Lord, we are a nation of Christians. If thine enemy strike thee on the cheek, turn the other to him. Smite our enemy, Lord, to the dust. We thank Thee for making our hearts meek and forgiving. Thou hast smitten our enemy in Spain and Portugal; smite him again in Spain and Portugal, Lord, *and* then we will thank Thee.'

Plymouth, 8th Aug. 1813.

At last I have a letter, and really not before I wanted one, for I was become quite anxious about you. I am now very happy, and more so since I knew you have people with you whom you like and who will take care of you.

Havelock[3] is a young and very fine lad of the 43rd to whom I once gave a very severe lesson, and he has, like a very proper spirited lad, proved by his attention and zeal that he knew I was right. I am sorry you did not get the note from Torbay; it was directed to Bunbury, and being written in a low moment I should not like it to be read by those whom it does not concern.

You may when you have time and money pay my tailor's bill, and tell him after you have paid him that he has made my clothes so ill, and treated me in such a manner, that I will change him. At the same time you need not pay him till you send me a copy of his bill to overhaul; and be *cool*, as I should not like to have the fellow saucy to you. Dick would do it better. A report of the most unfortunate kind has just been propagated here—that Lord Wellington has been taken. I hope to God it is not true Government could not exert its vigour better than to find the author, if false, and punish him. It is too rascally to set about any false report of that kind.

---

3. Brother of the late Sir Henry Havelock, mentioned in the *History* as *El Chico Blanco* at San Marcial.

Bellona Transport, August 9, 1813.
The wind is fair, and we are actually under sail. I have no time to write any more. God bless you!

Passages, 19th Aug. 1813.
After a very tedious passage we made this place this morning. I think it is the most romantic beautiful place I almost ever saw,—a long narrow arm of the sea, for four or five miles between very high and nearly perpendicular rocks surmounted by evergreens, and these again overtopped by the Pyrenees. We have heard nothing of our horses, but the regiment is only six leagues from this place, still at Vera. San Sebastian still holds out: the loss has been severe, and as well as I can judge it may hold out a month longer; the citadel is uncommonly strong. God bless you! &c.

Camp over Vera, Aug. 24th, 1813.
I have been here these four days, and have got your letters up to the 11th, the last of which makes me very uneasy, as I fear strongly for your health if you continue to have those nervous attacks. Can you not contrive to laugh always, or at least to get somebody to laugh for you and make you merry? I wish Emily would leave Ireland soon, or that Catherine Longley would stay on with you. Being by yourself is likely to give you gloomy thoughts, were you both in good health and serenity of mind, and now must be worse than bad for you.

They have refused the public monument for Macleod. Lord Bathurst wrote his letter in such a manner that Lord Wellington could not give him one. I am very much annoyed in every manner: first by that; next by the state of the regiment; then I can hear nothing of my horses; all my old bât-men are servants to other people; and to crown all, my liver is very bad.

Havelock was perfectly right about the plunder, and I am happy to say that the story about Madame Gazan and the other ladies is positively denied by all parties. The last battle[4] was very severe: Soult very nearly defeated Lord Wellington, as you may guess when I tell you that hardly more than one division was actually engaged, or could be so, against fully 50,000 men; in short, for the first three or four days Soult had the best of it, and nothing but Lord W.'s extreme activity and courage could

---
4. Roncesvalles and Sorauren.

have brought up sufficient troops to man the ground where the battle took place.

The position during the 28th was perfectly impregnable, and nothing but the extreme confidence the French always have in themselves, and the increase of that confidence from superior numbers, could have prevailed upon troops to attack it. They are now opposite to us on the French Basses Pyrenées—we on the Bas Spanish side, our picquets touching.

If you wish to know the place, read that book which Bunbury lent me, *Mémoires de la Guerre des Basses Pyrenées, par le Citoyen B———*. You will find all the posts described—Vera, St. Estevan, Orbaceté, Irun, St Sebastian, St Jean Pied de Port, &c. &c. It is very interesting.

There are many desertions from *both* sides. The French, it appears, are sending their men into the interior for clothing; they talk strongly of peace, and have even given us a sketch of the basis, *viz*. Russia to have Moldavia and Wallachia (this makes me doubt it); Austria to have Salzburg and the Tyrol; Italy to be a separate kingdom under Joseph Bonaparte; Jerome to have Holland; Westphalia to belong to the Confederation of the Rhine; Spain and Portugal to be free; Sicily ours; Malta the Grand Master's; and the W. Indian islands to be given back to France. The French army opposite to us is about 60,000 men, independent of Suchet, and neither Pampeluna nor San Sebastian yet fallen; so that the Speaker romanced confoundedly when he said that Spain and Portugal were freed by the decisive Battle of Vittoria.

Your arrangements are all very good, but I wish you would not let the word economy enter your head at all when you are upon your comforts or convenience in any way. You will make me very unhappy if I find you do not give yourself everything you can want. I have nothing more to say, save that I beg of you again and again to take care of yourself, and always to think me as fond of you as I could be of anybody.

Camp above Vera, 2 Sept 1813.

The posts are very uncertain; do not therefore conclude that I have either forgotten you or got myself hurt You will have heard before this reaches you that we have had another battle—the 43rd did not fire a shot. I was detached with half the regiment to keep open the communication of the army by Kempt, who is very zealous, but I think very inexperienced, as may be seen by that very order to me. The French army were in possession two hours before of the whole road, and I, of course, popped into the middle of them.

Three companies of the 95th, sent on the same errand by another road, supported by two Spanish regiments, were cut in upon by a French column. The Spaniards fell back; the 95th rushed on, joined me, and left the French to stand between two good things; in the meantime the French formed several strong columns and marched against me, who like a wise general put my tail between my legs and ran up a mountain, where I showed a very pretty front and frightened them away.

By this time a general called *Rain*, who I dare say you know is very formidable in mountains, accompanied by Lieut.-Generals Thunder and Lightnings set upon me without mercy for the whole of that day and night without ceasing, and, having no cover of any kind, they did considerable execution before morning. *A propos*, the priest of Vera, being asked how he got on in the valley between the French and us, answered, '*Even as Christ between two robbers*.' The same day a soldier of the 43rd, being asked how long his comrade had been dead, said, 'If he had lived until today he would have been dead a week.'

My horses have arrived, the grey mare crushed in every part of her body by being let to fall between the ship and the boat in disembarking; I am in some hopes she will recover.—Having now said my say about common affairs, I will upon another sheet of paper write to you about affairs of much more importance, in which you must give me your advice sincerely and without reference to any feeling of your own, with regard to doing what I wish. If you agree with me on the subject, you must write to George and speak to Bunbury upon it, who may be of use to me about it . . . .

I have a strong disposition to leave the army for the following reasons. In the first place I am 28 and only a major. I cannot rise to the head of my profession for want of time.—Next, I dislike the scenes I witness so much that nothing but the prospect of arriving at the head of my profession could make me endure it.—Next, my health is very bad, and getting worse. I am married to you whom I love better than anything else, and I give up your society and endanger your peace and happiness in order to acquire a little, very little, fleeting reputation or rank, dependent on the whim of Lord Wellington.

Certainly nothing ought to make me do this except the necessity of defending my country, but I think the war is not now carried on from any necessity of the kind; it is rather for the purpose of giving power to Lord Liverpool &c. to oppress Ireland, which is my country. Lastly, I have been ill used in the following manner. Lord Wellington wrote a letter saying he wanted 100 men and officers from the light division to lead the storm of San Sebastian: of course I volunteered to command them: I was accepted, and two hours after put in orders to take the command; but lo! when I arrived at the post appointed I found that the command had been taken from me and given to Hunt of the 52nd, a colonel by brevet, and nine children dependent on him for bread.

I went to Pakenham and Lord Wellington upon the spot with the order in my hand; was told it was hard and that I was ill-used, but that it must stand; thus I was cut off from promotion and one of the most splendid opportunities of gaining reputation that could have offered itself. Under all these circumstances I wish to quit the army, and I think for my wounds, for my loss of health and length of service, I am justified in asking leave to sell my majority. I should put it all upon my wounds and want of health; of course it is not necessary that I should be so explicit to the Duke as to you. The objections are as follows. Can you be content to live with me upon what we have? and do I do my duty to you and your children, if you have any, by retiring from the world at my age?

This you must answer me fairly, and you may consult Emily if you like upon it. There is plenty of time; I cannot do anything about it until the campaign is finished. If you have any more children, I am not too old or stupid to do something in other lines of life; if but one, I think we have enough; but your opinion will most undoubtedly decide me, both from my opinion of your judgment, and your being the most interested in the affair; for my own part, I have no other wish or desire than to render you happy in whatever way you like best I have only one thing further to say—the idea of your stopping my career must not enter into your thoughts. I *have no ambition*, and my inclination perfectly coincides with my judgment: whether it sways it or not I leave you to decide. If peace should be concluded I would not do anything about it until some time to come.....

September 5th, 1813.

I hope you have got my long letter about leaving the army; I have been very low-spirited since I wrote it, and with reason; I had not then heard of the result of the storming; our loss has been fully 1600 there, if not more. The 43rd gave one officer and 30 men volunteers; 21 including the officer have been killed or wounded. When I thought I was to have had the command, as I knew the eldest subaltern was old and stupid, I asked a young man of the name of O'Connell who had led two storming parties before, to volunteer, thinking that I could get him a company. He would not have done so had it not been for my sake, and he has been killed, leaving a mother who was supported by what he spared her out of his pay. Is this not very painful, and ought it not to strengthen me in my disposition to quit a service where friendship is a curse and kindness kills? however, I will not pain you any more upon the subject....

I send you a Spanish *Basco* or Basque inhabitant. Write over it *Uno Basco Español*; it is very like but badly drawn and worse coloured, as I did it on the hill where we are, in a few hours, and the rain and wind incommoded me much: when I come home I will make a good drawing from it Is not the air very fine, and the look altogether what that book I told you to get describes them to be? The French ones they say are still finer; the legs, large as they are, are not exaggerated, but one is longer than the other—my crooked eye! There does not appear much chance of entering France, more likely another attack of Soult upon us; he has still 60,000 men independent of Suchet.

Camp, Vera, Sept. 18th, 1813.

You give a great deal of pleasure in telling me you are so much better; your letter is very amusing. As to the little volume of poems, I am not at all surprised that you did read them through, but I am a good deal surprised that you liked them so much.

My moustaches are excellent, and I have also got a very fine King Charles.

Tell George, in justification of my abilities as a general (I told him I did not see how Lord Wellington was to cross the Douro this campaign), that I dined with Lord W. three days ago, and that after dinner he explained to me all his manoeuvres and arrangements for the campaign, and that deceiving the French and passing the Douro, turning their right by that movement, was the most difficult move he ever made,—that it was *touch and go,* and required more arrangement and more *art* than anything he ever did: had he been one day too late, he must have gone back. He made me laugh much. I asked him if it could not have been done by the other flank instead, and after some time considering he answered me with a great deal of malice, 'No, I'll be —— if my way was not the best.' He farther said that the French might have made a much better campaign of it, but that they were —— stupid and he was very clever. He was very kind and very glad to see me.

Little —— is here. I like him better than I expected. I believe they told lies about him. He is very modest, and good-natured enough to ride up to the top of one of the Pyrenees to give me Lucy's letter to him, saying you were well at St Anne's Hill. He dined with me, and told me among other matters that he liked me best, because Charles and George were too good, and liked beefsteaks as well as pies, but that I liked good living—further, that he liked command, and wished he was colonel, because he would then row the commissary and feed on livers and lights; he has a proper idea of obedience, and does not think himself a very great general yet;—these are good signs.

I think Bonaparte will beat them all; and if he does, what a short-sighted set they are who thought that Russia and Prussia were more than a match for him!

Camp of Vera, Sept 20th, 1818.

I have also adopted your plan of putting numbers to my letters, because I believe that there will be a number missing from the very irregular manner in which the posts go and come, or rather do not go or come. By this means you will give me credit for every letter that I do write to you, and not think me forgetful or ill-natured. I have received only as far as No. 4 of yours. We have a great many reports of battles here, and one French bulletin, which says the Allies lost 80,000 men. This of course will be voted a lie by the good people of London; for my part, I am persuaded that in the main points the French tell

the truth, allowing for a little exaggeration in the detail.
I have no map of Germany, and therefore I cannot give you my opinion of events, particularly from the crude unconnected reports of events that we get I think however that he will find most trouble from Bernadotte; but if he is able to check him he will march upon Vienna, and endeavour by fright, or other means, to draw Austria from the Confederation against him. What a ridiculous figure the account of General Gibbs and his army of 3000 men makes among the armies there! Oh! the wonderful works of Lords Bathurst and Liverpool! I am very anxious to get your opinion about what I proposed to do in my letter of August; I find myself more inclined than ever to quit the army: to tell you the truth, my health is really so bad, that my life is a perfect burthen to me; pain and lowness of spirits are my constant companions; and this, added to an eager restless impatience about you, totally unfits me for a military life.
God Almighty bless you, my own darling wife! You are the only comfort I have in the world; and I am determined that no silly hankering after fame shall prevent me from profiting by that comfort If you agree with me about it, pray ask Bunbury to sound Torrens about giving me leave to *sell* out; otherwise I cannot quit, as it would be reducing you to a situation of less comfort than I took you from, and that is what I will not do.

21st September 1813.

As the notice we get is in general so short that it cramps my ideas to write in time for the post, I have made a beginning to-day, and may perhaps finish this tomorrow or next day; thus you will have the benefit of the full and copious stream of my ideas. Having got thus far, I am sorry to say I find I have no ideas and must wait a little. *A propos*, the *Lengua Basquença* is I believe the Punic or Carthaginian; if not, it is still older, and must be the language of the aboriginal Spaniards. There is no grammar of it, nobody knows it, and everyone says it will take ten years to learn. I am a great proficient, having learnt seven words, *viz.*, *escacha polita*—pretty girl; *borster yeazaka*—half past five; *therimatea atoz*—come here, my darling; and *quensa*—come along.
We hear a great deal of news from the French. *Vandamme* seems to have been dished, or to have got *Van-dam* licking. There is a report that Boney has been beaten in person, and Marshal Ney

killed. I am sorry for the last, but I don't believe any of it; you know I am sceptical on that subject.

I have had a large swelling about four inches below my wound, accompanied with inflammation and some pain; the doctor thinks it is a small part of the ball or backbone coming away; in a few days I shall be better able to tell you. We are tormented here by constant desertion to the enemy, and the attendant upon it of shooting those that are caught You will hardly believe that the calculation of 500 men has been made as the number deserted from the army within these five weeks; and, what is very strange, the Portuguese go off faster than we do.

25th Sept.—I have got your letters up to No. 6; the advertisement is very funny, the watch-ribands very pretty, and majestic is not spelt with a g. *Vertot* I translated myself complete, and you may get it or not as you like. If *Washington's Life* is not the bad one I mean, you can have it too, and all Robertson, especially the *India*, I perfectly agree in your remark about the Review; the person who wrote it is probably just such another as Mr. —— and his friend appear to be. I cannot help looking on the Revolution as a blessing, (in spite of Mr. Eustace, who is as dull and as spiteful as any old querulous priest need be), were it only for crushing such spawn of hell as that society; for whatever crimes may have been committed in consequence, they are crimes that carry an air of grandeur with them, and have been attended with virtues and energy that will make them be regarded by posterity with admiration.

The *Review* chooses to call me stupid, who can't make out the story of the Giaour. Clearness I take to be a merit in all writing. I understand Homer and Virgil; why should Lord Byron be more obscure than they in a much less complicated poem? That it is obscure cannot be denied, or it would not have caused a sufficient number of people to assert it to make these domineering gentlemen take notice of the objection. For my part, I think that it and the Review of it are both equally obscure.

Old General Kemmis, who is a fine-spoken man, found a soldier very dirty. 'Take him,' said he to a sergeant, 'take him and *lave* him in the Tagus.' Some hours after—'Sergeant, did you do as I ordered you?'—'I did, sir.'—'Where is the culprit?'—'Sure I left him in the Tagus, as your honour ordered—up to his neck.'

The pain in my back continues, the swelling gone, and I don't know what it is.

Camp of Vera, October 1, 1813.

.........There is some talk of our invading France, but I do not think it can take place so late in the season and with such a force and position as Soult has in our front; besides, Suchet having been victorious in the south is very much against it. Bonaparte appears to have had too many people opposed to him, but that is no reason for supposing that he is ruined, which is all the talk nowadays. His chances are as follows—he has a better head than any of them, nearly as many troops, and all the fortresses.

"The enemy have some good heads, a great many bad ones, a great many troops with a better *morale*, but no fortresses: this morale of theirs is likely to evaporate soon, especially with the Austrians.

I see the papers praise a Mr. —— very much for bravely shedding his blood at San Sebastian, he being the son of Lord —— I returned Mr. —— when I was Brigade Major as a deserter from the 95th Regiment, and he was generally thought a ——; what a good scrubbing-brush a peer is!

I wait impatiently for your letter about my business, and am meanwhile—&c.

October 8, 1813.

Your letter from Mildenhall came to me on the 6th. The sense, the arguments, and the tenderness of it gave me a sensation that I cannot express to you. Certainly, my darling Caroline, there is nothing now that can either add to or diminish the love I feel for you; and the whole of your letter is as strong an argument in itself as you could use to confirm me in a determination which insures to me the society, and, I trust, the tranquillity of a woman that I love so much. About an hour before your letter came we had received an order to attack on the next day at 7 o'clock the position in front of us. I will tell you candidly I expected we should be cut to pieces, and I believe very few of us thought differently; it was however managed perfectly: great precision, great courage, great luck, and great numbers, enabled us to carry with little loss an immense mountain—entrenched with abattis, walls, rocks, and obstacles of every kind—in a space of two hours or less.

The 43rd lost few; the 52nd, under Colborne, were opposed in the strongest manner and carried everything with the bayonet before them. Our brigade under Kempt had apparently more difficult ground, but by out-flanking the enemy we did our business as easily; there were fewer troops and less courage opposed to us. Tell George of it; the position was stronger and higher than Busaco three times over; in short, if the enemy had put men enough into it we must have been beaten. I need not tell you I was not hit.

The plains of France lie before us, cultivated, enclosed, rich, and beautiful beyond description. The Spaniards, Portuguese, and I am sorry to say the British, are exulting in the thoughts of robbing and murdering the unfortunate possessors of what they see before them. Lord Wellington says *they shall not do it,* and I have great hope in General Pakenham; he is able from his situation, and most willing; he has already commenced by calling to account Colonel —— for permitting 140 of his men to remain unpunished who had already begun this villainous work; and he says he is determined to prevent it if possible.

Kempt I like very much, and he also is full of indignation at such conduct, and will be a powerful help. The cause of our country may justify our killing our enemies in battle, but it cannot justify our being even *spectators* of the merciless acts of a licentious army; and well I know there is no cruelty hell can devise that this army is not capable of and anxious to inflict upon the wretched people below us; but I trust in God we shall either from policy or principle find a sufficient number of people in power to prevent it. If it is not prevented, the vengeance for it will keep pace with the crime, and one continued scene of murder will be the consequence

I enclose you a paper of the Spaniards to entice the French to desert I can only remark that they neither pay nor feed their own troops; that Russia does *not* free Poland; that assassination is *not* virtue; and that the love of France is *not* very apparent in Moreau or Bernadotte; neither does it become a soldier to desert his country under any circumstances.

It has had *no effect.*

      Camp, French side of Vera, October 17, 1813.

Since I last wrote we have remained in the same position that we drove the French out of; they are in our front below us, in considerable force and strongly fortified, the weather extremely wet and disagreeable. The French attacked and took a fort from the Spaniards three days ago, which event caused me to be sent to support another batch of Spaniards on the top of La Rhune; and I was again discomfited by General *Rain* without cover from his fury. It seems to be my fate to remain with the unfortunate right wing of the regiment on the tops of bleak mountains without cover on rainy nights.

The pontoons are gone to the right, and we expect an attack will be made by General Hill and his division upon the left of the enemy. Should it succeed, of which there is little doubt, it will most probably give us the line of the Nivelle River and the town of St. Jean de Luz, with quiet for the winter.

March went home with the despatches. I have not heard from you since the 25th September. Your letters, I suppose from your being at Mildenhall, are always two days older than any other person's, which is rather provoking, as I am naturally more anxious about your health now than at any other time. I should be so happy if I was with you! I do not know if it is an increase of love towards you, or the very great difference I find in the regimental society, that makes me discontented where I am; but certainly from some cause or other I do not feel the same man that I used to do, and I am gallant enough to attribute it to love for you.

You are a good dictionary, and will, I have no doubt, find plenty of occasion to be useful, as my head is exceedingly conglomerated with love, war, politics, rain, and headache. General Pakenham[5] has taken my grey mare under his protection, which gives me some hopes of her final recovery. Did you ever take advice about ———? If it is not decidedly in my favour do not pursue the matter, as my anger has subsided into a settled hatred to all tradesmen which does not require the assistance of the law. I have had a very kind letter from George, and I enclose you an answer to him; I wish somebody would enclose me to you in a letter. I read the *Quarterly Review* upon the letters of Charles and Gilbert Wakefield.[6] The Reviewer says that Mr. Wakefield

---

5. Note by Sir W. Napier,—General Pakenham makes me now and then think that there are some good men in the world.

6. Correspondence of the late Gilbert Wakefield with Charles James Fox, *Quarterly Review*, vol. 9, pp. 118, 119—1813. The article was written by the late Lord Dudley.

had adopted the principles of the French Revolution in their vilest and most ferocious tendency;—and two pages after says that Mr. W. was a strictly moral and honest man! Are they compatible?

Camp, Puerta de Vera, Nov. 7th, 1813.

I am become quite as impatient as you can be for letters, not having heard since the 22nd of last month. I asked Lord Fitzroy yesterday if Major M—— was to get a lieutenant-colonelcy. He said Yes, and also that he had spoken to Lord W. for me, but that Lord W. thought I would not like it, as we had been so little engaged! After being 14 years in the army, having seen 15 engagements of different kinds, receiving two wounds, and being mortified by seeing nine younger officers in the light division alone put over my head, I did not expect to be told that; the greatest part of headquarters ought therefore to be ashamed to show their faces.

For my comfort, I am told I shall certainly have it next engagement. I shall not feel particularly grateful for it then, as, by their own account, I shall only then get what is due to me; I thank them much for the care they have of my modesty.—I have got my medal, and old Hearn is gone sick to England at last, intending to sell out The command of the regiment is mine again: this is some comfort at least, but it has not altered my opinion the least upon the subject of selling out if I am allowed: nothing can compensate to me for the loss of your society. . . . .

France, Camp 1 league in front of San Pé.

I am safe after a good deal of hard fighting. This I hope will reach you before the news of the battle, and save you the danger of a shock. I am much afraid that some foolish report will reach you, as I had a very narrow escape and it was reported during the action that I was killed. This is all I have to say for myself. Well I am not; my head is actually turning round with the misery I suffer from the death of some of my friends; at the head of them you will see Lloyd; but two really perfect friends, and one year has laid them both in the grave. Of two boys that I have brought up in my company for four years, who have been in every action with me, and who were my constant companions, that I looked upon as my younger brothers, one is killed, and the other so dangerously wounded that it is next to impossible that he can serve again.

Barnard, for whom I had a great admiration, and whom I really loved, is also wounded in such a manner that I expect to hear of his death every moment Captain Murchison, another friend and companion of 11 years' standing, with every good quality, died in great agony yesterday from his wounds. What misery, that the very number of my losses have left me hardly a point to fix upon to rest my grief! Poor Lloyd! this is the deepest; but I cannot understand that every friend is dead,—that five people whom I loved, and spoke to in health but a few hours back, should be all dead or dying.

How little should I feel the value of living longer myself if it were not for you! but there is a sensation for you that I feel keenly above any other feeling, which breaks through that dead horrible sensation that this crush of feeling has caused. God bless you! Pity your unhappy husband, but do not forget that your health and happiness are necessary to his existence.

CHAPTER 8

Battle of Orthes

When the necessities of his position induced Lord Wellington to force the passage of the Nive, and thus to separate his force into two parts, having between them a large navigable river over which the communication was always uncertain, and liable to entire interruption from the rising of the waters, the light division remained on the left bank of the Nive. Soult's position about Bayonne gave him the great advantage of a far more compact general position than that occupied by Wellington. Although it also extended on both sides of the river, the French possessed a constant and safe passage by the Bayonne bridge; they moved on a shorter line, and could therefore concentrate on either bank of the Nive far more quickly than the British.

Of these advantages Soult availed himself to make a sudden attack on the 10th of December with a greatly superior force on the British divisions between the Nive and the sea. Fortunately for them, Major Napier was on picquet in their front. The left wing, 43rd, was posted on the centre of three tongues of high ground which shot out towards the enemy; the right wing of the regiment was on the right tongue; the 52nd occupied the left tongue. There was no communication across the valley between the two wings, and each acted independently. Early in the morning, being with the most advanced picquet on the centre ridge, Major Napier pointed out to General Kempt and Colonel Charles Beckwith who were both there, that the French soldiers, while pretending to be skylarking with each other, continually jumped behind a hedge at no great distance below the picquets, and never went back again.

Feeling convinced the enemy meditated an attack, he urged this belief on General Kempt who at first was incredulous; but when the other showed him a French general officer behind a cottage at no great distance, he took the alarm, allowed Napier to put his reserve under arms, and went himself to counter-order the march of his brigade which was on the point of retiring to Arbonne. The brigade then occupied the church and village of Arcangues, and this precaution of Kempt's saved the position at that point on that day.

Major Napier placed the companies of his reserve in *échellon*; the right retired along the side of the valley which separated him from his right wing; and he had but just completed this arrangement when the French fell upon his advanced picquet with great fury, driving it back, and pressing vehemently along the side of the valley to cut off the retreat of the regiment on Arcangues; but the enemy was held in check by the *échellons*, which fired and retired in succession, thus giving time to the picquets to retreat, and finally, although hard pressed, the enemy never being more than 30 yards distant, he succeeded in drawing off all his men without losing a single prisoner to the church of Arcangues, the defence of which post was intrusted to Major Napier during the rest of the day.

Here he was twice wounded, once by a musket-ball in the right hip, again by the explosion of a shell which drove his telescope against his face. He did not however quit the field, and defended the church and churchyard until the 13th, when the fighting terminated by Lord Hill's glorious battle at St. Pierre. Although his wound in the hip was not healed for six weeks, he did not return his name among the list of wounded, because he was fearful of alarming his wife who was on the point of being confined. His cousin Tom Napier,[1] who was on Sir John Hope's staff, lost his arm in this action.

The day before the Battle of Orthes Major Napier was billeted in a village off the line of march; and while there he was disturbed by marauding attacks made on the village by stragglers from the army. After two attempts of this kind, finding the evil-doers got more daring, he took on himself to arm the villagers, and putting them under the mayor told him to fire on the first party that invaded them. They did so, killed one man, wounded another, and brought a third, a Portuguese, in a prisoner. Major Napier hastened to Lord Wellington to report what he had done; not without some fear that he had acted rashly.

But Lord Wellington on hearing his account ordered Colonel Waters to have the wounded man hanged by the roadside. He directed the Portuguese to be kept a prisoner, saying, in reply to the inquiry if

---

1. Lieutenant-General Thomas Napier, C.B.

he also was to be executed, "It is not so long since the French were in Portugal that I should hang this Portuguese." He at the same time enjoined on all the communes that they should treat marauders as had been done in the present instance.

After the Battle of Orthes, at which Major Napier was present in person although his regiment had gone to the rear for clothing, being deprived of the command by the arrival of Colonel Patrickson from England, and having been for some time seriously ill with dysentery, as well as suffering from the old wound in his spine, he consulted General Pakenham as to the propriety of asking leave to go to London for medical advice. The general told him at once he ought to do so, and in fact obtained the leave for him.

"Thus," he says, "I missed the Battle of Toulouse, for which I feel shame to this day; but neither I, nor any other person unless it was Lord Wellington, doubted at the time that the war was ended as to fighting."

He appears to have arrived in England in April or May, 1814; and he received the brevet rank of lieutenant-colonel at the termination of the campaign.

The following letters to his wife, for he appears to have had no other correspondent, refer to the period between the Battle of the Nivelle and his arrival in England.

Arcangues, Not. 24th, 1813.

We have had an affair yesterday which has caused me much mortification. We were meant to take possession of a ridge for our outposts, which we did with a loss of less than ten men; but no general that toe had understood what was wanted, and instead of halting us allowed us to halt ourselves. Some young sanguine officers who are more vain than good, concluded that with three or four companies they could drive the whole French army before them; the result was that I lost 75 men—more than I did in the last action; poor Bailey, who you will remember dined twice with us, was killed; and Hopkirk dangerously wounded, and is taken prisoner with a good many men; another officer also wounded.

And I run much risk of being called the cause of the misfortune, as I know that generals are sometimes not very scrupulous in blaming others to save their own credit. They have already thrown the whole blame upon those officers who went forward, forgetting that they themselves were the original and principal cause of it, all through ignorance in not knowing where to stop, or pointing out what they wished to have done to anybody; nay, I believe they did not know that any mischief had been done until they were told of it, for they came smiling up to me as if they had done great things in gaining 100 yards of ground with the loss of 3 brave officers and 75 men. I know not what Lord W. will say to it, but for my part I will not be abused for other people's faults.

Arbonne, France, Nov. 27th, 1813.

I wrote to you a hurried letter three days ago when my mind was agitated with the events that had just occurred; and I fear that all these letters of mine will do you harm. I believe I am a very weak-minded man to let the disposition of telling my feelings get so much the better of me as to run the risk of doing you harm. Not that I think it a weakness to confide to you any feeling or thought that I can have, and which I have a right to tell: far from it; I have the greatest confidence in your judgment, your love, and your principles; and it is the particular happiness of my life that I have a tender good friend in whom I can thus confide.

By this time I hope you are at Stone Hall, and that a few weeks will put an end to all my anxiety about you. I have heard from Hopkirk, who is not badly wounded, and whom I hope we shall be able to get exchanged: he has been as usual very well treated by the French, who, I am sorry to say, exceed us considerably in their attention to officers who are made prisoners. . .

. . . I am recommended for a lieutenant-colonelcy; and I trust a peace will soon put an end to all your anxiety. . . . . . I do not see the force of Emily's arguments against my leaving the army.

At all events, at 28 a man may be allowed to judge for himself. The profession of arms is a forced unnatural life, and only to be supported by severity which savours of tyranny. I believe China is the only part of the world where a man is forced to follow the profession of his father; and war is the most cursed of all trades. War is now unnecessary, and he who stops the tide of peace will stand as a mark for the curses of millions. . . . . I am very odd and not at all merry, notwithstanding my letter; I am besieged by a million of soldier's wives.

Lord Wellington has issued an order to officers commanding regiments to kill all the donkeys, and they bother me to be good to them; some threaten, some soothe.

Arbonne, Dec. 4th, 1813

I have just got your letter of the 17th. I fear you were still in town when the news of our last battle arrived. I was in great hopes you would be spared the uneasiness of the Park guns, &c., but comfort myself that you are so used to them that they will not have much effect upon you. And yet, as the navy knew of our action by seeing the firing, I fear much that some blundering captain with more sail than wit will have arrived with a hubbub account of a bloody battle fought for three days with alternate success, until the broadside of a brig of 16 guns turned the scale, the said broadside being fired with great precision at the distance of 16 miles from shore, and 36 from the place of the battle.

Arbonne, Dec. 14th, 1813.

At last I am able to write and relieve you from any fears on my account. On your own I hope you have less fear and reason to fear than I have for you. About this time my fate is decided, a fate that I am so little indifferent to that I could *now* with a great deal of pleasure compound for having no child to be assured of your safety. How much obliged I am to your uncle for giving you his house! I cannot write to him because it is not my way, but you must tell him it is not because I don't feel his kindness. We have had five days of constant fighting—sometimes one wing, sometimes the other, of the army.

Nothing decisive has happened, but both sides have suffered considerably; the enemy much the worst, but our loss is nevertheless about 5000 men as I should guess. Tom Napier is hit rather badly, his arm broke near the elbow, not in two, but the bone splintered; he will not lose it, however. I hope I have not been mistaken for him. I was slightly wounded in the hip, a ball having glanced from a gravestone in the churchyard and struck me there. I would not return myself for fear of alarming you; but I assure you it is no more than what I say; so you see I am not so vain as you imagine, having given up that feather in my cap to please the little lady in the straw.

My horse was wounded also the day before I was, so you must

divide your sorrow between us. I must not tell a lie, however; some vanity lies at the bottom. We Napiers are supposed to be always wounded: now, if I returned myself as such, and people saw me walking about, they would say *we* were a humbugging set, and that would not do. After all I believe I am as vain as my neighbours, and nearly as besotted about the name of Napier as some of my *cousins*[2] can be about the name of Fox.

I don't like Lord Wellington's despatch about the Little Rhune; I don't want to brag, but the best thing done on the 10th November, 1813, was the attack of the 43rd Light Infantry, and he has not done us the honour to mention our names. However, if he gives us a medal for the last five days, and one for the 10th, I shall only want one for a cross; and then what a fine wench you will be; only I *bar* giving my cross to the baby to bite after the manner of ladies in general, who think nothing too fine to put on their little ugly heads, nothing too good to wipe their little dirty noses, or too valuable to give them to put in their little mouths.

March is come out again; you never told me that he called upon you and saw you. If it was not that you are so ugly that I can trust him, I should be jealous.

Arbonne. Dec. 25th, 1813.

I am very well again. Poor Tom Napier has lost his arm, his left, above the elbow, but is doing as well as possible and is to get the brevet. The despatch with my recommendation was taken by the French, which accounts for the delay. We have had no fighting since I last wrote to you, and I hope we shall have none, as the speech of Bonaparte is so pacific; I suppose the Allies will not be fools enough to follow the ravings of our newspapers. I have had no letters later than the 7th December—a long time and a very anxious one for me, my love . . . . . . Is Bunbury out of office? I have been just breaking a muleteer's neck for beating his mule unmercifully. I pulled him off into the mud, and his head stuck so funnily in it that I forgot he was *killing*, but the doctor was by and he recovered. You know I am a *beast* about animals.

January 9th, 1814.

Your letters to 21st December have just arrived, and they would

---

2. His wife was his cousin, and a Fox.

be bad consolation if I had not better here. Lord Castlereagh has arrived at Morlaix to negotiate, and I think peace must be the consequence. We have had a bad four days' operations. Rain in bivouacs in January is bad fun, Soult made some move, and we opposed it; it ended in smoke, and the delightful news that my lord was at Morlaix, from Soult himself...... Your brother is very anxious for Boney's fame. Don't you think that a peace in good faith, and his great abilities applied to raise France, and that with success, would make him something more than a commonplace emperor? or had he better persist in the battle until he has the pleasure of ruining her and some other nations, and then, shooting himself, cry,—'I am a great man!'.... Fanny is the name I most admire in a woman if she is pretty; if ugly, it is the last I would give her.

Send me, or buy at least, and keep till further orders, a knife and fork like George's. I want to buy one for Tom Napier; it is a silver fork with a cutting edge on the side for one-armed people.

Arauntz, January 15th, 1814.

George came here about four days ago looking very well. He brought me the latest letter from you. Send the enclosed letter to Margaret, who has laid me under contribution for a correspondence on the state of George's health; but as I look upon it as a tyranny, I shall shake off the yoke as soon as possible, as the man is able and willing to write himself, and a schism in writing is a bad thing, as we might differ in our accounts, and she would at last believe neither and conclude that he was sick and me a *deceviour*.

Tom Napier goes home shortly, and you must have a knife like George's ready for him when he calls upon you. Patrickson I am told is going to sail for this country; when he comes I shall go home *cierto*. When I go I give my chestnut mare, which is without exception the best in Europe, to March, and my grey one to George, This is very extravagant, as they are worth 200 guineas; but March gave me one once, and George you know has a right to the other, and the —— money has made you so rich that we shan't starve; besides, my beasties will be better taken care of as gifts than they would be as sales: Margaret has persuaded George that he has no money and must starve in a little time, and it is very funny to see the distress he is in between his fears and his natural disposition, which leads him to be more than liberal. One of his ways to prevent expense was funny enough; for fear things should be dearer at quarters than at St Jean de Luz, he bought at the last as much as would feed his whole regiment for a month.

George tells me that Lord Castlereagh has been stout about peace; here they say he has gone over to the Continent to put them by the ears again; I should like to have reason to praise him for once.... Is it a patriotic wish that Bonaparte may give the Austrians a defeat about Dijon, by way of reminding them of their manifesto about peace; not enough to make him proud, but sufficient to make them humble? What do you think of giving him Italy? Naples independent under Marat; Holland free and independent, as she likes best herself; the Rhine the boundary-line; to have his fleets sent to him from the Texel and Scheldt, that is, all that are built with French money, those by Dutch to remain; Switzerland independent; and what could he or we desire more? To him would be given the most beautiful kingdom in the world (Italy); to us more than we could have dreamt of one year ago; and to the world—peace.

Poor Lady Elizabeth Monck's brother, Saunders Gore, was murdered in the most inhuman manner at Vittoria the other day by some Spanish soldiers.

Arauntz, January 22nd, 1814.

I have not received any letters from you, but I have seen in the papers that you are safe. I am so happy at this that I was not in a passion above an hour at your having a daughter! .....

Every day here gives us stronger hopes of a peace with France and a war with Spain. Bonaparte sent the Duke of San Carlos with the copy of a treaty concluded between him and Ferdinand, by which he guaranteed his dominions to the latter, and promised him an army to drive the English out of Spain. The Regency had just shame enough not to accept it.

February 6th, 1814.

I have not got any letters from you or anybody else by the last packet, which brought papers to the 17th: indeed, with the exception of two which Bunbury brought out to me, I have not had any later than the 4th of January. This is the curse of regular correspondence. I suppose the snow has been the cause of it, but I am rather uneasy notwithstanding. I wrote to you by Bunbury, a short letter: I had not much time to spare; but I will make up for it now with a very long one.

A propos, before I begin to you, make all the fine good speeches possible to Aunt Fanny for her letter to me; this I owe her for her goodness, and the more especially so as I took her originally for a *bête noire*, like a Goth and a Vandal as I was. What can I say to her to thank her? nothing I and when a man is very much obliged to a pretty woman, and has from the fullness of his feelings nothing to say, he can only kneel and make love with his eyes: being 500 miles off I can't do this, and if I could I suppose it would not be pretty behaviour, as she is too handsome and young to pass it off as the duty and affection of a nephew who was bred up in the most moral and proper manner.

Colonel Colborne somehow or other got hold of my review before I did myself, and kept it for a month. I have got it at last; Sir James Macintosh upon Madame de Staël's work strikes me as a piece of involved declamation, meaning nothing, except that he likes *Madame* herself. The review of Rogers is a determined lie, told in favour of their friend, with all the effrontery of which they are so capable. There is a very good one upon the law of libel, which however might have been enlarged upon with more force and without much difficulty; I should think written by Lord H——, from a certain sameness mixed with a little sarcastic playfulness that I have often observed in his speeches; the fact is, the subject appears to me one that it is impossible to fail in, and therefore I think the review good, but it might be much better.

The people of Bayonne sent word to their friends here last night that peace was signed upon the 1st of February: this I take to be premature, but I have no doubt it will take place soon. Does the baby continue refractory after the manner of its paternal race, or not? If it gives way an inch, it is not mine. By the bye, don't take any house for a long period, as I shall live at the seaside when I go home, and I suppose you will like to live with me.

February 12th, 1814.

Your fears of no peace seem to have too much foundation, but

I am rather amused at the march you have cut out for us across France, forgetting that it is 400 miles, and that one *Soult* has 60,000 men, whose leave we must ask first, and that we have not above 50,000 as a recommendation to him; nevertheless I will not conceal from you that I think it very likely we may make a march towards Bordeaux soon, but I hope the peace may still take place in time enough to stop us . . . . .

I don't think London is a likely place to improve a delicate child, as she will have to swallow at least a pound of sulphur every day in consequence of the smoke; could you not get a small cottage near London, or Stone Hall, until I come home? but do as you like best. . . . . I did not know a grandmother could be a godmother; make whom you please, only not the editor of the *Courier*, or *Times*, as I hate them both. Don't give the girl ten thousand names for goodness' sake, as she will have to pay for them as you did in the marriage articles; get her vaccinated as soon as possible, by Jenner if you can, if not by Moore; afterwards we will think of the petite *vérole* to prove it

Orthes, 28th February, 1814.

I have only time to tell you that I am not wounded. The regiment was in the rear for clothing. I was in the action. George is also safe; his horse was wounded. Poor March[3] was wounded very badly; I fear much that he will die. The only thing in his favour that I could see yesterday was that his face had no marks of immediate death about it; people mortally wounded have a very livid look about the lips, which he has not It will be sad that the best of so large a family should die so young; and doubly sad that the only person of rank I ever saw with everybody his warm friend, and nobody envious of him, should fall before his age gave him time to do that good which his noble disposition would lead him to do. Day after day the best of us go down, and still no remorse, no check of conscience to those ruffians who are constantly calling out 'War!'

Château Papreon, March 7th, 1814.

March is declared out of all danger although the wound is very severe; I am delighted; I cannot well tell you how much I felt when I saw him extended on the field with all the marks of death about him. I have another piece of news for you which I

---

3. Lord March—the late Duke of Richmond.

dare say you will not be sorry to hear. Patrickson has made his appearance in this country; when he joins I shall ask leave to go home; I think about that time March will also go home, in which case I intend to take care of him. We have been halted here a few days about Mont Marsan; what is to be done I cannot tell. I should think, if Lord Wellington does not decide to go either to Toulouse or Bordeaux, that Soult will put the question out of doubt and send us back to St Jean de Luz again; he expects reinforcements from Catalonia.

You may tell your brother Henry that the people here do not like Bonaparte; and if you may believe them, which I do not quite, they hate him. Peace they certainly desire ardently on any terms, yet the country is rich and flourishing, full of everything you could wish for, as cheap as you have heard of things being in England 100 years ago, and great numbers of young able-bodied men. It is astonishing to see the clockwork obedience and regularity with which everything is carried on by the people at the orders of the Mayor of any department Bonaparte's genius is truly wonderful; the whole country is like a regiment, and yet everything is done by the civil authorities, who are placed by the laws above the military, and independent of them.

Public works upon a very superb scale are going on in Mont Marsan, which is however only reckoned a small town; the conscription seems to be the great objection to his government—and all they say is not Gospel; as the proverb says, '*If you want a liar, a boaster, and a thief catch a Gascon.*' This night I give a ball at the castle to the village of Banco, of which I am the sole Governor at present.

The Duke of Angoulême, I am told, issued two days ago a proclamation declaring Louis XVIII. King, and Lord Wellington was very angry, and suppressed it Did you ever hear of such consummate impertinence? under the cover of an English army, with an English minister treating with Bonaparte at a Congress, to dare to publish a document of that kind without telling Lord Wellington of it! What would this stupid race of Bourbons not do if they had the power?

CHAPTER 9

Battle of Waterloo

On his recovery from a protracted illness resulting from wounds and exposure, William Napier, now a lieutenant-colonel, joined the Military College at Farnham. His brother Charles was there at the same time; and there they remained until the escape of Bonaparte from Elba roused Europe from its first sweet dream of peace. The motives which induced these men, who had commanded with so much distinction in the field, to shut themselves up for two years within the walls of a college, are well set forth in a letter of advice which thirty years later the conqueror of Scinde addressed to a young officer.

> By reading you will be distinguished; without it abilities are of little use. A man may talk and write, but he cannot learn his profession without constant study to prepare, especially for the higher ranks, because he there wants the knowledge and experience of others improved by his own. But when in a post of responsibility he has no time to read; and if he comes to such a post with an empty skull, it is then too late to fill it and he makes no figure.
> Thus many people fail to distinguish themselves, and say they are unfortunate,—which is untrue. Their own previous idleness unfitted them to profit by fortune.

Interrupted in his studies at Farnham by Napoleon's flight from Elba, Lieutenant-Colonel William Napier embarked at Dover on the 18th of June, 1815, to join his regiment in Belgium. We may imagine how his fiery nature would have chafed had he known of the scene which was enacting on the theatre for which he was bound. While he was putting his baggage on board the transport, the battle of the giants was being fought at Waterloo.

The following spirited account of the battle was found among Sir William Napier's papers: it was written by Captain Horace Churchill, lieutenant and captain in the Guards, and *aide-de-camp* to Lord Hill. He was afterwards General Churchill, and killed at the Battle of Gwalior on the 27th of December, 1843.

Le Câteau, June 24th, 1815.

I have not had time, my dear Father, to write you a more circumstantial account of our terrific day at Waterloo since my short note to say I was well.

Bonaparte on the 16th instant attacked our left (at Quatre Bras) before the whole of the troops cantoned on the right of the line could be brought up. The day certainly was to his advantage. The French cavalry behaved very dashingly and succeeded in breaking one of our squares of infantry. The Guards behaved with great bravery and covered themselves with glory. The same day Bonaparte attacked Blucher and the Prussians with part of his army. They beat Blucher during the day, but could not drive him from his position; and at night Bonaparte made one of the most extraordinary and brilliant movements ever heard of. He collected the whole of his cavalry m one great mass, charged through the centre of the Prussian army, took 18 pieces of artillery and the whole of the ammunition; and the Prussian loss was 15,000 men by Blucher's own account. The Prussians were *en déroute*.

The following day (17th), in consequence of the retreat of the Prussians, we retired to the position of Waterloo; a position nearly flat, quite open country—the whole one fine glacis; in the right centre a small wood with an old convent in it This point was the most essential for the enemy to gain. Lord Wellington sent the Guards into it with orders to defend it *coûte qui coûte*.

The evening of the 17th the French cavalry rattled in our rearguard and gained some advantages over our cavalry.

On the morning of the 18th we perceived at 11 o'clock the enemy's columns collecting in our front for the attack: the dispositions were immediately made; and at 12 to a moment the first cannon-shot was fired—an awful gun, for we perceived by the enemy's columns that his attack was in earnest, and it appeared as if the annihilation of our army must be the consequence of the shock. Our guns to the number of 100 were placed in front line—then squares of infantry to support our artillery—and the cavalry in intervals to act as they could.

The enemy began a cannonade from 250 pieces upon the front of our position, endeavouring evidently to cannonade our columns into confusion, and then for their cavalry to take advantage of it They attacked at the same moment the wood and convent, in order to *débouche* their columns from it when taken. The Guards foiled them in their attack. The cannonade continued and the butchery was terrible; but our columns remained firm; lucky they did so, for presently appeared their cavalry coming forward in the most brilliant manner, and in a body charged our centre in the very muzzles of our guns. They rode through us, passed our artillery, galloped through our intervals of infantry, went through some of our cavalry, and then attempted to form in our rear.

Nothing could ever be seen equal to the conduct of these troops. The whole of this first attack was made by *cuirassiers*. A most extraordinary circumstance happened now. Our artillery (Donald Crauford among them), after having been rode over and passed by the French cavalry, rose up to their, guns, turned them, and actually fired at the enemy when in our lines. Our artillery performed wonders of steadiness. Notwithstanding this, our squares of infantry remained untouched; our artillery was remanned, and again began the tremendous cannonade. A second body of the enemy's cavalry then repeated the bold attack and did exactly the same.

Then we saw their infantry advancing in one grand mass to attack us. They advanced under horrible slaughter from our guns, nearly gained our position; the day seemed to turn on a straw. Lord Hill then moved forward one division of his corps, before in reserve; the enemy could make no impression. Their cavalry charged our squares with the greatest determination—they could not touch them; there was one general row; the enemy was beaten back, or rather retired in very good order to his position. We now thought it was all over; it was about four o'clock. The enemy had made great efforts, but our troops foiled him everywhere; we could not follow him; he had retired rather than been beaten back, and his position was strong.

About six o'clock we perceived a formation of columns, cavalry and infantry formed in a grand mass. The enemy's artillery was brought to a more forward position, and again he began to cannonade us. He opened a fire, the most tremendous I believe ever known in the annals of war, 250 pieces, very close, throwing shells and round shot, grape and every instrument of destruction.

Thus it is not exaggeration to say, one could not ride quick over the ground for the bodies of men and horses. Under cover of this cannonade advanced Bonaparte at the head of his Imperial Guard; cavalry in a column on the left flank—the grenadiers of the Guard on their right flank. They advanced most steadily up to our line in one great mass—halted and commenced firing: our troops were literally mowed down; the fire was so great, nothing could stand. Our guns were moved close up to the flank of their column, *foudroyer* with grape into it Lord Hill moved a column, our *élite*, round the flank.

I brought up six squadrons of cavalry, and we made a general charge. The *cuirassiers* of the Imperial Guard had their ranks much thinned by our artillery, and went about; we with the cavalry pursued them, leaving the French infantry steady on our flank. Marshal Ney was with their retreating cavalry and I was within 20 paces of him; I could not get six of our cavalry to follow me or we must have taken him; he was alone with about six orderlies. I hollaed out to our rascals, but nothing could get them to face him.

Our cavalry then gave way and we were obliged to gallop. The enemy ran down about 20 of his guns and fired *such* a shower of grape! the infantry then opened upon us, and the French *cuirassiers* came clean into us. I was on my old brown horse; a grape-shot went through his body, and a round shot struck my hat at the same moment; he fell dead. I was a good deal stunned and could not get from under my horse. The French *cuirassiers* rode over me, but did not wound me. I lay there till they were licked back; they again rode by me; one of their *cuirassiers* was killed passing me—I seized his immense horse, and with some difficulty got upon him. I rode off, and hardly was I clear of them when a round shot struck my horse on the head and killed him on the spot.

An officer of the 13th Dragoons dismounted one of his men and gave me his horse: this was shot in the leg about half an hour after. The enemy was now beat back; Bonaparte had led his own Guards and been beaten. The Prussians now came upon the enemy's flank, and this obliged them to hurry their retreat. Our cavalry and artillery then advanced, the enemy was pursued, and his retreat became precipitate.

The fruits of this victory were about 200 pieces of artillery, four eagles, the entire baggage of Bonaparte and his army.

It is needless to enlarge on the conduct of the troops of the two armies. Lord Wellington calls it the 'Battle of the Giants.' I believe in the whole army Lord Wellington was the individual who *fought* hardest, and almost the only individual not touched. Currie was killed by a grape-shot close to me. Lord Hill in the grand *mêlée* with the Imperial Guard had his horse killed and was rode over; we lost him for an hour and I thought he must have been killed; I saw him at last knocking along a fresh horse. Of Lord Wellington's Staff, Colonels Canning and Gordon were killed; Fitzroy Somerset lost his arm; De Lancey badly wounded.

The admiration of the whole army was the gallantry and determination of the French cavalry, and the steadiness of our infantry. Three times the cavalry rode clean through our lines, and hardly a man escaped—they would not surrender. At one time the infantry of the two armies were all in squares. Never was such devotion witnessed as that of the French cuirassiers. I could not help exclaiming when the *mêlée* was going on, 'By God! those fellows deserve Bonaparte, they fight so nobly for him.' I had rather have fallen that day as a British infantryman, or as a French *cuirassier*, than die ten years hence in my bed.

I did my best to be killed, but Fortune protected me: I was struck by a ball on the side of my thigh, which did not even bleed me; one also struck me on the back of my shoulder, which I did not know of till after the action was over. Lord Hill was not touched though his cloak was *criblé de balles*. I rode over yesterday with Lord Wellington to see Blucher. I saw Bonaparte's carriage; his hat, coat, cloak, and all his orders were in it. His hat fits me exactly—would I had such a head under it!

Louis le Désiré comes here today—he will meet with bad reception I think.

Lieutenant-Colonel Napier sailed from Dover the 18th June for

Antwerp, and after a few days spent in Brussels accompanied the army to Paris, where he was a witness of the triumphal entry of Louis XVIII., whom he regarded with strong disfavour.

The following letters to his wife relate to his stay in Paris where Mrs. Napier joined him in August The first letter, written from Brussels one week after the great battle, expresses the ideas which existed as to the engagement in the rear of the army, many of which were of course erroneous and exaggerated.

Brussels, 25th June, 1815.

You will have known before this more of the battle than I can tell you. Poor Chambers has been killed and Simpson wounded. Tomorrow we march for the army, but from the distance they are in advance I think it impossible to join them before another battle is fought Lord Wellington's luck predominates over Bonaparte's; had the latter been two hours sooner in his advance, everything was lost; as it is I believe that a nearer thing never was; the loss in men I should think pretty equal. Bonaparte lost about 40,000, of which 7000 only are prisoners. We lost with the Prussians about 35,000; the latter lost 65 guns, but we have taken near 200. I have lost my two baggage-horses and canteens, and am in a very bad plight altogether; I fear the Prussians have robbed Southgate of them. The heavy cavalry behaved very well. All the French cavalry fought in the most astonishing manner. Bonaparte charged at the head of his own guards.[1]

Charles, I believe, was not in the action. Henry M'Leod was wounded in four places by the French lancers, but he is walking about and doing perfectly well.

Paris, 9th July.

I have not had an opportunity of writing to you before since I left Brussels. I am much annoyed at finding how completely the French nation has lost all sense of shame, and my admiration of Bonaparte is increased tenfold when I find what very contemptible stuff he had to work with. Yesterday the King made his *entrée*; I was on duty, and having placed myself between the palisades of the barrier had an opportunity of seeing everything! There was much shouting and noise, but it proceeded

---

1. This was not the case, but this letter represents the reports which circulated in rear of the army after the battle.

from a few women and gentlemen of his party, and from his bodyguard, which amounted to about 5000; he had also his bodyguard of Swiss and some artillery.

The day before at the same gate I saw the national guard and the mob seize upon two men with white cockades, tear them from their carriage and stone them, swearing that they abhorred Louis and that he never should enter Paris. The next day the same people tore the tricolour from their own hats and stamped upon it!!! The general opinion seems to be that he cannot reign longer than while the allied troops are with him; but who can reckon upon such a people? The soldiers are all gone behind the Loire, still faithful to Napoleon.

It is asserted here, but I do not believe it, that Napoleon is in Paris, and looked at the procession yesterday, laughing at the cry of '*Vive le Roi!*' It does not appear certain that the war is yet over. I went into the Louvre this morning; I was disappointed with the sculpture. I see nothing, save the Torso, equal to the Theseus and Neptune at Lord Elgin's; but the number of them dazzles me at present I confined myself to the Transfiguration among the pictures: *ma foi, que c'est grand!* I will tell you more in my next.

If we should be settled and quiet I must contrive to get you over here even if I go to jail for it; but at present it is impossible. The fortresses are all besieging, and the stragglers and parties of all nations make it very dangerous; but you had better enter into a negotiation about the little devils with some friend to take them in charge. Could not my mother live at Farnham and take care of them? People tell me I am like Bonaparte; and the 43rd soldiers gave me three cheers when I joined the regiment at Ghent,—*pleased* me.

July 20th, Paris.

I expected something like Emily's tumble before I got your letter, for I have had a run of misfortune for some time, and my devil would not let me rest. I am now quiet, and I hope there is an end for some time. As little beasty's head is not hurt I do not think you have anything further to apprehend. Charles's shipwreck was the first; then I got sick and lost my poor little ring; the next day I lost my green silk handkerchief, then a ticket for a tennis-match, then my gloves; my mare fell in the streets of Paris with me next, and rolled over my leg; and the same evening I broke my watch to pieces; your letter about Emily finished it.

If you have not set off before this arrives, don't wait one moment for Louisa or Dick, but come by yourself, sending me word, and I will meet you at Dieppe, Havre, or Rouen, whichever is most convenient I am the more anxious as the pictures and marbles are going fast from the Louvre.....

Paris, 23rd, 1815.

I have got your letter of the 17th with the good account of my little beast Fanny. It is strange you have not got any of my letters, as I wrote on the 7th. Tomorrow we are to be reviewed by the Emperor Alexander, and in about five days more we go into Normandy; thus my scheme about having you at Paris is knocked on the head. This day I met C——, who set me mad by his foolish observations; he said that he gave Napoleon no credit for his idea of an elephant for a fountain, as a whale would have been better, being more appropriate to water,— and this in earnest; is it not ridiculous?

It is impossible to describe this elephant to you, its magnitude and magnificence are astonishing; and after having exhausted my eloquence in describing it to a friend here he went to see it, and remained speechless; *voyez vous donc!* how impossible to write about it! Everything that I hear and see convinces me that, if there is any one thing in the world that Frenchmen can be steady to, it is the determination to hang that fat monster Louis as soon as we go from here; the red pink is the signal for the Napoleonites now, in place of the violet

This day I put on my *pelisse* (grey), a white waistcoat, and the red pink very conspicuous; I rode all over the town, and, although the king's orders are to arrest every person who wears it, not the slightest insult was offered, not one murmur, not a sulky look, but many smiles and many good wishes everywhere. ..... Some of the French army of the Loire gave the Austrians, who are called *les autres chiens*, a beating two days ago.

Paris, 25th, 1815.

Your letter of the 20th has just come to me, and nothing could make me more unhappy; your delight at the thought of coming to Paris gave me more pain than I can express, for the difficulty of accomplishing it increases. In the first place, the army has not yet surrendered, and the Prussians make it very unsafe for anybody to travel, so much so that until all that part is arranged you cannot come. Then as to the money, I have claimed another year's pay on account of my wounds, which if I get and the prize-money is paid, will enable you to come to me for a little while, but only a little, as a decent lodging costs 400 *francs* or about 20*l*. per month at the lowest calculation; however, you may begin and sell my pictures, that is the Rubens and Carracci, and the little pony, as soon as you like, which will help. I have a better pony for you here. Richard would be enough to take care of you, but what would you do for a maid unless you took a French girl?

Paris, July 27th.

I am very impatient to hear from the agents whether I shall get the money I expect; and also to hear something about the 2000*l.*, which Bunbury ought not to lose a moment about, as the exactions and robbery of all the Allies (us excepted) will very soon put an end to all chances of the country being able to pay the amount of the English debt Such a small sum as ours might however be easily got if asked for now; besides which the people must begin a national war soon, if the present system continues.

Even that old savage Louis begins to grumble; he has also begun the work of murdering his children as he calls them. You may probably have seen the list of proscribed people who are to be murdered; one would have thought that 100,000 killed since the war began would have satisfied a paternal king, without this additional mark of his affection.

I have seen —— here very often; she is old, fat, and for her ugly, with all her folly glaring in the noonday, stripped of its former ornaments. You may perceive I do not love her; I however esteem her more than I did, as I can now (judging with an unprejudiced eye) perceive that she is more fool than rogue and that her heart is light, but not bad. I will not insult you by telling you that I weighed you in the scale with her, but an involuntary feeling enforced your value upon my mind with a keenness that convinced me that I have thought too little of women in general, as there could not be so great a difference between two of them if their general worth was as small as I thought.

Paris, 30th, 1815.

I am astonished at the time letters take before they arrive in England from here; yours of the 24th came two days ago, and you had not then received mine later than the 8th. I have written nearly a dozen to you, and sent the draft back the same day that I got it If you can get money by any means I think you might at all events come by Dieppe to me. If we are in Normandy, where we are to march I am told in a few days, this will be some amusement to you even if we should not be able to see Paris.

I have not been to see anything since I wrote last; I have lost all interest in them and take rather an aversion than otherwise, since your letter; I cannot bear the idea of being amused at your expense; I, who ought not to see anything, have all the pleasure, and you, who deserve everything, remain at home wishing in vain. I have not called upon any English people here, as, if you can come to Paris, it will only be for a short time, and I think the sights will fully occupy that without visiting, which would besides be expensive; but if you think otherwise, say so, and I will cultivate for you; in short, anything you wish or that I can do for you......

Since writing I hear, but it is not certain, that our division, the 5th, is to remain in Paris: you had better get Louisa to take the babies as soon as possible Napoleon's letter makes me melancholy. What a noble mind he has! but I fear he mistakes the character of our government when he calls us generous. I have still charity enough to believe that the people are generous.

Paris, 2nd August, 1815.

I am able to get another year's pay and I shall be able to let you come to Paris; nothing that has happened to me this long time has given me so much pleasure, and your dream of Paris may be renewed. They have again told me I may have a pension for asking: shall I take it or not? Speak out to me upon it; I have no doubt but that of propriety; I do not mean nicety, but real propriety; a nice sense of honour unfounded would be an injustice to the little beasts. I hope we shall soon know where we are to go to in Normandy, as it will make much difference to you in land carriage to go from Farnham to Brighton or Portsmouth, instead of London or Dover. I will pay all Dick's expenses if he comes, lodgings and all, remember; so don't let him off on that score.

August 14th, Paris, 1815.

I am vexed to the very heart at this moment; within this hour I have lost your ring that you gave me. I was so fond of it, but I have been ill some time past, and my hand is thin; I lost it yesterday and found it again this morning; I missed it at breakfast; and although I have set about fifty soldiers to look for it and offered rewards, I fear I shall not see it again. I am very much vexed that I cannot keep what I love. I have your letters to the 6th.

With respect to travelling, take the first packet for Havre, or Dieppe, as they sail. If you go to Dieppe, post to Rouen, as from Rouen to Paris is not above eighty miles, and the best road in France. If you go to Havre you can travel by water to Rouen, and so on. If Richard is with you, well; if not, let me know in time, as I will meet you at Rouen; come as soon as possible, for I am very impatient to see you. Do not let anything hinder you, as we have plenty of money.

CHAPTER 10

Occupation of France

The records of the next three years of William Napier s life are but scanty. They are contained in the letters written to his wife from the quarters of the army of occupation on the north-east frontier of France. By the terms of the treaty which followed the downfall of Napoleon and the restoration of the Bourbons, it was stipulated that a portion of the allied army should remain in the French territory for five years. This force was placed under the command of the Duke of Wellington; the English contingent being quartered at or near Cambrai, Douai, Valeniennes, and Tournay.

The headquarters of the 43rd were fixed at Bapaume, a small town of about 3500 inhabitants, in the department of the Pas de Calais, about half way between Arras and Péronne. Here, chafing in inaction, and only consoled for the loss of those "crowded hours of glorious life" he had lately been living by his hatred for the inevitable horrors of war, William Napier cultivated his growing taste for painting, read Cobbett, and exhaled his soul in impatient longings for his wife and children. Fortunately the generous efforts of Wellington reduced the term of occupation to three years. It ceased November 30, 1818, and soon after the whole British army returned to their native land. The first letter was written to Mrs. Napier immediately on her return to England after a stay of some months in France:—

Bapaume, 13th March, 1816.

Changing quarters has prevented me from writing to you before. I got your two letters, one from Calais, the other from Dover, and the last did not at all surprise me. I was very ill indeed the three days after you left me, and being awake all the night I heard the storm. My familiar told me you had sailed that night, but it would not tell me whether you were safe. I was very unhappy until I got your letter...... I am going to practise portrait-painting and send you one as a specimen; the eyes will, I think, tell you who it is, they being peculiar.

When you are at Farnham look in the dictionary for Martin Voss, a painter of 1600 and something, as there is a picture of his here I have a mind to buy. I can get leave to go home when I choose now for six months, but I will wait for two reasons, *viz.*, one, in order that you may be settled first; the other, the large sum of money I give up, as all the allowances of those who go home are to be given to those who stop, which will make near a guinea a day to lose. Now, although I will and must see my babies, I must make some money for them too.

Bapaume, 22nd March, 1816.

.......Your friend, little pony, is now in such a state of fat that he can't get up when he lies down without he is on a hillside; he is called '*pone me pigris*,' which is Latin for 'place me on burning sands,'—very excellent for such a pig as he is. I was riding him a race yesterday, and when the other horse was beating him he caught him by the side with his teeth and stopped him, and then ran away neighing, meaning I suppose to laugh.

March 27th, 1816.

........I should like to have, two volumes *octavo*, price twenty shillings, Mr. Cobbett's paper against gold, or *Glory against Prosperity*, sold by Bagshaw and Sons, Bridges Street, Covent Garden—that is, when I go home in May, to read at home. The triumph of the income-tax *does not delight me*, nor the malt-tax either; it is only a means of putting off the reformation of the parliament and country for a longer period. Cobbett abused your uncle[1] falsely I think, said he was a pensioner; but he included him in the odium of the Grenville and Grey party, which I don't; but I should feel it difficult to defend him for acting with them, or rather for allowing them to act against his principles in his name....

Does Emily hold by her beak like a parrot? if she does she will be my favourite, as I always wished for a child who could do that, and you must confess that the accomplishment deserves any favour..... Brougham is out of my good graces for his

---

1. Charles James Fox.

speech about Bonaparte. If he is not satisfied yet that he was the only support of real freedom in Europe, I see no good to be expected from his politics: it smells too much of the Holland House opposition. Lord Holland, I observe, objects to the registry of slaves in the West Indies, the only means of preventing the clandestine introduction of them, and the good of which is amply proved by the eagerness of the planters to arrest it. . . . . Kiss my little babies for me; I want very much to see you and them.

Bapaume, 6th April.

Your letters give no information on the subject I am most anxious about—your health. I shall set off from here on the 1st or 2nd of May if I can; if you let the house, don't let the books with it. I do not much like to carry the whole brood (of children I mean) to the Isle of Wight, but I suppose I must. Cobbett likes horses and cats I see; so much the better for him.

I send you Carroll's two likenesses and an *egg* for Fanny. . . . . . I am not certain of getting the picture; I have offered three *Naps* for it, more I won't give; it is a coarse picture; the sky, the colouring, and one figure, struck me as good and Venetian. *Voilà un bon coup d'art d'amateur,*—it is Martin Voss. I send you. . . . .the first effort in the way of *dentelles*; it is twenty *francs* for the whole piece. I have some broader and finer at fifty-five *francs* for twice as much, which I will send by some other opportunity: will this be enough? I was getting well when Lord Liverpool's speech about Ireland threw me back again.

Bapaume, 14th April.

Did you see that poor Drouot, the general who followed Boney from Elba, is acquitted, and that the King's procurator had him detained notwithstanding in prison? also that General Travot had been tried? but the proceedings, being illegal even in their eyes, had been quashed, and an order sent down to Rouen to try him again, accompanied with another to execute him within twenty-four hours after sentence; anticipating the result of the trial as usual. The King has *ordered* M. Laine to continue to be President of the Chamber of Deputies. How independent of the Crown they must be under these circumstances!

Bapaume, 20th April, 1816.

Your letters (two) from London have arrived; my mother's was very agreeable, as yours do not come until two days after everybody else's. I am very glad to hear ——'s account of your health; ask him if sea-bathing this summer will do you good, as I must somehow or other get to the seaside, and I think of getting leave for three or four months for that purpose. Now if we could kill three birds at one throw it would be excellent. What do you think of you and me and Louisa at the Isle of Wight?

I have an excellent opportunity of going to Italy now, but I won't accept it; it is with Barnard and Beckwith, who are going in their own carriage, and with their own horses; but I would rather see the babies. . . . . Get the French money out of the funds as soon as possible; the government must go soon; they are frightened out of their wits now, and talk of arming all the people in these departments *en masse* to resist the '*vains efforts des méchants*.'. . . . I am doing a head of Carroll which is allowed to be like, and I say that it is better than anything I have done in the way of painting portraits yet—you shall have it.

Bapaume, April 21st, 1816.

Your letter of the 16th was just what I wanted, only that you have again left me in ignorance of the state of your own health. I perceive that at least four letters of mine have been lost, including the one with Cooke's arm. I am particularly sorry for the arm, as, independent of the goodness of the drawing, the arm itself is unique from strength and being a right arm. . . . . The bells and clocks of Arras have departed 'by the force of prayers' to Rome to be blessed; and as it will take a fortnight to bless them and perform the journey with comfort, the hours are struck by boys with mallets in the streets. *Voilà* the comforts of Legitimacy.

Did I tell you I shoot with a bow and arrow, and am become very expert at the same, frequently at 60 yards hitting a paper about the size of the top of a hat? . . . . . Your second batch of lace ought to have arrived, and if the first pleased you the last will delight you, being much prettier, broader, and better in every way. My application for leave went in yesterday, but I shall not get it for two weeks.

Colonel Napier, after spending six months with his wife and children in England, rejoined his regiment at Bapaume on the 30th November, and his correspondence with his wife is here continued.

Bapaume, 5th December, 1816.

Henry and I have been here these three days. 'Tis uncommonly stupid. I have not seen *Meere*[2] yet, and I am *ennuyé*. When I was last here the change from was so much for the better that I rather liked the place; and as you were going from an uncomfortable place to a good one, I cared less for that also. Now *tout est changé*, and certainly I bear the loss of your company less well than ever: formerly it was impatience, now it is melancholy, and if it increases I do not suppose that the army will be blessed with my presence if I can by any means get away from it.

I have written to Grant a flattering letter,[3] which will effect its purpose I think. I have forgotten my skates, and bought a large picture already for 25 *francs*, which you may expect some day in a long wooden box. I am as usual in the worst house in town, and am at present building fireplaces; the cold is great; much snow has fallen, and it is going to begin again.

God bless you, my dear Caro—I do love you better than anybody, and I am the more certain of this because no place and no society ever fills up the void or satisfies the longing that I feel when separated. We do not feel how much pleasure we are provided with in our existence until the absence of it causes pain; but a sore finger or the gout convinces us immediately that we are happiest when we least observe it

Bapaume, December 9th, 1816.

I wrote a letter to you four days past I have had one from you with a Cobbett Grant says he is delighted, and I really think he is pleased at being godfather.[4] I am going with Henry to see him for a few days. Meere has this moment arrived from Hair; the good beast is fat, and seemed to know my voice. I am vexed every day by new specimens of the manner of treating, or rather ill-treating, the soldiers, of the complete indifference to their comfort, and deference to the cheating of French and English contractors, displayed by everybody in power here, from the Duke to the Brigadier-General.

If I could fly, how pleasant to change at once to your society! . .

. . . Pray take care of yourself; if anything was to happen to you

---

2. His horse.
3. Afterwards Brigadier-General Sir Colquhoun Grant, whose adventurous career is sketched in the *Peninsular War,* Book 16, c. 7.
4. To his son John Moore Napier.

from your neglect of yourself, what life do you think I should lead; when you and my babies are now the only ties that make me wish to live and battle against the double depression of weak health and a mind dissatisfied with itself?

December 12th. 1816.

I have received your second letter, which makes me rather uneasy about the boy; but I hope it is only the fretting of the nurse. I feel more anxious about your health than his. I am going with Henry tomorrow to see Grant for three days.

Cambray, December 16th 1816.

I have been here for four days with Henry, and have in consequence lost the post at Bapaume, so that your letters are waiting for me to go back. The mania of seeing things has cost me rather dear, as I have been thrown back to at least the same situation I was in with regard to health two years ago. You need not wonder at it when I tell you that the first day's journey was riding through muddy heavy clay for 50 miles between breakfast and dinner; that Sir ——, with whom we dined, kept us up drinking until half-past one, and that I finished by getting wet through in a storm going home; that the next day proved so wet that we failed in getting to see the canal underground, *the only thing I wanted to see at all*; and that we finished by playing cards and drinking again until half-past two, with another wetting going home.

Thus everything has run counter; and when you add the internal vexation at doing what I did not like, you will not be surprised that my liver is swelled, my head aching, and my old regular liver cough come on. Grant has been as dull and good-natured as it is possible to be, but he, like all other people, mistakes my disposition, and imagines that a large party of what are called 'good fellows' must be delightful to me. Henry is pretty well, and will probably start today for Paris, and perhaps being quiet at Bapaume may bring me up again as well as I was when I first arrived, which was better than I can remember being for many years.

Bapaume, December 22nd, 1816.

A continual fight with Kempt, the Mayor, and the people of my house, which however has terminated in my favour in the three instances, prevented me from writing last post I am very glad that George is with you; pray tell him that Oglander will leave *Jomini* for him at my mother's house soon; he owes Oglander for it. You are quite right to have ordered that all beggars should be known to you before they are sent away; and that you may not be stinted in your bounty, I shall send you money every two or three months, out of which you may safely be charitable, as I am actually in possession of near £600 a year here while I command.

After I wrote from Cambray we endeavoured again to see the caverned canal, and succeeded, but got wet through, lost our way at night, and made a real party of pleasure for the devil who always delights in mischief,—no accident however. The canal is really wonderful; the first cut, four miles long; the second, a mile and a half through hills, at the depth of 240 and 100 feet below the surface, and the earth excavated was drawn out by baskets through small holes at the top, which now serve to ventilate it. It is 24 feet wide and 24 feet high, besides the watercourse arched with brick, and a stone pathway for men at each side, but no horses go; the whole finished in six years from the commencement. Still the sewers of ancient Rome are infinitely greater, if the account be true of them that they are 37 feet high and 37 miles long, arched with stone. . . . .

For myself, I am not well, but part of it I attribute to a fretful disposition which gains strength upon me every time I quit you, who are after all other pleasures pall the only real good I possess in the world. . . . Have you seen anybody that knows where places are to be sold, as I am more in fear than ever of the funds. The rows are nothing; and I do not fear for you, because it is everybody's interest to keep down such kind of vagabonds, who appear to me to be paid by the Government.

However, as things are, a revolution appears to me inevitable in England, and I cannot look forward without dismay; still, if we can save enough to give bread to our children, we may be happy, as we are not dependent on other people for amusement, and can I think both of us live contented in a Welsh cottage . . . . . When I called the rioters vagabonds I understood that they were principally pickpockets who had taken advantage of the time of the Spa-fields to maraud, not that they were really starving sailors and workmen. Could you not get Dick to walk now and then upon Westminster Bridge and give something for you and me to the poor creature Cobbett describes as lying there?

Bapaume, December 26th.

Your letter from St Anne's, the last that I have received, gives me a great deal of comfort both about you and the boy; but I hope you do not hurt yourself by too much watching at night,—such anxiety is very bad for you.......The Duke of Wellington set off for England two days ago suddenly; people say about the French contributions which cannot any longer be paid. Madame de Staël, I am told, said that the first year they would be paid in gold, the second in silver, and the last in lead. She certainly belongs to the brazen age herself; and if that metal would do, she might pay the whole in a month without materially diminishing her stock......

Bapaume, December 29th, 1816.

Every letter of yours adds to my satisfaction by the certainty they give me of your undiminished affection, which daily becomes more necessary to my happiness—every day convinces me of my own inability to attach friends, and of my natural gloomy unsocial disposition; and my surprise and gratitude to you for loving me is in proportion.... Henry I have at last heard from. He has given me a present that I am much obliged for, *Malbrook's Life*, the one supposed to be written by Napoleon, which I do not believe, as I find much inflated language about trifles which no real great man could have written. The observations betray a blind admiration of Marlborough, rather than the just praise of as great a mind as his own.

January 3, 1817.

My first letter of today did not contain half I intended to say to you, so I will write another through Mr. Arbuthnot, through whom I likewise send you the defence of Ney, which I found here amongst my papers. About a week ago I saw a bricklayer, an old French soldier, beating an English one in the street, your old friend that made you the fireplace at Villarapoli. This excited my rage, and, upon my interfering, the French gentleman informed me that he would serve me in the same way. This did not cool me, as you may guess, and I put myself in attitude, and we had a *fit*, which ended by my knocking him clean off his legs eight times following with as many blows, when he declined any more battle.

Mrs. Staples is quite right, for her only reason for being ministerial is a natural one—her father is one—and she did not believe the things she heard without seeing them, a common practice, which confines people's minds to a very narrow limit; although it ought always to be broken through with caution, as it cuts both ways.

Now she is convinced by ocular demonstration, and her rage is in proportion to her former blindness, and the novelty of her ideas relative to the author of the desolation she perceives around her adds poignancy to her resentment How many honest good people are deceived into supporting the wretches miscalled ministers, in the same manner as she has been heretofore!

Bapaume, January 6th, 1817.

We have no news here; but I know of a political story that is *authentic* and very diverting. Monsieur Decazes called upon the King and told him that His Majesty's postmaster, Emeral, was leagued with his enemies (that is the Prince's party), and that even the royal correspondence was not safe from their curiosity, and that he would prove it He wrote two letters, one a copy of the other, to a person in the south, abusing Louis grossly; got the King to direct it in his own hand, to put the private marks of royalty upon it, to seal it, and send it by his own servant.

Two days after, *Madame la Duchesse* made her appearance with a long visage, and a story about the King being surrounded with enemies, even his minister of police being a traitor; the King affected to be in great alarm, and out came *the letter*. 'Ah, *ma fille, mais j'ai ici le pendant de celle-là;*' and Louis showed her the duplicate. She fell sick; and Decazes is in greater favour than ever. I love you so much that my poetical brains have been called into action by it, and on the other side you will find what I call an *Ode to Love*, but I believe improperly, as it is an invocation. Read it and put it in my book, and tell me if it strikes you as original To myself it does not appear so; I hope I am wrong. It is a great proof of my untired love for you to be inspired in this manner, but I believe that the liver is a great steadier of people's minds, as I have been remarkably well these three weeks back, and so—I am a poet!

If you don't like the verses burn them, but give me credit for my endeavours, as I wrote it from a fullness of mind that I felt when thinking of you and all the goodness of your disposition.

Bapaume, January 9th, 1817.

Your letter of the 1st January! have had three days, and I do not at all understand how you come to be without mine later than the 21st December. Don't think I forget you: I have not much pleasure it is true in the act of writing itself but a great deal in doing what pleases you, and still more in hearing from you; so you also on your part must not forget me; your letters are as much my food as mine are yours, and your manner of writing is to me the pleasantest in the world, like talking to me, and such pleasing talk that when I read them it goes against my heart to burn them, which I do because you told me to do so, and I have as great an objection as yourself to their getting into other people's hands. Your reports about the troops have reached us; I do not know if they are true; I hope so: certainly the regiments in this country are to be reduced to 800 men each, as some of them have already received orders to that effect

I should like so much to be with you again that nothing but the absolute necessity of waiting for the events that are hanging over us could keep me wasting my life in this miserable place, and in such an unprofitable manner. What a difference between the company of Lock and other favourites of mine, and the Bourgeois de Bapaume,—between my own reflections or rather *ennui*, when I am by myself, and your face and conversation or my little Emily and Fanny talking to me!—not but I feel a charm in command even though it be during peace: still nothing compensates for the loss of the other pleasure, although it is a consolation not to be despised, quickly as it passes away and little remembrance as there will be of it when over.

What shall I do when Patrickson comes back? Idle as I must be, discontented as I will be, and tiresome as the place is always, I could almost wish the Bordeaux insurrection had taken place if it was only to give us a reason for quitting *les Bapaumois*.

January 15, 1817.

I write to you this day, which is one before the post, or rather half a one, as it is very late at night, because I have received the other for the reduction of the second battalion, and directions to pick and choose all the objectionable men, to discharge them, and to get handsome ones from the second battalion. That means to sign the death warrant by starvation of about 200 men because they are under five feet six inches high, or may have been worn out in an ungrateful service. This has taken me from the morning till the night of this day , and will also tomorrow, as I must send in a description-roll of them by the post—besides all the letters to be written; however, I have done a great deal, and found a good many more than I expected who wish to be discharged, and at all risks I am determined to keep a good many worn-out poor creatures who have served thirteen, and twelve, and eleven years, who would not get a pension under fourteen years' service, but whom it is expected I should thus *cheat* of their limbs, constitution, and money, because they are not tall people; I would sooner be hanged! Gore says that Talleyrand was asked by a lady the other day at a party how '*affaires*' went on now—'*Comme vous voyez*,' was the answer. N.B. She squinted horribly.

Bapaume, January 19th, 1817.

If I did not already love you as much as it is possible to love, your last letter would excite it; so natural, so frank, so tender, and so much simplicity of expression and feeling as it contains, it would be impossible to avoid loving the person who wrote it; to me it is very dear, more so than I can describe, because I know you, I know your mind and your disposition, and that the simple feelings and gentle tenderness of a child are supported by more sense and judgment than almost any woman I ever met is gifted with.

Your satisfaction at the verses is good news for me, and I can assure you that I felt very anxious for your approbation, not being at all *content* with them myself, while on the contrary, when I wrote the Plato, I felt more vain of my own talents than anything else, and thought I had conferred a considerable favour in writing such good verses.

I have had a regular attack again of the liver, and this day am not well by any means. The French people feel the effects of it; a quill-driving clerk, the largest man in the town, who was reckoned their bully, boasted for some months back that he would chastise any English officer that was saucy to him. In pursuance of his menace he has pushed several of the *small* officers off the pavement when he met them, and growing proud, he at last ventured upon me in one of my bilious humours, which cost him a good licking with a *green* ash walking-stick I had in my hand, since which the *bourgeois* say that he has lost *la gloire d'un brave Français*,' and he is always hissed when he appears. . . .

Valenciennes, April 17th, 1817.

The snow still continues to infest us by showers, and consequently my head is not much better. The duties of this town as established by General ———, and followed up by general power, in the plenitude of his blustering, are without exception the most absurd I ever met with: the more I see of the generals of the army, the more I regret Moore and wonder at Lord Wellington's success; Kempt will however be here upon the 24th and relieve us from the impertinent folly of the people here. I used to wonder a little at the idea in the army that Kempt himself was a great general; I do not wonder at it now.

The first day I came here I heard a great noise and tinkling in the Grande Place, and walked up carelessly to look what was going on; the grand guard was mounting, and just as I came up the field-officer, *kivered* all over with lace, rode up to me, dropped his sword, touched his hat, and asked my permission to march off his guard. My leave was easily obtained, but guess my horror at perceiving that 300 men and a proportion of officers, with this honest gentleman at their head, were all directing themselves in slow time upon me to salute. I was standing among some subalterns who rather hid me, and I took the opportunity of slipping away, leaving the *subbies* to receive the honours, to the dismay of the whole body. . . . .

I am in actual treaty for the picture; I think I can get it for 25 *naps*, which will be dirt cheap: it is the Marriage of Cana by a Dutchman or Fleming; the composition faulty, as there are two principal groups, the Jesus and the married couple; the dresses are Dutch also, or rather Spanish, but the faces, the draperies, the colouring, the depth of shadow, and all the minor ornaments, are *vraiment superbes*; it is six feet two inches by two feet four inches, as near as I can guess.

Valenciennes, April 24th.

I am going to buy the picture I wrote to you about; it is so beautiful I could not resist it; it will be about 25 *naps*, and is I think worth 500*l.*, which is next thing to cheating; but all is fair in pictures you know, or at least I know it if you don't. The Duke of Wellington is in England as I suppose you know, and as Patrickson came back last night I shall soon be there also, as I shall send in my leave tomorrow.'

April 27th.
Your permission to buy pictures came very *a propos*, as I had first paid 25 *naps* for him, and put him up in a box. I shall be very glad to quit this town, as I am decidedly agueish every day, and I am certain I should relapse very soon if I was to stop here.

I am much disturbed about poor old Lock's death. I was very fond of the old man, and should have been very glad to have shown my babies to him before he died; he was a true-bred Irishman of the best kind; he was fall of noble feelings and pride; very eloquent; and, if it had not been for his love of getting drunk, a very clever man.

His attachment to all of us was of a nature that made it impossible not to like him again; and the remembrance of him was one of the causes of my strong wish to see Celbridge again; this I suppose will never be, and I do not now regret it so much as I should have done had he been still alive to welcome you with all that vehement eloquence and energy which was so peculiar to him, and which would have made your blood curdle at times from awe. I have more recollections and associations of early ideas, old stories, and attachments to horses and dogs, connected with him than with any other person now alive, Doudeney excepted, and even with her they are of a less romantic kind than with him. He was a wild bard-like man, and I am very sorry for him.

Valenciennes, January 5th 1818.
Since I wrote last to you the picture mania has seized me again; it is in vain to struggle against fate. I have given six naps for a small picture by Casteliogi, after the manner of Correggio; it has, like all French pictures, been very much hurt by bad cleaning, but still it is of a roundness and plumpness so extraordinary and so beautiful, that it might easily pass for a true Correggio . . . I have been thinking of the verses upon Mr. Fox's death, and that the following alteration would be better; you might as

well show her the lines upon the peace which contain the verse about Lord Ellenborough; I think them the best I ever wrote.

I get exceedingly flattered here; I am told that I am very agreeable, that I am very handsome, and that I waltz better than anybody! the only effect it has is to make, me wish that you could see me.

Kiss my little babies for me, and cunning little Pucky particularly. I should like to see him riding upon Bull [the large dog], when he looks so funny upon the top of his kennel; something like this I suppose. [*Here is inserted a pen-and-ink sketch of the baby boy on a large dog.*]

Valenciennes, January 8th, 1818.

I was introduced to Lady —— the other night, who told me she '*waas vurry colt freend of yours, liked you vurry much, you waas so good, and so like your mother, who was best ooman evurr live.*' She made me like her by praising you so much; what do you think of her? . . . . . . If Fanny gets very tall you must give her ass's milk, as well as to Mr. Puck, and keep her out in the open air a good deal, with plenty of nourishing food. . . . . . I wish you would tell me of something you would like yourself, as I fear that pictures don't please you, and the idea of being selfish in my pursuits is not agreeable to me. . . . . . . My little babies give me a great delight, and I hope the same sensation will help to cheer you in all the trouble you have about the affairs of the house; and, indeed, my Caroline, the consciousness of being a good mother is worth a great deal of idleness, even should the idleness be accompanied by a great deal of amusement. . . . . . .'

Valenciennes, January 15th, 1818.

. . . . . . I have not seen Mrs. —— since I wrote last to you. I do not like her husband at all. He is gross in his manners, and coarse in his person, stupid in his mind, narrow and illiberal in his ideas, malicious in his disposition, mad in his looks, obstinate in his ignorance, and a rogue in his heart, *le gros coquin*! Mrs. —— is young, delicate, and almost very pretty in her person, perfectly ignorant of the world, innocent, simple, and *naïve* to the degree that borders upon folly, yet does not touch it, feeling that she wants something more than she has, but not perceiving that her brute is an unfit helpmate for her, and that she is entitled to something more intellectual.

Her sister is taller and more robust, not so much simplicity and *naïveté* yet enough of both to make her piquante, ignorant, and with a considerable share of folly, yet taking upon herself to direct her sister at all times and all things, the latter submitting more from not perceiving it than from any feeling of inferiority, which would be misplaced. . . . Mrs. ⸺ and her two daughters are the relict and children of a Major ⸺, who, being deceased, is called Major-General ⸺. They live upon *hopes and hope.*

The mother has two large gooseberry-coloured eyes, but you cannot say she has got no speculation in them; they follow and speak very plainly to every man of rank in the garrison, and they can perceive an order through any wall, and at any distance. She is tall, rawboned, and stalking; she is a wild and untameable hyena, who *oons, moans, groans,* and entices the little heedless officers into her house, and afterwards gives them to be devoured by her cubs; the last are two rather fine girls, one black, the other red, calling herself blonde, like the beauties of Rubens, with strong symptoms of the savage disposition of the mother in them.

The whole brood were engaged to a ball at Champs for a week before the time, but Sir Manly Power gave a ball the same night. The hyena came to the Champs and said her cubs had chilblains and were licking their paws at home. *Point du tout!* they were at the general's dancing. Like the primitive Christians they forgot all danger, sickness, or civility, at the sight of a cross.

Valenciennes, January 19th, 1818.
The description of my little funny Puck pleases me much, and I would also be very proud of Fanny's promising beauty, if I believed it. However, she may turn out a good mathematician, and she will be at least as pretty as Dalby. Have you been asked to subscribe to the Princess's monument? Do, if asked, but not otherwise, as they are foolish things I think; but I wish you, of all things, to subscribe a guinea to the committee for the relief of seamen in town; it appears the most praiseworthy and the best conducted thing I have heard of, and I am, besides, willing to show a little more liberality than the navy officers did at the meeting, where they abused the army very much, à *propos* to nothing but their envy and spleen . . . . . .

W. Pakenham came yesterday and told me that he was desired to say that my youngest daughter was everything that was delightful and good. What has the little she-wretch been doing, and who told him so? Don't imagine that I am uninterested in the girls, because I don't remark upon their progress and pranks so much as upon Puck's; the truth is, his little funny eyes catch my imagination more, and the ideas I form are more ludicrous; but I love the girls as much as him, be he never so pretty.

Valenciennes, January 25th, 1818.

I dined at Colonel Blair's, where I met —— and ——, with their two daughters, being on their road to Brussels, and having invited themselves. The old puffin was obliged to leave off her airs, and she behaved middling, was rather glad to see me, and did not talk of above half a dozen kings and princes when she first came into the room; however, she looked very like a pig who had strayed into a parlour, and was half inclined to grunt, but being struck by the novelty of the situation, remained silent.

—— looks haggard and very old, was dull and rather pompous, but at twelve o'clock dived down stairs to smoke and drink gin.

The young ladies came late for dinner, peering and stealing into the room like two young sick peachicks, looking very ugly and very much afraid of some of the officers pulling out their tail-feathers. Sir Alexander Dickson was there, and in the course of conversation he told me he knew that we had a particular method of mixing and making gunpowder, but he never could find out who had invented or introduced it

Now it was my father who did it, and I promised him a copy of the paper upon the subject, written for and printed in the *Transactions of the Irish Academy*. Will you get the volume and copy it for me in a good hand, and send it out? or will it add too much to your existing troubles? I don't like to give you the trouble, and if you feel any dislike, I am sure Henry will do it, as it concerns my father's fame in science.

I wrote last time to you about Mina I think, but I forgot to tell you a trait of Grant's character which will please you. He gave fifty *napoleons* to the subscription for Mina last year, and at a time when I know he had lost a good deal of money, and was just put upon half-pay.

Valenciennes, January 31st, 1818.

If Sir Humphrey Davy's work is very scarce, it would be good to get another for yourself, as that and Madame Marcet's conversations, with the scientific dialogues, would make a complete study of the first part of chemistry, and I believe you like that kind of study. I am reading them myself now, and, with a few instruments, we might make very pretty experiments together. I have read the *Edinburgh Review* about Sir Philip Francis, and I think it is quite conclusive, upon the whole, that he is Junius.

Valenciennes, February 9th, 1818.

If the change in your brother's destination is to do him service, I am very glad, but I fear it; for although Naples is as gay as Paris, it does not come in so agreeable a form, and, at all events, the expenses of Paris are so enormous, that I am sure 300*l.* a year will not half serve for his comforts, much less for his diversion, with his extravagant disposition. Sir Charles Stuart is the man whom he will find most agreeable and to his taste of all others—keen, shrewd, and manly, going his own way always, and allowing everybody else to do the same. He is, however, a good warm friend when he takes a liking to anybody, and particularly upright in his opinions without affectation.

The coalition with Lord North was a stroke of party politics which I think unworthy of your uncle's talents and character; but, at the same time, it was not an inconsistency on his part, as he did not join Lord North's politics, but made the latter adopt his, and that in an humble manner. The best defence of it is his own speeches, which you have, as well as those upon his India bill, which was a wonderful effort of genius, and as bold a stroke for establishing his system of politics as was ever tried before by any dealer in that trade.

The beauty of it was, that with his own interest he combined a beautiful system of just and humane government for India, and put an iron weight upon bad government and corruption in England. The people he chose for his committee, I think, he had too good an opinion of, and they would have been the stay and support of the aristocratic faction instead of the guardians of the people, which I really believe he honestly intended they should be; but the truth is, that he was rather too much engaged with that faction all his life, and he did not perceive that the people never really sympathised with him, although, from his talents and honesty, they sometimes appeared to be the same party.

The moment he died the party became contemptible, because, being without power and selfish, they could not join or would not join the people, and the king hated them. This it is which accounts for the great personal affection so apparent for your uncle, and the little interest and love for his party in the country; they liked him, but not his companions.

Valenciennes, February 16th, 1818.

Lord Wellington has been fired at at Paris, and what makes it very serious is, that although it only took place on Tuesday, we were told here and at Cambray that it had taken place upon the Saturday—that is, on Saturday the French news was that Lord W. had been fired at, and on the Tuesday following it actually happened. Louis's police have very coolly informed the Duke that the plot originated at Brussels, among the emigrant Frenchmen; that is, that having by their flight saved their heads from him, he is endeavouring to get them killed by us, by a false accusation.

For my part, I have no doubt that it originated with him and his ministers, partly out of enmity, and partly to have the means of attacking these poor devils in their retreat; the world will hardly be the dupes of such a gross artifice as this I hope, but almost anything will go down.[5] Mr. Phillips seems to have exposed the spy system completely in the House.

Will any honest man support ministers after that, or will it be passed over as just and fitting? For my part, I imagine a clever and bold man, being a tolerable lawyer, would be able to give them a great deal of trouble by accusing them at once of high treason upon oath, and proving the overt act by the conduct of their emissaries, who certainly, if their own necks were in danger, would not hesitate to denounce their employers.

The Prince of Hesse Homburg was the little fat ugly silly German monster who barked in a red volunteer sort of uniform with brown top-boots at Lord W's balls at Paris. You saw him talking to Miss Banks one evening about the Alps being *ver 'eye eel indid*.

---

[5] The assassin, Cantillon, was an undoubted Buonapartist, and rewarded for his attempt by a legacy of 10,000 *francs* left him by the Emperor.

Valenciennes, 2nd March, 1818.

The reports about going home are contradictory, but the most prevailing opinion is that we shall. Some people say that we are to be a corps of observation in Belgium. Will the King of the Netherlands like such inmates? If he does, the Belgians won't. Something unusual is however going on, as Lord Wellington comes back to Cambray the 26th of this month, and that is three months sooner than he intended when he went away. I send you a nice little ring that Charlie Gore gave me, of Bonaparte and Lord Wellington; you may wear it. There is at Guernsey, belonging to the Russian General, a little beautiful model in bronze of the Column of the Place Vendôme, about a foot high: you touch a little spring, and at the top out pops *le petit bon homme*, in gold, with his cocked hat and folded *arms*. There is nothing here of the kind, or I would get it for you.

12th March, 1818.

I am in very great pain and have had no rest for three nights back; I was very low at first, thinking it was the gout; but Hair seems to be decided now that it is the rheumatism. Blisters have no effect but paining me intolerably, and when I shall be well is very doubtful.

19th March, 1818.

I am much better as to pain, and of course my letter will be longer than the last, but not merrier, as I fear that it is actually gout that has caused my illness; there is some chance of its being rheumatism, but the choice is not agreeable. It is hard that I should have got the first without any of the luxuries that the world gives as the cause of it.

23rd March.

I am very low-spirited about my prospects; I am so shaken and so low, that although I have no pain I can hardly walk, and a sprain in the tendon Achilles is not a bit better, although I have put three successive blisters upon it

Valenciennes, March 26th, 1818.

I perceive in the list of new publications a *Life of the Elder Scipio Africanus* by the Rev. Edward Berwick; get it for me. Talking of Scipio, there is a French officer who calls himself Narcisse Achille Salvandy, and who is called Narcisse Achille Salmagundy, who writes a letter to Lord Wellington upon the occasion of the shot fired at him, in which he says, 'I have flattered your pride by calling you Hannibal. The French will pardon me a little pride when I regret being reduced to combat you with a pen; and Scipio was, when he conquered Hannibal, *à peu près aussi jeune que moi!!!*' I hear my picture is safe in London: our collection of pretty things *s'accroit*, even to our children, the last not the least pretty or expensive. Did you read the papers published by Las Casas? Pray don't forget to tell Miss Fox that I told her Sir Hudson Lowe's character early; and give my love to Mrs. Fox, who I believe is a good and sincere friend of yours and Bonaparte's, and either is a passport to my affections.

Valenciennes, March 30th, 1818.

Your letter giving an account of my poor little Emily's accident has just come, and has excited a great deal of uneasiness both about her and you. The poor little thing must suffer dreadfully, as there is no pain so great as a burn. I wish sincerely I was with you to look after my little baby, and take care of her as you are doing. I fear you suffer much yourself; indeed I cannot see how it should be otherwise. The simple description of her pain and her escape from death makes me creep with a sensation that I cannot describe. Kiss my little patient Emily for me......

Valenciennes, 30th April, 1818.

I have at last sent in my application for leave, and in ten or twelve days I expect to get it allowed. I think that the army will move before my leave is out, as the French seem to be determined to get us out; and having paid all their contributions with good faith, they say with reason we cannot have any good cause to remain in the country after the three years are out; and in order to back up their remonstrance they have ordered the garrisons of all their towns to repair to their different departments to get filled up by recruiting to two battalions, which at once doubles their army.

This last will, I think, prove the most cogent argument of any they may use, France being still the most powerful country of Europe, full of men and horses and warlike spirit and good officers; and I do not believe that any other country except Russia could go to war without great difficulty. The ministers of Prussia, and some say of Russia also, were pelted at Paris some time ago for being inimical to the evacuation of France. Lord

Wellington was in great favour......

On the return of the army of occupation in 1819 Lieutenant-Colonel Napier was quartered with the 43rd Regiment in Belfast. Although a lieutenant-colonel by brevet, he was still only a regimental major. An opportunity was now afforded him of purchasing the regimental lieutenant-colonelcy by the retirement of Colonel Patrickson, but he was unable to avail himself of it for want of means; and although Lord Fitzroy Somerset, with that overflowing generosity and kindness which made him beloved by great and small, pressed the required sum upon him as a loan, he declined it from a fear of his not being able to repay the money.

An officer who had seen little service, and that in a subordinate capacity, was about to exchange into the 43rd as major with the object of purchasing the lieutenant-colonelcy over the head of Napier, and the latter resolved to goon half-pay and seek for distinction in literature, since he was debarred by poverty from advancement in his profession.

Nearly every officer of his rank who had in any way distinguished himself during the war was at its termination rewarded either by being made King's *aide-de-camp,* and in this way several passed over his head; or by being made inspector of clothing, of inspecting field officer. He received nothing; yet he was highly connected, was second to none in merit, held in high estimation by the Duke of Wellington, had been thirty times engaged, had commanded a regiment in several general actions, and detachments nearly equal to a regiment in several others, had gained two steps and three decorations in the field of battle, and received three wounds, one of them so severe as to leave him for the remainder of his days only a miserably painful existence.

The circumstance is inexplicable except by the axiom *Nothing ask, nothing have*—for he was too proud to ask for any recognition of his merit, and he turned with a disappointed wounded spirit, but with the consciousness of power, to the task of immortalizing the deeds of that army which had been made so famous by its commander, and which in return made of that commander the foremost man in Europe.

Yet he was not wholly without compensation. When he quitted the 43rd all the officers who had served under him, even those who had quitted the service or gone on half-pay or into other regiments, subscribed to present him with a rich sword bearing on its blade the following inscription:—

Presented by Lieut-Colonel Patrickson, C.B., and the Officers of the 43rd Light Infantry, to Lieut.-Colonel William F. P. Napier, C.B., as a testimony of their sincere regard for him and their high admiration of the gallantry and conduct he ever displayed during his exemplary career in the 43rd Regiment.

In accepting this testimonial military propriety was not violated, because the man who presented it, and who headed the subscription list, was Colonel Patrickson, who was and had long been his commanding officer.

Before following William Napier into private life, the following letters are given, showing the opinions entertained of him as a soldier by those who served under his command.

FROM COLONEL CONSIDINE [6] TO COLONEL WILLIAM NAPIER.

(Written by him when about to leave the 43rd Regiment)

[*Extract*]

If you were our chief nothing would tempt me to leave the corps. There are very few here who are known to you, though to all *you* are known, as believe me you are often, very often, spoken of, proudly spoken of by those who knew you, and the name of Napier will not be forgotten in the 43rd.

In all my rambles I have never forgotten my old captain, and I have often congratulated myself that while yet a boy I was fortunate enough to be the *sub* and friend of one who confirmed in me what I deem my best and most chivalric feelings—who made me a soldier; this I have always felt and often spoken of to others, although not to you before. I am delighted to hear you say you have always the same friendship for me; you do not know how proud I am of it.

Another extract from the same to the same.

Here I am so far on my way to Constantinople, to look at the Turkish army, and subsequently command and drill them. I cannot leave England without communicating to my old captain and master in the art of war the present fate and destination of his former pupil. I need scarcely tell you, soldier as I am, how delighted I am at my trip and the compliment paid me. *You* first

---

6. Colonel James Considine was Napier's subaltern in the 43rd; afterwards Lieut.-Colonel commanding 53rd Regiment; employed later as British Military Agent at Constantinople and Commander-in-Chief of the Tunisian army. His early death was much mourned by his numerous friends.

made a soldier of me—you for whom I have a kind and affectionate remembrance as my old captain, whom I used to take as a model, and whose principles and lessons I have ever since endeavoured to follow as a soldier.

The following, from the same, relates to the storming of the "Petite Rhune."

My having commanded the two companies on that occasion was mere accident; when *you* were there my commanding the advance was of little moment; you commanded and led all.

FROM MAJOR SIR G. HOULTON[7] TO COLONEL WILLIAM NAPIER.

Farley Castle, 10th January, 1841.

I perfectly remember the circumstance at La Rhune to which you refer, and am proud to bear witness to that and to the many acts of bravery accompanied by humanity I never saw equalled, to all of which I was an eyewitness.

When we were fortunate enough to possess you as Commanding Officer, it was only to mention to the men that you were at their head, and a sort of frenzied courage immediately possessed them, so that they were equal to anything. Anything I can say must fall far short of my feelings with regard to you as a soldier: in fact, whenever I hear of a noble deed I exclaim, 'That's a Napier.'

FROM CAPTAIN PENRUDDOCKE, ROYAL NAVY, TO COLONEL WILLIAM NAPIER.

February 3rd. 1841.

As I understand you are making a statement of your services, a corroboration that proceeds from an eyewitness may be useful. A man named Walker told me that the bugle major 43rd, who attended you as bugler in the field, had spoken to him of you. I asked him what he said. '*That you knew what you were about, and were not afraid of anything.*'

Under any other circumstances you might think me impertinent in mentioning this to you, as you have avoided speaking of your personal exploits even when alone, and my curiosity was excited by the fact of your continuing in the command of the 43rd under Wellington so many years, you having only the

---

7. Served in the 43rd during the Peninsular war.

rank of Major.

Napier's modesty and silence with respect to his personal exploits were quite remarkable; and the statement of his services to which Captain Penruddocke alludes in the foregoing letter was only drawn from him in 1841 by what he considered an injustice inflicted on him by the operation of a new regulation, which will be referred to in its proper place.

FROM CORPORAL WILLIAM FOLLOWS,[8] 43RD REGIMENT, TO COLONEL WILLIAM NAPIER.

Honnored Sir,   Fermoy, 26th August. 1820.

I most humbly hope your honnur will not deem it too presumptive of your servant William Follows in adressing a few lines with my sincerest thanks for the many benefits and indulgences i receved from your honnor. it was greatly talked of your coming to join the Regiment again, but I am verry sorry and so is a great many and indeed most of the Regiment that it is not so. I hear the men when they would see the mare [9] wishing that your honnor was back again, but she is gone too so that there is nothing to remind them of you now but your honnors deeds of justice and vaulor witch will always be thought of by them that noes you. I hope Sir you will be pleased to give my duty to Mrs. Napier and i hope you will excuse my ignorant presumptive manner of writing, in witch i am very indolent, and is not able with my pen to express the warm sentiments of my mind towards your benevealent family whom everybody respecks. I have been Corporal better than 2 years, and I was Lance Sergeant but got reduced for a little misconduck to Corporal again, but i am verry comfortable with my wife and child. Your honnor will undoubtedly think me verry troublesum but i hope you will impute it to the weakness of your ever most humble and
    Dutyfull Servant,
     William Follows Corporal
      43rd Regiment Light Infantry.

It was such testimony as that contained in the foregoing letters, the unsolicited testimony of private soldiers, that Sir William valued

---

8. He was afterwards promoted to an ensigncy in the 53rd Regiment.
9. Formerly Colonel Napier's.

the most highly; and indeed justly, for they are always very impartial, and at the same time very rigid judges of their officers' merits in the field.

The following extract of a letter from General Shaw Kennedy addressed to the author is a curious evidence of the opinion entertained by the Duke of Wellington of William Napier when still a very young soldier:—

Bath, February 14th, 1860.

When I was *aide-de-camp* to General Robert Craufurd in 1809-10 Napier was a captain in the 43rd, and he sometimes saw and spoke to Lord Wellington at that time, and he sometimes told me what had passed in conversation between him and his lordship. As A. D.C to General Craufurd it was part of my duty to keep all the correspondence between them, which was very frequent and quite confidential; and I was necessarily often present when they met and discussed interesting matters personally. What struck me as most extraordinary was, that I found from Napier's conversation that Lord Wellington had said things to him which appeared to me of a more confidential nature than had even been communicated to Craufurd.

Napier was then a very young man, 28; had seen little, and had no military position: how then did it happen that Lord W., one of the most secret of men, should have discussed such matters with Napier? I considered then, as I do now, that this could only be accounted for by Lord Wellington having been drawn into it involuntarily by the talented observations of Napier.

With respect to William Napier's personal daring, General Shaw Kennedy related that a few days before the Battle of Waterloo, General Alton, who commanded the Light Division in the Peninsula, was passing in review the characters of the different officers of that division, and fixed upon Napier and Baring (his own A. D. C, who afterwards defended La Haye Sainte so desperately) as the two men of the whole division he would have selected for a desperate service.

Napier, in speaking of this, says, "This praise was unbought, for I was the only officer of the division who had refused to subscribe for a sword presented to him, and had given him my reasons in a letter; for we were never friends. It was very honourable of the old man to forget this."

CHAPTER 11

Collection of Materials for the History

After retiring on half-pay Colonel Napier took a house in Sloane Street and spent much of his time in painting and sculpture. In these pursuits, as in all others, he showed extraordinary perseverance. As a preparation he devoted himself to the study of anatomy and of the Elgin marbles, and his statuette of Alcibiades is proof of the progress he made. He became an accurate and vigorous draughtsman, was no mean colourist, and in the opinion of artists of great eminence, his natural powers and his indefatigable industry would have raised him to the foremost rank of living painters and sculptors, had he not been irresistibly led to exercise his talents in another field.

At this time he was leading an agreeable and rather a desultory though never an idle life, without any absorbing aim. Art was his principal pursuit, but he also read largely, and he mixed much in the society of a limited number of friends whose thoughts and pursuits were congenial to his own. His friend Colonel Shaw,[1] whose name will often recur in this biography, lived near him at Chelsea; and with him and other Peninsula officers, with Chantrey, Mr. George Jones,[2] Mr. Bickersteth,[3] and others of the same stamp, William Napier's time was principally spent. But he felt a want unsatisfied, just because he felt an undeveloped power within him struggling to come forth.

At this time Jomini published his work on the *Principes de la Guerre*, (also published by Leonaur as *The Art of War*), which contained the first exposition of Napoleon's system of warfare. Napier had studied

---
1. Afterwards General Shaw Kennedy.
2. Of the Royal Academy.
3. Afterwards Lord Langdale.

all Napoleon's campaigns thoroughly, and he wrote a very able review of Jomini's book which was published in the *Edinburgh Review* in 1821. The negotiation induced him to visit Edinburgh, where he became personally acquainted with Jeffrey and other literary celebrities of the northern capital. He also visited Paris in company with Mr. Bickersteth, and made acquaintance with Marshal Soult. The following letters were written by him at this period.

To his Wife.

Edinburgh, 25th May. 1820.

I had intended to wait until after I had conversed with all the great lions and heard them speak, before I wrote to you, but having been disappointed in hearing Jeffrey speak (all the others I have heard), I would not delay any longer. I meet them all at dinner today, and I am engaged to dine with Jeffrey on Saturday.

The town is extremely beautiful, the Old Town most picturesque, and the New Town the pleasantest to live in. At every turn or opening of both you find a delightful rocky and mountainous landscape, with the firth upon one side. To add to the beauty, the citadel and the Calton Hills are very like the Acropolis of Athens; and the people here intend to build upon the latter a facsimile of the Parthenon. Five minutes' walk brings you into the prettiest dells and walks imaginable from the very centre of the town. The air is cold and elastic, and health and happiness ought to be the lot of the inhabitants, and would be, if the crushing tyranny of Toryism was not so decidedly prevalent.

The most determined advocate for despotism that I ever met with in England, the most bigoted priest-ridden wretch I ever saw in Spain, the most violent ultra-royalist I ever heard in France, are nothing in the scale when compared with the detestable intolerance and cruelty of a Scotch ministerialist in power, and a load of my dislike to Scotch Whigs has been removed by finding what they have had to encounter in doing as much as they have done.

Edinburgh, 3rd June, 1820.

I am so ill and so tired that I have given up the Highlands, and intend to return with George. I dined last Saturday with Mr. Jeffrey, and again today I am to do the same; he is less clever and more agreeable than I expected, and must have a fund of good sense not to be utterly spoiled by the gross and ridiculous flattery that he meets with. He is a little nervous, and not fit to rule in a storm. His wife has been voted unfit for good society here by many people; her fault seems to be a small nervous catch in her shoulder, and an utter absence of affected vulgarity. I found her plain, natural, and intent upon making herself agreeable to her guests without formality or airs.

I dined with Mr. Cranstoun, who still holds the highest place in my esteem, both from his manners and talents, which appear to me to be of the highest order. The rest of the wise ones are active sharp men, with ready quickness, but nothing of the sublime in them; Rutherford, I think, promises to be better than any of them. I like Lady Robert Kerr exceedingly for an action which I saw her perform, and which put me in mind of you strongly.

******

Sir   London, June 17, 1821.

Having discovered that a negro named John Jackson, formerly a soldier in my regiment, had been convicted of a rape and condemned to die, I felt anxious to make some inquiry on the subject, because the man had always borne an excellent character (see No. 1. enclosure), and I was under some surprise that he should have thus suddenly plunged at an advanced age into such depravity.

The course of my inquiries having led me to wait upon you, you will remember in our conversation on the subject that, you dwelt much upon the strange uncouth gestures of the prisoner, which you thought at the time indicated a hardness and effrontery which you were surprised to find was not the case when you visited him in prison after trial; and you farther said that you thought an unfavourable impression had been made on the jury by this manner of his, which upon your description I instantly recognised as natural to him, because, having been employed as a player upon the cymbals, he, according to the custom of all regiments, had been taught to throw himself into a variety of uncouth and distorted attitudes, which, from long practice, had become habitual to him.

This explanation of one unfavourable appearance in the case

will, I trust, be of service to him; and as, from his poverty which prevented him from employing counsel, and from the shortness of time which prevented his seeking the assistance of friends, he was thrown bound hand and foot before the jury, it is not I trust too much to hope that the annexed affidavit (No. 3) will dispose my Lord Sidmouth, before whom I request you will have the goodness to lay these papers, to recommend the extension of His Majesty's mercy to this unfortunate African.

The mode in which I should like to press it upon his lordship's sense of justice is this:—It would appear that, although the man injured himself by the *manner* of making his defence, the judge charged the jury favourably for him. If then he had been able to procure counsel, and had called Patrick Robertson as a witness, could any jury have given a verdict against him? No prejudice would have been created by his uncouth manner, and his counsel with such a witness as Robertson must have been successful, unless the jury disbelieved this last-named man, which appears to me very unlikely.

   I am, &c.,

    W. Napier.

******

Sir,   London, July 2, 1821.
When you undertook the charge of teaching my son I placed him under your control with pleasure, trusting to the commendation which I had heard of your skill, and confiding in your profession of kindness the. more readily because your office of a Christian minister seemed to preclude the possibility of your giving way to the violence of passion, even if, as a man of honour and humanity, you could forget what was due to his helpless age and melancholy deprivation of hearing. That I have been cruelly deceived in my expectations is to your shame, and, I trust, is to your remorse; but under any circumstances, never shall you have anything more to do with him.

You must be aware of the quarter from whence I derive my information, the correctness of which I cannot doubt. How does it describe you? striking a child of four years of age with such fury as to dash its head against the ground with a violence that left it doubtful if the skull was not fractured, beating it cruelly yourself and permitting your female servant to do the same. I myself saw the mark of your violence with an uneasiness that I could with difficulty conceal, although informed by you that it was the consequence of boisterous play.

I have but one observation to make upon all this:—It is my business to remove my child beyond the reach of your power; to reconcile such conduct with the feelings of a man and the character of a clergyman is your task. I cannot conceive a more difficult one.

W. Napier.

To his Wife.

Paris, Sept. 26; 1821.

I have waited until after my interview with Soult to give you an account of it. Our journey was prosperous and pleasant in the extreme. I found your brother[4] looking very black, and he says very well; but he has the air of one rather disturbed in body and mind. He is known as a Radical here; and what is to be done for him with that imputation without a change of ministry, I cannot tell.

The Lady Harleys are here; they are in great beauty. I waited upon Soult yesterday at his country house. His *abord* was fierce and commanding. We talked a good deal, and parted apparently on very civil terms.

He gave me the idea of a great general of antiquity as much as any man I ever met with, rough in manner, bold, keen and simple at the same time, not quick, but the most determined grand face I almost ever saw; black, rather dirty, more from wearing coarse old clothes than actual dirt; he spoke with freedom and clearly, but not with the readiness of a man of the world. I pressed him upon war and upon his own campaigns, but he was dry in his answers; yet I contrived to get something out of him, and once or twice he spoke like a man of excellent heart in the midst of his sternness.

He spoke of Sir Robert Wilson's dismissal with indignation, praised him more than he deserved, and then by way of apology said, 'I have seen him serve like a good soldier, and when one sees that it creates an interest for him, even though he was my enemy; I can't help feeling it, and being sorry for him. This came out in a natural feeling manner, and did him great credit

---

4. Henry Fox, since minister at Washington and other courts.

His manner is like Lord Wellington's, but less careless and more reflective. Bickersteth formed the same opinion of him as I did, and we came away. much pleased.

To Captain Considine, 43rd Regiment.

Sir,   London, December 17, 1821.
In reply to your application requesting a certificate of your having commanded the advance of the 43rd Regiment in the Battle of Nivelle, fought on the 10th November, 1813, I have to state that, from the circumstance of Captain Murchison having been mortally wounded at the commencement of the action, you did command two companies on that day; and as it might appear to have been only a common advanced guard, I shall state the facts at some length, feeling that your constant assiduous attention to your duties during the period of the Peninsular war, in which you were present in every action notwithstanding the frequency and severity of your wounds, calls for every exertion on my part to assist and forward any application you may be disposed to make for promotion.

The position of Petite la Rhune which was stormed by the 43rd on the 10th November, 1813, was a mountain with a crest of large granite rocks in the form of a hog's back; it had been fortified by the French with great care, six weeks having been devoted to it, and it was occupied in force and presented but one point by which it could be assailed, and there only by sections: this point was at the extreme end of the hog's back, and the approach to it was covered by a marsh supposed to be impracticable; the regiment was consequently obliged to pass along the front of the works in order to penetrate between the assailable point and the marsh: this manoeuvre, which would have been a very delicate one, was rendered comparatively easy and safe by the able and gallant manner in which your two companies contrived to pass the marsh, seize the lower end of the position, and keep down the enemy's fire during the advance of the main body.

It would have been impossible for any officer less experienced in skirmishing to have succeeded with such rapidity under such difficult circumstances, more especially as the command of the two companies devolved on you during the action; and the severe wound which you received in the attack of the last fort occupied by the enemy gives you an additional claim to attention.

I am, sir,
Your obedient servant,
W. Napier.

In 1822 Colonel Napier undertook, at the instance of Jeffrey, to write an article for the *Edinburgh Review* on the politics of Switzerland, to which the following letters refer:—

COLONEL NAPIER TO FRANCIS JEFFREY, ESQ.

Sir,   London, September 19, 1822.

I have read with surprise the garbled portion which you have published of the article furnished to you upon the politics of Switzerland.

That article was written at your own request, and at the moment of undertaking it I distinctly told yon that unless I was permitted to treat the subject with freedom and impartiality according to my own views, I would not write at all, because I considered the principal publication to be reviewed as the work of a decided Austrian partisan, whose object was, not the freedom of Switzerland, but the slavery of Italy.

I also requested to have as much time as could possibly be granted, being, as I then informed you, unwilling to put forth a critique upon a celebrated campaign without due care and consideration. Too assented to my proposition, and you appointed the latter end of May as the utmost period of time to be allowed; that is to say, about 20 days, as it took above 10 days to collect the maps and books necessary to be referred to far the completion of the work.

The understanding between us was complete, yet at the end of more than three months you have, without any communication with me, published a garbled article which may suit your views, but which totally differs in spirit from that which I sent to you. Under these circumstances I disclaim it, and I must desire that you will not authorise any person to attribute it to me.

I am, Sir,
Your obedient servant,
W. Napier.

Colonel Napier to Francis Jeffrey Esq.

Sir,   London. October 9, 1822.

Your letter arrived in town at a time when I was absent, and, as it was not forwarded to me immediately, this must be my excuse for having delayed an instant acknowledgment of the candid, and liberal manner in which you have detailed the reasons which induced you to alter the article I sent you on Swiss politics; I now hasten to do so, but at the same time I must observe that it was the alteration (after the conversation I had with you) without any communication with me, that I complained of,—without the slightest idea of questioning your undoubted right as editor to alter, amend, expunge, or reject altogether any paper which might be sent to you for publication in the *Review*.

With respect to the proposal of putting a note in the next number relative to this affair, I have no wish that such a step should be taken; whatever measures you pursue must rest entirely with yourself; but I continue decided to disclaim the paper as it is published, nothing in Dr. Marcet's conversation appearing to me of sufficient weight to alter that determination.

I cannot conclude this letter without again expressing the sense I have of the frank and satisfactory explanation you have given me.

I am, Sir,
Your obedient servant,
W. Napier.

The death of Napoleon at St. Helena became known in England towards the close of 1821. When Colonel Napier first heard of it he shut himself up in his study, and, on his wife going to him there some hours afterwards, she found him stretched upon his sofa in an agony of grief. His worship of Napoleon was extraordinary, and he almost felt the extinction of that wonderful mind as a darkening of the sun for a time.

Early in the course of 1823 Colonel Napier was one day taking a walk with Lord Langdale in some fields, now built over and forming part of Belgravia; the conversation turned on Southey's late narrative of the war in Spain, and Lord Langdale was so much struck with Napier's remarks on the events of the war and the characters of the principal actors, that he urged him to write a history of the war himself.

The account he himself gave of it to his daughter just a year before he died is as follows:—

It was all owing to Lord Langdale I ever wrote that *History*; *he first kindled the fire within me.* I was living in Sloane Street on half-pay, and for the time just living a very pleasant, desultory life, enjoying my home and friends in London, dining out, going to the exhibitions, and talking to the officers I had known in the Peninsula, and consorting with Chantrey and Jones, and so forth, and painting a great deal. I had never written anything except that *Review*, when, soon after it appeared, I was walking one day with Bickersteth, and he asked me what I was thinking of doing. I thought he meant where I was going to dine that day; but he said No! what was I thinking of turning to as an occupation? and then he went on to urge me to undertake some literary work, telling me I had powers of writing yet undeveloped; that the *Review* proved it to him; that I must not waste my life in mere pleasantness; and he urged me so seriously and so strongly, suggesting the late war as my province, that it began to make me think whether I would not try; and what he said about not wasting my powers made a great impression on me.

On his return to the house from this walk which determined his future life, he told his wife what had passed and of his doubts as to his being equal to such an undertaking. She encouraged him strongly, and the idea, having once entered his mind, remained and grew there. He talked much of it and lay awake at nights thinking of it; and after a few days made up his mind to attempt the task, and immediately set to work to collect the materials. Those of his acquaintances who did not know him intimately were surprised, and looked on it as a piece of presumption in so young a man to think he could write such a history.

In truth his prospects were not very encouraging; he had many military friends, but he possessed no literary position, nor was his rank sufficiently high to give authority to his opinions. He found at the outset too that the two most formidable rivals who could have appeared were already in the field against him, *viz.* the Duke of Wellington, and his Quartermaster-General Sir George Murray.

His first step was to call upon the Duke of Wellington to announce the design he had formed, and to ask for his Grace's papers. The Duke's answer in substance was, that he had arranged all his own papers with a view to publication himself—that he had not decided in what form they should be given to the world, nor when; probably not during his lifetime; but he thought his plan would be to "write a plain didactic history," to be published after his death—that he was resolved never to publish anything unless he could tell the whole truth, but at that time he could not tell the whole truth without wounding the feelings of many worthy men and without doing mischief: adding, in a laughing way, "I should do as much mischief as Bonaparte."

Then expatiating on the subject, he related to Colonel Napier many anecdotes illustrative of this observation, showing errors committed by generals and others acting with him or under him, especially at Waterloo—errors so materially affecting his operations, that he could not do justice to himself if he suppressed them, and yet by giving them publicity he would ungraciously affect the fame of many worthy men whose only fault was dullness.

For these reasons he would not, he said, give Colonel Napier his own private papers, but he gave into his possession very important official documents, and gave him authority to get from the quartermaster-general all the Duke's "Orders of Movements." Among other documents thus acquired was King Joseph's portfolio, taken at Vittoria, and containing his correspondence with the Emperor, with the French minister of war, and with the marshals and generals who at different periods were employed in the Peninsula.

But although the Duke would not give his private papers, he said he would then and always answer any questions as to facts which Napier in the course of his work might wish to put "And," says Colonel Napier, writing after the conclusion of the *History*, "he has fulfilled that promise rigidly, for I did then put many questions to him verbally, and took notes of his answers; and many of the facts in my *History* which have been most cavilled at and denied by my critics have been related by me solely on his authority. Moreover I have since at various times sent to the Duke a number of questions in writing, and always they have been fully and carefully answered without delay, though often put when his mind must have been harassed and his attention deeply occupied by momentous affairs."

He next called upon Sir George Murray to get the "Orders of Movements," and to ask for the maps and plans illustrative of the operations in the Peninsula which were in his possession. This request Murray refused, stating distinctly as the cause of refusal, that he reserved them for that History of the war which he was himself about to undertake. For this refusal Sir George Murray was unjustly blamed. From his position at the time, as well as from that which he had held in the Peninsular army, and being moreover a man of considerable ability, he may well be pardoned for having considered that he would be more likely to do justice to the subject than a regimental major and brevet lieutenant-colonel, however distinguished.

The plans were public property certainly, but they had been executed through Murray's agency by an officer of his own department, and were intrusted to his keeping for the public benefit And so on fair public grounds he was justified in keeping them for the use of that History which ninety-nine men out of a hundred would have pronounced likely to be the more worthy record of English glory.

Be that as it may, it is certain that after the publication of the first and second volumes of Napier's *History* Sir George Murray renounced all idea of undertaking the work; and nothing more was heard of any intention on the part of the Duke of publishing or preparing for publication memoirs of the Peninsular war.

"What then was the cause," writes General Shaw Kennedy to the author after Sir William Napier's death, "of Wellington and Murray giving up an intention which each had fully formed, they being the very men who in the opinion of the whole army were the fit men to write the History of the war? The answer is dear and undeniable—they found that the ground was preoccupied, that the *History* had already been written with a truthfulness unknown to any previous history contemporaneous with the events described—in fact, with perfect truthfulness; and that besides this there was a soul given to it, and that it was animated by a genius of so surpassing a character as would have made any other *History* appear to be dull and insipid."

Colonel Napier now commenced the work of collecting materials from all quarters. He made another visit to Paris; on his return to England he took up his residence for some weeks in a farmhouse at Strathfieldsaye for the purpose of consulting the Duke of Wellington. From time to time also during the progress of the work he used to send to Lord Fitzroy Somerset questions on doubtful points, the Duke's replies to which were set down by his own hand in the margin. In the appendix will be found some of these documents, as well as notes of conversations with the Duke, which materials, as being the very core of history, will interest many.

From amongst these the following, from a letter to Lord Fitzroy, is extracted:—

I find that the siege of St. Sebastian was not carried on at all in accord with Lord Wellington's instructions, and that the deviations from them were injurious to the success of the operation, which I am sorry for, as I am quite tired of pointing out mistakes, but justice must be done and the saddle put on the right horse, or rather horses, though some of the defaulters are scarcely entitled to be likened to that particular quadruped.

And the following anecdote of the Duke's penetration and sagacity is interesting.

At the Battle of Sauroren, Wellington was anxious to let both armies see him, and they did. The armies were separated by a narrow valley not more than 200 yards wide. A double spy, called De la Rosa, whose real name was D'Olier, he being no Spaniard but a Frenchman, asked the Duke if he would like to see Soult.

"Yes."

"There he is, two hundred yards off."

Wellington looked and saw Soult writing orders and giving them to an *aide-de-camp*, and the distance was so short that he distinguished his features sufficiently to recognise him afterwards at any time. When De la Rosa left his side, Wellington, who more than suspected his good faith, said to one of his staff "Watch where that man goes to."

He went towards the weakest point of the position, and Wellington said "Soult will attack there." And he did attack there, but the English general had prepared accordingly.

To his Wife.

Petit Hôtel de Montmorency, Rue St. Marc, Paris,
Feb. 21, 1823.

I arrived here on Friday night after a pleasanter although more expensive journey than I expected. We found Mr. Tisdal going to Paris, and he proposed to us to join him in a hired carriage and to post it; we agreed, and, after an *orageuse* journey, *nous voici*. Tisdal attacked me about the game-laws; I attacked Young about politics; Young attacked Tisdal about everything. Sometimes I quarrelled with Young, sometimes with Tisdal, sometimes with both, and upon no one subject did we agree until we separated, when we agreed that the journey had been pleasant, which was strange but true; as the great object is to kill time, and quarrelling is as good as anything and very wholesome.

The confusion in Agramant's camp was nothing to our journey.

I found your brother in bed at two o'clock. I have only seen Lady Oxford yet, and have given no letters. Paris is detestable, wet, luxurious, filthy; the women ugly to the last degree; the men as usual fan of politics of all kinds; war with Spain certain and much disliked by the nation, and the fear of one with England has already given a severe shock to commerce.

All colonial produce has risen one half, and at Marseilles they could not muster a *bal masqué*, the prospect was so gloomy, '*et nos jeunes gens*' were too sentimental to dance '*et montrer de la joie dans un temps si grave.*' Queer devils! The Louvre is still superb: there are five or six paintings there that I study and gloat upon until I am ready to lie down and groan over my own want of power either to paint or buy them, or the like of them, which however are not in the world; there are two Correggios, and one Titaian, and two Rembrandts, and a Raphael, and a Paul Veronese; and then I shut my eyes and they swim before me in a vision, and I would paint them, and I open my eyes and the illusion vanishes, leaving me mournful.

A propos, I think of Bessie and Johnny always, they rank with the Correggios. I saw at Lady Oxford's three children Sir H. Mildmay's, and the youngest beats even Johnny in beauty. I don't think his face is quite as fine a character, and he is brown, but his dress suits in colour is very picturesque; and a beauty of expression that is peculiar renders him a very dangerous rival. He is a year younger.

                                        Paris, Feb. 24, 1828.

I have paid all my visits except Madame Ney and Count Daru. Jomini I saw for half an hour only; was going out of town for a week. Tomorrow I hope to see more of him. He resembles Tom Paine so much, the portrait in the latter's works might pass for his; Jomini's features are more delicate, and his skull rounder, his eyes not so piercing, but his mouth precisely the same with that remarkably cunning look of knowledge so conspicuous in Tom Paine. He received me very graciously, talked a great deal, and gave me hopes of getting a great deal from him. He also put into my hands a printed defence of himself which is very curious, and I think very strong.

Madame D'Esmenard and her daughters are very kind and very pleasant Lady Oxford took me to Soult's, whose pictures I saw, whose face I studied, and who received me very unusually well; his manner to most people being upon the borders of rudeness, if you can use the term to a man who has simplicity and grandeur combined in an extraordinary degree. I mean grandeur of mind; his neglect arises from his being above the forms of life, and probably from his contempt of his countrymen's obsequious and base conduct to everything possessed of power. Lady Oxford, as usual, imprudently asked him what he believed would be the result of the invasion of Spain; he laughed and said, 'I am like St. Thomas, I believe nothing.'

There was a picture of St. Thomas in the room. *A propos*, he has four pictures by Murillo that are exquisite; indeed it is impossible to describe them better than to say they are in the same taste and better painted than the Christ at Oxford, which I now feel must be his painting. Lady Oxford has asked me to give Lady Charlotte away; it was too flattering to refuse. She promises to get me all information upon the History, and I am in some hopes of being able to obtain something from Soult himself, who has invited me to go again next Friday.

The Ultras are mad with power and plans of conquest; they talk openly of England being *culbuté* and reduced to her proper situation of a second-rate power; and on the other side, the enemies of existing order speak out with so much boldness of certain events, that I think they feel sure of a change being at hand. Your brother is changing his politics; we are great friends at present. In one thing he is as usual; he keeps a cabriolet at ten francs a day, and he gets up at four o'clock in the afternoon. I saw Marshal Suchet; he looks quick and clever; but I felt my head, and thought I might perhaps beat *you* myself.

Paris, March 2nd. 1823.

I have seen Madame Ney who is a very ladylike agreeable woman, rather handsome; she asked me to her house where I was introduced to her sons. The eldest is stern-looking and has talent, but a repulsive look, and at present seems occupied in singing Italian music in which he excels. They say he is very fiery, which I can believe. The second is a tall every-day youth with a handsome face. The youngest that I saw (there are four) has an air of great character, but he is only twelve years old or thereabouts. I met at her house many generals, who all remembered Charles, and apparently with interest. Their names were Dalton, D'Albiac, and another, a very tall man whose name I forget.

I have found out my old friend Brossard who was our *parlementaire* in Portugal, and he has grown young and handsome; and being chief of the *Ecole Politechnique*, he has access to the *Dépôt de la Guerre*, and has promised me all sorts of assistance and even some curious papers. He is my mainstay, as Jomini has not got much, or at least won't give it to me. Daru I met at Soult's; he remembered you and asked after you; says Octavie is flourishing, and said he thanked me for the book long ago. I suppose his letter was lost. He told me he had a *petit paquet* to send to my lodging, which I conclude is his *History of Venice*.

Yesterday I dined with Vernet who is more amusing than ever. *Madame* just the same as usual, only more French if possible; she sent her souvenirs to you and a message to Pamela to say she would be too happy to see her in Paris. &c. &c.

Paris, March 6th, 1823.

I have been with Jomini, who told me a great deal of interesting matter relative to everything but Spain; and I despair of success, although I have plenty of promises. I told him I was the author of the last review; upon which he laughed and said that he had just been with a *monsieur*, who was consulting him upon the best means of preparing a *grande réfutation* of it. I talked a good deal with him, and he was clearly upon my side in everything but what regarded Italy's being free, which I guessed was because of the fear of the Emperor,[5] which is truly very strongly impressed upon the countenance and language of every man who has the misfortune to be under his control.

My doctrine respecting the neutrality of Switzerland being incomplete while the Austrians are able to penetrate, and the necessity of a more vigorous confederation, he says, is what he has a thousand times endeavoured to impress upon them himself, but in vain; but the funny part is that it was Mr. Pictet himself who wrote the book, and who also wrote that silly review upon it. My health is very bad, my spirits worse, and my expenses very great; books crowd upon me; I purchase all useful and even necessary, and as cheap as dirt separately, but very dear

---

5. Emperor of Russia. Jomini was in his service.

altogether. I have been assailed by half a dozen authors, offering me presents of their works, and praying that I would write *un petit mot* for, them in the *Edinburgh*.

Paris, 12th March, 1823.

Bunbury's offer is delightful;[6] and I will not lose the pleasure of being three months with you in the country and in a house without noise, for any other pleasure or advantage; we will, I hope, '*disport ourselves very pleasantlie*' together; it will be good for our health and the children's also. What a nice little twinkling thing Louy is with her songs! My information crowds thick upon me, and if peace continues I hope to be able in time to make out a history worth reading. Politics I don't write to you about, because, being in the ambassador's bag, I do not think it fair, and otherwise it is dangerous; plots are however thickening here, and I do expect some explosion at last.

Of one thing I am certain, that there are not more than *two* parties in France, *viz*. the Bourbons' and Napoleon's party. The first are in power, the last are the strongest, and the Liberals are about the strength, reputation, and honesty of Lord Grey's party in England—that is—nothing at all. Still they are good tools to work with; and thus they have an apparent importance, which is however only apparent, not real. I feel very anxious to be at Mildenhall with you; we will paint and walk, and read and write history.

16th March, 1823.

I am glad you have seen Grant I have no particular questions to ask him; but any papers, or information verbally, or references to men or papers for information, will be useful, particularly relative to the French position, numbers, and movements at any time during the war. Write to me in the ambassador's bag under cover to Harry. I understand every letter is opened now and read, and mine, from my intercourse with Lady Oxford, probably more than others. Spies abound, and I am told I am watched by them; but as I am very innocent I do not fear them; neither do I quite believe it, as I observe that people seem fond of thinking that they are of consequence enough to be watched. Sir Neil Campbell has been uncommonly kind and good-natured to me. That cursed war of Mr. Pitt's, and the pains the

---

6. Of his house at Mildenhall, Suffolk.

papers took to brutalise the minds of the English people, gave such a turn to the mind of many a good man, that I hated them when they deserved to be admired from their intrinsic good qualities Campbell is one of them; he has since the peace lost all his ultra prejudices, and shines forth now, like Bunbury, full of kindness and benevolence and gentleness to everybody within his reach. To do him justice he was at the worst of times a man of strict honour, though a prejudiced and an intemperate man in support of those prejudices; but now he is extremely amiable, and generous to a degree very unusual to find in a man of his age and experience of the world.

The Duke of Angoulême set off this morning for the army; and there is a report that the tricolour has been hoisted in the south by a Colonel Fabvier, a very clever man whom I have seen; they say he is at the head of a band of refugees from France; at all events he is on the Spanish frontier, if he has not yet entered France. I was engaged, the day that Manuel was expelled the Chambers, in a fine row in the Place Louis Quinze. I was riding with Lady Frances Harley, and as we came home she proposed to go and see what a French mob were worth in such a cause. This of course I acceded to.

The assembly would have cut a poor figure in London, being about as numerous and as wicked as Punch's auditors when he is in luck; all well-dressed people, however, for, as I said before, none of the real strength of France—that is to say, the peasants and workmen—take the slightest interest in the party calling themselves Liberal, always observing that they betrayed Bonaparte in 1815.

However, when Manuel came forth the mob shouted, and my horse plunged violently; a sort of hat-on-one-side bully, so common in Paris, struck him on the head with a stick. Thinking it might be done from fear of the horse, I spoke calmly to him, upon which he flourished his stick and called out in English, '*Damn you, Mr. Beefstik, and damn all the English.*'

I desired Lady Fanny to ride away, and keeping up the conversation with my friend until I had fixed him, I suddenly rode upon him and with a jockey whip cut him across the face so sharply as to make the blood spring out; he roared, and the mob fell upon me, calling out '*A la lanterne, à bas l'Anglais beefstik.*' My horse however soon cleared the crowd, and I found Lady

Frances in the middle of them addressing them in my favour. We afterwards rode slowly away pursued by the beasts, who were very noisy but offered no more violence. She thought they would take me to the police, but had determined to go there with me.

I never saw so brave and generous a girl in my life except one, and you know who that is, though I think you would be more nervous. For your comfort I can tell you that she was considerably frightened, though she conquered it, for which I admire her the more. What good-natured creatures they all are! At this moment they are copying for me all the different cramped French hands that my papers are written in. You will laugh at my despotism extending to them, but you must feel that it is very kind of them.

Paris, 20th March.

I send you by this day's post a packet of nine pieces for my *History*; more will arrive in time; one of them is a list of the things I am to do for my friend in return; his name is Koch. Read the paper, and if Grant or Bunbury or anybody can give you information about the contents, collect it for me.

Paris, 24th March, 1828.

I send you more historical pieces which you will put with the rest. I have had an offer so pleasant to me that you will, I hope, receive my refusal as a handsome homage to you. Captain Bacon and Lady Charlotte are going a cruise in his schooner to the Mediterranean, and mean to wait upon Lady Hester Stanhope, visiting Egypt and agreeable countries *en route.*

The only news that seems to be certain here is that the French army are in a very bad state, and unfit to make a campaign, from the total neglect, or rather the embezzlement, that has been going on of the stores, the contracts having been given for political services without any expectation of their being fulfilled.

Marshal Victor, the minister of war, has been turned out for peculation, and then he was appointed major-general to the army which he has just rendered inefficient by his rascality. This is rather an ingenious revenge, and looks as if they did not much expect to enter into a serious war.

Paris, 27th March, 1823.

Harry Fox wants so much to see the picture of Johnny, that I propose you should put it up carefully and enclose it to him through Mr. Rolleston. He will get it copied by Lady de Roos, and return it. Kiss the little fellow for me. I am in doubt if I shall be home this three weeks, as the *Dépôt de la Guerre* is open to me; and I am just come from five hours' work copying the most valuable materials; and these are so many that I trust to get a good collection, and perhaps I may never have such an opportunity again.

A conspiracy has just been discovered in the French army to place young Nap. upon the throne. This will do something at last, I believe; and I expect to see another revolution while I am here. Charles Napier's boy has got the scarlet fever, and I cannot worry him, poor fellow! I dined with him and saw his little girl who broke her arm; she is a little black-eyed child, as like him as possible. I have just heard from good authority that Lady Oxford is not suspected of being engaged in the conspiracy by the ministers, which I am glad of.

Paris is a delightful place for rogues, conspirators, gamblers, intriguers, painters, sculptors, charlatans, *gourmands*, drinkers, and speculators, but the devil for honest men and women."

Strathflildsaye, February, 1824.

It is my intention to stop until Charles comes back, because I have got into so regular a way of doing my papers that I should very likely lose if I was interrupted; and also because I am copying the pictures very hard, and I trust successfully; the famous Water-seller I have promised to the Duchess. She was so kind, and never asked for one, but so evidently wished to have it that I could not refuse her; when I said so she was quite moved. The Pope of Velasquez, if I succeed as well as the commencement promises, will be by far the best thing I ever did; and, as he is ugly and wicked-looking, nobody ever asks for him.

I have done—that is, arranged, read, and marked in an index—190 papers, many very long, and some in French and Portuguese; this has been hard work. I sat up sixteen hours without a check once; but having broken the neck it is easy to me to kill them now. As to your letter about Barton, it will break my heart to lose my little Bessie, but I am willing to sacrifice my own feelings about her if it is for her advantage.

I am anxious at what you tell me of Fanny; it is debility; don't teach her, and feed her well; we must get her into the country; if I cannot get a house I must send her under somebody's care. Remember me kindly to Brown, and wish him joy of his appointment to the Rifle Brigade. Ask him what the numbers of the battalions of detachments were when first formed. I will give Henry some papers in time, but I must first arrange them to know what I have got; and much obliged to him also. Terrible labour this arrangement, as you will say when you see my lists.

I fear you will not get the pope's head after all, as the Duchess told me that the Duke liked it so much, and repeated his admiration of it so often, that I could do no less than offer it to him; and she seemed to think he would be pleased; this remains to be proved.

I am in torture, and have been so without cessation ever since I wrote to you. I think I am all gout; if it was not for the very great kindness and good nature of Lord Douro, I do not know what I should do.

I am copying the pictures successfully; one, a head of Velasquez himself, I have in despite of all opposition reserved for you, refusing the repeated solicitation of the Duchess, and withstanding Pamela's half coaxing, half stealing manner. The Duke has been here these two days; and I got a long description of Talavera out of him, and would have had more but for interruptions.

I like the sons of the Duke much. Lord Charles I delight in; he is such a fine, laughing, playful, spirited boy, without the least pride or impertinence about him. Lord Douro is more grave, very amiable and gentleman-like, very much resembling the Duke without his *devil*.

Strathfieldsaye, 1824. (No further date.)

I was getting better but I am falling back again, owing to four successive nights of Strathfieldsaye, which however have repaid me if I am sick for six months. First, Lord Francis Leveson and his wife were there. She put me in mind, by her manner and a certain simple original look, of Fanny, and so I like her. The Duke appealed to me more than once at dinner to know if he was right about some events in the war. The instantaneous effect upon the whole company will make you laugh—silly people!

I mustered up nerve to ask the Duke about Sir John Moore, and he criticised his whole campaign. Beyond all question the Duke is a noble high-minded man, and I never will believe a story to his prejudice again; he said that Moore could not fight a battle, and that it was absurd to expect it; that the only fault he committed was when he marched to Sahagun, not having considered it a movement of retreat and prepared everything with that view. (This I know Sir John did, and told him so.) 'But,' says the Duke, 'this opinion that I give you is an opinion of a man who has had *great experience* in war, and *great experience* in the particular war necessary for that country where Sir John was for the first time, and moreover it is an opinion *après coup*.' Was not that very noble in him and very pleasant to hear, as I have not a single point of my own *History* which I do not find confirmed by his opinion? He has given me a long paper of conversation besides, and I shall make my way well and fast, I hope. Blanco[7] I have painted twice.

Strathfieldsaye, 1824.

The *History* has been cut up badly by twelve days of painting Blanco, and I was so intent and troubled about him that I did nothing; and worse than that, I shall be unsettled in my mind until he is revised by Jones[8] and framed. However, he is a *chef d'œuvre* in despite of his blue delicate white, which has been the devil to paint like, and give effect also. He has quite killed the portrait of Meere in my opinion, and he is, by the testimony of all the adepts, and Charles's servant also, as like as one cat to another, and I know he is well painted. I am glad your brother has got something good, but I suppose he would have been continued by Lord Granville if he had not got Turin, as he is looked upon, I find, as a very able man of business in his line.

TO THE DUCHESS OF WELLINGTON.

1824.

Lady Campbell informed me last night that you considered my note a *rude one*. As I wrote it in a hurry, and as it has appeared so to you, I must suppose that it is so, and I hasten to apologize for it; certainly I did never intend to have written or said anything bordering even upon rudeness; and as I am on the subject I will

---

7. His horse.
8. G. Jones, R.A.

frankly tell you what was passing in my mind at the time, and leave you to judge whether I might not have easily fallen into error on that head, when I only wished to inform you that I felt what you meant, and was ready to abide by it

It was impossible for me not to have perceived the extreme change of your manner towards me lately. I certainly did not intend to force myself on your attention, but I did not withdraw entirely, as I thought that very probably it was a passing cloud which it was wiser and more civil not to take notice of further. But when I was told by —— that you had expressed yourself in very strong terms relative to me, and declared that you would never ask me inside your house again, I could only suppose that an invitation sent half an hour before dinner, with the Duke's name especially marked in it, was meant by you as an intimation that the invitation came from him and not from you, and in my answer I really meant to convey to you that I accepted it as such.

I did accept it as such because the expression of commonplace opinions in politics was not a just cause for you to take offence, and I did not conceive that it could last long upon that point; however, you are the best judge of your own feelings. If it should continue, however unjust I may think you, my own part is very clear to me; and certainly rudeness or even anger would hardly enter into my mind, much less I trust be deliberately displayed towards a person from whom I have received a great deal of kindness, although mixed with some injustice; and least of all to the sister of Sir Edward Pakenham, for whom I had as much esteem and veneration as one man can have for another.

I am very sincerely yours,
W. Napier.

To Marshal Soult.

Mosieur le Maréchal, (No date, probably 1824.)
Avant de vous parler de ce qui m'engage à vous écrire, il est peut-être nécessarre de vous rappeler l'honneur que j'eus de vous être présenté et de vous voir plusieurs fois chez vous à Paris, et de vous remercier des bontés que vous montrâtes à mon frère le Colonel Charles Napier lorsqu'il était votre prisonnier à Corunna en 1809. Je m'occupe dans ce moment à recueillir les matériaux nécessaires à l'histoire des campagnes des armies Françaises et Anglaises en Espagne, que je compte écrire;

j'en ai déjà obtenu un grand nombre d'une grande valour: parmi les papiers Français je possède le portefeuille du Roi Joseph, pris à Vittoria. Dans ce portefeuille j'ai trouvé de vos lettres; elles ne sont pas aussi nombreuses que je pourrais les désirer; elles viennent de vous. Monsieur, et j'en connais l'importance.

J'y ai trouvé aussi plusieurs lettres du Roi Joseph à l'Empereur Napoléon; elles ne vous sont pas favorables; j'y remarque des injures les plus outrageantes centre vous pendant le temps que vous commandiez en Andalousie. Je puis contredire plusieurs de ces accusations par ma propre expérience, ce qui me porte à douter de celles dont je ne possède pas la réfutation. En fidèle historien je ne puis supprimer des faits importants—vous avant des obligations personnelles, il me serait très pénible de publier ces lettres—j'ai donc cru que la manière la plus franche serait de vous tout dire, et de vous demander si vous voudriez bien me procurer les pièces nécessaires à la réfutation de ces aspersions injurieuses.

Je ne m'étendrai pas davantage pour le moment sur les points en question; probablement vous les devinerez; ils portent principalement sur votre gouvernement en Andalousie en 1812, et sur la poursuite de notre armée et le passage du Tormes vers la fin de cette année. Si votre Excellence trouvait bon de me donner quelques renseignements sur cette époque, qui pourraient me rendre capable de mieux apprécier et écrire les operations de cette campagne, il est superflu d'ajouter combien j'en serais reconnaissant.

J'oserais aussi vous prior de me donner quelques lumières sur la poursuite de Sir John Moore, lorsqu'il faisait sa retraite sur Corunna, car je désire particulièrement rendre justice, par une relation sincère et vraie, a la mémoire d'un brave officier dont la réputation a souffert par les malignes et fausses attaques des détracteurs dans sa propre patrie; et J'éprouve d'autant plus de hardiesse en vous faisant cette demande, vous connaissant, Monsieur le Maréchal, pour ennemi généreux.

Meo beau-frère Mr. Fox vous fera parvenir cette lettre; il est attaché à l'ambassade; et toute réponse dont vous voudriez bien m'honorer, si vous aurez la bonté de la lui donner, me serait envoyée en sûreté.

"J'ai l'hoinnur d'être, avec les sentiments du plus profond respect, et avec les assurances de la plus haute considération que vous m'inspirerez toujours, &c. &c.

W. Napier.

To this letter Soult responded with the most generous cordiality, and sent all, and more than all, that was asked for. From first to last, and principally through the Marshal's means, besides an immense mass of official correspondence upon most of the great operations in the Peninsula which was sent to him direct. by Soult's orders, Colonel Napier had a direct correspondence with Marshal Jourdan; he had personal acquaintance with, and received information from, officers high on the staff of Marshals Ney and Masséna; he had copies of the official journals of military operations kept by the chiefs of Marshal Victor's and General Dupont's staffs.

In Paris he obtained admission to the "*Bureau de la Guerre*," and worked there for many weeks. Here, among other important documents, he had access to the muster-rolls of the French army in the Peninsula,—that is to say, to the real correct muster-rolls which were drawn up by Marshal Berthier every fifteen days during the war, for the special information of the Emperor Napoleon: for there were other muster-rolls, systematically fabricated to impose on the French people, and even on the armies; the distinction being that the true returns were bound in green, the spurious in yellow.

The two following letters were written during the progress of the first volume.

To Marshal Soult.

Monsieur le Maréchal,   Londres, 19 Mars. 1825,
J'ai gardé le lit plusieurs jours par suite d'une maladie grave, et je dicte toujours de mon lit, ce qui vous fera connaître pourquoi je n'ai pas encore fait réponse à votre lettre si pleine de bonté, renfermant celle que j'ai fait passer à mon frère. Il ne vous a pas donné son adresse parcequ'il est actuellement dans l'île de Céphalonie, dont il est Gouverneur. Constamment employé depuis la guerre, il n'a jamais eu l'occasion de remercier votre Excellence en personne de toutes vos bontés envers lui, et il sera charmé d'apprendre que cette circonstance, si fâcheuse pour lui, ne lui a pas fait tort dans votre opinion. Le message flatteur que vous lui avez envoyé dans la lettre que vous m'avez fait l'honneur de m'adresser, sera accepté de sa part avec la plus grande avidité.

Je viens de recevoir aussi dans ce moment votre seconde lettre, avec les renseignements relatifs à Dupont, Moncey, et Bessières, et je vous supplie, Monsieur le Maréchal, d'agréer les expressions de ma vive reconnaissance.

La bonté de votre Excellence en voulant bien m'encourager à vous demander sans crainte les renseignements dont j'ai besoin, m'a beaucoup soulagé sur ce point, car j'étais rempli d'une véritable inquiétude de vous être importun, et de me montrer trop empressé à saisir les occasions que m'offrait une bonté peu commune, entraîné comme je l'étais par le vif désir d'obtenir des informations d'une telle source.

Les détails des opérations du Maréchal Moncey sont intéressants. Je trouve dans les instructions secrètes de l'Empereur au Général Savary (dont je possède le manuscrit corrigé de la main de Napoléon) que les divisions de Caulaincourt, de Gobert, et de Frère, étaient très harassées par des marches et des contremarches procédant des ordres qui leur venaient de Madrid, et que Moncey fut aussi commandé d'aller une seconde fois à Valentia. Le tout est critiqué très amèrement par l'Empereur, et en cela il me paraît qu'il y a quelque obscurité, parceque, quoique l'Empereur lui-même ait donné des ordres aux divers généraux, le Général Savary paraît avoir pris sur lui de donner aussi des orders, et de faire même des changements asses importants.

Je trouve dans les instructions dont j'ai déjà parlé les mots suivants: 'C'etait une autre erreur que de songer à faire aller le Maréchal Moncey à Valentia, pour ensuite le faire marcher en Murcie et sur Grénade. C'était vouloir fondre ces corps d'armée en détail et sans fruit.' Je ne comprends pas très exactement si la division de Frère était isolée, ou appartenait à l'armée d'observation des côtes d'océan.

Je désire beaucoup avoir des renseignements sur les opérations du Maréchal Lefevre centre l'armée de Blake à Durango, Espinosa, &c. &c., et si ce Maréchal est entré en opérations trop tôt et centre les intentions de l'Empereur, et s'il a par ce moyen offert un contretemps aux progrès de la campagne; aussi l'ordre des mouvements du Maréchal Lannes centre les armées de Castaños et de Palafox pendant la bataille de Tudela et dans la poursuite.

J'ai l'honneur, &c.

W. Napier.

TO THE SAME.

Monsieur le Maréchal, (No date, probably 1827.)

It was with great pleasure I received your Excellency's letter of the 10th January; it relieved me from the fear that I had taken too much advantage of your former kindness, and overstepped the bounds of decorum in my eagerness to obtain the valuable information with which your Excellency has hitherto favoured me.

My work is not yet in a state for publication, because I seek for the truth in all quarters, and my materials are often more complete in the later occurrences of the war than in the earlier transactions: what I have written is therefore in detached pieces, and must of course be carefully revised after the connection has been made out. I have, however, completed the transactions of Spain and Portugal up to October, 1808, and I am on the point of finishing that which relates to the campaign of Sir John Moore, and the victories of your Excellency and the other Marshals commanding corps against the Spanish armies of Andalusia, Estremadura, Gallicia, &c. &c., in the month of November, 1808.

The march of your Excellency against Oporto will next occupy me; and I am in hopes that I may be able to place the difficulties overcome by your firm and decided character in their true point of view. In Mr. Noble's account of that campaign I can trace two hands—the one feeble, unjust, and inaccurate; the other masterly, concise, and vigorous; but there are some parts which indicate rather than explain the conspiracy which evidently cramped your Excellency's movements. I know, what perhaps your Excellency does not;—that an English officer was disguised in your camp, and treated with some officers of your army relative to a defection.

The Sieur Argenteau was the agent through whom the affair was conducted. I am perhaps now presuming too far in touching upon this matter, but I know enough to pique my curiosity without satisfying my reason, and I trust your Excellency will excuse me. The peculiar manner in which your advanced guard was formed in your retrograde movement appears to me to have had some relation to this affair; at all events, the commanding character displayed by your Excellency throughout this difficult campaign must strike the most superficial observer. I cannot understand why the division of General Lapisse and the 1st Corps d'Armée did not support your movements in the manner which the Emperor evidently intended they should have done, and which circumstances so loudly called for.

The proposal which your Excellency has made to me on the part of le General Comte Mathieu Dumas is a flattering proof of the interest you feel in the success of my work. I accept the offer with joy, well knowing that Monsieur Dumas is capable of giving my production a value which it would not otherwise have; and I trust that the veracity and good faith with which I shall write upon the campaigns of Spain will compensate for want of talent, and render my *History* worth the attention of the justly celebrated author of the *Précis des Evénements Militaires*. I shall also feel pleased—as it will be impossible for a soldier to avoid a certain enthusiasm for his companions in arms—that any undue bias may be corrected by the notes of an impartial and able historian such as Monsieur le Comte Dumas.

When any portion of my work is prepared for the press, I shall certainly give your Excellency notice, and arrange the mode of transmitting the sheets to Monsieur le Comte in the most convenient manner.

In the meantime I have to reiterate my acknowledgments of your continued goodness, and to subscribe myself, &c. &c.

W. Napier.

Besides the materials supplied by Marshal Soult and the Duke of Wellington, Colonel Napier collected an immense mass of documents in the shape of letters and journals from officers of all ranks in the service, conveying narratives of events which passed under their personal observation in different battles or combats. In many instances, as was to be expected, the same event was related very differently by two different writers, and probably the most difficult as well as delicate task of the historian was to arrive at the real truth, and relate it without giving offence. It was however unavoidable that offence should be given in some cases, and the controversial correspondence thereby entailed, and in several instances the challenges incurred, were of themselves enough to furnish sufficient employment to the historian.

It is indeed doubtful if he could have borne up against the incessant labour, aggravating the attacks of painful illness which yearly became more frequent, but for the aid of his wife, the importance of which will be best described in his own words.

> When the immense mass of King Joseph's correspondence taken at Vittoria was first placed in my hands, I was dismayed at finding it to be a huge collection of letters, without order, and in three languages, one of which I did not understand; many also were in very crabbed and illegible characters, especially those of Joseph's own writing, which is nearly as difficult to read as Napoleon's; the most important documents were in cipher, and there was no key! Despairing of any profitable examination of

these valuable materials, the thought crossed me of giving up the work, when my wife undertook, first to arrange the letters by dates and subjects, next to make a table of reference, translating and epitomizing the contents of each; and this, without neglecting for an instant the care and education of a very large family, she effected in such a simple and comprehensive manner, that it was easy to ascertain the contents of any letter, and lay hands on the original document in a few moments.

She also undertook to decipher the secret correspondence, and not only succeeded, but formed a key to the whole, detecting even the nulls and stops; and so accurately, that when in course of time the original key was placed in my hands there was nothing to learn. Having mentioned this to the Duke of Wellington, he seemed at first incredulous, observing I must mean that she had made out the contents of some letters; several persons had done this for him, he said, but none had ever made out the nulls or formed a key; adding, 'I would have given twenty thousand pounds to any person who could have done that for me in the Peninsula.'

Lady Napier's mode of proceedings she thus described:—

'Many letters amongst Joseph Bonaparte's correspondence were entirely in cipher; perhaps about one-half of the contents of some letters were in that form; others had only a few words occasionally in cipher. These few words proved in many cases to be either the name of some particular general or *corps d'armée*, or the numbers of the particular army which was the subject of the letter. No key was at first sent. Lady Napier began her attempts to decipher by these occasional words, judging by analogy with respect to the remainder of the letters what they were likely to be, and guessing several monosyllables and short words which she found occurred very frequently, such as No. 13, which she imagined meant "*de*," No. 514 "*armée*," &c. &c. A little trouble and patience confirmed those guesses, and these first discoveries were of great use in the prosecution of the task; No. 13 not only meaning "*de*" as a single word, such as Duc *de* Dalmatie, *corps d'armée*, &c., but representing *de* as the component syllable of longer words, such as in*dé*pendant, *dé*sordre, &c.

'When a certain number of these discoveries had been made, Lady Napier found a few letters in which the short sentences had already been deciphered, and the translation written over them; these confirmed her own previous guesses, and some new syllables were added to her vocabulary. Thus she had discovered in a great measure a key to this mode of ciphering, and had made considerable progress in translating both the mixed and the entirely ciphered correspondence, when the key of the cipher was found and sent to General Napier. Afterwards the task was of course comparatively easy, though, from the multiplicity of numbers, and the minute, intricate, varied subdivision of words, it was still a work of time and patience.

'In the course of the early attempts Lady Napier remarked several numbers often recurring which she believed to be *nulls*, unmeaning, and at all events forming no part of any words or sentences, and as such she discarded them. On examining the original key, she found that most of these meant full stops, commas, marks of interrogation, parentheses, &c.; and a few of them were intended to nullify the number that preceded them.'

To this simple account of a task requiring wondrous subtlety, it is necessary to add that she made out all my rough, interlined, and illegible manuscripts, when I could scarcely do it myself, and wrote out the whole work fair for the printers, it may be said three times, so frequent were the changes made; but her statement conveys no just impression of the concentrated thought, the patient acuteness, the quiet perseverance and constancy required, and for many years exercised, unabated by severe suffering from illness and heavy grief. A strong heart, an unclouded brain, and invincible resolution, enabled her however not only to do this, but to make other exertions of a different nature, requiring such an enduring fortitude, that the power exercised seemed even to those who beheld it scarcely credible.

In Napier's account of the capture of Badajoz he states that the fort of San Christoval, to which the governor had retreated, surrendered the morning after the assault, "upon summons to Lord Fitzroy Somerset" But before he could state this fact, that the fort surrendered to Lord Fitzroy, he was obliged carefully to wade through a controversy on the subject, for another officer claimed the credit of the surrender; just as at Ciudad Rodrigo Gurwood and Mackie both claimed, and each fully believed justly, to have captured the governor of that fortress. The following letter, which decided the question with the historian, is here published both on account of its intrinsic interest and for that which attaches to the late Lord Raglan:—

Lord Fitzroy Somerset to Colonel Napier.

My dear Napier,   Dover, October, 1834.

It is certainly true that Colonel —— was present when the governor of Badajoz surrendered in front of San Christoval, and that he was senior to me in the rank we then respectively held; but in my opinion the circumstance of his presence or his seniority does not affect the question at issue.

In order that you may clearly understand the matter, I will briefly relate what I did after I entered the town.

Having heard while sitting with Barnard and the remains of the Light Division that Badajoz was in our possession, I immediately proceeded with Captain T. Stewart, the assistant quartermaster-general of the division, towards the place, and, passing across the ditch and up the great breach, entered the town. I in the first instance directed my steps to the house which Lord Wellington had occupied as his headquarters, conceiving it to be the residence of the governor. I was right in this conjecture, but I could hear no tidings of him there. He had gone out when the attack commenced and had not returned.

I went from thence to the castle, not without the apprehension that the governor and a portion of the garrison had escaped, for though, as I walked along, I fell in with detachments of prisoners, yet I did not see anything like the number I knew that the garrison consisted of. On my arrival in the castle which I entered by the gate opening on the town, I learnt to my astonishment that the troops which occupied it were not aware that we were in possession of the place. I hastened to make known the fact to Colonel Campbell of the 94th (now Major-General Sir James Campbell), the senior officer present, and then continued my researches, accompanied by Sir Alexander Dickson, who had been put into the castle on duty connected with the artillery.

I am not certain when Captain Stewart left me to return to his division, but I think it was at the castle.

I proceeded with Sir Alexander Dickson towards the bridge over the Guadiana, near which we found a considerable force, composed of the several regiments of the 5th Division. Nobody had passed the bridge, or could say where the governor and his staff had taken refuge. Under these circumstances, I requested Major Loftus of the 38th to collect a few men, and come with me across the bridge in order to summon the guard at the *tête-de-pont*, and eventually the fort of San Christoval. Some little delay occurred in forming this detachment and in finding a drummer, and in the interval Colonel —— came up to me, and asked what I was doing or where I was going. I told him I was looking for the governor, of whom I could hear nothing, and that I was going across the bridge, and he said he would accompany me.

We went accordingly, Colonel ——, Sir Alexander Dickson, myself, Major Loftus, and his detachment of the 38th, and the drummer (a little Portuguese boy). The guard at the *tête-de-pont* immediately surrendered, and we continued our march towards San Christoval. On approaching the glacis we beat the *Chamade*, the French in the fort hoisting a white flag, and sending out a drummer on their part In a short time the governor, General Philippon, and the lieutenant-governor, General Veillande, came out, and, on its being announced to them that the town was in our hands, they said they had no knowledge of the fact, and would not surrender until they should be acquainted with it; but they were willing to go to Lord Wellington's camp to arrange the terms of capitulation.

A warm discussion ensued, in which Colonel —— and myself took part; he, if I recollect right, being disposed to agree to their proposition; I, on the other hand, being violently opposed to it, and declaring that they should not stir from the fort otherwise than as prisoners. In the end they agreed to surrender; horses were brought out for them and for us, and we set out for the headquarter camp; where, on arriving, I deposited the two generals, and then proceeded to the works to report to Lord Wellington, and Major Loftus took possession of the fort and its garrison, which was considerable.

I cannot say precisely when Colonel —— announced to me that he, as senior officer, should take possession of the swords of the officers; but if I mistake not it was immediately before the governor and lieutenant-governor came out to the conference. I at once protested against his having the smallest claim to the swords, or any right to interfere in the operation, which

I had undertaken as one of the staff of the commander of the forces, and I appealed to Sir Alexander Dickson, who coincided with me. Colonel ——, however, got possession of the swords, which he delivered to Lord Wellington.

From this narrative it would appear that from the moment I entered the town I had but one object in view, and that I steadily pursued that object until I accomplished it. It will also be evident that Colonel —— joined me by mere accident, and that, whilst it was strictly in the line of my duty as *aide-de-camp* to Lord Wellington to make every exertion to ascertain what had become of the governor, Colonel —— was not in a position, as *aide-de-camp* to a general officer who had nothing to do with the siege, to interfere with me, or direct the employment of troops; and indeed I very much question whether, if he had ordered Major Loftus to move a detachment across the bridge, that officer would have obeyed him,

I never mentioned the subject to Marshal Beresford, but as a proof that he viewed the question in the same light as I did, I beg to state that he sent Colonel Arbuthnot to me the following day to say he was very sorry to find that his *aide-de-camp*, Colonel ——, had interfered with me, and that he entirely disapproved of his conduct.

Sir Alexander Dickson happening to be at Dover, I have read this letter to him; and he is perfectly satisfied as to its accuracy as far as the events to which it relates came under his observation. You are at full liberty to communicate it to Colonel ——.

Yours very faithfully,
Fitzroy Somerset.

The following is from Colonel Hunt, already alluded to as having led the stormers of the light division at the assault of St Sebastian:—

Colonel Hunt to Colonel Napier.

My Dear Napier, July, 1839.
Yesterday I had the pleasure to receive your letter; the pleasure however was mingled with sorrow at hearing so bad an account of yourself. I would fain hope that when your 'work' is finished the worrying will cease and your health improve. That your intention was to write the truth I am certain; but where pretension abounds, truth will not satisfy. Why then mind their cavilling? To your queries.

1. What brigade of the 5th division first advanced?
General Robinson's, I believe.

2. When were the volunteers let loose?
Soon after, on its being seen that the troops made no progress.

3. At what time did the great explosion happen? was it before the volunteers advanced or after? Or was it at the time Snodgrass crossed the river, or after, and how long after?
The explosion happened some considerable time after the volunteers and advanced and Snodgrass had crossed the river.

To explain my answers more fully I will give you a brief extract from the notes I made a few days after the *to me unfortunate* event, for from being then disabled my prospects were destroyed.

28th August, 1813.—Colborne being out of camp, received an order to furnish a certain number of volunteers for an enterprise of moment. At Mein's desire, put down his name; but being told that a field-officer, much his (and *your*) senior, had volunteered, and *he* being disliked, put my own name in place of Mein's. (I do not forget my dear Napier that you were at *the time* displeased with me for interfering with you, but it was to prevent the Major alluded to from having the command that I offered; and having once come forward I could not withdraw with honour.)

August 30th.—Reached St. Sebastian. Having preceded my party, I thought I observed that the troops engaged in the siege were dispirited from their former failure; accordingly halted my people a few miles distant and bivouacked. At about midnight received orders to move my people into the trenches.

August 31st—At 7 a.m. was ordered to attend at headquarters for my instructions; found on arrival Sir James Leith and heads of corps, &c., of the 5th Division assembled. Sir James observed that they were at a loss to conceive why Lord Wellington had thought fit to send us, as the 5th Division were fully equal to the undertaking; but being come, he intended that the volunteers of the light division should be stationed in the advanced part of the trenches for the purpose of keeping under the fire of the enemy; and upon my representing that my character and experience were well calculated to lead the assault, he rather angrily replied, 'That would be an affront to the 5th Division.'

About 11 a.m. the 5th Division (preceded of course by their forlorn hope, with whose commander, Lieutenant Magenis, I was much struck) and storming party advanced to the assault, but owing to the rocky ground reached the breach much broken, and perceiving them stopped (repulsed), I urged Sir James Leith to back them, for I feared they would come away. While speaking a shell burst and wounded him; he then desired me to lead on my men. On reaching the breach I found the men of the 5th Division were making no progress, but rather were crouching under cover of the fallen; we tried in vain to rouse them, and seeing a little to our right some men making head, we moved towards them.

At this time our artillery opened, and a cry arose to come away as our batteries had opened on us. My men were too good soldiers not to know that the fire was not at us, and remained. In attempting to make a lodgement in some ruins *within the wall*, I received a wound which disabled me; almost all the officers and great part of my men had previously fallen. I was carried into the trenches, where I met Sir Richard Fletcher. I told him the troops had made a lodgement, and nothing would drive them out The great explosion *then took place*. Fletcher was killed soon afterwards.

Whether the fire of our artillery had ceased or not I cannot say; but I verily believe that, if it did not cause the explosion directly, the latter was the *consequence* of their fire, from the surprise and confusion it created among the enemy. The artillery certainly deserved credit for their practice; but what troops but Britons would have persisted, with cannon-shot from their own batteries flying a few feet overhead?

Thanks be to God for it, I enjoy good health; but the crosses and losses I have met with in latter life make me look back to those early days with peculiar pleasure; in short, I live upon the past. In the sincere hope that I may meet you again in renovated health and spirits,

    I remain, my dear Napier,
        Yours truly,
           T. P. Hunt.

It is extremely interesting to compare the foregoing letter with Napier's account of the storm; and Colonel Hunt's account itself is a most vivid word-painting of the scene. It brings out strongly the coolness, daring hardihood, of "the fierce rugged veterans of the Light Division," and the almost sublime confidence in them of their experienced commander, "the daring officer who had already won his promotion at former assaults;" who, while being carried to the rear severely wounded, told the engineer that his men had made a lodgement, *and nothing could drive them out!*

For his narrative of the Battle of Salamanca the historian entered into a correspondence with twelve British officers who had been engaged in that battle. Here, also, there were discrepancies and disputes as to the exploits, and credit claimed for different regiments, particularly with reference to the cavalry charge of Le Marchant's heavy brigade. All this was in addition to the French documents relating to the battle, as well as to those supplied him by the Duke of Wellington, having reference to the general transactions of that day.

The following note was written by Colonel Napier to his wife from Strathfieldsaye, without date.

NOTE. SALAMANCA.

The contradictory statements of the *U. S. Journal*, and of the cavalry generally, are intolerable. Colonel Moore, who was in the great charge of cavalry at Salamanca, tells me that the Heavy Dragoons were not alone, that Anson's brigade was with them on their right. He doubts if Sir H. Watson charged the square at all. The heavies had the worst part of the cavalry charge to do, but there was no heavy body of French ridden over; they were loose and unprepared, and threw down their arms and surrendered in crowds, blinded with dust outside of the wood, although not inside of the wood. Preserve this note for me. It was Sir Stapleton Cotton who ordered the charge and who led it General Le Marchant was killed. I shall have to alter all my fine writing. What a bore! however, truth is the thing.

W. N.

Later evidence however satisfied him that Sir H. Watson did charge the French square, though unsuccessfully, and that a very heavy body of French infantry in compact order was ridden over by the heavy brigade, as he has related in the *History*.

The two following letters from Sir Charles Dalbiac will be read, particularly the first, with great interest

General Sir Charles Dalbiac to Colonel Napier.

My dear Sir.   24th August 1833.

You would have heard from me sooner, but that I have been busily employed on a tour of inspection. Let me now express my thorough obligation for your letter of 28th July. It will be very gratifying to me to see recorded the heroic conduct of a wife whose devotion to her husband scarcely knew a parallel. It will also be gratifying to a daughter (an only child) and to an aged father still living. You must speak of her, however, not as *Lady*, but simply as *Mrs*. Dalbiac, for I had to deplore her loss before His Majesty was pleased to confer upon me a title.

I have no desire that you should introduce into your work anymore of Mrs. Dalbiac's Peninsular history than what relates to the 22nd July, 1812; though for your own information I will briefly state that she accompanied me through the Peninsula from the period of the retreat to the Lines in October 1810, until the month of May 1813—excepting only the winter months of 1811-12, during which the 4th Dragoons, of which I was second lieut.-colonel, remained in Portugal for the most part inactive.

Whenever the regiment took the field Mrs. Dalbiac accompanied me on horseback; and such was the case on the day of the Battle of Salamanca up to the moment when the action commenced. She then remained near the extreme right of our position, whence the heavy brigade of cavalry had moved to the attack, and whence she could distinctly discern most of the operations in that quarter; namely, the commencement of the attack by the 3rd Division on the enemy's left, the movements of the enemy on that flank, the advance and the charge of the heavy brigade, and the advance and attack of the right wing of the Allies. Here she had the fortitude to remain during the whole of the action, though so completely within cannon range that shots from the enemy's guns frequently raked up the earth near her horse's feel It was to this spot that the heavy brigade returned at nightfall after the action ceased.

Early in the subsequent morning a cousin of Mrs. Dalbiac's. Lieutenant (now Major) Norcliffe, who was serving in the 4th Dragoons, and who had been left on the field where the heavy brigade had charged, was brought in dangerously wounded by a musket-shot in the head. Mrs. Dalbiac conveyed him into Salamanca, where she sought out Lord Wellington's surgeon, Mr. Gunning; she assisted in dressing his wound, and having otherwise administered to his comfort (to which care Norcliffe may be said to owe his existence), she left Salamanca to overtake the army, which she effected early on the 24th, near the spot where the German heavy cavalry had attacked and captured the enemy's rearguard.

Of this incomparable wife I will only add that, with a mind of the most refined cast, and with a frame of body, alas! too delicate, she was when in the field a stranger to personal fear.

I cannot refrain from seizing the present occasion to say a few words regarding the share which the heavy brigade of cavalry bore in the battle of Salamanca, which I have less hesitation in doing because the 4th Dragoons was not commanded by myself, but by Lord Edward Somerset, then senior lieutenant-colonel, myself being only second.

I entertain no doubt that you are prepared to record with your usual justice and ability all the particulars of that memorable day, so far as information may have been procurable. But owing to the circumstance of General Le Marchant's death, no special report was ever made to Lord Wellington of the particulars of the charge of the heavy brigade at Salamanca. The consequence was that his Lordship's despatch did not, I think, do full justice to that brigade, of which I believe Lord W. was some time after quite aware. The despatch should have reported, not that '*Sir S. Cotton at the head of the cavalry*,' but '*Sir S. Cotton at the head of the heavy brigade*,' did so and so; which brigade (composed of the 5th Dragoon Guards, the 3rd and 4th Dragoons) brought into action only eight squadrons, amounting to no more than 750 sabres.

Having been in the forenoon on the very position which was subsequently (but previous to the battle) occupied by the enemy's left, and having been sent by General Le Marchant just before the action commenced, to reconnoitre the intermediate ground over which the heavy brigade was expected to move to the attack; having moreover been in a situation fully to observe the previous march and advance of the 3rd Division, I think I can speak with some accuracy of the manner in which the attack was directed prior to and including the charge of the heavy brigade.

The 3rd Division (which had been left in the morning at Cabrarizos, whence it had been ordered to march by the rear and towards the right of our position), having moved round the foot and under cover of a small height which sloped upwards in the direction of the enemy's left, commenced the attack, and completely succeeded in turning the enemy's left flank. During this operation Bull's troop of Horse Artillery moved up to the crest of the height alluded to, and performed excellent practice on the enemy in his attempt to throw forward a part of his left to repel the attack of the 3rd Division; which attempt having failed, the heavy brigade of cavalry advanced in an oblique direction, between the left of the 3rd Division attacking to the flank, and the right of the division which formed the right of the first line attacking to the front; and having shot ahead of those divisions, it encountered first a raiment (I believe the 66th French), formed on the slope of the French position, every man of which was cut down or taken prisoner.

The brigade continued to advance, and shortly after charged two, if not three, distinct bodies of the enemy formed in square or in column, the whole of which it cut through and defeated, carrying off from the field 2400 prisoners and six or seven guns. Throughout these charge on the enemy the heavy brigade was unsupported by *any other portion of the cavalry whatever*, but was followed as rapidly as it was possible for infantry to follow by the 3rd Division, which had so gloriously led the attack in the first instance, and had so effectually turned the enemy's extreme left.

I must here in strict candour admit that the enemy had taken up the ground on his left in a very loose and slovenly manner; owing to which circumstance, and to the alarm consequent upon so unexpected and so decisive an attack, may be ascribed that the resistance offered to the heavy brigade was not at all points of that determined character which is to be expected from French troops. Still the loss of the heavy brigade, amounting, I believe (for I have not the returns with me), in men and horses taken together, to more than one-fourth of its numbers, and which was sustained in the course of a very few minutes, sufficiently attests that the success of that brigade was not achieved without considerable opposition and difficulty.

Should there be anything essentially wrong in this statement,

Lord Combermere, Lord Edward Somerset, Sir J. Elley, and many other officers now living can correct it.

Believe me to be
Your sincere and obliged,
J. C Dalbiac.

The date of the second letter from Sir C. Dalbiac shows that the historian had not been able, in the interval of sixteen months which had elapsed since the first, to satisfy his mind on the details of the battle.

GENERAL SIR C. DALBIAC TO COLONEL NAPIER.

Slemingford Hall, Ripon, 17th Dec. 1884. When I get to town I can send you a return of the killed and wounded of Le Marchant's brigade. I believe 750 sabres were quite as many as we had in action, because Major Onslow with one squadron of the 4th had been detached about noon far to the rights and was not in the action.

You should have had the enclosed rough reply some days sooner, but that I have been intensely engaged electioneering in this borough, where my colleague, Mr. Pemberton, has 230 well-assured votes, and I 250 (exclusive of half a score of neutrals), out of a constituency of 377.

QUESTIONS AND ANSWERS ENCLOSED IN THE ABOVE.

Questions by Colonel Napier

1. Was the charge of the heavy cavalry ordered by Lord Wellington or by Sir S. Cotton, or was it a voluntary of Le Marchant?
2. Did Sir S. Cotton head it himself?
3. What time did Anson's cavalry join D'Urban's on the right of the 3rd Division?
4. When Anson's cavalry took the place of the heavy dragoons, after the brilliant charge of the latter, what became of the heavy German cavalry? And what position in Lord W.'s advancing line did the cavalry occupy during the remainder of the action?

Answers by Sir C. Dalbiac.

1. The charge of the heavy cavalry must unquestionably have been preconcerted by Lord Wellington to combine with the attack of the 3rd Division, so soon as the latter should have commenced the action. Perhaps there never was seen a more perfect

combination of the three arms than that of the 3rd Division, Bull's troop of horse artillery, and the brigade of British heavy cavalry. In proof of the said charge having been preconcerted by Lord W., I should mention that about an hour before the charge took place Le Marchant ordered me to the front and to the right, to reconnoitre the ground over which the heavy brigade would have to advance, and to drop *videttes* where impediments, if any, should be found.

2. He must have headed it, or joined early during its advance upon the enemy.

3. The 3rd Division, which had been left at Cabrarizos in rear of the left of the army in the morning, moved by the string of the bow along the rear towards the rights where the attack was to commence; and I have little doubt that Anson's and D'Urban's cavalry fell in on the right of the 3rd Division at about three-quarters of a mile from the point of attack. I conceive the movement of the light cavalry above named to have been quite beyond the extreme left of the French position. It bore *no part* of the brunt of the charge with the heavy brigade.

4. I neither saw nor heard anything of the German heavy cavalry on that day, nor do I believe they were engaged at all. I always conceived they were near the left of the army. Le Marchant's brigade collected as well as they could after the charge, and remained on the ground where their attack and their advance had ceased until near sunset. It then fell back about three-quarters of a mile to the same ground whence it had previously moved for the attack, and there lay all night.

J. C. Dalbiac.

Sir J. Scott Lillie to Colonel Napier.
(Salamanca.)

Sir, London, Dec. 1835.

As you stated in the letter you did me the favour to address to me on the 18th *ultimo* that you would be always glad to receive documents to support general statements in your *History of the Peninsular War*, I beg leave to mention some circumstances connected with the Battle of Salamanca, in case you should consider them deserving attention.

The Duke of Wellington's headquarters, some hours previous to this battle, were with the 4th Division to which I belonged, in front of the hills called the Arapiles, the more distant of which was close to a thick wood which concealed a corps of the enemy without our knowledge. I received orders through the Duke of Richmond to occupy this latter with a detachment of the 7th Caçadores, and on arriving close to it I found it too steep to ascend on horseback, and consequently rode round, while my men made the best of their way directly to the top.

I was not aware of any enemy being in the immediate vicinity, as some Spaniards had been there a short time previous; thus, when I came suddenly on some troops advancing from the opposite direction, I took them for Spaniards, and questioning them in Spanish, they replied *that they were Spaniards*: they were partly covered by the high corn and the uneven ground, and I rode up in the same direction with them until we met our men at the top of the hill, when all doubts on the subject were removed by their opening a fire on us at a few paces distance.

We contested the point so long as anything like an equality of numbers permitted us; but as their numbers rapidly increased, and we found that we were encountering the head of a brigade, we were overpowered and closely pursued in the direction of the other Arapiles, for which the enemy made a push, and which they would have succeeded in taking had not the fusilier brigade and the Duke himself been sufficiently near to arrive the first, where I found them on my return; and this induced the enemy to resume possession of the former hill, which they retained much to our annoyance (from their artillery) during the remainder of the day.

If you will permit me, from the situation in which I was placed, I will add what perhaps few survivors can state respecting the subsequent attack of Pack's brigade on that hill—that it was in my humble opinion an injudicious one, having been made at the point where I could not ascend on horseback in the morning; injudicious also as to the time when it was made, for the enemy's centre and left were giving way; consequently either a flank movement, or a little longer delay, must have rendered the loss of life that took place unnecessary. I happened to be at the time with some companies of the *Caçadores* and the 40th Regiment on the enemy's left, and we moved after Pack's brigade was repulsed towards the enemy's rear, which obliged them to evacuate the position.

This was one of the few occasions on which I saw the bayonet used; the 40th British under the late Colonel Archdall, having come into close contact with Bonnet's French brigade in consequence of this movement, which was directed by General William Anson in person; he was moving on with the 40th, leaving the Arapiles on his left and in his rear, on which a corps moved from behind the hill in rear of the 40th for the purpose of attacking it, the regiment being at the time engaged in front I happened to be between the 40th and the enemy, and rode after the former to tell Colonel Archdall of his situation, on which he wheeled round and charged the enemy's column with the bayonet and thus terminated the contest at that point.

As I find in the Duc de Ragusa's despatches giving an account of this battle, that he mentions a Lieutenant Guillemot of the 118th French Regiment as having taken a flag with great bravery from the British, I beg to observe that I understood the 100th, 118th, and 120th French Regiments to have been those stationed at the Arapiles; and if so, there certainly was no flag taken by them in that quarter; but I can answer for one having been lost by them in this affair with the 40th, as I happened to be the first to come up with the officer who carried it, without claiming to myself any merit for so doing, as he was wounded at the time and unable to defend himself or his flag, which I secured and sent next day to headquarters.

Your very faithful servant,
J. Scott Lillie.

The following was found among the Salamanca documents. It, and the letter next in order, are a fine example of the *esprit de corps* which is the animating soul of the British army:—

(11TH REGIMENT, SALAMANCA.)

My Dear MacGregor,   Canterbury, 8th June, 1835.
The time that has elapsed since the Battle of Salamanca makes my memory no better for the wear; however, what I recollect you shall have. At the time our brigade advanced in contiguous columns ascending a rising ground, you may recollect that just before we reached the top the 4th Division came over it in a state of disorder, the enemy close upon them, the French officers in advance, and actually making use of their swords against our retreating men: our brigade was immediately halted and

began to deploy. By the time three companies had formed, the portion of the 4th Division opposite to the 11th passed round the right flank; these companies at once opened their fire and swept away nearly the whole of those officers; this checked them, and after some firing they turned about and fled.

I believe it was at this point Cuyler was wounded; I know that the whole regiment had not deployed when I was told that the command rested with me. The brigade now advanced in line, and when we rose the hill a body of French cavalry was coming up at a hard canter, either to cover their retreating infantry, or to put a finishing hand to the 4th Division; we at once halted and gave them a volley which sent these cavaliers to the right-about in much quicker time than they came, leaving several horses and men on the ground. The brigade then again advanced in line and entered the plain in front of the enemy's position, and within range of their batteries, which commenced a fire upon us.

We advanced but a short distance before we were halted by Headquarter Staff, and in this situation remained considerably more than an hour, waiting as I understood for the movement of the 3rd Division to turn the left of the enemy's position. During this time their artillery played incessantly on us with shot and shell, by which I lost about forty men; and the loss increased so fast by their getting the range, that I told Hulse[9] something should be done, either in retiring or by the line lying down. The latter he agreed to, and we had hardly a casualty after. During all this time Pack's Portuguese brigade corresponded in their movements with ours, they on our right flank, and Hind's brigade again on *their* right

The next advance of the 6th Division was to the attack of the French position. As soon as the French saw this, a cloud of their skirmishers came down to the foot of the hills forming their position, and as we neared them opened their fire, supported with terrible effect by their artillery with grape; however, the brigade kept moving on, and in spite of every obstacle carried the position. Not a shot was fired by the 11th until we reached the top, when we gave them a farewell discharge. By this time the loss of the 61st and 11th was most severe: the Portuguese brigade in attacking their portion of the position found the

9. The brigadier.

ground steeper and more difficult of access, which enabled the enemy to retain that part, and eventually the French came down and attacked them in turn.

I saw this and proposed to Hulse to wheel up the 11th to their right and attack them in flank, but for the present he declined, thinking we were too much reduced. After a while poor Bradford, the assistant adjutant-general, came up, and instantly went to the rear and brought up to our support a brigade of the 4th Division which had been reformed; the 61st and 11th then changed their front to the right, and attacked this hill and carried it. This was the last of the engagement, and at this period the 61st and 11th had about five officers and eighty men each left. The loss of the 11th was sixteen officers and 333 sergeants and rank and file. I believe the 61st was much about the same. The 53rd after we entered the plain was not in my sight, being separated from the brigade by undulating ground, but I know they kept moving on until attacked by a body of cavalry, which they kept at bay amongst some inequalities of ground though repeatedly attacked Nothing could exceed the conduct of the other two regiments, suffering as they were; and the expressions used by Hulse and other staff officers was most flattering—*the 11th had indeed their full share of applause*;—poor Cotton! I shall never forget the enthusiasm with which he spoke of them.

Colonel Beresford, who was also on the staff, was very pointed in his expressions, and I recollect his saying a day or two after that he would take care the public should be acquainted with their conduct I think you might gain some useful intelligence from him; he was living a short time ago near Lichfield; but so many witnesses of material consequence have gone to their long home, that I fear little can be done now to put the gallantry of the brigade before the public with any great effect. Hulse's conduct during the whole of the battle was beyond praise.

   Yours sincerely,
    J. L. Nott.

CAPTAIN FORD TO COLONEL NAPIER
(79TH HIGHLANDERS, TOULOUSE).

Sir,   Royal Hospital, Chelsea 12th May, 1840.
You must excuse this attempt of an old subaltern of the 79th to point out a few inaccuracies in your account of the battle of

Toulouse, so far as relates to that corps.

The 79th did not on this, or any other occasion that I am aware of *support* the 42nd.

The 79th *alone* carried the Calvinet redoubt, but did not, as stated, *retake* the Colombette redoubt.

I shall only state what I witnessed at the Battle of Toulouse.

After crossing the River Ers, that excellent officer General Clinton assembled the commanding officers of regiments, and gave particular directions to those who should be on the right flank of the 6th Division to be prepared for an attack of cavalry—a timely and valuable precaution, for we were on the right. After crossing the Ers River we advanced by threes in double time in a line parallel to that river (and a fatiguing run it was), to avoid unnecessary exposure to the fire of the Calvinet redoubt, from which General Coles' division had previously suffered severely. The 79th were on the right, as I have said, when a body of French cavalry appeared debouching from one of the deep farm-roads which crossed the Plateau de Calvinet, and leisurely marching towards us. Lieutenant-Colonel Neil Douglas immediately formed a hollow square, ordered out Ensign Balfour with the regimental colour to the front as a directing point, and then gave the word 'March.'

We thus continued our march in the original direction. To see Balfour some distance in front, marching erect, pointing his toes with as much precision and care as if at a formal parade in England, with the colour inclined forward, which required strength of arm (for we had no shoulder-belts to support them), and the French leisurely walking their horses towards us, was a *beautiful sight*, and reminded me of what I had read of the days of Marlborough when such daw movements were common. The square was halted, Balfour called in, and a volley fired by the right face, and the enemy immediately wheeled about and slowly retired, without loss to either side.

The following bit of *gasconade* from the '*Précis Historique de la Bataille de Toulouse*' must apply to the 79th square, as there was not any other square formed on that side of the Garonne:—

> [Extract.] '*Les Ecossais manœuvraient sur la droite du 115me pour se rapprocher de la Tour des Augustins (Calvinet), alors le Commandant Dorsenne détacha les Capitaines Lassé et Pomard, pour aller charger, en sortant des retranchements, le*

> *carré qu'ils avaient formé là à bout touchant; ces deux compagnies brûlèrent quatre-vingt cartouches par homme, ce qui fit perdre aux Ecossais au moins 600 hommes dans deux heures que dura oette attaque!'*

The 79th then proceeded to join the division, and marched up one of the deep farm-roads which crossed the Plateau de Calvinet, and remained some time in it till the order was given to form a line, advance, and attack the Calvinet redoubt The 42nd formed line at the same time, gallantly advanced, and attacked the Colombette redoubt. The two redoubts were carried by these regiments, and it was *here* both suffered The 79th on the morning of the 10th April had 414 rank and file, and of that number 199 and eighteen officers were killed or wounded in carrying the Calvinet redoubt

The French attempted to retake the redoubts, drove the 42nd out of the Colombette, and, falling back upon the 79th, that regiment was also obliged to evacuate the Calvinet redoubt: both regiments retired and reformed. This success of the enemy was only a momentary affair, for General Pack brought up the 91st and other regiments and the enemy immediately retired, and the 79th was ordered by General Pack to occupy the Colombette redoubt, the rear face of which commanded Toulouse.

When the enemy attacked to recover the redoubts I was in a kind of *flèche* or outwork of the 'Calvinet,' separated from the main work by a deep farm-road, and one French regiment marching up by that road cut off my retreat and that of seven men who were with me. One of the men who first saw the enemy advancing on our left had the presence of mind to cry out, '*The French!—sit down!*' and had the words come from a general officer they could not have been more promptly obeyed; we sat down close to the parapet. At this moment we heard a cheering, and that portion of the enemy *then close to us* appeared panic-struck and went to the right-about.

One French officer looked at us and shrugged up his shoulders, supposing we were wounded, and thereby intimating that he could not afford us any assistance, and one French soldier attempted to pull off Captain John Cameron's epaulettes (he commanded my company) as he lay dead a few feet from us, but did not succeed. Their success was altogether momentary:

the cheering came from the 91st then advancing to meet the enemy, for Lieutenant A. Robertson at the head of a party of that regiment immediately entered the work, and, surprised at seeing us *there*, said, '*Ford, are you wounded?*'—and we then joined our regiment where it had reformed.

Before we ascended the Plateau de Calvinet the whole division witnessed a singular scene. The light company of the 61st were skirmishing, when a French regiment in close column descended by a road intending to deploy at the foot of it. A soldier of the 61st advanced and shot the commanding officer at the head of the column, and the instant he fell the regiment went to the right-about and retired.

From what I have seen I think the French officers rashly and unnecessarily exposed themselves, or that such conduct was necessary to get their men forward. To see them rushing forward and jumping about, waving a handkerchief or a sword, vociferating, '*En avant! en avant!*' formed such a contrast to our line that it could not pass unnoticed. In one instance (Fuentes Oñoro) a French officer stood upon the top of a dyke waving his handkerchief *and* sword, *alone*; not another man being viable; and there he stood exposed to our troops till knocked over—he seemed to court death.

It would be a good thing if someone would undertake the labour of ascertaining the *average* number of British troops effective after a month, six months, and a year's campaigning and marching, excluding severe epidemics such as the Walcheren fever, and the killed and wounded, so that the rising officers might form an opinion from the past experience of others what number of *effective* men they could probably calculate upon for any operation.

In the south of France we were reduced to between four and five hundred men capable of any duty, veterans in every sense of the word. Having thrown off all our weak and sickly men, this little body could have marched from one end of Europe to the other without leaving scarcely a man behind.

For example, a regiment joined our division in Spain, and on the first forced march left one hundred men on the road, while at roll-call we had not a man missing. The people of England have a very foolish notion on this subject, believing that every man embarked is *an effective soldier*; an opinion as ridiculous as that of my little boy who said to me, 'Papa, after you soldiers fight a great battle, do you sit down to a feast or a good dinner?'

Pardon this digression and nonsense, and believe me

Your faithful servant,

J. Ford,

Captain Royal Hospital.

Extract of a letter from Lieutenant A. Robertson, 91st Regiment, to Captain J. Ford, late 79th, 1831.

(Battle of Toulouse.)

As a member of the 91st Regiment, I feel indebted to you for the candid manner in which you take notice of the conduct of that corps. Certainly it did not fall to their lot to have much to do, but what they did I believe was performed with sufficient spirit and gallantry. You forget that the 11th was also left out of the despatch when deserving to be noticed more perhaps than the 91st

I think you will agree with me that in talking or writing on such subjects it is too frequently the case that minor points are dwelt on particularly, while more important ones are entirely overlooked. There is an instance of this sort in Malcolm's reminiscences when narrating the operations at Toulouse. He writes of what he saw to be sure, and of that only he tells us. Now, on that particular occasion he sees nothing but what relates to himself or his own corps, the 42nd, while everyone in the division must have observed the spirited and well-ordered conduct of the 61st who led the way, and the fall of their gallant Colonel Coghlan in taking the first redoubt Coghlan found a grave not far from the spot where he and his undaunted little battalion proved so quickly victorious, that scarcely a Frenchman but the dead or wounded was to be seen on the ridge by the time we reached it.

It was the Duke of Wellington's pleasure, however, to have the body disinterred and conveyed to the cathedral at Toulouse in procession; attended by himself and staff.

I say, my dear Sir, that the conduct of the right brigade and of that regiment in particular were circumstances not to be overlooked in any narration.

THE EARL OF STRAFFORD TO COLONEL NAPIER.

My Dear Colonel Napier,　　　　　London, May. 1840.
I cannot refrain from writing how much gratified I feel by the truly friendly manner you have received and acted upon a communication made to you by Colonel Moore respecting myself. I would not have had you annoyed on the subject; but from what Moore said of your desire upon all occasions, and as respects every one, to do full justice—having received an addition to my arms for the act referred to—I could not but naturally wish it might have place in what I consider is now the best history of an interesting period, and which I think will go down to posterity so considered. With your proposed addition in a second edition I am more than satisfied.

I wonder much at your general accuracy in the many affairs of Lord Hill's corps: there are only two to which I could offer addition or correction, and that too trifling to require notice.

　　　　Believe me, yours sincerely,
　　　　　　　　　　Strafford.

The following is selected from among other letters of a like nature, as an example of the difficulties of the task Colonel Napier was engaged in, and for that reason is, like many of the preceding ones, inserted here without reference to date.

Sir,　　　　　　　　　　London, October, 1832.
I have just received a letter from my brother-in-law. Sir ———— ————, dated Missouree, the 17th April last, in which he informs me that it was only on the day before he had read a paragraph in your third volume of the *Peninsular War* reflecting upon his conduct at the Battle of Barrosa. He desires me to inform you without delay, that immediately on the termination of his military duties in India (which will take place in the latter part of the next year) he will return to this country and require from you that satisfaction which is due from one officer to another for this most unfounded calumny.

I have the honour to be, &c. &c.

———— ————

To Colonel W. Napier, C.B.

Colonel Napier to ——— ———, Esq.

Sir,   Freshford, October, 1832.

I yesterday received your letter of the 18th instant, but not in time to answer it by return of post

The message conveyed by you from Sir ——— ——— shall be duly honoured whenever it may suit Sir ———'s convenience to act upon its tenor. Meanwhile I take occasion to observe for his information that in my third volume of the Peninsular War I have stated only three circumstances having reference to him:—

1st That some Spanish troops did, without orders, come back to assist the British at Barrosa.

2nd. That it was expected Sir ——— ——— would have done as much.

3rd. That no sabre-stroke was given that day by the Spanish cavalry in aid of the British.

Now, whether these things be or be not injurious to Sir ——— ———'s reputation, they were substantiated to me as facts by several eyewitnesses. I believe that they cannot be disproved; and, until they are, I repel with contempt the assertion that I have published '*an unfounded calumny.*'

I have the honour to be, &c. &c.

W. Napier.

His military duties detained the challenger in India. He only landed in England in July 1835, nearly three years after the delivery of his first message to Colonel Napier, and he then went immediately to an officer of rank (who was fortunately also a friend of Colonel Napier), to request him to act as his friend in the matter.

That officer in writing to Colonel Napier, said,—

It seems by what has passed between us, that he is not hurt at what you have said in your account of Barrosa, but he is hurt at thinking and believing that reflections had been cast on him by others for not having charged with the Spanish cavalry under his command at a particular moment of that battle. In speaking on that subject he said to me, 'I do not in the slightest degree impugn the veracity or correctness of Colonel Napier's statement as regards my conduct; that conduct was in obedience to peremptory orders from General La Peña, my commander-in-chief, but was by no means the result of my own inclinations.

Had I followed them, my conduct would have been very different. To this I will add from myself, that having seen —— in action both at Talavera and Castalla I can bear personal testimony to his gallantry; and I will here add that having served a considerable time with him I know him to be an officer of high talent. Yet here is my friend who is possessed really of a sound judgment and very good sense, admitting that *he does not impugn your veracity or correctness*, and in the same breath wanting to call on you to give him a hostile meeting, for no other reasons that I can discover than because *somebody else* may have impugned his courage for not having charged the French in disobedience of the orders of the Spanish commander-in-chief, he —— being an officer in the Spanish service.

I have pointed out to my friend the impossibility of my becoming a party to such a view of matters by acting otherwise than as a friendly mediator, which I hope you will allow me to be; and the first thing I have to do is, to ask your consideration of the enclosed paper which —— put confidentially into my hands in contemplation of a meeting with you, and which he hopes you will do him the favour and justice to insert in the Appendix to the edition of your *History* now in the press.

In delivering this paper to me, he said, 'I have no wish that Colonel Napier should alter his book in the text—all I ask is that he will publish my statement now delivered to you, omitting only the last sentence as to my not intending to return Colonel Napier's fire, which it must be evident is not matter for publication.'

I am really vexed my dear Colonel to add myself to the number of those who have broken in on your valuable time, and added to the delay of your work, for the completion of which everybody is anxiously looking forward. &c &c.

Colonel Napier to General ——

My Dear General,   Freshford, July, 1835.
Sir —— has placed me in a very strange position. I cannot deliberately commit murder by firing at a man who admits that I have done no wrong, and who declares that he will not fire at me. The copy of Sir ——'s communication to me which I enclose will make you understand what I am going to say.
Sir —— must withdraw his letters, or rather messages, sent

through Mr. —— and he must especially withdraw the imputation cast upon me, namely, that I have published '*an unfounded calumny,*' before I can enter into any further communication with him. This he can of course have no difficulty in doing, because he has already acknowledged that I was right in point of fact, and that he had no ground whatever of complaint against me.

And this withdrawal must be made known to Mr. ——.

I trust you will feel my difficulty of position. The withdrawal is absolutely necessary to my honour, but the peremptory tone which I am forced to adopt is irksome to my feelings. You will therefore consider this as confidential, but a *sine quâ non*.

Yours sincerely,
W. Napier.

In reply to a second letter from General ——, in which, he enclosed a retractation addressed to himself of the charge against Colonel Napier, the latter wrote the following:—

(TO GENERAL ——. PRIVATE.)

My dear General,   July. 1835.

Sir —— has not withdrawn his challenge, nor has he made Mr. —— write to say he is aware of the fact You will excuse me for sticking so formally to the thing, but I have had enough of experience from Mr. ——'s affair, which is not yet quite developed to the worlds to suffer myself to be placed in the same situation again. When Sir —— withdraws his challenge, and through Mr. ——, I will willingly receive and insert so much of his statement as relates to Barrosa; that will be justice, but all that relates to Talavera is quite another thing; I am not bound to mention officers' wounds, or even their exploits. As a favour I will consent to say. Sir —— *commanded the two regiments; but his wound, &c., I will not put in.*

Yours sincerely.
W. Napier.

The challenge was then withdrawn, as Colonel Napier required, and Sir —— stated he was "quite satisfied with the mention Colonel Napier purposes to make of Barrosa, and of my having commanded *the two regiments* at Talavera."

CHAPTER 12

Bromham and London

In the spring of 1826 Colonel Napier and his family went to Tunbridge Wells. During this visit his children fell ill of whooping-cough, and one of them, Henrietta, a child of five and a half years, died. Colonel Napier was at this time in straitened circumstances, owing to the largeness of his family. Although bearing in his body a French bullet which rendered his whole existence a painful one, he had no pension for the wound, and all the pecuniary benefit he derived from his good service was a major's half-pay of 9s. 6d. a-day. The following letter to Lord Fitzroy Somerset shows his delicacy of feeling, and explains itself:—

TO LORD FITZROY SOMERSET.

My dear Lord Fitzroy.   Battle House, Nov. 30. 1826.

I think it is Bacon who says that '*the man who takes the advice of a judicious friend doubles himself,*' and, in the belief that it is true, I am going to ask your advice on a subject of some importance to me, but involving a question of delicacy which I feel reluctant to decide for myself. I am perhaps taking too much advantage of your uniform kindness by thus intruding my private affairs upon you, but as I know your sense of honour will lead you to determine rightly, so I trust your friendship will find an excuse for the confidence with which I put it to the test.

You are aware that a year's pay was granted to officers for each wound received in action. I was wounded three times, but I only received the allowance for two wounds, as may easily be proved by the books of the War Office and Medical Board. Many officers have lately claimed and received the allowance—I mean within a year or two; but there are some circumstances attending my case which I wish to put you in possession of. My third wound I received in the churchyard of Arcangues; and you yourself can vouch for the fact as you saw me bleeding, and the Duke desired me to go to the rear thinking it was worse than it really was.

A musket-ball glanced from a tombstone and struck me on the hip; it was flattened, and a cannon-shot rebounding from the church wall at the same moment struck the ball and drove it into the flesh. The wound was at first, though a very painful one, not sufficient to justify my going to the rear, but two days afterwards the bruise of the cannon-ball sloughed and it was six weeks before it healed, as Hair who attended me can vouch for. I did not return myself wounded, partly because it was becoming rather a fashion at that time to return very slight hurts as wounds, but principally because Mrs. Napier was on the point of being confined and I feared the effect it might have upon her.

The scar is from the nature of the wound more like that left by a sore; and having no vouchers with me when I claimed for the other two wounds, and the Medical Board, from the number of deceits practised on them, being very indelicate in their inquiries, I feared insult and said nothing about the third wound. I have however been lately struggling (without much success) against untoward circumstances; and as the allowance *was* my undoubted right, I think justice to my children requires that I should overcome the repugnance I feel to make a claim attended with so many peculiarities and of this nature, at so late a period, when the country is suffering.

I think I have a right to it, but necessity is a bad counsellor on such occasions, and the consciousness that I am urged to think of it by the want of money renders me exceedingly doubtful of the propriety of stirring about the matter. My wounds were certainly very severe; my backbone was fractured by one of them, and the effect of that has been great weakness in the lower extremities ever since.

I never laid claim to a pension for that wound as it did not come under the letter of the regulation, and therefore I think I am not overstepping the right line in asking for a third allowance, which is strictly within the regulation, although at a late period. Your opinion, if you will give it, will decide me; and in

the meantime I am
Yours sincerely,
W. Napier.

Lord Fitzroy's answer urged Colonel Napier to make the application, and the allowance for the third wound was obtained.

The following letters were written during the year 1827; some during occasional absences in London, some from home to his wife at Dawlish:—

London.

Shaw has been appointed assistant-adjutant-general in the north of Ireland, and goes there in a week or two. The —— family sent one of their members post haste to London to ask for it before it was vacant; —— backed him up; but the Duke, on looking at the name, said, '—— family—live in the north of Ireland—wants to draw pay and live at home—no—give it to Colonel Shaw, he has asked for nothing.'

London.

..... I saw the Duke; he received me very kindly and asked me to dinner, but I was engaged, which was disagreeable. Soult's son is in town, a very agreeable modest young man, very like his father, but softer looking; he is going to Bath, and, if possible to put him up, perhaps we may have him at Bromham. This I would not have thought of if I had not seen that he is a young man who would not care for bad accommodation.

London.

......Lord Bathurst gave me leave to copy his papers; I wrote to him to say I would not without first apprizing him that I had found fault with his administration in what I had already written, and he has withdrawn his leave as far as concerns his predecessor's time, but continues his leave for his own time; this I cannot blame him for.....

London.

..... I write in a happy humour because I have just had the pleasure of stuffing a little child, less than Pammy, with buns. It was stretching its little hands to the cakes in a pastrycook's shop, and whining to its father, on whose back it was strapped, and it looked pale and starved, poor little thing!

Lord Goderich is to be Premier. This I suppose to be temporary; he can never maintain that place. Lord Wellington *said* to be Commander-in-chief. This would do.

...... Bickersteth and I dined together; he is, I am delighted to say, still Radical, and dislikes Canning. It was not Burdett but the present Chancellor that got him the silk gown. He asked for it as a matter he was entitled in justice to, and Copley had the good sense to give it him. The soldiers and their wives have found me out in Brompton in two hours after I arrived, and daily besiege me. Everybody says I am the author of *Cyril Thornton*. Am I? ..... If the Duke does not come in Colborne is to succeed Sir Herbert Taylor: this is excellent.

June, Bromham.

No letter from you since you arrived at Dawlish. Sirs. Moore came yesterday, and the fair would have gone off well if she had not heard of her sister being ill again, but that made her low. The people of the fair showed all the inherent mischief of the English character, but, being of more than even Wiltshire stupidity, were unable to give it vent beyond groaning and shouting and breaking palings. The children bought as many dolls as would people a desert island, as many cakes as would feed a populous one, and as many drums and whistles as would frighten any island from its propriety. I have resolved to mend and beautify Fanny's room, but don't tell her till she comes back. I hear Lord Londonderry has published a *History of the Peninsular War*.

Fanny's room is much improved, but of course winter is trial time; even the drawing-room is comfortable now. Anastasia Moore gets evidently better. The rooms are beautiful to look at I have read the *Fairy Tales of Ireland*; they are stupidly done, especially *Mr. Rusty-black Eagle*, but the inherent fun amuses you justly in spite of its dullness.

The time of haymaking makes this place more beautiful than you can imagine, and sweeter than Arabia. I have weeded your garden, and made a walk across the grass for you. I am going to give a tea-party this evening to Mrs. Moore, Mrs. Phipps, and the Baileys. I shall be Jack among the maids, the husbands being in London. The Duke of Wellington has beat the Ministers on the Army Bill a second time; I rejoice thereat. ...... Jones has been employed to paint a national picture for Greenwich; he made a bargain that no naval captain, or higher rank is to direct him how to paint, and strange to say it was assented to. This, if it is the consequence of the change in the Ministry, is the best sign I know of the times.

.... Mrs. Moore's sister is dead and she is in great distress; Anastasia is getting better daily. I have done no history worth speaking of; and worse, I cannot settle to it yet—my mind is distraught.

I have read Moore's book, *The Epicurean*; I think it the most learned, beautiful, and interesting romance I ever read. It will be a standard work, and discovers better taste and more genius than anything he has yet written, but the end of it half killed me. When you read it you will understand why. The description is true, not to the life, but the death.

The agitation in favour of Roman Catholic Emancipation, which gave occupation to all political parties during the ensuing three years, roused all Colonel Napier's deeply-rooted feelings and sympathies for the Irish. He did not stand forward to take a prominent part in politics until after that measure was carried, but he felt a keen interest in the struggle. He distrusted the honesty of O'Connell however, and the following note found among his papers in his own handwriting goes far to justify his opinion:—

(*Note.*)—Lord Nugent tells me that he heard O'Connell urge upon Burdett the payment of the Roman Catholic clergy, &c., called *the Wings*; that Burdett said if it would forward the Catholic question he would support the measure, and he would take O'Connell's assurance to that effect O'Connell went back to Ireland and found Shiel and Jack Lawless spouting against these *Wings*, and in command of the populace thereby; whereupon O'Connell turned round and publicly declared Burdett to be a "*spotted traitor*," an enemy to the Catholic religion, for supporting the Wings; that is, for doing what O'Connell himself had urged upon Burdett in London.

W. N.

In the spring of 1828 the first volume of his *History* was published, and Colonel Napier found himself possessed, at a bound, of a high station among historical writers.

The following letters to his wife were written during the course of its publication, which he superintended in. London:—

London, [No date.]

The following table of contents is the shortest way of explaining my adventures to you.

Author got to London well—dined with James Moore—quarrelled—Jones praised work too highly—slept at Gloucester Coffee-house—wet bed, fever, no lodging—met Cooke[1]—got his bed—continued fever—Murray praised book highly—offered 500 guineas for copyright—took no notice—gout, laid up—pain, feyer, and irritation—unable to write—Cooke very kind—got lodging—opened intercourse with had hopes 1500*l.*—could not manage the negotiation in person—agent made some mistake of little consequence—anxious to buy, but tried tricks—enraged, kicked him to the Devil—wrote a peremptory note to Murray—he came forward handsomely—bargain struck, printed in three weeks or a month, but continued gout irritates and interferes dreadfully—1000 guineas for the copyright, Murray to have the option of purchasing the other three volumes at the same price—all the money yours, darling—twelve copies, and the right of sending proof-sheets to Soult, mine. I shall get a present out of him, bound for you, I think——

Pray make out a French letter to Soult, thus:—Say that I am ashamed of the time that has elapsed since I had hoped to be ready to print; that booksellers and various difficulties have delayed me; that I am at last ready to send him the proof-sheets if he will indicate the most secure way of their reaching him; that I hope he will approve of what I have written; that my wish has been to do justice; that I have been obliged to sell the work m England to a bookseller, and that consequently I have no control over it, but that I stipulated that he, Marshal Soult, should have the proof-sheets as they come out, and consequently the means of translating it, if he thinks it worthwhile, before any other person.

Put all sorts of compliments, and say that I hope my arrangement will meet his wishes, but that I have had great difficulty in getting it done, as the right of sending it to him was much cavilled at by the booksellers; indeed it was the principal hitch with ——. In explaining this difficulty you must be delicate to him, and you must be quick, for Murray is upon the wings of

---

1. Major Cooke, late of 43rd Regiment.

desire and talks of getting it done in three weeks.

P.S.—I am mad about the plates, and Sir H. Dalrymple, and Bickersteth. Murray roars out for the manuscript, I roar out from the gout, and neither Sir Hew nor Bickersteth has seen the work. I shall go quite mad—I am half so already. Without Cooke's activity and kindness I should have been ruined."

London.

Your brother[2] is appointed Secretary of Embassy at Vienna. He had his choice of that, or again at Buenos Ayres. There was no time to be lost and Lord Stuart chose the first for him; he was right Buenos Ayres would be so expensive, that his 2800*l.* would not go so far as 1200*l.* at Vienna, and in other respects there could be no question.

London.

I only found yesterday that your brother had rejected Vienna, and chosen Buenos Ayres, partly, I suppose, for the sake of the larger salary, and partly to be alone. I think he is wrong; but he ought to be the best judge. He has applied for leave to go from a Continental port without coming to England, which Lord Stuart got for him, so that I fear you will not see him for a long time.

London.

The King's Speech calls Navarino 'an untoward affair.' The Duke has resigned the Army. This certain, and you have the first news of it—tell Moore.

The report goes that Beresford, Murray, and Sir H. Taylor are to be in commission; this will be destruction to the army, and to my prospects. The dispute at present is whether the Duke is a d—d idiot or only a common idiot. Mark me! he gives up the Commandership-in-chief because he is determined to take the affairs of this country up in earnest; he will be found to be a master-hand and a strong one. I date the crisis from this moment.

London.

I have had a strong discussion with Murray, but it is all settled amicably. On Tuesday he signs the legal part; 350*l.* in four months, 350*l.* in six months, 350*l.* in eight months.

---

2. Mr. Henry Fox.

London.

Lord Londonderry's narrative differs *toto cœlo* from mine. I hear he abuses the Convention of Cintra. This is also pleasant, as the Duke will be on my side. I am disturbed at not hearing from Soult; I fear the book does not please him.

The book gets on slowly; about 100 pages are finished. I was going to send you the first proof-sheet of the *quarto*, but I thought that it would, perhaps, make you sorry that it was to be in *octavo*. The Duke wished to keep the Commandership-in-chief, but his friends pressed him to give it up. A pity! it would only have been a nine-days' wonder, and the Duke of Marlborough had it when chief, or one of the chief Ministers.

London.

Small cares thicken on me, and I have had another gout for two days; but the book gets on.

I made two good sayings lately. I was at Crockford's as a sight: the looking-glasses are numerous. It was said 'The gentlemen must be vain.' 'No, it is to watch their neighbours cheating.' 'That would not do for Crockford.' 'Why not?' 'The Devil has no shadow, Crockford can have no reflection.'

Second good saying. 'A woman is a biped that wishes horses to go faster than coachmen like, ships to carry more sail than sailors wish, generals to fight more battles than soldiers desire, and dandies to make more love than reasonable men find convenient.'

London.

I am very busy. Book 160 pages corrected—letter from Soult—four sheets gone to Mathieu Dumas to translate. When the money is paid, set apart ten guineas for the poor people, over and above the usual charity; it is right to do so. The printers say I am very troublesome in correcting; you could have told them that before. The Duke is fighting everybody. I dined with the Blencowes. They are good, sensible people, and the party was sensible and pleasant. Everybody talked politics; all were evidently, of different sides, yet I came away without knowing what any man was, so gentlemanlike and agreeable all were. I never saw it before, but the Duke seems to have killed party feeling. Huskisson is knocked on the head, but I hear he intends to revive this night.

London.

I am weary of my life; for the last week I have been rolling in agony with the gout; the pain was incessant for 36 hours, which never happened before. I am better now, but I feel as if a fresh fit would come on every moment.

To mend the matter the printers are getting slow and careless, and the time flies. The Duke of Wellington has been near dying; he is hardly recovered. War seems to be certain. France will have Egypt, depend upon it. Nobody seems to think of that quarter.

COLONEL SHAW TO COLONEL NAPIER.

Manchester, 16th May, 1828.

Having read your first volume with every attention, I sincerely congratulate you on your having written a history which I am fully convinced will be read with admiration by the present and by future ages. As a military history nothing in our language can be placed in comparison with it. So the Duke does not admit all the criticisms as to the movements at the periods of Roliça and Vimiero; I suspect, however, that in the midst of the French army as ours was at four o'clock after the action of Roliça, there were good gleanings to have been got.

I see some minds are struck by your saying that the Duke committed faults. Turenne points out the only case in which a commander does not commit faults, '*quand un homme n'a point fait de fautes à la guerre, il ne l'a pas faite longtemps.*' A man who conducts military operations must be most extraordinarily stupid if he fails to discover that before long he has committed many errors; the Duke must like the frankness of your observations, it makes your praise of him valuable.

Your work is very generally read here; all the Messes have got it; the mercantile men have got it in their libraries, and several of the mercantile people have spoken to me of it, after having read it with great interest, and anxiously asking for the second volume.

William Campbell[3] writes me such an excellent criticism on your work that I must give you a literal copy of it. 'Have you begun Napier's book? I am delighted with it. By Jove! I do not think such a history has appeared since that of Xenophon. The

---

3. Major-General Sir W. Campbell.

writing is beautiful, and though entirely free from affectation he says the best things short, pithy, and to the purpose. There never was written anything of more rapid current, and in his course he flings to right and left the dirt and filth of prejudice; lays bare the baseness and corruption of the Juntas, &c, and exposes, alas! the blindness and folly of our military agents—the madness or imbecility of our Government! and all this done with good taste, and from undoubted documents, quoted in the margin. All as it ought to be; the subject deeply considered, the whole evidence well sifted, and the presumed troth impartially told. I am charmed. This is History. Mr. Southey should have waited; he would then have published only his historical essay, which is amusing enough.'

COLONEL GEORGE NAPIER TO COLONEL WILLIAM NAPIER.

Grosvenor Street, May 18, 1828.
I returned late last night I was highly delighted with Paris, and everything. Marshal Soult's reception was the kindest you can imagine; I saw him every day, dined with him, and met many Generals: among others Clausel, who seems a proper clever fellow. Soult desired I would give his best regards, and said, 'Your brother's work is perfect; it does honour to his head and heart, and must be as satisfactory to the French army as it is to the English; it is the work of a just and honourable man, whose only object is to tell the truth without fear or vain boasting; and as to his remarks at the end of the chapters, they are most scientific, and require no comment from me or any other military man—they speak for themselves.'

He afterwards said to me, 'Your brother is the most candid, fair, and honourable man I ever saw, and his *History* is truth, and cannot be contradicted' In short my dear William your whole conduct has been such as to gain forever not only Marshal Soult's friendship and admiration, but that of every officer I conversed with in Paris. The Marshal presented me with a beautiful print of himself the day I came away; in short, he was most kind and friendly, and most sincerely do I thank you my very dear William for your kind letter to him. He lives *en prince*, I like his daughter very much, she is a handsome woman. The Duchess was very friendly indeed, and I rattled oat execrable French without fear, jumbling tenses, genders, and numbers in one confused mass; however, what with shrugs and grimaces, I contrived to make myself understood, and I understood them pretty well.

Old Lafayette desired I would remember him to you; he is a fine old fellow, but I should doubt his cleverness; very good-natured, and a little vain. I see he is held in high respect. Count Dumas, with whom I talked for an hour or two, said he had written to you respecting the stops in the English edition; he showed me twenty-five sheets already printed of the French translation; and as far as I could judge from a hasty view, he appears to me to have caught the spirit of your style very truly, and done the thing uncommonly well.

He said, 'I have written a few lines to your brother upon the very few points on which we may have a trifling difference, but, on the wholes I pronounce the work a model of truth, skill, and eloquence. As to the retreat of Sir John Moore, the battle of Corunna, and the General's death and character, it is perfect; not a single false idea; and the eloquence with which it is written; although I am an old author and have met with much approbation, I do not feel competent to criticise it, indeed it is impossible.'

All this being said in English I know to be correct He also said, 'Your brother is the only historian who has been able to comprehend the ideas of the Emperor on entering Spain, and he is the only man who has done Napoleon's genius justice; all he says is new to France and to Europe, and is all true.'

He told me to entreat of you to get another volume out in two months. I said I feared that was impossible but I would give his message. He repeated several times, 'Pray make him work to bring out the second volume immediately. I hope my dear William you are at work, for rest assured your fame will be immortal by this *History*.

I enclose you a letter from old Desmenard, who is as good a fellow as I ever met. I went every day to his house; his nice nieces sent all kinds of loves, &c., as did *Madame* their mother. I like the family very much. They begged their best compliments and all kinds of French sayings to dear Car.; it would do her heart good to see how highly respected and esteemed you are my dear Podge by all the French. As to Paris itself, it is delightful, and I saw everything. What I admired as most splendid to the glory of the French nation was the beautiful column in the Place Vendôme; I went to the top of it. What a mean, rascally revenge, to take down the statue of Napoleon, who had led the armies whose victories ore there embossed!

Lord Strangford is going to attack you: he is in a great rage, I hear. And now God bless you my dear William! and work hard as Dumas begs.

The following letter from "Tom Moore," refers to one of the numerous controversies imposed upon him by his publication.

My dear Napier,   June 6.1828.

I enclose you a note which I have just received from Wilson, and which, as I am not returning so soon as he thinks, I enclose to you. I find the feeling he expresses relative to your note upon Strangford and Strangford's answer very prevalent, and I think it right you should know it. If you have it in your power to give a complete and documentary reply to Strangford's pamphlet (for the mere questioning his veracity will not do), I say again, what I said when you mentioned the substance of your note to me, '*Let him have his deserts, coûte qui coûte.*'

But the next best thing to being able to answer him is to say honestly and frankly that you have been mistaken, and the rest of your book will but rise the brighter and more trustworthy for the concession. I have not time to write more on the subject, but Wilson's note very much expresses all that I feel on it. There is, in fact, no middle line left you between a complete and instantaneous answer, or as complete and instantaneous an *amende.*

Ever yours most truly,
Thomas Moore.

NOTE BY COLONEL NAPIER ON THE ABOVE LETTER.

Colonel Napier did answer Lord Strangford effectively; and when the editor of the *Sun,* commenting on the controversy, condemned his lordship, and used terms so strong as to draw on himself a prosecution, Lord Strangford's advocate admitted the truth of Colonel Napier's principal accusation, and, attempting to justify it, was publicly rebuked by Judge Bailey. The verdict was for the editor.

Colonel George Napier to Colonel William Napier.

Barèges. Aug. 1, 1829.

I long to hear of your second volume. Is it out? . . . . . We have got acquainted here with many pleasant Frenchmen, among others little Las-Cases, who tells us many interesting things of Napoleon to whom he seems uncommonly attached. He does not think well of Gourgaud. We have also a Count Canonville, who was Napoleon's Maréchal de Palais, and with him everywhere. He is a complete Napoleonist and has told us many curious facts. I am reading Bourrienne's *Memoirs*; the first four volumes are lately published; he was Napoleon's schoolfellow and private secretary for years.

Canonville tells me that nearly all of it is true, but that there are also many false statements, and that it should be read with the knowledge that Bourrienne was punished at last by Napoleon for misapplication of the public money, and therefore he writes evidently with a wish to lower Napoleon's private character, at the same time that he exalts his talents to the highest pitch. However, the book is well written and extremely interesting and curious. He takes every opportunity of holding Sir Walter Scott's book[4] up to the ridicule it so justly merits.

I went over to see Alava[5] at Bagnères. He swears you are blind to that *coquin* Napoleon's conduct in Spain, and believe in all the dam French rascals like ———, &c., and by ——— I am angry with William, but by ——— the military part is to me better and dearer than Polybius; by ——— George, I tell everybody no such book in Europe! By ———, William would make the best minister in the world, and by ——— he is equal to command any army; he is one dam clever fellow, the cleverest fellow, but dam rascal to the Spaniards.'

And then he jumps up on his one leg, and sputters out French, English, and Spanish, to the utter incomprehensibility of any human being. He is a fine fellow! his health is much better, but his hip is as bad as ever, poor fellow! he sends his best love to you.

The only really unfair and uncandid criticism of the book ap-

---
4. *Life of Napoleon.*
5. The Spanish General Alava, attached to the Duke of Wellington as Military Commissioner in Spain.

peared in the *Quarterly Review*, but the spirit of the work was too much opposed to the prejudices and feelings of the day to make it generally popidar. The publisher who purchased the first volume had the right of refusal for the second. When the latter was nearly ready a friend informed Colonel Napier that he did not think his publisher would purchase the second volume, because he had heard him say that an officer of high rank, connected with the ministry, had declared it was not *The Book*. The following letter from Mr. Murray assigns a more substantial reason for his refusal to publish the second volume upon the same terms as the first.

> My Dear Sir,   Albemarle Street, May 13, 1829.
> Upon making up the account of the sale of the first volume of the *History of the War in the Peninsula*, I find that I am at this time minus 545*l.* 12s.
> At this loss I do by no means repine, for I have derived much gratification from being the publisher of a work which is so intrinsically valuable, and which has been so generally admired; and it is some satisfaction for me to find by this result that my own proposal to you was perfectly just.
> I will not however venture to offer you a less sum for the second volume, but recommend that you should, in justice to yourself, apply to some other publishers. If you should obtain from them the sum which you are right in expecting, it will afford me great pleasure, and if you do not, you will find me perfectly ready to negotiate, and in any case I shall continue to be, with the highest esteem,
>   Dear Sir,
>   Your obliged and faithful servant,
>   John Murray.

Colonel Napier published the second and all the succeeding volumes of the *History* on his own account.

The following letters to his wife refer to the publication of this second volume.

                                                                June,

I am too late for a frank but I do not like to keep you in suspense. I have settled to print on my own risk. I have got good security as to character of my agent, and the calculation will, if I sell 3000 copies, give me 950*l.* profit, the copyright remaining with me. I hope it will do. If I fail in this plan I will never write another line; for submitting to the insolence of such fellows as —— is out of the question. When I have set the printers to work, I shall go down to Wiltshire, and correct by post; it will be cheaper even by coach-parcels than living in London, and I cannot stay long away from you without pain.

Fanny's letter has relieved me from a state of great uneasiness,[6] but I am impatient to hear from Brabant. I was twice on my way to the coach-office last night to go down to you. I am glad now that I did not, as it might have disturbed you; and I will not go now till I have completed the business here, for I have had a letter from Dumas, complaining of delay and wanting me to make an apology to the public, and promise to be a better boy at my lessons in future. What a very funny idea! I shall teach him better things in time, but I must get his part settled before I go down to you, and I think that as quiet is necessary for you it may be better; but if you have the least desire to see me, say so, and in twelve hours I will be with you. Tell Fanny I thank her for writing to me—she is a good girl.

Lady Lansdowne was so kind as to send a servant to Craven Hill to look for me, and from thence to Edward Street, with an invitation to her music party; but I could not raise spirits enough to go. It shows that she is not too fine a lady for her country friends, and I like her for it. I had a long conversation with the Duke of Richmond. He is a very reasonable, honest man, and everybody says he is to be Prime Minister. I warned him not to look for it, and he seemed to feel my reasons.

His friend Colonel Shaw was at this time Military Political agent at Manchester, for which post he had been recommended to the Ministry by the Duke of Wellington, and the following letter gives an interesting account of the state of that town during the Reform agitation.

Colonel Shaw to Colonel Napier.

My Dear Napier,   Manchester. Nov. 30, 1829.
Since the 3rd I have been on a Court of Inquiry on which we were occupied during the whole day, having no time for anything else. I ought to have written long before, but my attention was constantly kept on the alert by a strange state of things here. There are twenty thousand people out of work for months, and

---

6. His wife had had a severe attack of hay fever.

this contest between the workpeople and their employers continued till October; in the latter part of its continuance it was of course greatly more dangerous than at any other time, for the workpeople became more and more exasperated as their wants and miseries daily increased from so long a want of wages.

For a great many weeks we were kept in momentary dread of scenes of violence, and I felt a great responsibility and anxiety to accomplish the two not very reconcilable objects of protecting the lives and properties of the employers, and of avoiding the necessity of actively employing the troops in support of the civil power. The chief means taken to accomplish these two points was that of establishing piquets of cavalry and infantry in the parts of the town that were threatened, and having the police and one of the magistrates constantly in readiness, so as to proceed instantly to any place where a mob was assembling. A mob here, being allowed to collect and proceed to commit excesses, soon gathers into such a storm that there could be little chance of its being stopped without lives being lost; I cannot doubt therefore that the most humane course to pursue, and that which will also best protect property, is to overcome the mob by their seeing that you hold in readiness such a force as can instantly support the civil power, and that the civil authorities; acting in understanding with the military, instantly proceed to meet and suppress every scene of riot that may take place, only showing the military when the civil force is evidently inadequate; for showing the military in time has the effect of intimidating the rioters, and encouraging the constables, to such a degree that the former in general disperse.

It was upon this principle that we acted for a great many weeks here every day and every hour, and you will see that to carry the thing into practice was, in fact, to lie in an unceasing state of watching. If you happen to recollect it when you write, you may mention what you think of this notable theory as to civil commotions. The people here since the disturbances have consented to prepare a place; in the centre of the town where a considerable body of troops may be lodged within an enclosure, which separates them entirely from the people, and in good rooms and stabling: this was agreed to with the utmost unanimity; but previous to the riots when I proposed it to the authorities, they approved but said, they durst not even mention it The dispute between the masters, and their workpeople is for the present completely settled; the workpeople in this instance were, I conceive, completely in the wrong, and the masters beat them.

Neither, the notice which has appeared of your second volume in the *United Service Journal*, nor any other, that I have seen, deserves the name of a review. In the first paragraph (*U. S. Journal*) they raise you above Caesar and Napoleon, and all others who ever approached the subject of war; in the three next paragraphs is thrown some disparagement, which is to a certain extent popular, however unjust, from the idea that you lean too much to the French owing, to your getting so much information from them, and particularly from Soult.

That you have unguardedly adopted anything from the French Generals, the reviewer does not offer the remotest instance; and I apprehend that the result, so far from turning out 'galling,' will be quite the reverse, for truth requires that the French should be shown to have been highly skilful and most formidable opponents; and surely on their having been so, and being so represented, depends the glory of the British arms.

Nothing I assure you could have, given me greater pleasure and gratification than the perusal of your second volume; you have got, and I conceive must ever maintain, the highest place among military writers.

There is a gentleman here who lately travelled with, and saw a great deal of General Sebastiani. From what he says it is evident that Sebastiani is a hater of the English. I was glad to find however that he had the candour to praise very much your work, and to call you a very able man.

    Yours sincerely,
        J.Shaw.

COLONEL SHAW TO COLONEL NAPIER.

My Dear Napier,   Manchester, Nov. 22, 1830.
Since receiving your last note I have looked at Bonaparte's own account of his proceedings against the Sections at Paris. You will see from that account that he occupied the Pont Neuf, which surprises me; I think that under the circumstances on the morning when he placed his guns, the Pont Neuf was *out* of his position: I see that on the other side he occupied the

Louvre and the Place Louis XV., and consequently the whole line to the Champs Elysées, and that he commanded the Rue St Honoré by the points which he held.

I see from what you say that we agree in the main points; that the streets (*i.e.* the town) should not be abandoned. The idea that it should, has I see become common with military men. Abandon the town, and you at once give up everything you have to contend for; the moral effect would be fatal; it would encourage all the bad to the utmost, would discourage those otherwise willing to protect property, and leave them to be even forced to act against you; it would deliver over to pillage the property you wish to protect, and give those within time so to prepare the town that you could not again enter, at least without destroying it. It is clearly right to hold an important and commanding portion of the town you wish to protect, and also to command an outlet: now this latter condition materially affects one of the principles you mention,—that of keeping very concentrated, for you must have a good and open part of the town, and yet you must keep up a communication through it so as to get out in case of need.

This may and must sometimes force you to occupy a longer line than you would otherwise wish, and it is a difficulty I have had before me for some time. The practical remedy I conceive to be that of occupying and fortifying strong and important points on the line of communication; if the line is to be intercepted those points must be attacked; so be it, but when the attack upon them becomes serious, move your disposable force from your main position and fall upon the assailants; and in this encounter probably the whole affair will be settled.

Again, there is another important modification as to the extent of the position you may occupy in a town. It may with greater safety be more extended when the streets are broad and straight, so as to be easily raked and commanded by artillery.

A concentrated and strong position is evidently essential when affairs get serious, and the troops are likely to be overpowered by numbers; and as, when any movement of a great town begins, you cannot tell how far it may go, such position should always be clearly fixed upon, and the important points in it held from the first. But I should altogether deprecate the remaining in such a position with the troops at the commencement of a popular tumult; in that case strike blows as rapidly as possible at the assembling bodies, disperse them, and retire to your intended position the moment you have done so; repeating these blows when called for, and trusting to your activity and vigour to secure getting back to your position, and also using great discretion not to leave your position when you find that your first vigorous efforts have not put down insurrection, and that matters were become too serious for detailed attacks.

The defence of the points you occupy in a town seems an easy matter; strong buildings cannot be taken from you; occupy the projecting houses of all inlets in the squares and open spaces which you have with a small force on the side of the square, and they will be completely barred. When you issue from your position to do anything offensive, three cases may be supposed; 1st, that you are to act against an assemblage not occupying buildings; 2nd, against an assemblage occupying isolated buildings; 3rd, against an assemblage occupying whole streets, and having both streets and houses barricaded.

The first case must be easily disposed of, if there be any adequate force to protect your guns.

The second Bonaparte disposed of solely by the use of artillery, as it ever ought to be disposed of; for one factory, defended decently even by a rabble, mighty were you to attack it rashly, defeat any force you might attempt to storm it with.

The third case can only be disposed of by burning, and total destruction to the buildings by that means and by artillery.[7]

As to a whole country rising in rebellion against its government, that is a different affair; the position is in fact an absurdity in itself, as at once appears by asking the question—Does the army and government belong to the country, or does the country belong to the army and government? It would be the contest of one limb against the whole body. There is one case, however, which actually may occur in this country, in which I would act even at the risk at least of destruction to a place, which you think too horrible to be attempted. It is not at all an

---

7. Colonel Shaw must here have written hastily. Later experience teaches us that barricades defended by any mob may be carried without guns and without destroying houses. The troops force their way into the nearest houses on both sides of a street so occupied, and break a way through the partition walls, from house to house, until they torn the barricade.

impossible thing to occur that, were much commotion to take place in this vicinity, the plundering mob might seize upon a town.

I think that in such a case they should be powerfully attacked and dislodged at all hazards to property: the good people would have fled, and the existence of such an example would endanger all the property in the district I may expect therefore that my being hanged in such a case would meet with your approval. I shall think it very hard if I am hanged at last for any acts of the troops in which I may be concerned; for I have spared no pains to pre vent, collision between the troops and the people; and this is chiefly to be effected by such good understanding with the magistrates as will prevent their committing the imprudence of calling out the troops unnecessarily; a great deal may be done also by the way in which the troops are stationed, so that they may not be placed in actual contact with the people where irritation most exists, but sufficiently near to reach such points speedily and in force, if absolutely necessary.

Yours sincerely,
J. Shaw.

The following is from Colonel Napier's brother.

COLONEL CHARLES JAMES NAPIER
TO COLONEL WILLIAM NAPIER.

London, August, 1830.

Talking with Lord Aylmer about your *History*, he told me that about three years ago he met with a Mr. Blancheton at the baths of Enghien. This gentleman in high in the confidence of Masséna, and secretary to him in Portugal He now lives in the Rue de Lycée Valois, in Paris. Lord Aylmer says he has more information on the events of that campaign than most people, and that he is very communicative. Being blind, he has no pursuit, and likes talking of past days; and, therefore, if you like to write to him, making use of Lord Aylmer's name, Mr. Blancheton will be both able and willing to give you all the information you can require on the French side. He told Lord Aylmer that Marmont superseded Masséna during the Battle of Fuentes d'Onoro, and that he believes Masséna's anger prevented the attack on the right from being followed up, as it was at that moment that Marmont arrived.

I suspect Paris is '*as quiet as a barrel of gunpowder*.' King Philippe had better take care how he smokes his pipe! I know nothing to detract from the merit of the Parisians except Mr. Bowring's praises, and I have not so much confidence in the town as in the country. I would rather trust the people of France than the people of Paris. Were I King Philippe, I would take delight in great reviews at Paris, and much pleasure in country amusements at all other times. Slipping one's king is like slipping one's shoulder, after the first time a trifle does it. I believe it is better that Charles's head continues where it is; yet if there was any justice in beheading Charles the First and Louis, I do not see why this man should escape; Johnny Crapaud is very good-natured. God bless your honour!

C. J. Napier.

To his Wife.

London, December.

Lord Althorpe appears honest to me, he may yet save us. Lord Douro found me out, and is just the same excellent, honest, sensible young man as when I last saw him; he wishes me to go with him to Strathfieldsaye, and I have agreed to do so. His politics are decidedly adverse to his father's, and he is for a thorough reform. He dislikes London society for its heartlessness, and as good as told me Sir John Moore was as great a man as his father: this shows how keen he is in observation. What he liked best in Sir John Moore was his kindness of disposition.

December?

Charles tells me (for Moore) that Major Sirr fired at Lord Edward [Fitzgerald] through the hinge of the door, and then ran down stairs and sent a sergeant of the Derry Militia up, who found Lord Edward holding both Ryan and Swan down on the floor, kneeling on one of their breasts, and trying at the same time to lift the window. The sergeant called to him to surrender, or he must kill him: he said he would not, and held up his left hand, which the sergeant split, up the fingers, at one blow, and with a second cut his head open, when he was taken, having fallen down.

Charles saw himself the bullet-hole through the door at the hinging of it; and Lieutenant Stone of the Derry Militia, who had the care of Lord Edward, told Charles that after he was taken he called for some water, and when it was brought to him Major Sirr dashed it away and said, 'You damned rebel, you shan't have any.' Lieutenant Stone, however, insisted upon its being given to him. Moore may depend upon this as fact, and there, is another curious fact for him. The dagger which Edward used was given to him suddenly at night in the streets, a few days before his arrest, by a stranger, who said, 'You will have occasion, for it in a few days,' and then walked on.

I have been in bed for a week past with a cough rheumatism, and gout all together, and of course my spirits are not very high, and not raised by the dangerous state Emily[8] is in at Barton; she has a very severe illness and gets worse. Charles Bell is gone down to her, and Charles, Henry, Louisa, and Caroline have also gone there. Tomorrow I fear we shall have bad news, yet I hope not; I shall keep this open until the post from Barton tomorrow.

Friday.—I am much alarmed at no letter from Barton. I fear all is over and that I shall never see my poor Emily again. It is very alarming: yet I do not feel that internal sense of misfortune that generally gives me notice of approaching distress. The facts are all very threatening, yet I am calmer than I can understand. God send it may be a good omen!

Perhaps Bunbury thinks I am out of town and has written to you.

Jan. 6, 1831.

How strange that my letter telling you of Emily's safety should have been delayed! She is going on quite well. I am walking about again. Have you seen in *The Times* a letter from me against Mr, Sherer? It is an impudent forgery; I have said so in a letter which will appear tomorrow. Was there ever anything so impudent?

January.

Henry is made post-captain by Sir James Graham; the very first commission he has signed, and he has spoken to him in the handsomest manner besides; and notwithstanding my roughness to him he spoke of me with great respect, and decidedly bears no malice. Now, as I bear so much myself, I have an esteem for those who do not and I must henceforth respect him.

---

8. His sister.

January

Emily much better. Mind you give me an account of Fanny and the ball.

You will soon receive a book of Mr. Herschel's, to whom I have been introduced. Everybody says it is the most delightful and the cleverest book ever written, my own not excepted. I daresay it is true; he has the head of a very great man, as well as the character of one. The Whigs are persecuting Cobbett—*true Whigs*.

I open my letter to tell you the news. The National Guards at Paris have risen, driven out the Ministers, and put Soult at the head of the government, *i.e.* the Ministry. War seems certain. The King is not deposed. Ask Mr. Salmon if I am right.

January.

When you write tell me more about the ball, I like to hear of it.

I hope your party will go off well, and that Fanny will do the honours like a lady as she is. . . . . . Bickersteth is reading Beresford's pamphlet, and seems at present against taking any notice of it, but he has not finished it. I have had another long talk with Douro: he is very clever and subtle, yet honest.

The *Athenaeum* says my second letter is the forgery. Rather funny that!

January.

Your account of the birthday was very agreeable to me: and I am so glad you like your chair. Henry shall not pay any of it, it shall be all my own present to you. War is fast coming. The papers tell you of the insurrection at Petersburgh, which is, however, more serious than is said. In Ireland the Green and Orange flags are joined, and the people demand under them a reduction of *rents and tithes*. In France they are collecting troops *on the side of Piedmont*. This last is private news, quite true, but not known; you may use it to get yourself a name for political sagacity; before spring all Europe will be in war and turmoil.

Here in London men speak sedition openly in the clubs and secretly in the streets; every person is prepared or preparing for a great change; in short, what I told you as far back as when we were in Louverval *château* is coming to pass. In a little time show of any kind will be dangerous. In the country people go on in their old hush drum way about politics, but in London treason is not thought of, and you will be surprised to learn that I am reckoned too moderate; in short, public opinion is at last ripe for a revolution, and the first great man that steps forward will be sovereign of this country or he will found a republic.

January

Lady H. Hoste has ordered me to wait upon her at three o'clock on Tuesday, that she may consult me upon the publication of her husband's *Life*. She is a Walpole.

Jan. 13.

I am not well: how can I be in London, and foreseeing so much mischief in the world to come? I wish I was not a politician,—I should be happier. You see I was right about the fires; they are increasing, and the bloody proceedings of the Ministry will make them increase.

Henry's little things are not well at all; they evidently suffer from the change of climate, and he is already regretting that he ever came away from Italy. The boy is the nicest pretty little thing in the world; but he is very sick. Gougou is, as I told you, a nice little girl, though not so pretty as the boy. The account of your party pleased me, though how you got fifty-four people into the house I don't know! I have just received a letter from Dumas, kinder than ever. The book goes on faster now.

Jan. 27.

Preserve this as a memorial of my military *coup d'œil*. The Russians will move in three columns: one direct upon Prague, by the left of the Bug; one by the right bank of the Bug upon the Bolra River to near Seirock or Pultusk; the other upon Ostralenka, and by the right bank of the Bolra upon Pultusk; they will then fix their depots at Ostralenka and Pryanie and besiege Modlin. If they have enough men they will attack Praga at the same time and take Warsaw. The Prussians will then aid them, I think. The Poles ought to fix a bridge and *tête-de-pont* at Seirock, beat the force that comes by the left of the Bug, or, if that is too strong, pass the Bug at Seirock, and fight either at Pultusk or at Ostralenka. Warsaw, I think, will be taken and burnt under any circumstances; Praga is the fortified suburb of Warsaw. Time will show if I am right.

Feb. 1.

I have seen Lady Harriet Hoste for two hours. I could only promise to look over her work, and it is to be sent to me in June: what could I do? Besides, she wants support in a right cause, for her relations are attacking her to suppress his cause of discontent with the Admiralty; and she says that she wants my opinion to set against theirs. She is so right and they are so wrong, that I felt I should be wanting in good faith to a right cause to refuse what she asked. There is very little of her writing and a great deal of his, and I think it will be interesting to read. Poor thing! it was very melancholy to see her, and she is quite crippled in her limbs besides.

We have admired Johnny's beauty and other children, but all must hide their heads when her youngest boy is seen. He has his father's dark hazel eyes, golden locks, and a beautiful rich, though fair, colour in his cheeks; but his face is so oval, his features so beautiful, his look so sweet, so innocent, that I thought it was a girl, and such a girl as never was seen on earth before. He is five years old, large and well made, but scarcely human in grace and loveliness. Jones has read the third volume: he says there is not a word to change, and that it is by far the best of the three.

I have read over many hundred sheets of Lady Harriet's, and given her my, not her own, writing, for the whole thing is an ill-assorted heap of his letters from the time he was a boy of twelve years old until the peace of 1814. They are interesting certainly, because they show his mind to have been very content, very good, and gentle to the greatest degree, never changing, and always right in feeling with relation to service, and to his family and friends; but they have rather lowered my opinion of his talents. He was unquestionably a very able seaman, a very bold man, persevering, full of resources, and capable of inspiring his men with confidence to undertake anything.

But then I find no trace of any general views of politics or of war. His speculations on affairs are very few, but always belied by the result, and there is a contracted judgment about Napoleon and the French, and about England, which is quite worthy of Lord Nelson's school. Everybody opposed to England are always 'rascals,' 'damned rascals.'

Napoleon is a *charlatan*, until the splendour of his actions at last reluctantly forces from him the confession that his talents are wonderful. The naval battles are always won by 'treachery and bribery,' and the world can't be at peace until '*Boney is killed*,'—and such trash as that; yet it is evidently the result of his bad education, for naturally his disposition is generous, and his actions always so, and he never breathes an expression of cruelty. The idea of vengeance, or of any other mode of venting his enmity against the French but that of hard fighting, never enters his mind. He is also free from the love of money: still he is not a great man.

His descriptions of actions are meagre, dull, and *borné*; he seems never to have taken a view of the causes of success or defeat, and yet his own actions show that he could think of them well; but he was evidently a man of perception at the moment rather than of deep thought. His admiration of England is lower than the *Morning Post's*, and more devoid of reason; one example will suffice. At Goree, on the coast of Africa, he sees some miserable black slaves to a black woman. That is to say, the most miserable degraded people in the world on the most miserable spot of land in the world. Well, what reflection does he make on their state? 'That people in England, who grumble at taxes and the distress of war, should see these people and be content.'

As if nobody ought to complain whilst there are any worse off in the world, and that to prove our sense and public virtue we should quietly permit Ministers to reduce us to the lowest possible condition short of absolute starvation, and that while any part of the human race are raised above that state they have no business to complain or exert themselves to prevent suffering.

Yet he is often complaining himself of his own poverty and the want of promotion, and the dislike he has to salt provisions!—If this sort of reasoning had been when he was young there might be some excuse, but it was when he was captain of a frigate. Again, he is always launching out in abuse of the French tyranny, and plunder of the statues, &c., their contributions, &c., at the very time he is selling the prizes he takes, and affects to pity the poor owners, some of whom are aboard, as if this was not worse than the French land plunder of statues, &c.

The latter were the public property, the former were private property. Yet his mind does not enable him to see this, and, blinded by this custom and by prejudice, he calls one robbery, the other fair play. It is from such specimens that I have lowered my opinion of his intellect. Still he was a fine fellow, and would, under a better master them Lord Nelson, and in a better school than our navy, have been a *very* fine fellow, and his disposition was very amiable indeed. His love of his friends and his gratitude to anyone who takes notice of him and his bluff manner of expressing it are very like George. . . . I have given her my advice freely and honestly, and if she don't follow it I can't help it. The children are all well: Norah very fine; Catty so good that she extorts involuntary praise from nurse.

Feb. 21.

The news I gave you is not confirmed in all its extent, but the people have restored the sculpture of Napoleon's victories to the Arc de Triomphe, and the revolution is going on well; you will hear news very soon. I dined yesterday with Bickersteth. The Harleys were there, but the party was disagreeable to me because Burdett, as I knew he would, commenced attacking the Irish question and Cobbett and contrived it so that I was obliged to take up the cudgels, which brought Bickersteth upon me and of course I had a hard fight to make. I kept my temper well and beat Burdett certainly, as even Bickersteth turned against him about Cobbett a little; but it gave a disagreeable turn to the evening.

I must, however, say for Burdett that it is impossible to argue with him on equal terms; his language is so eloquent, his manner so perfectly gentlemanlike, and his whole demeanour so void of offence or harshness, that his opponent must always feel that he is appearing to disadvantage; and when you beat him, he withdraws in such a dexterous and delightful way from the dispute that you feel he is paying you a compliment, and assuring you that he would rather be beaten than disturb your equanimity.

Feb. 25.

I have taken mine and Henry's places for Saturday morning. The subscription is over two thousand two hundred and forty copies taken off at once, and one hundred and sixty-seven of second volume sold *en passant*. So great a subscription was hardly ever known; *bon*. Give the poor something; I like to mix up other people's good fortune with my own; it brings a blessing on one, and gives a reason for rejoicing without feeling too selfish: feed some little children that are hungry, it is always good to do that

In April, 1831, Colonel Napier received through his friend Colonel Evans,[9] a man of the same political creed and of equally pure and disinterested views, the offer of a seat in Parliament, at a very trifling expense, which the latter had been authorised to make him by Sir Francis Burdett. To this offer the following reply was returned:—

COLONEL NAPIER TO COLONEL EVANS.

My dear Evans, April, 1831.
I have eight children, and scarcely enough money to feed and clothe them; it would therefore be madness in me to stand an election, especially as the old plan of buying the electors to sell again is not the thing nowadays. Moreover, I have not the qualification necessary to take the oaths. I feel, however, very much obliged to you for remembering me, and I hope you will return my thanks to our common friend, whose name I guess.
I was glad to see by your letter in the papers that you had brought up some of those gentlemen who think that a long prescription of wrongdoing entitles them to abuse those who do right.
Yours very sincerely,
W. Napier.

The third volume of the *History* was published in this year, (1831) and the following extract from a review of Audubon's *Birds*, in *Blackwood's Magazine*, July, 1831, shows the sort of effect produced by the "heroic" style of description in that volume:—

Peace be to the manes and fame to the name of Sir Sidney Beckwith! a man, as Napier says, who was equal to any emergency, and more than once in Spain retrieved a disastrous day. As for Napier himself, his Spanish campaigns are immortal. His famous passage about the 'astonishing infantry,' the 1500 unwounded survivors of the 6000 British heroes, crowning the hill with fire and dyeing it with blood at Albuera, will be quoted as long as we are a military people (and that we trust will be

---

9. Lieut.-General Sir De Lacy Evans.

till we fade away within the Millennium), as the most spirit-stirrinig specimen in any language of the Moral and Physical Sublime.

COLONEL GEORGE NAPIER TO COLONEL WILLIAM NAPIER.

March 25. 1832.

Lord Hill has given George[10] an Ensigncy in the 28th, and, as it is one of the best regiments in the service, I am delighted. Sir Edward Paget has written to me most kindly, saying he is delighted to have a son of mine in his regiment. He is going to take Billy[11] into the Military College next year, and has shown great interest about it; indeed his friendship to me has never altered.

I shall make George come home by Bath to stay some days with you, and I hope, my dear Bill, you will impress upon him some lessons of military discipline, &c.; and do give him what I know is your opinion as well as my own respecting *kindness of manner* and of speaking to the soldiers, and not supposing they have not the same feelings as officers, because they are privates; in short, my dear William, a few words from you, to whom, as well as to Charles, I have taught him to look up as military characters, will do him more service than anything.

Pray also warn him against idleness and *billiards*; he will be more impressed by what you will say to him on that subject than by any other person, because in you he will see an example[12] that the man who has true, honourable feelings can overcame any habit of that kind when he determines to do so, and turn his splendid abilities to the good of his country and the honour of the Service.

I wish you would also point out to him that the free and easy manner in which young officers of a month's service give their opinion of the military conduct of their superiors, and address them by their surnames as if they knew them all their life, is in the first case very presumptuous, and in the second vulgar to a degree.

I know, my dear William, you will not mind this trouble on your nephew's account, for I am fully persuaded you will be as

---

10. Afterwards Major-General George Napier, C.B.
11. Afterwards Colonel William Napier, Commandant Staff College.
12. See William Napier's letter to Captain Charles Macleod, of July, 1803.

anxious about his doing credit to the name as I can be myself. My boy John[13] is studying hard; he is the cleverest, most ambitious, and most persevering, and will make a proper soldier. God bless you, my dear William!

In the Appendix will be found an interesting paper which Colonel Napier, in 1832, addressed to some periodical on the military operations in Ireland at the time of the French invasion under General Humbert, and in justification of the proceedings of Lord Cornwallis during that period

The following correspondence took place about this time.

ELIAN [14] TO THE EDITOR OF THE BATH JOURNAL.

Sir, April, 1832.
In a recent number of your paper there is an extract from the *Life of George IV*. which relates to the Duke of Wellington's position at Waterloo. The writer, who is evidently not a military man, has treated the matter with greater boldness than discretion. He says that 'any person who had ever seen the wood at Soignies could at once decide that it would ruin a beaten army;' and he doubtless thought he might safely say so because it is a fashion now to hail any detraction of the Duke of Wellington, and because Napoleon has given an opinion to the same effect.

Lord Wellington asserted that the wood would have covered his retreat. Napoleon asserted that it would have prevented all retreat. Between such authorities it is dangerous to offer an opinion. Nevertheless it may, I think, be shown that Napoleon was not so well entitled to speak authoritatively as the Duke on this particular point. There is no doubt that a close wood would greatly impede the retreat of a beaten army. There is no doubt that Napoleon was the man above all others who gave his enemy least hope of escape. There is no doubt that the French are the most dangerous soldiers in a pursuit that the world can produce.

But this wood of Soignies was open. There was no brushwood, no difficulty for infantry, and not much for horsemen, to pass through it, and it was pierced by broad highways. Now then, let us see what might have been done in case of disaster; and first of

---

13. John Moore Napier, afterwards Captain 62nd Regiment, died of cholera at Kurrachee in 1846.
14. A name under which Colonel Napier occasionally wrote.

all the author should learn that an army may be beaten and yet not dispersed. Seldom does it happen that a disciplined army is so completely broken, that neither rearguard nor reserve are left to cover the rout; and of no troops can it be more safely predicated than of the English, that there will be many men to turn and die in opposition rather than in flight In all pursuits the cavalry are the most formidable because most rapid. The infantry, tired with a long battle, heavily loaded, and probably wanting ammunition, move slowly on and scarcely see a retreating enemy after the latter have fairly turned their backs.

The Duke of Wellington never spoke of flight; he knew his troops too well; he was only considering an orderly retreat in presence of a daring enemy. What then could the French cavalry have done? Wellington would have sent his artillery and all his disordered troops by the high roads, and then, forming a rear-guard of the best men, have filled the wood on each side of those roads. If the French cavalry charged amongst the trees, their destruction would be certain. If they pushed along the road, the fire of the men from each side would be equally fatal to them. The British rearguard must therefore have been attacked with infantry and artillery, but this would have required some disposition, which always costs time; and as the battle was not decided until the evening, it is but reasonable to suppose night would have set in before they could be entirely dislodged. The Duke would thus have gained several hours, and his retreat as far as the wood was concerned would have been secure.

In writing thus, I do not mean to place Wellington's military genius on a par with Napoleon's. The latter was original, powerful, dazzling! His like on a field of battle, unless Alexander of Macedon be the man, has never been, and probably never will be: but Wellington is also great and of a peculiarly correct judgment; and I believe that in this instance he is quite right Thousands may have seen the wood of Soignies, but how many were able to judge of what they saw?

Elian.

"A WATERLOO MEDDLE," TO THE EDITOR OF THE
BATH JOURNAL.

Sir,

Your correspondent Elian, whose letter appeared in your last, must have a very imperfect knowledge of the wood of Soignies, so frequently mentioned in Waterloo reminiscences, or he is a most determined apologist of the 'Great Captain' whose success in his *last battle* depended certainly on the cast of a die. He had 'set his life upon a cast,' and he won. I have always called him 'the Fortunate Captain,' particularly in the affair of Waterloo; for had Grouchy arrived on the ground before Bulow, the Duke might have bidden *adieu* to all his 'greatness' and his army to boot I could say much on this subject; but, not to occupy too much of your columns, I shall confine myself to the wood of Soignies, which the army of the Duke could no more have traversed, *even without arms and baggage,* than twenty thousand men could have passed out of a single door of a theatre on fire, without being nearly all burnt.

The wood of Soignies extends in length from three to four miles, and in breadth from one to two. It is thickly set with trees of no great size, intended chiefly for fuel, and encumbered with underwood. There is only one road through it, leading from Waterloo to Brussels, which is partly paved in the middle, about ten feet in breadth, like most of the roads in the Netherlands; but at the time of the battle it was in excessively bad condition, torn up by the passage of artillery and baggage waggons passing to the scene of action, and softened besides by continual heavy rains. The soil is loose earth mixed with sand; and even before the battle it had been found very difficult to proceed over it with heavy carriages; the stones of the paved part of the road being displaced in such a way as to form nothing but hillocks and holes.

Off the paved road it was impossible to travel at all, either on horse or on foot, as the sides were perfect quagmires, in which wheels instantly sunk to the axle-trees. The question was therefore, How could the English army find refuge in it? and not, How would the French be able to follow? There was no other means of retreat; and the whole army must have been taken prisoners by the French, if the unparalleled strength of arm, courage, and devotion of British *soldiers* (to whom the success of the battle is due) had not formed an impenetrable barrier against the charges of the French until the Prussians made their appearance.

The frequent exclamations of the 'Great Captain,' 'Oh that

night or Bulow would come!' sufficiently explain the *delicacy* of his situation; and his reiterated orders to those colonels who reported their regiments to be almost annihilated, 'to stand their ground even to the last man,' are quite unequivocal in explaining the forlorn situation in which the British army stood during the whole of the day of the engagement. I am no apologist for either side, but I wish to 'give the Devil his due.'

   I am, Sir, &c.,
    A Waterloo *Meddle*.

 "Elian" to the Editor of the Bath Journal.
Sir,   Bath, April 26, 1832.
In replying to 'A Waterloo Meddle,' I must premise that I will not write more than this letter on the subject: your correspondent wanders too much from the point

The question is not whether he has the habit (people acquire bad habits sometimes) of calling the Duke of Wellington 'the Fortunate Captain,' or any other name; it has nothing to do with the supposition of Grouchy's arriving before Bulow, nor with the reports (if such were made) by the colonels of regiments during the action; neither has it any connection with the 'unparalleled strength of the English soldier's arm,' even though it be true, as I have sometimes heard, that the glory of the day equally illumined Wellington's head, Anglesea's leg, and Shaw the Life Guardsman's fist. Finally, it has nothing to do with the Duke of Wellington's exclamations, if he made any, during the battle, but with what he could have done to save his army in the event of a defeat

'Waterloo *Meddle*,' gives a wonderful description of the wood of Soignies. The Hyrcanian forest was nothing to it! only one road through it; nobody could get on to that road, nobody could get off it! nobody could get forward! nobody could get backward! 'Of a surety it is prodigious!' as the Dominie saith. But, sir, Ferrari's map will show you that there are four great *chaussées* or paved roads, and innumerable bye-roads, through it, and two of those '*chaussées*' were available for a retreat

The first by Waterloo, was behind Wellington's right wing; the second, by La Hulpe, was behind his left wing which covered Ohain. Near Ohain, Vandeleur's brigade of cavalry (which by-the-bye has never had justice done to it) remained in observation until late in the day. By Ohain Bulow arrived, by Ohain the left wing could have retired to La Hulpe, while the right wing went by Waterloo; and I still maintain that the wood would have furnished means to cover the retreat.

My personal knowledge is indeed confined to a ride through some parts of it three days after the action; but I have heard experienced staff officers, who had professionally examined it both before and on the day of the battle, say that it was perfectly practicable for infantry, and in parts for cavalry; and this coincides with my own observations. I saw no incumbrance of underwood, and found no difficulty in passing off the high road. It is further confirmed by the fact that the Belgians and other fugitives, and there were many, did, as is well known, find their way in crowds to Brussels. Baggage, horsemen, waggons, cavalry, and infantry contrived to get along this terrible forest, through 'field and footpath, wild forest black, and quagmire deep.' It is '*an unhandsome fix,*' as the Yankees say, where an infantry soldier can neither fight nor run away.

Elian.

The increasing frequency and severity of Colonel Napier's violent attacks of illness, from one of which he was then suffering, joined to his straitened means, led him in the spring of 1833 seriously to contemplate leaving the army. His whole military pay amounted to 171*l.* *per annum*, and, if he died, the value of his commission would be lost to his family. By the sale of his commission he could realise 3200*l.*

The following letter from Mr. Bickersteth, whom he again consulted on this occasion, shows that he had actually forwarded his official request to be permitted to sell out, but that Lord Fitzroy Somerset would not act upon this without first remonstrating with him and asking his reconsideration of the subject.

MR. BICKERSTETH TO COLONEL NAPIER.

Mr Dear Napier, May 13. 1833.
Your letter was by mistake left at my neighbour's house, and not sent to me till late on Saturday night Thinking myself obliged to send your answer to Lord Fitzroy Somerset by the time you limited, and being unable to make up my mind that you ought to quit the army, I sent your note B, consenting to remain, to Lord. Fitzroy, and at the same time took the liberty of requesting him (notwithstanding, the note) to permit the question to

remain open for a few days longer; and this request he has been so obliging as to comply with. I have, therefore, the opportunity of telling you what I think, and leaving you to decide for yourself afterwards.

The only advantage obtainable by quitting the army is securing the price of your commission for your family, and for this you propose to relinquish the position and the chances which the commission affords. I will not say that you ought not to make a sacrifice for the sake of securing a considerable sum for your children, but in this case, as in all others of the like kind, the welfare of the father is the interest and welfare of his children; and unless I could clearly see that you personally would be made happier and more comfortable by quitting the army, I should not think that the price of the commission would make it their interest that you should do so.

It is very true that the chances of promotion or of active service, when strictly examined, appear at present to be but small; but still, there they are, these chances; and how is it with us all throughout our lives? the possibility of some remote contingent advantage being at some time or other realised, dwells in the mind, and affords from time to time a source of hope and pleasure, which would be wholly wanting in the dull and cold certainty of having nothing to look forward to. These low spirits, the natural consequence of sickness, ought to be struggled with, and may be overcome.

Suppose yourself again in health and vigour,—how would you feel on finding it no longer rational to enliven your studies by the imagination that you might one day be in a situation to apply your knowledge in the most important circumstances—on finding the links which bound you to your old friends and companions broken—in seeing others preparing for honourable employment, and doing things to make your heartstrings thrill, whilst you were excluded from all participation! Suppose, in short, a conscious ability in yourself to do all that might be required from the position you now occupy or may fairly look forward to, that an opportunity offers, and that you are wholly shut out by a step taken in a moment of despondency!

You will say that your health does not permit you to suppose a complete recovery; to which I answer that your opinion only shows you are in low spirits: there is no organic mortal disease;

and that being so, you ought by all means to expect a recovery; you ought to do everything in your power to raise your spirits and be cheerful, and to avoid everything which seems like giving yourself up, abandoning your chances, and forsaking the course. I doubt not but that you have within you the means of rendering good service to the world, and I object to your taking a step which would, as it seems to me, tend to increase a despondency which ought to be resisted.

I believe that I should preach longer if I had more time and room. You must necessarily write your final determination to Lord Fitzroy. I have been a sufferer by this influenza, and have had its full complement of gloomy thoughts and dark forebodings, with which I had to buffet as well as I could, and I am now going out of town for our few days' vacation.

Very sincerely yours,
H, Bickersteth.

Colonel Napier to the Duchess d'Abrantes.

Madam, Sept 11, 1833.

In the eighth volume of your *Mémoires* I find the following passages:—

> *Toutefois, pourquoi donc m'étonner de la conduite des Portugais? N'ai-je pas vu, ici en France, un des frères d'armes de Junot souffrir qu'on imprimât, dans un ouvragé traduit de l'Anglais, des choses révoltantes de fausseté sur lui et sur le Maréchal Ney? .... Cet ouvrage, fait par un Colonel Napier, et qui a trouvé grâce devant le ministère de la guerre parcequ'il dit du bien du ministre, m'a été donné, à moi, à moi, la veuve de Junot, comme renfermant des documents authentiques. J'ai dû y lire une indécente attaque contre la vie privée d'un homme dont on ne pouvait dire aucun mal comme militaire dans cette admirable, affaire de la Convention de Cintra, puisque lea Anglais ont fait passer à une commission militaire ceux qui l'avaient signée pour l'Angleterre; et les beaux vers de Childe Harold suffisent seuls à la gloire de Junot, quand l'original de cette convention ne serait pas là pour la prouver. Heureusement que je le possède, moi, cet original, et même dans les deux langues. I'l n'est pas dans M. Napier.*

It is not permitted to a man to discover ill-humour at the expressions of a lady; yet, when those expressions are dishonouring to him, and reputation and wit joined to beauty give them a wide circulation, it would indicate insensibility to leave them unnoticed.

To judge of the talents of a general by his conduct in the field has always been the undisputed right of every military writer. I will not, therefore, enter upon that subject, because I am persuaded that your Grace could not mean to apply the words '*revolting falsehoods*' to a simple judgment of the military genius of the Duke of Abrantes.

Indeed you intimate that the offensive passages are those directed against his private life, and touching the Convention of Cintra. I think, however, your Grace has not perused my work with much attention, or you would scarcely have failed to perceive that I have given the Convention of Cintra at length in the Appendix.

But in truth I have only alluded to General Junot's private qualities when they bore directly upon his government of Portugal, and, with a fresh reference to my work, you will find I have affirmed nothing of my own knowledge. The character of the late Duke of Abrantes given by me is that ascribed to him by the Emperor Napoleon, (see Las Cases), and the authority of that great man is expressly quoted. It is against Napoleon, therefore, and not against me who but repeat his uncontradicted observations, that your resentment should be directed.

If your Grace should deign to dispose of any further thought upon me or my work, I would venture to suggest a perusal of the Portuguese, and English, and Spanish, and German histories of the invasion of Portugal; or even a slight examination of only a small part of the innumerable, some of them very celebrated, periodicals which treat of that event. You will then be convinced, that, so far from having wantonly assailed the character of General Junot, I have made no slight effort to stem the torrent of abuse with which he has been unjustly overwhelmed; and believe me, madam, that the estimation in which an eminent man will be held by the world is more surely to be found in the literature of different countries than in the fond recollections of his own family.

I admired General Junot's daring character; and having enough of the soldier in me to like a brave enemy, I have, wherever the truth of history would permit, expressed that feeling towards him and towards other French generals whose characters and whose acts have been alike maligned by party writers in this country; such indeed has been my regard for justice on this point that I have thereby incurred the charge of writing with a French rather than a national bias, as your Grace will discover by referring to my Lord Mahon's *History of the War of the Succession*, in which his Lordship has done me the honour to observe that I have written '*by far the best French account* yet published of the Peninsular War.'

For my own part, I still think that to refrain from vulgar abuse of a gallant enemy will not be deemed un-English, although Lord Mahon considers it wholly French; but his Lordship's observation incontestably proves that I have discovered no undue eagerness to malign any of the French generals. And with respect to the Duke of Abrantes, I could show that all the offensive passages in my work rest upon the published authority of his own countrymen, especially the Emperor Napoleon; and that they are milder in expression than those authorities would have warranted.

It is, however, so natural and so amiable in a lady to defend the reputation of her deceased husband, that, rather than appear to detract in any manner from the grace of such a proceeding, I choose to be silent under the unmitigated severity of your observations.

Not so with respect to that part of your remarks which relate to Marshal Ney. After carefully re-examining every sentence I have written, I am quite unable to discover the slightest grounds for your Grace's accusations. In all parts of my work the name of Ney is mentioned with praise. I have not indeed made myself a partisan of Marshal Ney in relating his disputes with Marshals Soult and Masséna, because I honestly believed that he was mistaken; neither have I attributed to him unbounded talents for the higher parts of war; but this is only matter of opinion which the world is quite capable of appreciating at its true value; upon all other points I have expressed admiration of Marshal Ney's extraordinary qualities, his matchless valour, his heroic energy!

In the hope that your Grace will now think it reasonable to soften the asperity of your feelings towards my work, I take my leave, with more of admiration for your generous warmth in defence of a person so dear to you, than of resentment for the harsh terms which you have employed towards myself.

    I remain, Madam,
        Your very obedient servant,
            William Napier, Colonel.

COLONEL NAPIER TO LADY CAMPBELL.[15]

[No date, probably 1833.]

That you thought your letter long is not surprising; I know your dislike to writing at all, and I feel the effort you have made the more sensibly. There is a great deal in it, a great deal to read, and more to think about; and I do not know whether the past, present, or future comes oftenest into my mind when I read it There is one thing however that never quits it, and that is the kindness of your feeling towards me, and above all other parts of that kindness the confiding way in which you have what you call 'twaddled' about your children. You well knew you were safe from any reprimand on that score from me. I could hear the praises without fatigue of uglier children, and from people far less entitled to exact a patient hearing than you are. . . . . . .

I believe you are quite right about Mr. Stanley, but he is doing the Devil's work in Ireland; and as I have not the counterbalance of knowing him personally, I hate him for it. Of all the people you have mentioned to me as acquaintances, the one I like, and am most jealous of, is Mr. Hamilton the *savant*. I have an awful sense of his talents and *agrémens*; and an agreeable mathematician is such a formidable fellow ! there is no getting the better of him in reasoning, because he proves everything; and to overcome the dullness and savageness engendered by such a study, indicates so much natural talent for society, that once set a-going he must be like the locomotive machines on the railroads.

As to the *History*, God defend the right, for I fear I shall never finish it, and that the falsehoods of the English press, and English politicians, and English prejudices, will remain without any further exposure. It is now two years since the third volume came out, since which I have written *one book*, or a fourth part of the fourth volume; but then I have changed my home, and *written a Reply*, and made speeches, and corrected and published second editions of the two first volumes, and copied out

---

15. Daughter of Lord Edward Fitzgerald.

a whole volume of secret and important correspondence between Lord Wellington and the English, Spanish, and Portuguese Governments, all of which is arranged for printing. I have therefore not been very idle, but my mind is harassed, and not in a state to remember all the little parts which go to make up the mosaic of History.

I am, however, now bent seriously on finishing the fourth volume at all events. As to the Beresfords, I thank you for believing that I am not tamed. You are right in supposing that I shall say more because he was never again intrusted by Lord Wellington with a command, and I have nothing to say against him except in the capacity of a Commander-in-Chief.[16]

Talking of tameness, I am told that my Reply disappointed the military world by not being trenchant enough. I thought I should have got credit for my moderation; besides, Beresford was *not the aggressor*; my subject obliged me to attack him, and in supporting my attack I was, I think, bound to avoid all appearance of personality. I say all this to you because I like to chat with you, and because I have a great respect for your judgment in books as well as in many other things.

What does Guy[17] think of the Reply? everybody knows he can be sharp enough if he chooses, and therefore his opinion in favour of moderation would be conclusive with me. For my own part, I do not think I have much turn for light sarcasm. I can I know be bitter, and with diligence and time I can concoct a disagreeable paragraph, but it is not natural to me, and therefore my praises of moderation are to be suspected, like the fox's observation about the grapes; but Guy's talent and taste for a *soothing* observation to an impudent fellow are indisputable.

What a rigmarole story I am writing to you, dear Pamela, instead of talking about what is pleasanter to you and really more

---

16. Napier has been charged with injustice to Beresford, especially in his account of the Battle of Albuera. What says Wellington on this subject? "The Battle of Albuera was a strange concern. They were never determined to fight it; they did not occupy the ground as they ought; they were ready to run away at every moment from the time it commenced till the French retired; and if it had not been for me, who am now suffering from the loss and disorganization occasioned by that battle, they would have written a whining report upon it, which would have driven the people in England mad. However, I prevented that,"—Wellington's *Supplementary Despatches*, vol. 7, p. 177.
17. Sir Guy Campbell.

interesting to me,—I mean your little boys and girls.

Edward,[18] Guy told me, is a page, and slept like a page in his spurs the first night of his appointment Does it give him anything now in hand, or are all his advantages fastened to his heels? You will get the better of little Guy very easily, particularly if you appear not to expect any resistance or particular atrocity from him. It is surprising how children set up their bristles against people who tell them they are bad, even though it be the truth.

Your little goddaughter has been made a very nice, obedient, affectionate little body by a contrary system, though she promised at first a deal of trouble; but I need not preach to you who are so affectionate and kind to everything, and I dare say the little fellow will not turn out a difficult job. Some minds are so forward in perception that the judgment is distanced at first, but it will afterwards come up and all will be right Of one thing I am quite sure, namely, that children should be *tamed* instead of being broken in. I don't mean tamed down, but tamed to their work, that is coaxed to it

If your affairs and inclinations should ever let you write me another long letter, or even a short one, it will be a great pleasure to me. To have a letter from an old friend is like going to the fire on a cold day.

    Yours affectionately,
      W. Napier.

In the course of this year, 1833, Colonel Napier's eldest daughter, aged nineteen, died; mention is made of her in his letter to Lady Hester Stanhope in 1839. The author of this biography has indeed grievously failed in the delineation of his character if it is here necessary to tell the reader how overwhelming was the blow to the bereaved father. But he sought to stun his grief by increased labour at his *History*, and early in 1834 his fourth volume was published, containing the descriptions of the Battle of Albuera and the sieges of Badajoz and Ciudad Rodrigo, in language of extraordinary sublimity.

FROM COLONEL SHAW KENNEDY.

Sept. 6, 1834.

I was in Scotland when your fourth volume came out and did not see it till after my return here: you must not suppose from

---

18. Later Lieut.-Colonel Sir Edward Campbell.

my silence that I thought less of it than of the three preceding ones; I on the contrary think it the superior composition of the whole; and no historical descriptions have I think ever exceeded in spirit, truth, and beauty, those of the sieges as contained in that volume. I must certainly ever feel highly gratified to see that you have introduced my name in one of the most finished and beautiful descriptions that have ever been penned of any military operation.[19]

COLONEL GEORGE NAPIER TO COLONEL WILLIAM NAPIER.

Pisa, Oct. 5, 1834.

I now turn to a more pleasing subject, which is to thank you my dear brother most affectionately, for the justice you (who are the first historian of the war) have done me in your clear and beautifully written account of the siege of Ciudad Rodrigo. You have said everything I could *possibly wish*, and more than I had any right to expect: and to be mentioned in such a gratifying manner by my brother, my friend, my comrade, and the first military writer of our times, when other writers did not think my conduct worth notice, is to me a *triumph* and an *honour* that I would not exchange for all those writers could possibly say, were they to ransack the English language for terms of eulogium on me.

Their trifling, partial, feeble accounts will be forgotten ere their own lives are terminated, while your incomparable History will remain a model of truth and justice, and a record of the achievements of the two greatest nations in the world, as long as history is read! therefore again I say my dear William accept my sincere and grateful thanks for your honourable and gratifying

---

21. In this dreadful situation, while the dead were lying in heaps and others continually falling, the wounded crawling about to get some shelter from the merciless shower above, and withal a sickening stench from the burnt flesh of the slain, Captain Nicholas of the Engineers was observed by Lieutenant Shaw of the 43rd making incredible efforts to force his way with a few men into the Santa-Maria bastion. Shaw immediately collected fifty soldiers of all regiments and joined him; and although there was a deep cut along the foot of that breach also, it was instantly passed, and these two young officers led their gallant band with a rush up the ruins; but when they had gained two-thirds of the ascent a concentrated fire of musketry and grape dashed nearly the whole dead to the earth; Nicholas was mortally wounded, and the intrepid Shaw stood alone! With inexpressible coolness he looked at his watch, and saying it was too late to carry the breaches, rejoined the masses at the other attack."—Siege of Badajoz, *Peninsular War*, book 16, chap. 5.

mention of my name.

I have read this volume through with great care and unbounded delight, for in it you have had opportunities of recording the many glorious military achievements of the four nations engaged, and you have not let slip one occasion of rendering every justice to those Spaniards whose patriotic conduct deserved it, as well as of bringing forward the gallantry of individual officers and privates of whatever nation; and I have had great pleasure in making Sarah translate to many of my Italian acquaintance that beautiful passage relative to the gallant conduct and death of poor Bianchi, the Italian soldier.

I think, if possible, you have surpassed your other volumes; and as to the writing, your account of Badajoz is splendidly exciting; it makes me regret, bitterly regret, I did not, wounded as I was, remain with my regiment, and have either fallen gloriously or done something *worthy your pen!* And you may rely upon this, William, that if a war should again break out, and that you are alive, the feats of gallantry that will be achieved in the hopes of their being recorded by your pen, will surpass all that ever was done before; and in after ages I look to your *History* as a clear guide to statesmen; an incomparable military map for the general in forming his plans for campaigns, and a perfect example for their execution; and last though not least a glorious incitement to the army to do its duty as well as ours did in the Peninsular War.

There is a friend of mine here, an old General Macaulay of the East India Company's Service, a devilish clever old fellow who has *seen much* and *knows more*; he is delighted with what you say about the ministry of that day. He also highly admires the way in which you pass your criticisms on the Duke's conduct before and after the two sieges: he says nothing can do so much good as to see the bold, decided, but respectful manner in which you have pointed out the military faults of the Duke.

The General is an old friend of the Duke's, and corresponds often with him; he has told me many curious anecdotes of his Grace, all tending to show the acuteness of his genius and the vastness of his mind even when a very young officer.

    Yours affectionately,
      George Napier.

In 1832 Colonel Napier, always watchful for the fame of Sir John Moore, had published a pamphlet, *Observations illustrating Sir John Moore's Campaigns*, induced thereto by the remarks on that general which appeared in a book published at the time by Major Moyle Sherer, entitled *Life of the Duke of Wellington*.

The following letter refers to the circumstance.

MAJOR MOYLE SHERER TO COLONEL NAPIER.

Dear Sir,   Claverton Farm, Nov. 7. 1834.

I have considered well the frank offer you made me of inserting any reply of mine to your *Observations illustrating Sir John Moore's Campaigns* (pamphlet, 1832) in the Appendix of your *History*. As, however, I suffered those *Observations* to pass without notice at the time of their appearance, my proper course now is to wait until, if such should ever be the case, a second impression of my book should be called for.

Acquitted in my own heart of the slightest prejudice against the noble man whose fame is guarded with such vigilant jealousy by your powerful pen, I was not very careful of the opinion that might be formed by the public on the remarks (upon a passage of mine) in the pamphlet which you put forth. But I was never for a moment indifferent to what you yourself thought, and when I heard from your lips on Tuesday last that I was not considered by you as having written in a spirit hostile to the venerated memory of Moore, it certainly gave me very high contentment

I have perused your *Letter to Lord Beresford* with great interest; but as I have never seen his *Refutation*, I am not of course competent to judge of the *Letter* in all its parts; yet, from the whole, it is clear that his third lance is shivered.

Your treatment of Marshal Beresford in your *History* I have always thought hard. His difficulties and perplexities, and manifest inability to sustain them, demanded at your hands more allowance than you were willing to make. In controversy he has invited and therefore merited hard measure.

I cannot close this note without thanking you for the pleasure and privilege of being introduced to the repeat in which you carry forward your great and severe labours. It has been seldom allowed to an historian to be so aided and cheered at his own fireside. A sad seal of separation has for the most part been stamped upon the forehead of immortal authors.

As minds of the very loftiest order may take invaluable hints from those of a meaner capacity, let not my entreaty be lost upon you; go higher up the mountain than you have yet gone, and seating yourself in those silent and severe solitudes where around and above all is cold, clear, and serene,—suffer the mists of present time to roll disregarded beneath your feet The muse of History should be passionless, and then, indeed, the clangour of her trumpet becometh solemn as that of a commissioned angel.

Connect my present presumption with that which may have fallen from me without due respect on Tuesday last, and pardon them both. I think for myself in all things, and have sentiments upon many subjects which can hope for no sympathy but from those who share them. Therefore my path is somewhat lonely; but if your walk ever extends to Claverton, my farmhouse lodging will afford a chair for rest; and it will be an abiding comfort to me to know that if I meet you in my walks it need not ever be in future with a doubtful feeling.

Having entered the lists on every occasion against Sir John Moore's real or supposed enemies, he felt himself now called upon to defend him from his friends.

A biography of Sir John Moore by his brother had lately appeared, and Colonel Napier was so dissatisfied with its execution, that he undertook to notice the work in the *Edinburgh Review* of April, 1834. The article contains an admirable exposition of the manner in which a great man's biography should be written.

> We had often considered the mode in which such a man's life could be best written to bring into full relief its numerous excellences. The rules of good composition require that there should be a principal action of the piece, and we had endeavoured to decide whether it would be more judicious, and more just, to give the preference to his brilliant talents, or to that stern, that inflexible virtue, which was inherent in his lofty mind. Turning to the great models of antiquity, we saw the fiery breath of Tacitus animating his idol Agricola, admirable in speech, in camps a hero, in retirement a philosopher; how he made him frowning and dreadful in the front of battle, sedate on the judgment-seat, cautious within the snares of a court, calm and serene upon the

bed of death; in all things exciting our sympathy.

Yet we could not but fed that here the genius of the writer had overlaid the genius of the warrior; that it was Tacitus rather than Agricola we admired. Again, when we looked at the mild and philosophic Plutarch, selecting a few distinguishing traits of private character, mixing them lightly up with great actions, skimming off the results with a dexterous hand, and pouring them forth to his readers with the gracious benevolence of a benign old storyteller, we were pleased with the writer, but felt that neither would this method, so agreeable where other records failing a number of great men's actions were thrown together, serve for one life; because Plutarch has made but a collection of slight sketches, fit enough to excite noble thoughts, yet without one finished portrait by which the particular man might be known in the crowd.

It was in the natural, the simple, the powerful writings of Xenophon, we thought we had discovered the secret of representing a great man truly; and hence that, if any one should undertake to portray Moore's character such as he would be desirous it should appear, that is, such as it was upon all occasions, it would be necessary to resort to himself; that to write his life justly he must be made, like Xenophon, to speak for himself. And we knew that he had so spoken. We knew that ample materials were in existence, so ample, so complete, that the dullest of writers, honestly using them, could not fail to produce a work deeply interesting and instructive, treating of great events full of sense and honour.

CAPTAIN J. H. PRINGLE TO COLONEL WILLIAM NAPIER.

Sir, London, Oct. 2, 1835.
Feeling that the present hour is the proper period communicate to you the substance of this letter, I beg to call your attention to some observations you have made, in your *History of the Peninsular War*, upon my kinsman the late Earl of Chatham; the memory of which noble gentleman, to use the mildest terms that courtesy can invent, you have loaded with unmeasured censure. In a few hours, Sir, I shall follow all that remains of the Earl of Chatham to his grave; and though there are now but two remaining male descendants of his blood, I cannot see the vault closed upon his coffin without making an appeal to you;

and one which I make in the full persuasion that the delicate feelings of a gentleman will prompt you at the earliest opportunity to expunge from your work a passage so offensive to the friends and so insulting to the family of my departed kinsman, as the one alluded to in this letter.

Your *History*, Sir, is a work that may live with the language of our country; but I think. Sir, that reflection will suggest to you that the house of Chatham never has deserved to be and never should have been mentioned but with honour: and I presume, Sir, that you must be aware, had not my noble kinsman been suffering for some years under sickness and infirmity, you would have received an appeal from him in person far different from mine, and shaped in any form but that of a request Now, Sir, I have said my say, and have only to repeat my faith in your feelings as a gentleman, and to request an early notice of this communication, with which remark I remain, Sir, &c. &c

P.S.—The observations alluded to by me are in the 2nd vol. 355th page. *Hist. P.War.*

FROM COLONEL WILLIAM NAPIER TO CAPTAIN J. H. PRINGLE.

Sir,   Freshford, Oct 4. 1835.

Your letter of the 2nd has only just reached me, and in answer I must request you to reflect further on the subject of it. The passage which you refer to imputes military incapacity to the late Earl of Chatham, and nothing more; for the addition that it caused the title of Chatham to be scorned, is merely and literally the assertion of a fact, in reference to the newspapers and speeches of the day, and to hundreds of publications, ephemeral and permanent, all of which scoffed at his conduct of the Walcheren expedition.

Under these circumstances I cannot admit that the passage will bear the imputation of being insulting to the family of Lord Chatham. Military incapacity is a matter of opinion dependent upon facts; the expression of that opinion is no insult; and if the expedition caused the public to scoff at the leader of it, the mention of such a fact is certainly not an insult; and I must really and earnestly beg of you also to consider that the passage complained of has been six years before the public without the slightest notice being taken of it by Lord Chatham himself.

You say that he was for several years suffering under bad health;

but if I am not very much mistaken, his lordship was, at the time of publication, Governor of Gibraltar, and in person doing the duty of that situation. I cannot therefore admit your right as a relation of Lord Chatham to call upon me after such a length of time, when his lordship himself did not think such a proceeding called for at the time.

I will however in consideration of your appeal to my feelings go so far as to say, that if by mutual agreement and as a matter of courtesy, I can so shape my expression as to make it less painful without sacrificing the fact, I will willingly do so, as a proof that I have no personal motive whatever, save a love of truth.

Captain J. H.. Pringle to Colonel William Napier.

Sir,   London, Oct. 5, 1835.

I beg to acknowledge the receipt of your letter of the 4th instant, which reached me this morning. You request me, Sir, to reflect further on the subject of my last communication, and you remark that the passage to which I refer 'certainly imputes military incapacity to the late Earl of Chatham, but nothing more, for the addition, that it has caused the title of Chatham to be scorned, is merely and literally the assertion of a fact, in reference to the newspapers and the speeches of the day, and the hundred publications, ephemeral and permanent, all of which scoffed at the conduct of the Walcheren expedition;' and that you, Sir, cannot admit that the passage will bear the imputation of being insulting to the family of Lord Chatham.

With regard to the justice of your judgment or the expression of your opinion on the military capacity of the late Earl of Chatham, I have never presumed to offer an observation. With regard to the decisions in the newspapers and speeches of the day being a sufficient groundwork for the historian to build his censure and record his facts, whatever ideas will present themselves to my mind, I admit, Sir, that you are the most experienced judge; but. Sir, to say that the title of Chatham has been scorned, yet that such expression is not insulting to his family, does appear to me most strange.

You must allow me, Sir, calmly and with due consideration to differ from you; and as I presume not to remark in any way upon your opinion of the military incapacity of my kinsman, so, Sir, I must maintain that I am the most complete judge of what is due to the honour of my family; and I must observe that I have yet to learn what greater insult can be put upon a gentleman than to treat his title with scorn, excepting, Sir, that one should record that it was so treated; and further, Sir, Lord Chatham never shrank from any inquiry into his conduct, and never, from the King, parliament, or military authorities of Great Britain, did he receive any censure.

Subsequent to his return to England from the Walcheren expedition, he was intrusted with the government of a most important military possession—I mean Gibraltar; and, as the most honourable tribute to his memory, the King's carriage followed his mourners to the grave. These circumstances, Sir, tally ill with the supposition that in any way he has brought scorn upon his name. If the words '*be scorned*' were expunged, then I should feel that all just cause of complaint Would be immediately removed; and I do not doubts from your friendly expressions, that you will gladly consent to this.

COLONEL NAPIER TO CAPTAIN J. H. PRINGLE.

Sir,   Freshford, Oct. 6, 1835.

Your letter of yesterday's date reduces the subject of our correspondence to a very simple affair.

It is true that I do still hold my view, as to both the particulars touched upon in my former letter, to be the correct one; and under other circumstances I was prepared to maintain it I will not, however, dwell upon these points, because I understand your present letter to be entirely a reasonable appeal to my good feelings upon a subject that has given you pain. This appeal you have an undoubted title to make; and I reply that it is right I should respect your feelings when no principle is thereby sacrificed. It is sufficient, Sir, that the word 'scorned' gives you and your family pain to induce me to expunge it You are of course aware that nothing can be done before a new edition is published, but I believe that will be soon, and it shall appear without the obnoxious word.

CAPTAIN J. H. PRINGLE TO COLONEL NAPIER.

Sir,   London, Oct. 7, 1835.

I have received your letter of the 6th instant, and I beg leave to return you my sincere thanks for the fine and gentlemanlike manner in which you have relieved me from a most painful position.

GEORGE JONES, ESQ., R.A., TO COLONEL WILLIAM NAPIER.

My dear Napier,   Oct. 8, 1835.

I think you have done wisely and virtuously in the affair of Captain Pringle; and I feel for him and with him that the word 'scorned,' appearing in such a *History* as yours, would be humiliating to any family to which it might be applied. I cannot either acquit you of rashness in using the term, for scorn should only attend premeditated crime; consequently I think your intention of expunging the word to be both just and generous.

I think, my dear Napier, you know that I prize honour infinitely above life; but it is that honour which will bear no stain on itself, nor inflict any spot on another that is not provoked by delinquency which calls for the just reprobation of man, and is in opposition to the law of God. Firmness in the truth of these sentiments makes me hope that no chimerical notions will induce you ever to risk inflicting a twofold evil on any family. Too often your duty as an historian calls upon you to inflict wounds, but *when possible* let your pen be like the spear of Achilles.

Mr. Jones was through life one of Sir W. Napier's dearest friends, and in their high and noble feelings they were worthy of each other. Mr. Jones thus writes of his friend to the author of this biography:—

William Napier was one of the most vehement of men, and one of the most warm-hearted, so that an error on his part became an agony. I have seen him throw himself on the ground, bathed in tears, when he thought he had done an injury. A late instance: when he learned that he had inflicted a pang on the mother of Sir James Outram, his grief was extreme, and he did all he could to make atonement. He once told me that he had endeavoured to make his *History* as truthful as possible, yet he found that it was full of lies; but, he added, all history is so! Of course he meant errors—how can it be otherwise?

The correspondence with Mrs. Outram above referred to will be given in its proper place.

During this year, although closely engaged in the continuation of his *History*, Colonel Napier did not neglect the public duties of a good citizen, by endeavouring to promote with all his talent and energy those public measures which he believed would tend to improve the condition of his countrymen, as well as to promote the cause of humanity generally over the world. In July he was invited to take the chair at a public meeting of the Bath Auxiliary Society for the Extinction of Slavery and the Slave Trade.

COLONEL NAPIER TO LADY CAMPBELL.

Freshford. Nov. 1835.

The sight of your handwriting is always balm to me, and I know you are quite right—that O'Connell is not a great man; but I don't agree with you that he gets his money wrongfully or meanly; he has undertaken a great and excellent work, the freeing of his country from the most diabolical and horribly mean tyranny that ever was endured, and, as he is unable to do it by arms, he must do it by art. Hence many things he must submit to; many mean acts he must commit; because he has to deal with the meanest and basest of men.

You judge him hardly; he does not do the thing in the noblest way, but he does do it If he did not take money he would have been driven from the field long ago. If he fought he would have been killed long ago. He is a general; to be guarded and paid for the sake of his army and his cause. Don't run him down, or you run down the only chance the poor starving wretches have whose fate depends upon his success.

We have had our dinner here, seven hundred and fifty *eating persons* in one vast room; five hundred ladies, at least females, looking on from a gallery, and two thousand gaslights. Food excellent, waiting excellent, the order and propriety perfect The cheers ought to waken even the Lords. I was very well received,—better I think than the others; at least the cheering was longer and louder. I send you the *Bath Guardian* with my speech. Tell me if you like it.

Have you seen Picton's *Life*? I will answer it in my fifth volume. All the attacks on me are so false that I shall have nothing to do but print other people's (eyewitnesses of the facts) testimony; I have already collected a good many. Only think of the *Times* newspaper saying that Lord Wellington's letter to the author of the *Life* completely refutes my statement that he and Picton had quarrelled,—I having never made any statement of the kind, nor anything like it!

Shall I see you? Ah, well! next summer will come, and I *hope* the book will be finished; *at least I hope so*, and hope is warmed by wishes. I am better in health now than I have been for years. I know not if it is the dry weather, or a change from long suffering that is to be permanent, but I am better; and the manner in which I sway the political multitude of Bath is a helper also. It is a very grand feeling to make a thousand people shout and toss up their hands and appear like bedlamites. &c. &c.

The following letter to his wife was written towards the end of this year (1836).

London.

I am sitting by Bunbury's desire to Mr. Jones for an oil picture—a portrait. It is very like, and I like it better than any that has been done of me. It is a full-length; there is to be a bust of Lord Wellington and a map of Spain to mark my pursuits, and Jones wants my fine 43rd sword also, but I dislike all that, and I have insisted upon something of Napoleon being in. It is to be his bronze figure, and the silver eagle.

I have no pleasure in sitting for this picture, except to please Bunbury. I wish to finish my *History*, and have done with this world; but I am pursued now when I have no ambition by all sorts of honours. I have had deputations to ask me to stand for Westminster against Sir G. Murray, who is canvassing. I am told that myself and Mr. Ward of St. Alban's are the only persons in England that would be certain of being elected. I refused plumply; I told the proposers that I should sacrifice both my constituents and my children by accepting the offer. The reply was characteristic: 'Oh! his children are nothing; but his constituents,—that is a reason.'

Since I wrote to you I have been introduced to the King of Oude's Ambassador, a very good-humoured, gentlemanlike, and rather clever-looking man, and a great poet in his country. He told me his master had desired him to translate six works into Persian for him, and that my History was one of them. I of course gave him a copy, and he says he will make a private translation himself to give to the king.

Shortly after, Colonel Napier was attacked by an illness of a like nature to those from which he had so long suffered, but of peculiar severity and obstinacy. To restore his strength, which had been fearfully reduced, he was advised to try the warm baths of Barèges in the Pyrenees, and thither he went in June, 1837. He was accompanied by his wife and one daughter, the remainder of his family spending the period of his absence at Drumcondra near Dublin, the residence of Sir Guy Campbell.

All this time his literary labours continued unabated. While prosecuting his great work he still found time to write for the *London and Westminster Review* an article on the *Despatches of the Duke of Wellington*, undertaken at the request of the editor in order to prove that a radical magazine could appreciate the genius of the great soldier. Nor did he disdain lighter works of imagination, for in April he contributed to *Bentley's Magazine* a tale called *Griffone*, which is replete with beautiful fancies and imagery.

In March, 1838, his second surviving daughter was married to the Earl of Arran.

CHAPTER 13

Marshal Soult in England

In the summer of this year Marshal Soult visited this country as the representative of Louis Philippe at the coronation of Queen Victoria. An article in the *Quarterly Review*, which appeared at this time, drew from Colonel Napier the following letter which was published in the newspapers.

Freshford, June 24, 1838.

An elaborate article has just appeared in the *Quarterly Review*, professedly written to prove that the Duke of Wellington was not beaten at Toulouse, for which his Grace must be truly thankful. The real design of the reviewer is the base one of reviving national animosities by insulting and if possible causing others to insult a venerable warrior, who comes to offer the right hand of peace and good fellowship to his ancient adversaries.

To insult a man who comes as the guest of England!—to insult the veteran Soult, incontestably the most eminent from talents and great exploits of all the distinguished foreigners now assembled in London for the purpose of gracing the approaching coronation!—to insult an aged warrior, whose name is, in the mind of every British soldier who served in the Peninsula, as surely and closely associated with the recollection of hard-fought battles, as crashing bullets are with the recollection of artillery!—yes, to insult this man while he is the national guest, to create heartburnings, to revive ignoble prejudices, and perpetuate malice between two friendly people, is the object of the *Quarterly*.

Soult was the first *marshal* who attacked our army in the Peninsular war; Soult was the last man who resisted that army in that memorable contest; and that he was the most skilful, persevering and formidable enemy we encountered during the long struggle none can doubt His troops were often discomfited, and the glory of England shone the brighter therefrom; but he himself was never quelled in spirit, his proud head never bowed in despair; he had the will and he found the way to give blow for blow to the last

That he was a magnanimous enemy is evinced by the monument he ordered to be erected to the memory of Sir John Moore. That he was a generous enemy to his prisoners one of my own family can vouch from personal experience, and so can many other persons. That he was a sturdy foe in battle every British soldier who served against him will acknowledge: He comes now in his old age on a mission of peace and good-will to this country, which has ever honoured a brave and noble opponent—respecting most at the board him who struck hardest in the field

Marshal Soult has been the gallant enemy of England in the field. He is now her guest. How will he be treated? Surely in the way that will most honour him and his host,—treated as one of the bravest and ablest soldiers in Europe should be treated! Grey-haired and covered with honourable wounds he comes, nothing doubting that his greeting will be such as becomes the gallant high-blooded people of England to offer him. He knows, none better, how sternly and strongly they throng together in battle; he will now learn that they bear no malice after, or the national character is changed.

It is said, nay it is known, that the Duke of Wellington, with that proud delicacy which is more than life-blood to a thorough English gentleman, has delayed the publication of the eleventh volume of his *Despatches*, because while Soult is in the country he would not let a word, a sign escape him, calculated to wound his former opponent, or to recall past asperities. *He* means to honour the soldier guest of England.

Shall this noble sentiment or the malignant vulgarity of the *Quarterly Review* be the guide for Englishmen? It would be a national insult to express a doubt!

W. N.

Mon Cher Colonel, *Londres, Juin 29, 1838.*

Depuis mon anivée à Londres j'ai fait chercher partout de vos nouvelles, et tout à coup j'ai appris par l'article si remarquable que vous avez fait paraître dans le Morning Chronicle, en réponse au Quarterly Review, que vous étiez à la campagne loin de la capitale de l'Angleterre. Je ne soupçonnais pas l'existence de l'article du Quarterly Review auquel vous avez si dignement répondu. Si l'on m'en avait parlé auparavant, j'aurais dit que je ne m'abaissais jamais à faire attention aux turpitudes. Vous le savez mieux que personne, vous qui avez écrit avec tant de loyauté et en langage si noble une partie de ma vie militaire; aussi je n'ai point été surpris en voyant avec quelle chaleur vous avez pris ma défense.

J'éprouve un besoin de sentiment de vous en faire mes remercimens les plus sincères. Dans cette circonstance vous avez été l'interprète fidèle du public Anglais, qui par ses manifestations m'a prouvé hier, dans le cours de la mission que j'avais à remplir près de S. M. la Reine Victoria, qu'il ne partageait pas les passions haineuses des écrivains qui ont répandu la calomnie sur mon compte, et cherché à pervertir l'opinion à mon égard, dans l'espoir peut-être d'arrêter la marche des progrès sympatiqies qui rapprochent de plus en plus nos deux pays. Mais grace à vous mon cher Colonel, et grace aussi au public de Londres, j'en suis vengé aujourd'hui, et c'est dans l'effusion de la reconnaissance qui m'anime que j'en dépose avec bonheur l'expression dans votre sein.

Si par événement, ou par des raisons de santé, vous ne venez pas à Londres pendant que j'y serai, procurez-moi au moins le plaisir d'avoir de vos nouvelles, afin que je sache quelle est votre situation, et si bientôt vous mettrez la dernière main à votre si intéressant ouvrage sur la guerre de la Péninsule.

J'ai l'honneur de vous renouveler, mon cher Colonel, l'assurance de ma haute estime et celle des sentiments de considération toute particulière que je yous ai vouée.

Ml. Duc De Dalmatie.

TO HIS WIFE.

London, July, 1838.

I will give you a journal of events. The railroad coach is an actual lolling sofa; no shaking, less noise than a common carriage, no smell, and the first stage at the rate of sixty miles an hour, ten miles in ten minutes. I got to dinner in exact time. On Saturday I went to Mr. Leader, who was excellent in disposition; he will follow the matter up for me on Monday, or, if not then, the first opportunity. I found Trelawny with him, a very handsome dark Greek-looking fellow—indeed, quite a picture and dressed in Greek costume; that is, in a bedgown like mine, and a Greek nightcap. I liked him and he took to me. Leader wants me to go down to him at Putney.

After that I went with Richard and Henry to call upon Soult. He was shaking hands with Sir Edward Codrington when I came in, and when he saw me he came running to me, called me his '*enfant*,' and demanded an embrace *à la Française*. After being kissed on both cheeks I was delivered over to his staff for a moment The Marquis was glad to see me, but his son-in-law, the Marquis de Mornay, jumped into my arms, and old Hodez was delighted to offer me his homage. I immediately asked him for my papers; he had forgot them all! I blowed him up and told Soult, who blowed him up also. In fine, we were all excellent friends in a moment

There was however one *aide-de-camp*, a young, clever-looking man, who scowled upon me the whole time with as much ferocity as the devil himself could give out by looks. I don't know why. Soult would not believe I was sick, and was very anxious that I should try homoeopathy in Paris, and live with him. I told him I could not stir until the book was finished; and as Hodez had forgot the papers, I charged my bad health upon him, and so he got another blowing up.

Soult told me that he could not tell what day he could spare, but the first he could fix upon must be a Napier *tête-à-tête*, a *déjeûner* for all my relations and friends, '*parceque vous êtes tous mes enfans*.' He is very old and dried up, but looking more good-natured and less stern than before. Then came my miseries; all London, strangers and all, desire me to get them tickets for Soult's ball next Tuesday. —— sent a note to me this morning to settle that an invitation must be got for him.

To all I have answered '*No*! I don't know Marshal Soult well enough, and he has not yet asked *me* to his ball;' which is true, for I told him I did not wish it. Lady —— told Louisa as a positive fact three days ago that I had apartments in Soult's house and was employed constantly writing for him! Louisa's denial went for nothing. I have not yet seen Hopkins or Brotherton or any friend but Sutton Sharpe. This morning however I met

Macaulay, who was delighted to see me, and we talked together for three hours; he was very agreeable, but is grown fat and, I think, nervous. He says he will not go into the House of Commons again; I believe it but the world don't.

I believe it because I think his nerves are shaken and that his fat is disease. I saw Jones, who was as he always is. He approves of the letter about the statue. Soult went down to Woolwich and saw an artillery review. The Queen only is able to compete with him in popularity. There were four thousand soldiers at dinner in the open air after the review at Woolwich; they all spontaneously rose and gave him three cheers. He is enchanted with England and the English. Liverpool has invited him to a feast there on the 21st, after which he goes back, but he tells me his intention is to return *en bourgeois* to visit us.

The reviewers are still busy calumniating Soult It is now whispered about that he ordered his troops to give do quarter to the English at Toulouse, and that the proofs will be given in the 11th volume of the *Despatches* when he is gone. This is a lie; and the 11th volume is referred to merely to give credency to the falsehood now. There will be nothing of the kind in it, and, if there should be, how will Wellington look? He lets the Queen receive as ambassador, and he himself receives as guest and pays court to a man who ordered our soldiers to be butchered unfairly. Bah! it won't do. . . . I am getting ill again according to custom, and I expect to be obliged to go back before Soult's breakfast.

I went to the review this morning in Hyde Park. I saw Macdonald riding with a young man; I called to him, and he asked me if I was come to see the review. 'No, thanks to you and your d—d ministerial set, I can't You will only let generals beyond the line, and you won't make me a general after thirty- eight years' service and thirty battles!' I went on in this way for some time; at last Macdonald introduced his friend as Lord Howick. This did not change me as you may suppose, and Lord Howick seemed highly amused. Immediately after. Lord Fitzroy came galloping up to me, and I told him what had passed; he laughed and said that Lord Howick was angry at the brevet also; that it had just stopped short of all the officers who had distinguished themselves, but the Government said they were too poor.

I told Fitzroy that Lord Durham's four secretaries' salaries would pay the expense; this tickled his fancy, but he told me positively that the next brevet would take me in. Soon after, I saw Soult riding at the head of his staff. The mob cheered him and so did I; he saw me and shook hands; and his staff gathered round me, and carried me in beyond the legal bounds. Arthur Upton and others came to talk to me, and I was a lion, but the horses pranced and I could not get out of their way; whereupon Arthur Upton gave me in charge to one of the princesses' coachmen to take care of me, exactly as if I had been a child.

While I was laughing at this, all my great friends disappeared, and my honours ceased rather disgracefully, as I was discovered by the police and turned away to the ranks of the *canaille*; whereupon I walked away with great dignity, such as I suppose, Captain —— displayed when he was kicked at Detroit.

TO THE SAME.

London

Soult has invited me and my brother to breakfast on Saturday, and Naudet has made me a present of a nice little book of fables in verse, written by himself. I think it ought to be given to Pammy. Richard has heard from Sir John Herschel that George's reply approved of what was the exact thing to do. Herschel said that he looked forward to George's reply as decisive of the fate of the colony, and he was in raptures at it He explained the reasons, which proved to be exactly what I had thought before, judging only from the address and answer before me.

You have of course seen the shindy I kicked up in the House about Sir George Murray and the plans. The whole House were against him, and everybody treated the subject exactly as I told Hume he ought to treat it Leader has given notice of a further motion, a very galling one to Murray, for Thursday; and I have been all the morning concocting the plan of proceeding with him.

—— —— is secretly very angry with me because I would not ask Soult to invite him to his ball. I told him that I had not been invited myself, which is true. Whereupon he said 'Oh! of course then you could not do anything for others; but I thought as a matter of course that Soult would behave well to you; I naturally did not think that he would behave like an ungrateful brute!' 'Oh! he has behaved precisely as he should do to me; I don't like balls; and moreover the only acquaintance I have with Soult is asking and receiving from him many favours, which gives him a right to ask for an invitation to my ball, but does not give me a right to invite other people to his ball.'

There is nothing new stirring, but I am sorry to tell you that everybody says the Duke of Wellington is broken down and will soon go. Have you seen Soult's answer to the City about the Duke and the dinner? At the review the people insisted upon shaking hands with Soult, and when he got tired he ordered his staff to shake hands for him.

A few days later the Marshal invited Colonel Napier to accompany him on a visit to Liverpool, where he had been asked to a public dinner. Admiral Charles Napier was also of the party.

Conversations With Marshal Soult During a Journey to Liverpool.

"Grouchy," he said, "was not a traitor, he was unequal to his situation,—that is to say, he could not command more than a few thousand men. I calculated (said Soult) the value of the French generals by the number of men they were capable of commanding. I name nobody, but there were amongst them men who were worth ten thousand men, who were worth fifteen thousand, twenty thousand, thirty thousand, forty-five thousand, or even in case of necessity, sixty thousand. The art of commanding armies becomes more difficult as the numbers increase. It is very different to command eighty thousand, and to command a hundred thousand. Pass a hundred thousand, and the human mind is scarcely equal to the task.

"Napoleon committed a great error in giving so many men to Grouchy. 1st. That general was not equal to the command. 2nd. Ten thousand men would have been sufficient to impose on the Prussians. But the Emperor seemed at times to be changed; there were moments when his genius and activity seemed as powerful and as fresh as ever; at other moments he seemed apathetic. For example, he fought the battle of Waterloo without having himself examined the enemy's position. He trusted to General Haxo's report. In former days he would have examined and re-examined it in person.

"Ney was the evil genius of the campaign; he neglected his orders at Quatre Bras, and again at Waterloo; he attacked Wellington's position beyond La Haye Sainte contrary to orders, and too soon; but he is dead, he was unfortunate. I do not like to speak of his errors.

"The reserve cavalry of the guard was engaged without orders. There was no intermediate corps between the main body and Grouchy's corps. The latter had forty-three thousand, and the former was sixty thousand."

[*Note*,—Napoleon says Grouchy had thirty-three thousand, and himself sixty-nine thousand, and that there was a small intermediate corps. Napoleon's version agrees with the report of Colonel Grant, who directed the secret intelligence of Wellington's army. Soult appeared to me somewhat confused in his recollection on this point.]

"The wood of Soignies would have proved Wellington's destruction."

[*Note*.—I could not avoid disputing this point, and Soult certainly did not give any conclusive reasons in favour of it]

Generals of the Revolution,

Hoche: Soult knew him well. "I was with him" (he said) "when he died; he was poisoned by the Directory; I thought so at the time, I think so still, and for the following reasons: 1st He was so vehemently opposed to the council, that when he heard it was on the point of being overthrown he, though dying at the time, exclaimed 'I shall recover now.' The council knew of his enmity and that he was seeking means to overthrow their power. Here then was cause for the effect. It is true that Hoche was a libertine, and that he and Championnet, who was of the same stamp, had some short time before his illness been engaged in continual orgies of a sensual nature for a week; but those pleasures do not kill suddenly.

"Hoche was formed like Hercules, and his constitution was as strong as his body. His sickness was short, and when he died, a friend of mine, an eminent surgeon living in the town, was at my instance called in to assist at the autopsy of his body. The stomach was marked with livid spots, indicating, said my friend, the action of poison. There were five surgeons or physicians present, three of them ignorant commonplace officers of the army, the other two of eminence in private practice; the three first declared the spots were nothing, the two last insisted that they indicated poison. Numbers carried it, and the *procès verbal* only noticed the opinion of the majority. I believe he was poisoned. He was a man of great talent and considerable acquirements, perfectly understanding war on a great scale; and if we except his debauchery, he was a man of a great and noble disposition, generous, humane, and patriotic. He was a little jealous of Napoleon's reputation, but he was not equal to the Emperor; at least, I think so."

Napoleon: "Marshal! Was not Napoleon the greatest genius of all the men France produced?"

"Ah! bah! Yes! there was no comparison."

"Was he not a good and kind man also?"

Here Soult raised his head with great eagerness, and exclaimed in an emphatic manner, "*Napoléon n'a jamais perdu personne de son propre mouvement,—jamais, jamais, jamais! It was necessary, when once you were known to him, to commit faults, nay even crimes, over and over again, twenty, thirty times, before he could bring himself even to punish. Non, jamais; l'Empereur n'a jamais perdu personne de son propre mouvement.* But wicked people sometimes deceived him. He had many false friends; many persons opposed him who owed everything to him; his relations were not true to him; his brothers were his worst enemies. They were continually opposing and thwarting his plans, and they and his sisters always spoke and acted as if they had been legitimate monarchs, reigning by hereditary right, and fixed in the affections of their faithful subjects.

"One day Caroline, the wife of Murat, vehemently addressed Napoleon in this view; she was very clever and very eloquent, and her reproaches were strong, and continued with all the warmth and variety of which a woman is capable, for more than half an hour. The Emperor listened calmly until she was exhausted, and then asked her in a gentle tone, and with an affectionate manner, if it was from their father, the late king, that she had gathered those doctrines. Louis, Joseph, Lucien, Jerome, all behaved ill to him; they even, especially Joseph and Jérome, entertained thoughts of opposing him by force."

Joseph: "At the Battle of Ocaña Joseph was at my side, and so meek, so quiet, I could have put him in my pocket. After the battle was gained and that we had supped, instead of conversing upon the action and the war, he altered into a vehement allocution against the Emperor, and told me that he had written to him a letter which he would show me. It was menacing, urgent, insolent; and his discourse went to sounding me upon exciting the army to resist Napoleon. I rose from my chair and addressed him thus: 'Sire, you speak and act in such a manner that you give me the right to treat you without reserve or ceremony; and first, it is fortunate for you that I choose to speak to you as a private person, and not as a Marshal of France, What! you imagine that the *éclat* of such a victory as Ocaña renders you so dear to the French soldiers, that they will support your absurd and rash notions? Suppose it were true: have you gained the affections also of the rest of the French army in Spain? Are you sure of those who remain to France out of Spain? You are woefully deceived: beware of how you try what you are thinking of, even with the army here under your orders; it will be dangerous. And then you menace your brother! You! you menace Napoleon! Oh! Sire! you shock me.' (Here Soult put himself into the attitude, and used the same gestures as he had to Joseph, and they were very striking; he covered his eyes with one of his hands, and with the other seemed to repulse some horrid image, and his colour and looks were very animated.)

"'Who are you? what are you? who has made you? Your brother; and you menace him! Burn your letter, Sire, and think again.' 'What! (exclaimed the king) am I not his elder brother, the chief of his family?' 'Yes, Sire, but you speak not as a brother, you speak and would act as a king; and you are not the chief of monarchs. Burn your letter.' He did so, and wrote another; it was better, it was decent, but it was not what it ought to have been. Napoleon loved his family, he was ready to do everything for them, but he always insisted upon their accepting power from him as a gift from their superior, and expected them to be grateful. If they were humble, there were no bounds to his generosity and affection, but they never were; they always took as their right what was his gift, crowns amongst the rest"

Marceau: "Marceau was clever and good, and of great promise, but he had little experience before he fell."

Moreau: "No great things."

Augereau: Ditto.

Junot: Ditto.

Gouvion St. Cyr: "A clever man and a good officer, but deficient in enterprise and vigour."

Macdonald: "Too regular, too methodical; an excellent man, but not a great general."

Ney: "No extent of capacity: but he was unfortunate; he is dead."

Victor: "An old woman, quite incapable."

Jourdan: "Not capable of leading large armies."

Masséna: "Excellent in great danger; negligent and of no goodness out of danger. Knew war well."

Marmont: "Understands the theory of war perfectly. History will tell what he did with his knowledge." (This was accompanied with a sardonic smile.)

Regnier: "An excellent officer." (I denied this, and gave Soult the history of his operations at Sabugal.) Soult replied that he was considered to be a great officer in France; but if what I said could not be controverted as to fact, he was not a great officer, his reputation was unmerited. (The facts were correctly stated, but Regnier was certainly disaffected to Napoleon at the time; his unskilful conduct might have been intentional.)

Desaix: "Clever, indefatigable, always improving his mind, full of information about his profession, a great soldier, a noble character in all points of view; perhaps not amongst the greatest of generals by nature, but likely to become so by study and practice, when he was killed."

Kleber: "Knew him perfectly; colossal in body, colossal in mind. He was the god of war; Mars in human shape. He knew more than Hoche, more than Desaix; he was a greater general, but he was idle, indolent, he would not work."

Berthier and Clarke: "Old women—*Catins*. The Emperor knew them and their talents; they were fit for tools, machines, good for writing down his orders and making arrangements according to rule; he employed them for nothing else. Bah! they were very poor. I could do their work as well or better than they could, but the Emperor was too wise to employ a man of my character at a desk; he knew I could control and tame wild men, and he employed me to do so."

OPERATIONS IN THE PENINSULA.

"My army was at one time very sickly in Andalusia from fever and ague. It was in the heats of summer; the money and clothing which should have come from France did not arrive, and I was obliged to take clothing from the country for the soldiers. I had considered the subject, and ordered the clothing to be made entirely of the brown thick Spanish cloth which the peasants make their clothes of; and at the same time I ordered that neither officer nor soldier should wear, or even possess, a linen jacket or linen trowsers. The whole army were ready to mutiny; they cried out as if they were on the rack; they bullied, complained, screamed out enough to split their own heads; I did not listen to them. The thick clothing was put on, and in a month after there was neither fever nor ague. I know how to rule an army."

"You had some difficult jobs?"

"Yes, at Oporto especially; that was the most critical period of my military life. You, Monsieur Napier, have written that well, but you do not know all. There were a great many more traitors than D'Argenton, and Lafitte, and Donadieu, General Quesnel was a traitor; he was placed on the river by me to report any movement, any attempt of Wellington to pass, and he did report to me, but not till Wellington had thrown two thousand men into the seminary on my side, and all was lost General Mermet was a traitor. In fine, all the generals of the 8th. corps which had been in Junot's army were traitors; they wished to force me to capitulate in order to justify their own Convention of Cintra, which was a shameful one; *mais, ma foi!* they did not know their man.

"Yet, what a situation I was in! knowing all the traitors, and yet obliged to trust them with the most important commands, and to trust them as if I admired, trusted, and loved them. Loison was the greatest traitor of the whole, and I was obliged to send him to Amarante, the key-point of my retreat. I gave him orders to defend it to the last extremity. He had two divisions, and trusting to his sense of shame, I marched, but he abandoned the place and the bridge to a few peasants and militia. I heard of it when I was with my army retreating from Oporto, and in a narrow defile; and, as misfortunes never come single, at that moment my horse threw me on to some loose stones and hurt me so severely that I could scarcely bear even to be moved in a recumbent posture. The rain was terrible. The army was excited by the traitors and fearful. I said to myself 'What is to be done? I will not yield, but what is to be done? Soult, you must show what you have in you.'

"And I did so I collected all the baggage, and burning my own first, destroyed all, and gave the sumpter animals to carry the sick men and the ammunition. I destroyed artillery also, and then led the way up the narrow path over the mountains. The energy which a consciousness that I was right and capable of meeting the crisis, gave me, restored me to strength. I scarcely felt my hurt until I reached Carvahal. There I met the traitor Loison. He did not expect to see me, but I dissembled, and applauding him for having his division in hand, destroyed his artillery, and placed him in the advanced guard. We moved to Ruivaens; the people had all fled; however, one peasant was taken. 'Do you know the Ponte Nova?' 'Yes.' 'Is it destroyed?' 'No, but they are destroying it.' 'Who?' 'The peasants and militia.' ' Are there any regular soldiers?' 'No' 'That will do. Dulong (he was a great soldier), take twenty-five men,' &c" (Then Soult told the story as I have told it in my *History*, 2nd vol.)

"I thus escaped, but I was never in such danger and never showed more vigour of character. After this I co-operated with Ney, until the Emperor gave me the command of his and Mortier's corps with orders to move into the valley of the Tagus. Mortier obeyed my orders with alacrity and good will. Ney absolutely refused to march. I told him at last that I gave him positive orders, and would in the name of the Emperor order his troops to march; if he stopped them it would be at his peril: I should march myself; and if the operations failed he must answer it to the Emperor. This decided him, but he acted unwillingly, and we lost a great chance."

"Marshal, why did you not pass troops over the Tagos at Almaraz,[1] and seize Mirabete and Meza di Ibor before the allies got possession of those positions?"

"I ordered Ney to do so, but he did not."

"But that was later than I mean; you should have done it before Lord Wellington crossed the Tagus; what hindered you?"

"I could not; my troops in consequence of Ney's delay were marching by divisions, and were not numerous enough in advance to detach men across the Tagus, and I did not know the real state of affairs, nor where Victor was."

Joseph: "He was a vain weak man, not of a bad disposition, but meddling. He hated me and endeavoured to ruin me with his brother, but he failed. The Emperor, when he sent me to take the command after the Battle of Vittoria, gave me power to arrest Joseph if I found it necessary to prevent him from doing mischief. He was at Bayonne, and might have stopped with the army if he had pleased and been content to remain quiet; but that was not in his nature, and pretending to be afraid of me, he quitted the army secretly and went into the interior. I did not prevent him; I was glad to get rid of him."

1. After Talavera.

Soult's Ministry after the Three Days of July.

"I was made minister of war. The crisis was awful; the monarchs of Europe were ready to pounce upon France, and she had no means of defending herself ready. I first ascertained that her resources were equal to her safety if drawn forth, and immediately set diligently to work to bring them out, and meanwhile I boasted that they were so drawn out However, the Opposition in the Chambers asked many questions difficult to answer, and made great clamour. 'France,' they said, 'was menaced, and there was really nothing to support her; there was no army, and what was to be done to save her?' They were right in fact, but not in wisdom. I became excited; I could not answer them; but the crisis of my reputation as a statesman was come; it was the *pendant* to the military crisis at Oporto.

"I mounted the tribune, and with a calm confident manner asked them what they wanted? what they feared? 'Let all Europe,' I said. 'come against us; we are prepared. I have already five hundred thousand soldiers organized, armed, and clothed. What do you want more?' This was pure invention, but it succeeded. The Opposition stared, but were silenced; my supporters cried out 'A wonder!' and the monarchs of Europe were deceived and trembled, for they said that a man of my reputation and character would never commit himself in the face of France by assertions which could be so soon disproved if unfounded; and in a certain degree they were right, for I would not have said so if I had not before taken means to fulfil my boast, and been sure of success. I gained time by the declaration, and before its falseness could be discovered I realized the vaunt.

"Now Monsieur Napier, I tell you for your instruction that I am following the same plan now. I have boasted that France and England are excellent friends, and they will be so. France and England would have *bon parti* against Russia. I have considered the subject and come to that conclusion; we shall see. Meanwhile, I believe that I have said more on that subject than I can well prove. It will however have its effect on the Russians, and I trust a good one. A great crisis is brewing. The declaration of independence by Mehemet Ali will probably bring it to a head."

[*Note.*—The meaning of this I could not well make out, for there were in the carriage Admiral Napier and the interpreter Manby. If he meant to quiz me, he did not succeed, as I never attempt to divine the tricks and designs of politicians, which depend upon cunning or falsehood for success, independent of the nature of things. I gave no weight to his discourse, and only repeat it now because he said it. I however think it probable that Soult, who was the principal cause under Napoleon of gaining the Battle of Austerlitz, does not like the preponderance of Russia—that he has a personal feeling as well as a political feeling against her, and is really willing to check her. Still, why did he tell me? Did he imagine I was going to publish his conversation? if so, he was speaking foolishly for his professed object; and if he thought I would keep the matter secret, why tell it me at all?]

Chapter 14

Lady Hester Stanhope

COLONEL NAPIER TO LADY HESTER STANHOPE.

Dear, dear Lady Hester,   Freshford, March, 1839.
I wish from the bottom of my worn-out heart that I could once more see and talk to you, the friend of my youth, when I was full of hope and cared little for the frowns and pains of the world. I too could tell of many things that would be strange, strange as belonging to that England which you and I once thought we knew, a proud and generous nation. It is not so now. Gold is an Englishman's god—gold and ostentation of gold; for this they live and die. Generous sentiments are scarce, magnanimous actions scarcer. Napoleon was cast to perish on a rock under brutal insult; you, the niece of Mr. Pitt, are subject to the persecutions of Lord Palmerston.
Yet we are on the eve of great and terrible changes—I fear not for the better, because gold is still the moving power. But there are powerful passions excited. The working men of England, driven by long oppression to violence, are arming universally, and as they have bad leaders blood will flow without utility. You demand a history of me and mine. It is painful to relate, to me painful.
My old mother died long ago, she was eighty-four. Two of my sisters live, one unmarried; the other has been for years married to Sir Henry Bunbury. His first wife was my wife's sister, his second my own sister; he has four sons by his first marriage, none by his second. My eldest brother Charles has been twice married; he has two very young children, girls. It was he you heard from in the Ionian Isles, where he has by his talent,

activity, and good government, and by the great public works he carried on, left a good name that will not be suffered to die away by the Greeks. His numerous wounds, seven and very severe, have not impaired his activity or whitened his head

This month he takes the command of the northern district of England; it is a fearful command at this time, but he is modelled after your men of the *far East*. His book would entertain you much; it is full of painful interest also, for he writes well and acts well; nevertheless, I believe that it is not his book that you have heard of, but my book; of that hereafter. My second brother George has lost his arm; like a brave man he lost it on the top of the breach at Ciudad Rodrigo in 1812.

He married a Scotch lady, and has three sons and two daughters, the youngest about eighteen; his wife died after the birth of the last child, and he, with a steadiness of sorrow and principle not common, devoted himself to the education of his children. He and Charles are generals and Knights of the Bath, and George is Governor of the Cape of Good Hope. Two of his sons are with him. His policy is to protect the Caffres from the gold-seeking rapacity of the English and Dutch settlers. He has a hard task, but his soul is honest and his heart true and firm as steel, and he has withal a good head.

Richard did not pursue the law. He married a widow, a very clever and beautiful person; his pursuits and his wife's are alike; they have both great talent, great learning, have high and warm imaginations, delighting in poetry and noble writing, and he is by nature a poet himself; yet their particular pursuit, strange to say, is political economy, and I think it is not unlikely be may someday publish on that subject.

Henry, the youngest of us, is a post captain of the navy. He married his cousin. He was rich, happy, and his wife good, affectionate, and one of the most lovely of God's creatures. Alas! she died suddenly about two years ago, leaving him with four children, a broken-hearted miserable man. He devotes himself to his children; their mother was but thirty when she died. He has written a *History of Florence*, but it is not yet published.

What now shall I tell you? My own tale? I like it not, yet I will tell it to you, and truly; but first permit me to join to my brothers' history that of our cousin Charles, 'Black Charles' they call him. He is not a brother, but I claim a place for him because he is a great man, though a strange one. A life of daring and enterprise in our navy as a captain created him a name which attracted the Portuguese Emperor Don Pedro's attention. Black Charles was offered the command of his fleet; he accepted it, and in one action, against the most overpowering advantages on the enemy's side, decided the fate of Portugal. He is now going out in command of the *Powerful*, 74, to the Levant, and you may perhaps hear of him again; a rough black diamond, but a sure hand in war.

Thus you see that we have not let our name sink in the world, and yet we have been honest, and what has been a sore stumbling block in our way, independent; always opposed to the powers that be, and yet able to force our way to notice though not to riches. I would willingly dwell longer upon his exploits, but they must have reached you even on Mount Lebanon. Now again for myself. Why did you ask me? I must rip up old sorrows and probe wounds that have never healed. I am a broken man; broken, though not bent,—the world has failed to do that; and I can still make my enemies beware of treading on me. But I will tell you all truly; I have played my part and continue to do so in the world.

It has been in my power to raise a civil war, and it may be so again, but I abhor such a proceeding. Yet I am both courted and feared, without reason; for sorrow and pain, continual sorrow and continual pain, have almost if not quite unsettled my reason; at least I am conscious that I had another mind once. I do not think I was married when you left England; my wife was the daughter of General Fox, and niece of Charles Fox. She lives to take care of me when I want care, and she is a person capable of great things; fortitude and judgment, and energy mental and bodily, she possesses in an extraordinary degree. When I married I was sanguine and confident that I could go far in the world.

Secretly I thought God had given me the head and heart of a warrior, and my body was them of iron. Well! I won my spurs honourably. Three decorations and two steps of rank I gained in the field of battle—Wellington gave them to me; and I am a Companion of the Bath,—no great thing; but I could have safely rested my claim upon the testimony of my soldiers. Ah! those soldiers, the few that are now living, are poor and miserable, for England despises her former defenders.

My regiment, the 43rd, was one of the three regiments that formed the Light Division, always in contact with the enemy; those three regiments were avowedly the best that England ever had under arms; this is no idle boast; war was better known, the art more advanced, under Napoleon than in any age of the world before, and the French veterans, those victors of a thousand battles, never could stand an instant before my gallant men. Curse on the liars, the cowardly calumniators, who have told you that Irishmen are cowards! they are equal to the English in bravery, superior to them in hardihood of sufferance and in devotion to their officers in the hour of trouble; and they are superior to the Scotch in everything, and yet there are very good soldiers among the Scotch; I like them not, but I will not belie them. Was not mine a fair start for distinction?

Peace came, and I am a colonel still! I had no money; and younger officers, some of them bad, were ready to purchase over my head; others were thrust without money over me. I had gained the brevet rank, but I could not gain the regimental rank; the first was to be got on the field, and I got it; the second was to be got by money or favour, and I had neither, so I went on half-pay, and tried to still the gnawing of the worm by occupation of a different kind. I painted in oils, and was elected a member of the Royal Academy. I modelled in clay, and Chantrey, the first of modern sculptors, proposed and got me elected as a sculptor in the Savants' Club, called the Athenæum.

But the worm gnawed still. I wrote reviews, and I was successful; my first was to defend Sir John Moore. To you I need not speak of that great and heroic man, nor of his wrongs. Southey wrote a *History of the Peninsular War*; it was smooth and clear in style, but nerveless as the author's mind, except where his political rancour broke out to destroy Sir John Moore's reputation and to calumniate the French army.

For the latter I cared only as it was disgraceful to any country to malign a brave though vanquished enemy; but for the first I felt as you would have felt. I was going to write a commentary, but I soon saw that to beat the false history I must write a true one; the task was formidable, but I have done it; I have beaten the calumniator and established my *History* in the world's good opinion. I have done more; without yielding one jot of England's glory I have by just and fair admissions of the prowess of France obtained the public assent of the French generals to the truth of my relation; I have thus solved the difficult problem of recording the defeats of a vain, proud, fiery, and learned people, without losing their approbation; I have obtained their testimony to the glory of the British arms, and thus placed the latter upon a rock.

Many enemies in England I have created by this; I should have doubted the value of my work if it had not been so. Truth must be offensive to many. But I have also many supporters, because truth is powerful; and though my *History* wants one volume still to complete it, the first five volumes have been already translated into French, into Spanish in South America, and reprinted in North America; it is also translated, or being translated, into Italian and German; and I have been elected a member of the Academy of Military Sciences in Sweden.

My English enemies are virulent and numerous, but I have met them all, and hitherto triumphed, and I will meet them as long as I can speak, write, or pull a trigger. I like not republicanism; I desire to see men of all classes as God designed them to be, free in thought and unabashed in mien, but virtuous and obedient to the just institutions of society. I do not spurn at kings and nobles, but I like not that they should spurn at me. Would that we had a great man I Changes are at hand; the masses are in movement, but there is none to guide them, and they will clash for mischief. I am well pleased to do some good, but what can a man do who dare not encounter a shower of rain lest he should lose the use of his limbs for six months?

Where is Wellington at this crisis? you will say. Alas! he is only great by the head, not by the heart, and that is only half the greatness required. He is of commanding intellect, commanding courage, commanding honesty; but he despises the people, has too many prejudices opposed to their feelings, and they hate and fear him. He cannot work with them because he will not work for them. The rest are nothing. I have, as I have told you, great influence with the people, but it will not last; I can do evil, but not much good; I know well what to oppose, but not what to assist, for there is much evil stirring on all sides, and my worn-out body will not allow me to engage in anything requiring exertion of limb. Do not mistake me or imagine that I mistake myself. I do not suppose myself a great man, but I have certain talents and knowledge which have given me a power in the present conjuncture that might be turned to good or bad if I had bodily strength, and I have it not.

Well! enough of this matter. I strive to put off the tale of my sorrows as long as possible. I have had ten children; seven still live, six girls and a boy, but he is deaf and dumb. Three girls died—the first young, very young; it was written; I wept for her, and so it ended. The next died at five years old. She also was deaf and dumb, and that caused her death. I will not tell you how; I cannot; but twelve years ago she died, and I have not been as I should be since. Should I tell you how more than human her beauty was, and how exquisite her intelligence, notwithstanding her deafness, you would not believe me, but though I am at times insane I am not doting.

Six years after her death my eldest child was torn from me by consumption; she was fair and joyous as the day, tall and beautiful, strong of heart, and dear of head; yet a few short months sufficed to send her at the age of eighteen from the admiration of the world to her grave. I would tell you more about my dear children, only I cannot. I have seven still. . . . . . .

Lord Chatham, *the* Lord Chatham's Correspondence is being published by his grand-nephews. Captain Pringle of the Guards and his brother. Two volumes are out, but as jet there is not much interest attached to them, so I suppose the valuable papers are reserved for the other volumes; when I say interest, I mean proportionably to the man's fame, for there is curious reading in them. Pringle I have had some dealings with, and I think, judging from his correspondence (for I have not seen him), there is a vein of the good Pitt blood running through him.

Your men of the East are, I believe, superior individually to the men of the West, but each man stalks through the world like a lion; they do not herd together, nor work together, and so like lions they live and die and are forgotten. The horse is a better animal than the lion. You love the brute creation, and so do I, and I love you that you do love them. The brute is of the same essence as man,—an essence however more restricted, confined by the inferior organisation of their bodies, therefore more condensed and honest What are we of the human species? angels or devils, or a compound of both? There must be I think two governing principles, God and demon, and we partake of both. This doctrine is Eastern, and I think it more reasonable than any other.

I wonder whether you would like my *History*? It is no whining affair. There is much in it that you would not like, but nothing I think that would lessen your friendship for me; you might be angry, but you would not cease to be my friend; and surely there is nothing that you could say or do, however passionate at the moment, that would ever hinder me from being your friend, esteeming and reverencing you as much as I do now and ever have done. The time I passed with you at Mr. Pitt's home at Putney, and the few short hasty periods in which I had the happiness of being received by you after his death (for me at least they were few, too few, and too short), are among the moments of my past life remembered most vividly and fondly.

This letter tubs on. How shall I send it to you? I think I shall be able to transmit it officially, for I have still some friends at court who can separate the politician from the man. Do not start at my consideration for your pocket; yon live in the East, but I live in England where money is the great god; I hate their god, but I must worship sometimes lest my impiety should be observed and punished. Yes, I think of money. Is not poverty demised, wronged, insulted? and shall I not tremble lest my good, my innocent, my beautiful girls, and my helpless boy, should be consigned to such horrors?

My life is not worth a year's purchase; who shall protect them after my death if they be poor? For their sakes I live; for their sakes I gather money by my labours; and for them I keep it as well as my nature will allow me. Ah! you are a living example of the generosity of Englishmen towards helpless women. . . . .

Your nephew, Lord Mahon, is an author, and in his book sneered at mine, went out of his way to say that it was the best French history of the war; this he thought smart, but I replied I had always thought the doing justice to a vanquished enemy was thoroughly English until my Lord Mahon assured me it was wholly French. Was I right? I tell you this that you may know me; I am not changed in feeling or sentiment, but you should know what I have said or done that might offend you, or I should be going to you under false colours.

Much do I like your Beni Omaya, if they be truly heroic; but beauty and courage are only gifts, not virtues. Are they compassionate? Are they just? Are they mild or cruel to their vanquished foes? Are they gentle or harsh to women and children? Do they admit women to have rights? Do they govern them by their affections or by their fears? Do they make chattels of their persons, and kill them in their tyrannical jealousy? If they do they are not heroes for me. Women are gentle, and should be free human beings, and the peculiar guardians of children, the most helpless and the most beautiful of God's creation; there can be no virtue, no generosity, where they are oppressed. I know nothing so degrading to England as the treatment of women and children.

There is a factory system grown up in England since you left it, the most horrible that the imagination can conceive. Factories they are called, but they are in reality *hells*, where hundreds of children are killed yearly in protracted torture, that the cotton lords may extract gold from their bones, and marrow, and blood. Patience! patience! There will be a day of reckoning for all things; it approaches. Farewell, dear Lady Hester. God knows whether I shall ever hear from you or write to you again, but never believe that I have not a true and deep feeling for you.

W. Napier.

During this year, (1840), Colonel Napier was employed in putting the finishing touches to his *History*, and in the autumn the sixth and last volume was published. A French translation of the work by Count Mathieu Dumas, the celebrated French military chronicler, appeared shortly after; and a critical review of the *Peninsular War*, written by M. Jules Maurel, contains the following panegyric on the *History*:—

> With regard to the book itself, it would be but meagre praise to say that it is superior to everything that has been written on the same subject; it is simply a *chef-d'œuvre* of style, criticism, and narrative. It combines the most opposite kinds of merit; the most exact spirit of investigation, even to the most minute detail; large and elevated general views; infinite suppleness in controversial analysis; admirable power in the recital; the most sincere devotion for the glory of his country, combined with the most noble impartiality and the most chivalrous homage to her enemies. There are certain passages, such as the storming of

Badajoz and the Battle of Albuera, that will stand comparison with the finest pages of the historians of antiquity.

The following letters are here given, because, although not written until 1850, they refer directly to the veracity and impartiality of Colonel Napier's *History*; and because they contain an enumeration by himself of the principal French sources from which he derived his information with respect to the numbers and proceedings of the French armies; because, also, when a writer of M. Thiers' celebrity could write in the *Times*, that "the opinion which all men well informed on the subject have for a long time entertained of General Napier's work absolves me from the necessity of answering the attack which he makes on my book in the *Times* of ———" it is incumbent on the biographer to show that this contemptuous mode of dismissing the subject by M. Thiers was simply adopted by him to cover his retreat, when he had literally no defence against the statements of the English historian. And any person who should first read this correspondence, and afterwards M. Thiers' *History*, will only find the latter confirm at every step the grave doubts with respect to the author's credibility and candour in relating military operations, which must inevitably be excited by the letters given here below:—

To the Editor of the *Times*.

Sir,   Feb. 11, 1865.

M. Thiers, in his ninth volume of the *Consulate and Empire*, claims for himself the secret of the Peninsular war, having found it in certain papers to which he only has had access. That may be; but I ask if he is incapable of drawing false conclusions from secret materials, to support perverse assertions. To answer with good warranty let us examine how he deals with authentic documents, not confined to his secret repertory.

Thiers.—'30,000 brisk resolute Frenchmen' opposed 15,000 English at Roliça.

Reply.—The Duke of Wellington judged the French to be 6000. Laborde, then commander, denied that he had 6000, thus tacitly admitting he had 5000 or more.

Thiers.—The English had 400 cavalry.

Reply.—The English Adjutant-General's return gives 250.

Thiers.—Laborde wounded or killed 1200 or 1500 English at Roliça.

Reply.—The Adjutant-General's return gives 479 killed, wounded, and missing.

Thiers,—Junot collected 9000 some hundred men to fight at Vimiera.

Reply.—The French order of battle found on the field gave 14,000.

Thiers.—22,000 French embarked under the Convention.

Reply.—The official French embarkation return gives nearly 26,000 men and officers.

Thiers.—Only 26,000 men followed Junot into Portugal.

Reply.—The Imperial muster-rolls give 29,584 effective in Portugal, 23rd of May, 1808.

Thiers.—The French army of Spain, under Napoleon, was 250,000 strong, of which 200,000 only were assembled there the end of October, 1808.

Reply.—The Imperial muster-rolls show, on the 25th of October, more than 319,000 effective; on the 15th of November, more than 335,000 effective.

Thiers.—Sir John Moore's troops arrived at Salamanca exhausted by their long march and by privations.

Reply.—Moore's despatches say his troops were in better case than when they started from Lisbon; they suffered no privations, and their excellent condition up to Sahagun was notorious.

Thiers.—Moore advanced to Sahagun with 29,000 English troops and about 10,000 Spaniards.

Reply.—The Adjutant-General's return of the 19th of December gives 23,583 of all arms; Moore had no Spaniards, and Romana, who did not act in concert, had only 6000.

M. Thiers cannot deny the authenticity of my numbers, seeing they were taken from the original Imperial muster-rolls in the French war-office—not the yellow, but the green rolls; the officers of that office will appreciate the distinction of colours. M. Thiers cannot plead ignorance. All the documents are printed in my *History*, and he had access to the French originals.

So much for quantities. Let us examine him as to qualities.

Thiers.—Wellington has a 'contracted intellect;' Sir John Moore was 'irresolute in council;' the English soldier is 'beaten almost to death for the least fault;' 'he is little practised to march;' 'is inanimate, feeble, when forced to move to attack;' 'he has no vivacity, no audacity, no enthusiasm, no hardihood, no enterprise;' 'to beat him he must be forced to. take the initiative in attack.'

Reply.—Wellington's intellect, measured by M. Thiers' imagination, must appear very contracted. Yet it is strange, that with a few troops, having no enterprise, no hardihood, and fearing to be beaten to death for trifling offences, he should have maintained the war for five years successfully in Spain, against enormous numbers of soldiers and officers, the best and most skilful in the world according to M. Thiers, and finally should carry the war into France! Strange that troops unable to march should have moved in face of an enemy from Lisbon to the Agueda, from the Agueda to Madrid, from the Douro to the Adour, from the Adour to the Upper Garonne!

Stranger still, if to beat those troops it was only necessary to make them attack, that they should have attacked successfully at Roliça, where the French hill was five times more steep, rugged, and difficult than the English hill at Vimiera which the French unsuccessfully attacked; that they forced the passage of the Douro, and drove Soult out of Portugal; that they attacked Masséna at Redinha, at Casal Nova, at Fonte d'Aronce, at Sabugal, and drove him also out of Portugal; that they attacked and retook the key of the position at Albuera, which the Spaniards had lost; that they attacked and defeated Marmont at Salamanca—the King at Vittoria, driving him out of Spain; that in the second fight near Pampeluna they attacked Soult's mountain position, and drove him out of Spain; that they forced the intrenched mountain position at Vera, and his fortified mountain lines on the Nivelle, covering Bayonne; that they passed the Gave de Pau in face of the French army, and defeated that army at Orthes; that they passed the Garonne, and forced the intrenched camp at Toulouse, thus terminating the war! M. Thiers is not happy in his military reveries. Brilliant phrases, condemnatory of revolutions which he could neither arrest nor guide, are more consonant to his genius.

Thiers.—Sir John Moore was 'irresolute in council'—'he yielded to the imperious admonitions of M. Frere'—'papers published by his family prove this.'

Reply.—The papers published by Moore's family prove that he repelled M. Frere's arrogance with calm dignity; did not follow his plans, and changed his own because fresh events called for change. His irresolution in council exists in M. Thiers' imagination—nowhere else. Those who knew Sir John Moore will laugh at such a silly assertion. M. Thiers has not been so remarkable for political resolution himself as to give him a right to censure others. In what council known to him did Sir John Moore display irresolution? Those who have read that general's journals know of several held with Mr. Pitt, Lord Melville, and others, wherein his ability, unhesitating vigour, and readiness to undertake what he advised, the sure sign of resolution, were signally manifested. But M. Thiers speaks afterwards of his 'prudent firmness.' Prudent firmness combined with irresolution! Indomitable resolution, both in council and in the field, was Moore's characteristic—Napoleon himself was not more decided

One more example of unfounded censure. 'Sir John Moore said his advance served the Spanish cause, by drawing Napoleon to the north, and giving the south time to rally.' This M. Thiers calls a 'presumptuous manner of presenting the affair to cover a disastrous campaign.'

The best reply to that presumptuous remark is M. Thiers' *History*, wherein he distinctly shows that Napoleon did turn all his forces from the south to the north in consequence of Moore's advance to Sahagun—an advance which that general had previously declared he would make to produce such a result .Verily M. Thiers must amend his manner of treating known accessible facts, if he would have his authority accepted for the unknown and inaccessible.

William Napier.

A MONSIEUR W. JEFFS, À LONDRES.

Monsieur, Paris, le 26 Février. 1850.
Je vous remercie de la communication que vous avez bien voulu me faire. Il est impossible d'écrire l'histoire sans rencontrer des critiques, mais l'opinion que tous les hommes bien informés au sujet de la guerre de la Péninsule ont depuis longtemps conçue de l'ouvrage du Major-Général Napier me permet de ne pas m'arrêter aux attaques qu'il dirige contre mon livre dans le Times du 11 de ce mois. Partout où j'ai

eu à indiquer un nombre de troupes, j'ai toujours consulté, avant de me prononcer, la correspondance des gouvernements et celles des généraux placés à la tête de ces troupes; c'est à l'aide de ces documents contradictoires que j'ai établi les nombres que j'ai donnés. M. Napier n'a eu pour écrire son Histoire aucun document Français officiel, et ce n'est qu'à des officiers du Maréchal Soult qu'il a dû peut-être quelques communications sans caractère authentique.

Quant aux jugements que j'ai émis sur le Duc de Wellington et sur l'armée Anglaise, ils sont exprimés dans les termes qui marquent tout mon estime et pour les troupes Anglaises et pour le grand homme de guerre qui les a commandés dans la Péninsule. Je me suis préscrit la loi d'être toujours impartial et juste; aussi de tous les écrivains de l'Europe je crois être celui qui a parlé des armées étrangères et de leurs capitaines avec la plus grande impartialité, et qui leur a rendu le plus largement justice. Je n'ai donc rien à retirer, ni des chiffres qui se trouvent dans le neuvième volume de mon 'Histoire du Consulat et de l'Empire,' ni des appréciations auxquelles je me suis livré à l'égard des généraux et de leurs troupes; je tiendrais en conscience mon temps pour mal employé si je consacrais une partie à réfuter les assertions de certains critiques ignorants ou intéressés.

Agréez, monsieur, l'assurance de ma considération très distinguée.
A. Thiers.

To the Editor of the Times.

Sir, March 27, 1850.

Previous to noticing M. Thiers' observations which Mr. Jeffs has published in your journal of this day, I dare offer the following consolation to the last-named gentleman:—A person wishing to purchase M. Thiers' ninth volume was told by his bookseller that my criticism in the *Times* had caused every copy to be sold off—he had not one remaining! I heartily wish it had done as much for my own work. My conscience not being burdened therefore with sin or sorrow on account of Mr. Jeffs, I can with greater ease of mind meet M. Thiers, whose work, sparkling with paste brilliants, wants that real jewel—truth. M. Thiers has himself confirmed my judgment of his infidelity to facts, and his unsound peremptory assertions.

What does the analysis of his letter to Mr. Jeffs present in answer to the long list of errors I charged him with?

1. That he has always consulted for his numbers the govern-

ment correspondence and that of the generals commanding the armies.

2. That I had no official French document to guide me, but had *perhaps* some communications, non-authentic, from some of Marshal Soult's officers.

3. That his judgments on the Duke of Wellington and the British troops were expressed in terms marking his esteem for both.

It is then a mark of esteem for a general and his troops to deny to the first an enlarged capacity, and to the last nearly all the essential qualities of soldiers.

Perhaps it is a proof also of his esteem for French generals and soldiers to tell them by implication, as M. Thiers has certainly done, that they were overcome, not once and accidentally, but during series of years, by a military chief of a contracted mind, and an army incapable of doing anything better than standing still to be shot; for to that conclusion M. Thiers' History inevitably leads.

But I, an English historian, having seen what French generals and soldiers can do in the field, tell M. Thiers, the French historian, who has not I believe ever served, that his country's generals and soldiers are most formidable men to deal with in the field; and that the general and soldiers who face them must be fitted to encounter all that genius and the sternest hardihood can effect in war.

M. Thiers speaks of French governments' and French generals' correspondence, as conclusive in support of his statement of numbers. They could not be conclusive as to the English numbers, which he has misrepresented as much as he has the French numbers.

The question is however not what M. Thiers consulted, but what he has published. And there I am forced again to say that he must amend his treatment of known accessible facts, if he would have his authority accepted for the unknown and inaccessible.

He says I had no official documents—meaning, of course, the correspondence he has consulted—to guide me; nay, that I had only some unauthentic communications from some of Marshal Soult's officers. But if I show him that I also have seen most of his governments' and generals' correspondence; and that my communications were with Marshal Soult direct, not with his officers; he will perhaps allow some weight to my authority. Any person looking at my *History* will find all my obligations to French generals and officers acknowledged. But my business here is to show how M. Thiers, while thinking to dispose of me as lightly as he does of facts, entirely confirms my judgment of his reckless dogmatism, when he says I had no official French documents.

1. I had direct communications from Marshal Soult, who, when Minister of War, sent me through General Pelet, with whom I also had personal communication, an immense mass of official correspondence upon most of the great operations in the Peninsula.

2. I had the correspondence of King Joseph with the French marshals and generals, and with the Emperor, during the greatest part of the war. This correspondence, ciphered and deciphered, was captured at Vittoria, and was lent to me by the Duke of Wellington.

3. I had a direct correspondence with Marshal Jourdan.

4. I had personal acquaintance with, and received information from, officers high on the staff of Marshal Ney and Marshal Masséna; and I had copies of the official journals of military operations kept by the chief of Marshal Victor's staff and General Dupont's staff, and several others, as may be seen in my *History*.

From all these authentic documents I also was enabled to establish the numbers I have given. I was also enabled to compare them with the information obtained in the field by the Duke of Wellington. But I did not rely, as M. Thiers seems to have done, upon an estimate obtained from a comparison of contradictory documents—'*documens contradictoires*'—these are his words. I went directly to the fountain-head; I got admission to the French '*Bureau de la Guerre*.' I worked there for many weeks with General Pelet, who was then engaged in seeking authority for his really sound and truly excellent *History of the Emperor's German campaign of 1809*—a work I recommend to M. Thiers, as having no false brilliants, but yet of inestimable worth.

Well, then, from the Emperor Napoleon's muster-rolls, made every fifteen days by Marshal Berthier—not those bound in yellow, as I have before said, but those bound in green for his peculiar information—I extracted most carefully the numbers of the French armies throughout the war, and I have published them in my *History*. Comparing them with the Duke of Wellington's field estimates, and with statements of the generals commanding corps found in Joseph's portfolios, and with the official journals of operations, and with the Emperor's plans of operations transmitted to the King, in which he details the numbers even to a squad of a few men—for I found a correction even of such a small matter in his own handwriting on one of these memoirs;—comparing, I say, all documents together, I found the accuracy of the muster-rolls confirmed, as indeed they were sure to be, for what general dared to make a false return of numbers to the Emperor?

If, then, the correspondence of Napoleon, of Wellington, of Soult, Jourdan, and King Joseph be official authentic French documents, I was in as good a position as M. Thiers to arrive at accuracy; and I repeat my censures upon his inaccuracy, leaving the world to judge.

M. Thiers says his time would be ill employed if he devoted a part of it to refute the assertions of ignorant or interested critics. I entirely agree with him; it would be much better to employ it in writing his own *History* in a manner to avoid the just censures of honest and well-informed critics.

W. Napier.

CHAPTER 15

Remarks on the *History of the Peninsular War*

The merit of the *History of the Peninsular War* is best proved by the fact of its steady growth in popularity and fame; for seldom has a book been commenced with less immediate promise of circulation and favour. Even after the appearance of the first volume had proved the incontestable ability of the writer, the book had to fight its way to public favour against the prejudices which its peculiar political opinions created. The spirit of the work was directly offensive to the opinions of those times.

It affected[1] Englishmen, because it assailed the still dominant policy of Toryism, and conceded infinitely more credit to Napoleon, to his system, and to the French army, than the still rabid anti-Gallic feelings of the country could pardon. It offended Spaniards, for it brushed away the brag of the nation, and reduced the enthusiasm and efforts of the patriot armies to dimensions more consistent with fact. Frenchmen it might possibly conciliate, for it recorded their military merits with a chivalrous appreciation to which they were wholly unused in English writers; but to no other sympathies did it seem addressed.

These opinions brought down on the author a perfect storm of obloquy. Among other imputations, he, the grandson of a duke and the great-great-grandson of a king, found himself charged with a malignant hostility to aristocratic birth,—an attack which he quietly repelled by observing that he was at least

---
1. *Times*, Feb. 14, 1860.

as nobly connected as the people he was accused of decrying. But, however the author might be infected with political heresy, his characteristic dedication of the work to the Duke, and the genuine sentiments with which its every page was underlaid, soon proved that its real and sole object was to erect a fitting monument of British glory achieved by British arms; and as the development of the History showed it gradually and triumphantly attained, the angry clamours of the Strangfords, the Beresfords, and the Percevals were left to die unheeded away.

Against the current of popular and political prejudice, the work forced its way by its intrinsic fascinations to the summit of public favour; and though the ground had been occupied by favourite and attractive writers, the supremacy of Napier's *History* soon became incontestable. The truth is, besides the genuine nationality of its object and its tone, there was a dignity in the treatment, and a living verity in the descriptions, which led the mind unresistingly captive. Never before had such scenes been portrayed with such wonderful colouring. As event after event was unfolded in the panorama, not only the divisions and the brigades, but the very regiments and regimental officers of the Peninsular army, became familiarized to the public eye. Marches, combats, and battles came out upon the canvas with the fidelity of photographs; while the touches by which the effect was produced bespoke, not the ingenuities of historic art, but the involuntary suggestions of actual memory.

The shrillness of Craufurd's scream at Busaco, as he ordered the Light Division to charge, was probably ringing in the author's ears as he wrote; and the whole scene upon the Coa, with the little drummer-boy beating the charge, the French officer, 'in a splendid uniform,' leaping on the bridge, and the surgeon tending the wounded in the midst of the fire, must have risen before his eyes as he drew it. For the sake of painting like this, for the sake of an eloquence unknown before, and devoted unreservedly to the recompense of British valour, people readily forgave the pre-possessions or deficiencies of the work. If its spirit was haughty, it was also so national and so public that the very haughtiness was becoming; if its style trenched upon bombast, such loftiness of language did but correspond with the grandeur and heroism of the deeds described; and when the magnificence of its diction culminated into sublimity in the stories of Albuera and Badajoz, every reader felt that the theme and treatment were consistent with each other.

By the completion of this work Colonel Napier's fame as an author was completely established. The style was universally admitted to be as nearly perfect, regard being had to the nature of the subject, as any writing could be.

> There is certainly no great quality in which it is deficient; it has ease, animation, brevity, correctness, and vigour, and these, taken together, in a greater degree than any other historical writer of English, except Raleigh and Hallam.[2]

Its historic accuracy as to facts was only established the more firmly by the inevitable attacks of men who, having been actors in the scenes described, found the parts they had played unnoticed, or thought them undervalued.

The only important criticism which has survived to the present time is that, owing to the author's partiality for Napoleon, he both laid out of sight the detestable criminality of his first aggression on Spain; and, still more, that he undervalued the patriotic efforts of the Spaniards, and dealt out very harsh judgement upon them. This opinion found so many supporters that Colonel Napier's biographer will here endeavour to show by a few extracts that these charges have no sound foundation.

But before proceeding to do so it may be well to ask if the supporters of those charges were not themselves in the position of jurymen who come to try a cause with a strong prejudice in favour of one of the parties to the suit; and whether, while condemning the historian for unfair bias in favour of the French and against the Spaniards, their own judgement was exempt from strong national anti-Gallic prejudices, and unwarped by the romantic interest with which the general rising of the Spanish nation and the holiness of their cause invested the efforts of the patriots.

First, as to the charge that the author glossed over the criminality of Napoleon's aggression. In the very first chapter of his work are found the following paragraphs.

> Hence the craving of his (Napoleon's) military and political system, the dangerous vicinity of a Bourbon dynasty, and still more, the temptation offered by a miraculous folly outrunning

---
2. John Stirling, in *Athensaeum*.

even his desires, urged him to a deed which well accepted would have proved beneficial to the people, but enforced contrary to their wishes was unhallowed by justice or benevolence. In an evil hour for his own greatness and the happiness of others he commenced the fatal project. Founded in violence, attended with fraud, it spread desolation through the Peninsula, was calamitous to France, destructive to himself; and the conflict between his hardy veterans and the vindictive race he insulted was of unmitigated ferocity; for the Spaniards defended their just cause with proverbial hereditary cruelty, while the French struck a terrible balance of barbarous actions. (Vol. 1.)

A cause manifestly unjust is a heavy weight upon the operations of a general; it reconciles men to desertion, sanctifies want of zeal, furnishes pretexts for cowardice, renders hardships more irksome, dangers more obnoxious,, glory less satisfactory to the mind of the soldier. The invasion of Spain, whatever its real origin, was an act of violence repugnant to the feelings of mankind. The French were burdened with a sense of its iniquity, the British exhilarated by a contrary sentiment. (Vol. 1.)

Read also the concluding words of the second chapter.

With a strange accent he (Joseph) called from the midst of foreign bands upon a fierce and haughty race to accept a constitution which they did not understand, his hope of success resting on the strength of his brother's arms, his claims on the consent of an imbecile monarch and the weakness of a few pusillanimous nobles, in contempt of the rights of millions now arming to oppose him. This was the unhallowed part of the enterprise; this it was that rendered his offered constitution odious, covered it with a leprous skin, and drove the noble-minded far from the pollution of its touch!

But a dislike to the war prevailed in the higher ranks of the French army; the injustice of it was too glaring.(Vol. 1.)

His invasion of Spain was at first viewed with anxiety, rather than with the hope of arresting it; but when the full extent of the injustice became manifest, the public mind was vehemently excited; and when the Spanish people rose against the man feared by all, the admiration which energy and courage exacts even from the base and timid, became enthusiastic in a nation conscious of the same qualities.(Vol. 1.)

Again:—

> This constancy, although rendered nugatory by the vices and follies of the Juntas and leading men, hallowed the people's efforts, and the *flagitious violence of the invasion almost justified their ferocity*. (Vol. 2.)

That it cost the writer a struggle to write thus of the man he almost idolized is beyond a doubt, but it would be difficult to express reprobation more distinctly or in stronger language; and having thus delivered his verdict on the act of wicked aggression which produced the war, he proceeded to describe the struggle itself irrespectively of its origin, proclaiming however, in the second extract above given, that the arm of the invader must be weighted throughout its whole duration by a sense of the iniquity of his cause, while that of his opponent would be nerved by a contrary sentiment; and it is manifestly unreasonable and unjust to blame the author for not returning again and again during his narrative of the war to the consideration of its origin which he had dismissed.

Turning now to the charge that the author undervalued the patriotic efforts of the Spaniards, and showed a strong bias against them, the following extracts, out of many others of a similar tendency, are taken from the *History*.

> There is not upon the face of the earth a people so attractive [as the Spaniards] in the friendly intercourse of society. Their majestic language, fine persons, and becoming dress, their lively imaginations, the inexpressible beauty of their women, and the air of romance which they throw over every action and infuse into every feeling, all combine to delude the senses and to impose upon the judgement. As companions they are incomparably the most agreeable of mankind, but danger and disappointment attend the man who, confiding in their promises and energy, ventures upon a difficult enterprise.[3] (Vol, 1.)

> The genius of the Spanish people is notoriously ardent, subtle, and vigorous. (1.)

In another place the author speaks of:

> . . . . . . that susceptibility to grand sentiments which distinguishes the Spanish peasants. Although little remarkable for

---
3. These are taken from the first edition, which called forth the criticisms.

hardihood in the field, their Moorish blood is attested by their fortitude; men and women alike, they endure calamity with a singular and unostentatious courage. In this they are truly admirable. (3.)

In bearing such privations (hunger, &c.) the Peninsular race is unrivalled. (4.)

The Spaniards, with whom the sentiment of honour is very strong, when not stifled by the violence of their passions. (5.)

So much for general attributes.

In extenuation of their shortcomings:—

Constituted as modern states are, with systems ill adapted to nourish intense feelings of patriotism, *it would have been miraculous if real grandeur had been displayed by a nation which for two centuries had been debased by civil and religious despotism.* The Spanish character in relation to public affairs is marked by inordinate pride and arrogance. Dilatory, improvident, singly and in mass, they cherish an absurd confidence that everything suggested by their heated imaginations is practicable; they see no difficulties, and the obstacles encountered are attributed to treachery; hence the sudden murder of so many virtuous men in this commotion. Kind and warm in his attachments, savage in his enmity, the Spaniard is patient under privations, firm in bodily suffering, prone to sudden anger, vindictive, remembering insult longer than injury, bloody and cruel in revenge. With a natural perception of what is noble, his promise is lofty, but, as his passions always overrule his reason, his performance is mean.

When all patriotism is lost among the upper classes, it may still be found among the lower; in the Peninsula it was not found, but started into life with a fervour and energy that ennobled even the wild and savage form in which it appeared; nor was it the less admirable that it burst forth attended by many evils; the good feeling displayed was the people's own; their cruelty, folly, and perverseness were the effects of a long course of misgovernment. (1.)

Under such a system the peasantry could not be rendered energetic soldiers, nor were they active supporters of the cause; yet with a wonderful constancy they endured for it fatigue, sickness, nakedness, and famine; displaying in all their actions and in all their sentiments a distinct and powerful national character. This constancy, although rendered nugatory by the vices and follies of the Juntas and leading men, hallowed the people's efforts, and the flagitious violence of the invasion almost justified their ferocity. (2.)

With reference to the demeanour of the Spaniards during the struggle: —

In Catalonia, the Somatenes were bold and active in battle, the population of the towns firm, and some of the Juntas apparently disinterested. The praise merited and bestowed upon the people of Zaragoza is just, yet Gerona more justly claims the admiration of mankind.(1.)

At Gerona—

They fought bravely, they endured unheard-of sufferings with constancy; and their refusal to accept the armistice offered by Augereau is as noble and affecting an instance of virtue as any that History has recorded. (3.)

At Badajoz—

The soldiers fought with surprising ardour, but the entire want of arrangement on the part of the generals, unworthy to command the brave men under them, ruined all. (3.)

At Albuera—

The Spaniards had been feeding on horseflesh, and were so attenuated by continual fatigue and misery, that, while enduring such heavy privations, it was a great effort of resolution and honourable to them that they fought at all. (3.)

It must not be supposed that, because the guerrilla system was in itself unequal to the deliverance of the country, and was necessarily accompanied by great evils, that as an auxiliary it was altogether useless. (4.)

The calm resignation with which these terrible sufferings were borne was a distinctive mark of the national character; not many begged, none complained; there was no violence, no reproaches, very few thefts. But with this patient endurance of calamity, the Madrilenos discovered a deep and unaffected gratitude for kindness received at the hands of the British officers. (5.)

The Madrilenos have been stigmatised as a savage and faithless people; the British army found them patient, gentle, generous, and loyal. (5.)

The Spaniards, who cared so little for their own officers, with that noble instinct which never abandons the poor people of any country, acknowledged real greatness without reference to nation. (6.)

Hear in conclusion the author's own defence, published in the 3rd volume:—

I have been charged with incompetence to understand, and most unjustly with a desire to underrate, the Spanish resistance; but it is the province of History to record foolish as well as glorious deeds, that posterity may profit from all; and neither will I mislead those who read my work, nor sacrifice the reputation of my country's arms to shallow declamation on the unconquerable spirit of independence. To expose the errors is not to undervalue the fortitude of a noble people. In their constancy, in the unexampled patience with which they bore. the ills inflicted alike by a ruthless enemy and by their own sordid Governments, the Spaniards were truly noble; but shall I say that they were victorious in their battles or faithful in their compacts; that they treated their prisoners with humanity; that their Juntas were honest or wise, their generals skilful, their soldiers firm?

I speak but the bare truth when I assert that they were incapable of defending their own cause! Every action, every correspondence, every proceeding of the six years that the war lasted, rises up in support of this fact; and to assume that an insurrection so conducted did or could possibly baffle the prodigious power of Napoleon, is an illusion. Spain baffle him! Her efforts were amongst the very smallest causes of his failure. Portugal has far greater claims to that glory. Spain furnished the opportunity; but it was England, Austria, Russia, or rather fortune, that struck down that wonderful man. The English, more powerful, more rich, more profuse, perhaps more brave, than the ancient Romans,—the English, with a fleet, for grandeur and real force, never matched; with a general equal to any emergency,—fought as if for their own existence.

The Austrians brought 400,000 good troops to arrest the conqueror's progress; the snows of Russia destroyed 300,000 of his best soldiers; and finally, when he had lost half a million of veterans, not one of whom died on Spanish ground, Europe in one vast combination could only tear the Peninsula from him by tearing France along with it What weakness then, what incredible delusion, to point to Spain, with all her follies and her never-ending defeats, as a proof that a people fighting for independence must be victorious!

Let us now turn to the Duke of Wellington, and ask what were his opinions as to the aid he derived from Spanish co-operation. Here follow a few of them.

Extracts from Lord Wellington's Correspondence, 1809:

I come now to another topic, which is one of serious consideration—that is, the frequent, I ought to say constant and shameful misbehaviour of the Spanish troops before the enemy; we in England never hear of their defeats and flights. In the Battle of Talavera, in which the Spanish army with very trifling exceptions was not engaged, whole corps threw away their arms and ran off in *my presence*, when they were neither attacked nor threatened with an attack, but frightened I believe by their own fire.

I have found, upon inquiry and from experience, the instances of the misbehaviour of the Spanish troops to be so numerous, and those of their good behaviour to be so few, that I must conclude they are troops by no means to be depended upon.

The Spanish cavalry are, I believe, nearly entirely without discipline; they are in general well clothed, armed, and accoutred, and remarkably well mounted; but I never heard anybody pretend that in any one instance they have behaved as soldiers ought to do in presence of an enemy. It is said that sometimes the infantry behave well, though I acknowledge I have never seen them behave otherwise than ill.

Nothing can be worse than the officers of the Spanish army; and it is extraordinary that when a nation has devoted itself to war, as this nation has by the measures it has adopted in the last two years, so little progress has been made in any one branch of the military profession by any individual.

I cannot say they do anything as it ought to be done, with the exception of running away and assembling again in a state of nature.

The Spaniards have neither numbers, efficiency, discipline, bravery, nor arrangement to carry on the contest.

1810.—

The character of the Spaniards has been the same throughout the war; they have never been equal to the adoption of any solid plan, or to the execution of any system of steady resistance to the enemy by which their situation might be gradually improved.

The Spanish nation will not sit down soberly and work to produce an effect at a future period. Their courage, and even their activity, is of a passive nature; it must be forced upon them by the necessity of their circumstances, and is never a matter of choice or foresight.

There is neither subordination nor discipline in the army either amongst officers or soldiers; and it is not even attempted (as, indeed, it would be vain to attempt) to establish either. It has, in my opinion, been the cause of the dastardly conduct we have so frequently witnessed in Spanish troops, and they have become odious to the country. The peaceable inhabitants, much as they detest and suffer from the French, almost wish for the establishment of Joseph's government, to be protected from outrages of their own troops.

I am afraid the Spaniards will bring us all to shame yet It is scandalous, that in the third year of the war, and having been more than a year in a state of tranquillity, and having sustained no loss of importance since the Battle of Ocaña, they should now be depending for the safety of Cadiz—the seat of their government—upon having one or two, more or less, British regiments; and that, after having been shut in for ten months, they have not prepared the works necessary for their defence, notwithstanding the repeated remonstrances of General Graham and the British officers on the danger of omitting them. The Cortes appear to suffer under the national disease in as great a degree as the other authorities,—that is, *boasting of the strength and power of the Spanish nation till they are seriously convinced they are in no danger, and then sitting down quietly and indulg-*

ing in the national indolence.

The above extracts might be multiplied, but enough has been said to prove that if any bias hostile to Spaniards existed in the mind of Colonel Napier it was shared with at least equal force by the Duke of Wellington. But the truth is, no such bias existed; and there is not to be found in the History one statement in disparagement of the Spaniards which is not borne out by irrefragable facts. By furnishing the opportunity to England, Spain did certainly contribute to the overthrow of Napoleon, but it was in the same sense only as the boy who blows the bellows contributes to the magnificent anthem which peals from the organ.

In many instances the author has been remarkably lenient, as, for example, in his observation above quoted in apology for the dastardly behaviour of the Spanish troops, both officers and men, at Albuera, which so nearly lost the battle. Also let the moderate remarks in the History on the behaviour of the Spanish troops at Talavera be contrasted with the Duke's strong expressions in the above extracts.

Again: with respect to the barbarities committed by the Spaniards, the reader is referred to the opening of chapter 3, vol. 1, for an account of the murders and massacres which took place at Cadiz, Seville, Carthagena, Grenada, Valencia, Badajoz, Talavera, and Corunna, &c., at which last-named place the able and honest Governor Filanghieri was tossed aloft and transfixed in his fall on the bayonets of the wild beasts who formed its garrison, and left to die. "Oh! mere misdirected energy," say the apologists, "and the certain deplorable result of centuries of political and priestly oppression."

Be it so: but this misdirected energy is not a fit subject for historic laudation; and a nation, prone from ignorance and ferocity to such excesses, as the Spaniards were universally, would be pronounced *primâ facie* by any student of history as utterly incompetent, without many years of discipline, which should elevate them from the condition of moral infants to the standard of men, to organize and sustain such a struggle as was required to make head against such a power as France.

As regards the governing bodies of the nation, with few exceptions, no words are too strong to characterize their arrogance, folly, cowardice, treachery, and ingratitude to their deliverers, the British army and its great commander. As instances of the last vice may be cited their shameful conduct with reference to the British hospitals at

Fuenterabia and at Santander. At the latter place the authorities, resolute to drive the hospitals from their town, suddenly, and under the false pretext of a contagious fever, placed all the British hospitals, with their officers and attendants, in quarantine.

This was in January, 1813.

> Thirty thousand men had been wounded since June in the service of Spain, and the return was to make those wounded men close prisoners, and drive their general to the necessity of fixing his hospitals in England.

In chapter 6, book 22, and chapters 4 and 5, book 23, will be found ample confirmation of these remarks.

It will there be seen that, when preparing to enter France, the Duke was provoked to tell the Council of Regency that he had been most unworthily treated, even as a gentleman, by the Spanish Government; that he was compelled to tender his resignation as *generalissimo* of their armies in consequence of their repudiation of engagements entered into with him by their predecessors; that his resignation was actually accepted, although a new Cortes afterwards requested him to keep his command, and decided that the Regency was to be bound by its predecessor's acts; that when he invaded France he did so in greater dread of the enemy at his back than of the foe in his front; and that, even while encamped on French territory, he was induced by the menacing action of the Spanish authorities to warn the English ministry against the possible contingency of a war with Spain, and to propose seizing St. Sebastian as a security for the safe withdrawal of the British troops to England.

One of the ablest reviews of Napier's *History*[4] contains the following passages:—

> Now, it really seems a little unreasonable that men of skill and authority, overflowing with Jomini, and science, and literature, with Hannibal, and Frederick, and so forth, at their fingers' ends, should very violently condemn the unfortunate Spaniards because they had not knowledge and discipline by instinct.

> And again: when the historian narrates, with the horror of a chivalrous soldier, the cruelties committed by the Spaniards on the French, why does he represent the cruelties of the French as mere pardonable retaliations for these?

---

4. In the *Athenaeum*, republished in Stirling's *Essays and Tales*.

For the first of these strictures there is not the smallest particle of foundation to be discovered in any line of the *History*. The extracts which are above given from it sufficiently prove that the author, while stating the fact of the absence of military knowledge and discipline, explained that it was impossible the Spaniards should have had those qualities at the commencement of the war. After it had continued three years, however, and it was apparent that Spain, torn by factions, continued as helpless as at the beginning, and that neither shame for her deficiencies nor any desire to amend them was visible; it would have been to abdicate the functions of an historian if the author had failed to mark with deserved reprobation the indolence and arrogant self-confidence out of which her incapacity arose.

With reference to the second stricture, let the author speak for himself in his reply to a similar charge urged by the *Quarterly Review*.

> The critic accuses me of an unnatural bias, and an inclination to do injustice to the Spaniards, because I have not made the report of some outrages, committed by Soult's cavalry, the ground of a false and infamous charge against the whole French army and French nation. Those outrages which I did notice, and which he admits himself were vigorously repressed, were committed by troops in a country where all the inhabitants were in arms, where no soldier could straggle without meeting death by torture and mutilation, and, finally, where the army lived from day to day on what they could take in the country. I shall now put this sort of logic to a severe test, and leave the Reviewer's patriots to settle the matter as they can. That is, I shall give from Lord Wellington's despatches through a series of years, extracts touching the conduct of British officers and soldiers in this same Peninsula, where they were dealt with, not as enemies, not mutilated, tortured, assassinated, but well provided and kindly treated.

> Here follow twelve extracts, extending over three years, from the Duke's despatches, from which the two sentences following are alone quoted:—

> *June*, 1809. [To Lord Castlereagh.] There is not an outrage of any description which has not been committed on a people who have uniformly received us as friends, by soldiers who never yet for one moment suffered the slightest want or the smallest privation.

May, 1812. [To Lord Liverpool.] The outrages committed by the British soldiers have been so enormous, and they have produced an effect on the minds of the people of the country so injurious to the cause, and likely to be so injurious to the army itself, that I request your Lordship's early attention to the subject.

Colonel Napier then goes on to say—

Having thus displayed the conduct of the British army, as described by its own general, through a series of years; and having also, from the same authority, shown the humane treatment English officers and soldiers, when they happened to be made prisoners, experienced from the French, I demand of any man with a particle of honour, truth, or conscience in his composition, whether these outrages, perpetrated by British troops upon a friendly people, can be suppressed, and the outrages of French soldiers against implacable enemies enlarged upon with justice?—whether it is right and decent to impute relentless ferocity, atrocious villainy, to the whole French army, and stigmatise the whole French nation for the excesses of some bad soldiers, prating at the same time of the virtue of England and the excellent conduct of her troops; and this too in the face of the Duke of Wellington's testimony to the kindness with which they treated our men, and in the face also of his express declaration (letter to Lord Wellesley, 26th January, 1811) that the majority of the French soldiers were sober, *well disposed, amenable to order; and in some degree educated?* But what intolerable injustice it would be to stigmatise either nation for military excesses that are common to all armies and to all wars; and when I know that the general characteristic of the British and French troops alike is generosity, bravery, humanity, and honour.

The truth is, that Colonel Napier, abhorring from his soul every act of cruelty by whomsoever perpetrated, beheld the turmoil from the philosophic height and related it with the impartiality of the historian, while his critics threw themselves into the press, and regarded the various incidents with the eyes of partisans.

As a sample of Spanish ferocity towards their invaders, and as a melancholy cause for the terrible balance of barbarous actions which the French unhappily struck, take the following extract from the *History*:—

On the line of march, and in Andujar, he had terrible proofs of Spanish ferocity; his stragglers had been assassinated, his hospital taken; sick men, medical attendants, couriers, staff-officers,—in fine, all who were too weak for defence,—had been butchered with extraordinary barbarity; four hundred had perished in this miserable manner since the fight at Alcolea. The fate of Colonel René was horrible. Employed on a mission to Portugal previous to the breaking out of hostilities, he was on his return, travelling in the ordinary mode, without arms, attached to no army, engaged in no operation of war, yet he was first *cruelly mutilated, then placed between deal planks and sawed in two!* (Vol. 1.)

Few books that have ever been published afford so true on index of the mind and character of the writer as does the *History of the Peninsular War*. Hatred of cruelty, love of clemency, pity for the oppressed, righteous uncompromising hostility to tyrants, chivalrous appreciation of an enemy, charity to the poor, tenderness to the weak, and general benevolence towards all mankind except the evil-doers, speak out from his pages in ringing accents. His political opinions, notwithstanding their unpopularity in high places, were set forth with the utmost fearlessness and honesty, careless whom he might offend when he was speaking truths, the acceptance of which he believed essential to the wellbeing of his countrymen and of the world.

Colonel Napier's radicalism had for its principal characteristics a hearty appreciation of all that is grand and beautiful, and a firm faith in the glorious results to be achieved by the spread of education among the millions and their political emancipation. To raise the many, and not to annihilate the few, was its main object; and the foundation of his political creed was an undoubting belief in the capacity of human nature for progressive improvement in liberty and virtue.

The following extracts from his work will illustrate his political opinions; they are set forth in the story of his life, because many of them are such as would be little expected from him by those who may have been accustomed to confound him with the great mass of miscalled Radicals or Liberals.

Evils of Aristocracy.

Napoleon's troops fought in bright fields, where every helmet caught some beams of glory; but the British soldier conquered under the cold shade of aristocracy; no honours awaited his daring, no despatch gave his name to the applause of his countrymen; his life of danger and hardship was uncheered by hope, his death unnoticed.

In Spain, in 1813, Wellington was inimical to the constitution, because it admitted a free press, and refused to property any political influence beyond what naturally belonged to it—that is, it refused to heap undue honours, privileges, and power upon those who already possessed all the luxury and happiness that riches can bestow; it refused to admit the principle that those who have much should have more; that the indolence, corruption, and insolence, naturally attendant upon wealth, should be sup- ported and increased by irresponsible power; that those who laboured and produced all things should enjoy nothing; that the rich should be tyrants and the poor slaves.

But these essential principles of aristocratic government have never yet been, and never will be, quietly received and submitted to by any thinking people—where they prevail there is no real freedom. Property inevitably confers power on its possessors; and far from adding to that natural power by political privileges, it should be the object of all men who love liberty to balance it by raising the poorer classes to political importance; the influence and insolence of riches ought to be tamed and subdued, instead of being inflated and excited by political institutions.

The emigration of the royal family of Portugal forced men to inquire how subjects were bound to a monarch who deserted them in their need? How the nation could belong to a man who did not belong to the nation? It has been observed by political economists that where a gold and paper currency circulate together, if the paper be depreciated it will drag down the gold with it, and deteriorate the whole mass; yet, after a time, the metal revolts from this unnatural state and asserts its intrinsic superiority; so a privileged class, corrupted by power and luxury, drags down the national character. There is, however, a point where the people, like the gold, no longer suffering such degradation, will separate themselves with violence from the vices of their effeminate rulers. Until that time arrives, a nation may appear sunk in hopeless lethargy when it is capable of great and noble exertions.

The French Revolution was pushed into existence before the

hour of its natural birth. The power of the aristocratic principle was too vigorous, and too much identified with that of the monarchical principle, to be successfully resisted by a virtuous democratic effort; much less could it be overthrown by a democracy rioting in innocent blood, and menacing destruction to political and religious establishments, the growth of centuries, somewhat decayed indeed, yet scarcely showing their grey hairs.

It seems nearly certain that one of his (Napoleon's in 1813) reasons for replacing Ferdinand on the Spanish throne, was his fear lest the republican doctrines, which had gained ground in Spain, should spread to France. Was he wrong? The fierce democrat will answer Yes! But the man who thinks that real liberty was never attained under a single unmixed form of government, giving no natural vent to the swelling pride of honour, birth, or riches—those who measure the weakness of pure republicanism by the miserable state of France at home and abroad when Napoleon, by assuming power, saved her—those who saw America, with all her militia and her licentious liberty, unable to prevent three thousand British soldiers from passing three thousand miles of ocean and burning her capital—will hesitate to condemn him.

And this without detriment to the democratic principle which in substance may, and should always, govern under judicious forms. Napoleon early judged, and the event has proved he judged truly, that the democratic spirit of France, however violent, was unable to overbear the aristocratic and monarchic tendencies of Europe; wisely therefore, while he preserved the essence of the first by fostering equality, he endeavoured to blend it with the other two; thus satisfying, as far as the nature of human institutions would permit, the conditions of the great problem he had undertaken to solve. His object was the reconstruction of the social fabric which had been shattered by the French Revolution, mixing with the new materials all that remained of the old sufficiently unbroken to build with again.

Such were the men, calling themselves statesmen, who then wielded the vast resources of Great Britain.

. . . And to reduce these persons from the magnitude of statesmen to their natural smallness of intriguing debaters, is called political prejudice! But though power may enable men to trample upon reason for a time with impunity, they cannot escape her ultimate vengeance; she reassumes her sway, and history delivers them to the justice of posterity.

Such was the denuded state of the victorious Wellington at a time when millions, and the worth of more millions, were being poured by the English Minister into the Continent.

...And all this time there was not in England one public salary reduced, one contract checked, one abuse corrected, one public servant rebuked for negligence; not a writer dared to expose the mischief, lest he should be crushed by persecution; no minister ceased to claim and to receive the boasting congratulations of the Tories; no Whig had sense to discover or spirit to denounce the iniquitous system; no voice of reprehension was heard from that selfish faction, unless it were in sneering contempt of the general whose mighty genius sustained England under this load of folly.

The English are a people very subject to receive and to cherish false impressions; proud of their credulity, as if it were a virtue, the majority will adopt any fallacy, and cling to it with a tenacity proportioned to its grossness.

A weak man may safely wear an inherited crown—it is of gold, and the people support it; but it requires the strength of a warrior to bear the weight of an usurped diadem—it is of iron.

Gold is not always the synonym of power in war, or of happiness in peace.

Most surely all generals and politicians of every country, who trust to sudden popular commotions, will find that noisy declamations, vehement demonstrations of feeling, idle rumours, and boasting, the life-blood of such affairs, are essentially opposed to public exertions.

In large communities, working constitutions are the offspring, and not the generators, of national feelings and habits. They cannot be built like cities in the desert, nor coat as breakwaters into the sea of public corruption; but gradually, and as the insect rocks come up from the depth of the ocean, they must arise, if they are to bear the storms of human passions.

In 1813, the Portuguese Government neglecting to pay their

troops, Wellington made an appeal to the honour and patriotism of the Portuguese soldiers whose time had expired. Such an appeal is never made in vain to the poorer classes of any nation; one and all, these brave men remained in the service, notwithstanding the shameful treatment they had endured from their own government. This noble emotion would seem to prove that Beresford, whose system of military reform was chiefly founded on severity, might have better attained his object in another manner; but harshness is the essence of the aristocratic system of government, and the Marshal only moved in the straight path marked out for him by the policy of the day.

The great mass of men in all nations are only endowed with moderate capacity and spirit; and as their thoughts are intent on the preservation of their families and their property, they must bend to circumstances; thus fear and suspicion, ignorance, baseness, and good feeling, all combine to urge men in troubled times to put on the mask of enthusiasm for the most powerful, while selfish knaves ever shout with the loudest.

Bad government is more hurtful than direct war; the ravages of the last are soon repaired, and the public mind is often purified and advanced by the trial of adversity, but the evils springing from the former seem interminable.

The Americans.

A people who, notwithstanding the curse of black slavery that clings to them, adding the most horrible ferocity to the peculiar baseness of their mercantile spirit, and rendering their republican vanity ridiculous, do in their general government uphold civil institutions which have startled the crazy despotisms of Europe.

Colonel Napier's admiration for—not Napoleon—but for the ideal Napoleon he set up for himself—was unbounded. The stupendous intellect and genius of the great conqueror, which were realities, were credited by him with all the unselfish desire for the improvement and happiness of mankind, which would have been his own motive of action had he possessed Napoleon's power. So it was that his Napoleon was an ideal character, and, like all his ideals of greatness, grand, good, and beautiful. He has himself supplied the reasons for this worship of his hero.

While he (Napoleon) sacrificed political liberty, which to the great bulk of mankind has never been more than a pleasing sound, he cherished with the utmost care equality, a sensible good that produces increasing satisfaction as it descends in the scale of society.

Self had no place in his policy, save as his personal glory was identified with France and her prosperity. Never before did the world see a man soaring so high, and devoid of all selfish ambition. Let those who, honestly seeking truth, doubt this, study Napoleon carefully; let them read the record of his second abdication published by his brother Lucien, that stern republican who refused kingdoms as the price of his principles, and they will doubt no longer.

There is nothing more remarkable in Napoleon's policy than the care with which he handled financial matters, avoiding, as he would the plague, that fictitious system of public credit so fatuously cherished in England.

The annual expenditure of France was scarcely half that of England, and Napoleon rejected public loans, which are the very life-blood of state corruption. He left no debt. Under him no man devoured the public substance in idleness merely because he was of a privileged class; the state servants were largely paid, but they were made to labour effectually for the state. They did not eat their bread and sleep. His system of public accounts, remarkable for its exactness, simplicity, and comprehensiveness, was vitally opposed to public fraud, and therefore extremely unfavourable to corruption.

Napoleon's power was supported in France by that deep sense of his goodness as a sovereign, and that admiration of his genius, which pervaded the poorer and middle classes of the people; by the love which they bore towards him, and still bear for his memory, because he cherished the principles of a just equality. They loved him also for his incessant activity in the public service, his freedom from all private vices, and because his public works, wondrous for their number, their utility and grandeur, never stood still; under him the poor man never wanted work. To France he gave noble institutions, a comparatively just code of laws, and glory unmatched since the days of the Romans.

His *Cadastre*, more extensive and perfect than the *Doomsday Book*, that monument of the wisdom and greatness of our Norman conqueror, was alone sufficient to endear him to the nation. Rapidly advancing under his vigorous superintendence, it registered and taught every man the true value and nature of his property, and all its liabilities public and private. It was designed and most ably adapted to fix and secure titles to property, to prevent frauds, to abate litigation, to apportion the weight of taxes equally and justly, to repress the insolence of the tax-gatherer without injury to the revenue, and to secure the sacred freedom of the poor man's home. The French *Cadastre*, although not original, would from its comprehensiveness have been, when completed, the greatest boon ever conferred upon a civilized nation by a statesman.

To say that the Emperor was supported by his soldiers is to say that he was supported by the people; because the law of conscription, that mighty staff on which France leaned when all Europe attempted to push her down,—the conscription, without which she never could have sustained the dreadful war of antagonistic principles entailed upon her by the Revolution,—that energetic law which he did not establish, but which he freed from abuses, and rendered great, national, and endurable, by causing it to strike equally on all classes,—the conscription made the soldiers the real representatives of the people.

The troops idolized Napoleon; well they might: and to assert that their attachment commenced only when they became soldiers, is to acknowledge that his excellent qualities and greatness of mind turned hatred into devotion the moment he was approached. But Napoleon never was hated by the people of France; he was their own creation, and they loved him so as never monarch was loved before. His march from Cannes to Paris, surrounded by hundreds of thousands of poor men who were not soldiers, can never be effaced or even disfigured. For six weeks, at any moment, a single assassin might by a single shot have acquired the reputation of a tyrannicide, and obtained vast rewards besides from the trembling monarchs and aristocrats of the earth, who scrupled not to instigate men to the shameful deed.

Many there were base enough to undertake, but none so hardy as to execute the crime; and Napoleon, guarded by the people of France, passed unharmed to a throne whence it required a million of foreign bayonets to drive him again. From the throne they drove him, but not from the thoughts and the hearts of men.

The foregoing extract contains almost the only instance of special pleading to be found in the *History*; the French soldiers may, indeed, in consideration of the incessant activity of the conscription during the reign of Napoleon, be said in one sense to have been representatives of the people; and that the soldiers adored him is true; but it was for the glory he gave them as soldiers, the first object of a Frenchman's worship, not necessarily for the excellence of his moral qualities. And it is strange that the writer did not perceive that the system of conscription—an excellent, just, and beneficent system in defensive warfare—becomes, when combined with wars of aggression and conquest, the most hateful instrument of tyranny.

In Napoleon's council were persons seeking only to betray him. It was the great misfortune of his life to have been driven by circumstances to suffer such men as Talleyrand and Fouché, whose innate treachery has become proverbial, to meddle in his affairs, or even to approach his court. Mischief of this kind however necessarily waits upon men who, like Napoleon and Oliver Cromwell, have the courage to attempt, after great convulsions and civil wars, the rebuilding the social edifice without spilling blood. Either to create universal abhorrence by their cruelty, or to employ the basest of men, the Talleyrands, Fouchés, and Monks of revolutions, is their inevitable fate; and never can they escape the opposition, more dangerous still, of honest and resolute men, who, unable to comprehend the necessity of the times, see nothing but tyranny in the vigour that prevents anarchy.

There were many traitors likewise to him and to their country, men devoid of principle, patriotism, and honour, who, with instinctive hatred for a falling cause, plotted to thwart his projects for the defence of the nation. In fine, the men of action and the men of theories were alike combined for mischief. Nor is this outbreak of passion to be wondered at when we consider how recently Napoleon had stopped the anarchy of the revolution, and rebuilt the social and political structure in France. But of all who, by their untimely opposition to the Emperor, hurt their country, the most pernicious were those silly politicians whom he so felicitously described as 'discussing abstract systems of government when the battering ram was at the gates.'

Such, however, has been in all ages the conduct of excited and disturbed nations, and it seems to be inherent in human nature, because a saving policy can only be understood and worked to good by master spirits, and they are few and far between—their time on earth short, their task immense. They have not time to teach; they must command, although they know that pride and ignorance, and even honesty, will carp at the despotism that brings general safety.

It was this vain short-sighted impatience that drove Hannibal into exile, caused the assassination of Caesar, and strewed thorns beneath the gigantic footsteps of Oliver Cromwell. It raged fiercely in Spain against Lord Wellington, and in France against Napoleon, and always with the most grievous injury to the several nations. Time only hallows human institutions. Under that guarantee men will yield implicit obedience and respect to the wildest caprices of the most stupid tyrant that ever disgraced a throne; and wanting it, they will cavil at and reject the wisest measures of the most sublime genius. The painful notion is thus excited, that if governments are conducted with just the degree of stability and tranquillity which they deserve, and no more, the people of all nations, much as they may be oppressed, enjoy upon an average of years precisely the degree of liberty they are fitted for.

National discontents mark, according to their bitterness and constancy, not so much the oppression of the rulers as the real progress of the ruled in civilization and its attendant political knowledge. When from peculiar circumstances those discontents explode in violent revolutions, shattering the fabric of society, and giving free vent and activity to all the passions and follies of mankind, fortunate is the nation which possesses a Napoleon or an Oliver Cromwell 'to step into their state of dominion with spirit to control, and capacity to subdue, the factions of the hour, and reconstruct the frame of reasonable government.' Nor do I hold the conduct of Washington to be comparable to either of those men. His situation was one of infinitely less difficulty.

No one can have read Colonel Napier's writings without being struck with the unaffected love and admiration he had for the soldiers of the British army. Both his practice and theory were calculated to elevate not only their material condition but also their moral tone. In his earnest, lofty enthusiasm, he believed them capable alike of the most heroic actions, and of the loftiest sentiments; a wiser and nobler creed than that of those who hold that rice and ruffianism are necessary adjuncts of a soldier's character; for such a belief in men by a commander of the stamp of William Napier would go far to make them what they would feel proud of being thought to be.

The few extracts following from the *History* instance the feelings of the historian on this point, and his opinions with reference to war in general, and to our army in particular.

> It is said that no soldier can be restrained after storming a town, and a British soldier least of all, because he is brutish and insensible to honour. Shame on such calumnies! What makes the British soldier fight as no other soldier ever fights? His pay? soldiers of all nations receive pay. At the period of this assault (St. Sebastian) a sergeant of the 28th Regiment, named Ball, had been sent with a party to the coast from Roncesvalles to make purchases for his officers. He placed the money he was intrusted with, 2000 dollars, in the hands of a commissary, and, having secured a receipt, persuaded his party to join in the storm. He survived, reclaimed the money, made his purchases, and returned to his regiment. And these are the men, these the spirits, who are called too brutish to work upon except by fear! It is precisely fear to which they are most insensible.
>
> Captain Brotherton of the 14th Dragoons, fighting on the 18th at the Guarena amongst the foremost as he was always wont to do, had a sword thrust quite through his side; yet on the 22nd he was again on horseback, and, being denied leave to remain in that condition with his own regiment, secretly joined Pack's Portuguese in an undress, and was again hurt in the unfortunate charge at the Arapiles. Such were the officers. A man of the 43rd, one by no means distinguished above his comrades, was shot through the middle of the thigh, and lost his shoes in passing through the marshy stream; but refusing to quit the fight, he limped under fire in rear of his regiment, and with naked feet and streaming of blood from his wound, he marched for several miles over a country covered with sharp stones.
>
> Such were the soldiers. And the devotion of a woman was not

wanting to the illustration of this great day (Salamanca). The wife of Colonel Dalbiac, an English lady of a gentle disposition, and possessing a very delicate frame, had braved the dangers and endured the privations of two campaigns with the patient fortitude that belongs only to her sex; and in the battle, forgetful of everything but that strong affection which had so long supported her, she rode deep amidst the enemy's fire, trembling, yet irresistibly impelled forward by feelings more imperious than horror, more piercing than the fear of death.

As specimens of heroic portraiture, in which Napier has probably never been surpassed by any profane writer, the reader is referred to the *History* for the characters of Sir John Moore, Lieut.-Colonel Macleod who fell at Badajoz, Lieut.-Colonel Lloyd and Lieutenant Freer, who were killed at the Battle of the Nivelle.

As examples of the evil of committing the conduct of a great war to men ignorant of its first principles, take the following:—

> The slightest movement in war requires a great effort, and is attended by many vexations which the general feels acutely and unceasingly; but the politician, believing in no difficulties because he feels none, neglects the supplies, charges disaster on the general, and covers his misdeeds with words.

> The want of transport had again obliged the allies to draw the stores from Elvas, to the manifest hazard of that fortress; and hence here (Badajoz), as at Ciudad Rodrigo, time was necessarily paid for by the loss of life—or rather, the crimes of politicians were atoned for by the blood of the soldiers.

> Why were men thus sent to slaughter when the application of a just science would have rendered the operation comparatively easy? Because the English ministers, so ready to plunge into war, were quite ignorant of its exigencies; because the English people are warlike without being military, and, under pretence of maintaining a liberty they do not possess, oppose in peace all useful martial establishments. Expatiating in their schools and colleges upon Roman discipline and Roman valour, they are heedless of Roman institutions; they desire, like that ancient republic, to be free at home and conquerors abroad, but start at perfecting their military system as a thing incompatible with a constitution, which they yet suffer to be violated by every minister who trembles at the exposure of corruption.

Every British officer of rank knew that without powerful interest his future prospects and his reputation for past services would have withered together under the first blight of misfortune,—that a selfish government would instantly offer him up a victim to a misjudging public and a ribald press, with whom success is the only criterion of merit.

The secret of making perfect soldiers is only to be found in national customs and institutions; men should come to the ranks fitted by previous habits for military service, instead of being stretched as it were on the bed of Procrustes by a discipline which has no resource but fear.

War tries the strength of the military framework; it is in peace that the framework itself must be formed, otherwise barbarians would be the leading soldiers of the world; a perfect army can only be made by civil institutions, and those rightly considered would tend to confine the horrors of war to the field of battle, which would be the next best thing to the perfection of civilization that would prevent war altogether.

England stood the most triumphant nation in the world; but with an enormous debt, a dissatisfied people, gaining peace without tranquillity, greatness without intrinsic strength, the present time uneasy, the future dark and threatening. *Yet she rejoices in the glory of her arms! And it is a stirring sound! War is the condition of this world. From man to the smallest insect all are at strife; and the glory of arms, which cannot be obtained without the exercise of honour, fortitude, courage, obedience, modesty, and temperance, excites the brave man's patriotism, and is a chastening correction for the rich man's pride. It is yet no security for power.*

Napoleon, the greatest man of whom history makes mention—Napoleon, the most wonderful commander, the most sagacious politician, the most profound statesman—lost by arms Poland, Germany, Italy, Portugal, Spain, and France. *Fortune, that name for the unknown combinations of infinite power, was wanting to him; and without her aid the designs of man are as bubbles on a troubled ocean.*

In one point, and in one point only, did Colonel Napier violate the dignity and high judicial functions of the historian, in the bitter unmeasured censures he passed against Canning and Perceval; censures which bear the appearance of being directed not only against the political bat also against the personal character of those ministers. That ample grounds existed for his censure of the rashness and ignorance with which they commenced the struggle in the Peninsula with 9000 men against the whole might of the French Emperor is certain; but it is a blot on his great work, that the historian, while condemning the folly and mischief of their proceedings, should have omitted to attribute their shortcomings to ignorance, to our system of government, to other than moral defects, and to give them credit for that warm and generous sympathy with the Spanish patriots which was the undoubted spring of their actions.

That he should have been indignant with the statesmen who directed the war from home was just and natural. They are convicted in the *History* of such astounding ignorance of the first principles of war, of such amazing credulity in Spanish professions, and of such shameful mismanagement of the immense sums which were lavished on Spain at the outset of the struggle, that the successful prosecution of the war appears miraculous. Take a very few instances among many.

Sir Arthur Wellesley sailed from Cork in July, 1808, to land in Portugal, and drive the French out of the Spanish Peninsula. His force consisted of 9000 men. He was informed that General Spencer, who was on board ship at Cadiz with 5000 men, was at his orders.

General Spencer however had received instructions empowering him to act in the south, at his discretion, without reference to Sir Arthur's proceedings.

And Admiral Purvis was also authorised to undertake any enterprise in the south he might think promising, and even to control Sir Arthur's operations by calling for the aid of his troops, which aid the General was enjoined to give if demanded.

Sir Arthur had scarcely sailed when he was superseded and reduced to the fourth rank in the command of the expedition, by the appointment of Sir Hew Dalrymple as chief, and of Sir Harry Burrard and Sir John Moore as subordinates superior to himself.

The instructions given to Sir Arthur were absurd The arrival of Sir Harry Burrard off the coast after Wellesley's victory of Roliça stopped him from inflicting a serious blow on the enemy; the arrival of the same general on the battlefield of Vimiero stopped him from following up the retreating French; and by the arrival of Sir Hew Dalrymple on the following day, the army thus fell successively into the hands of three men coming with different views, habits, and information, without any previous knowledge of each other, and brought together at a moment when it was probable they would all disagree.

Later, when the ministry ordered Moore to march into Spain, Sir David Baird was directed with reinforcements to Corunna, there to land, and thence to march through a most difficult country to join Sir John Moore, who, to effect this junction, must himself march over 250 miles of difficult country, and with the possibility that the point of concentration might be in possession of the French before either he or Baird could reach it.

Although Moore had been kept almost destitute of money, the ministers had saturated Spain with gold for the Spanish Juntas, which Sir John Moore was now actually obliged to get back for the subsistence of the British army in loans.

When Baird arrived at Corunna, he also was destitute of money, and all that Moore could spare him was 8000*l*. Mr. Frere, however, who arrived at Corunna about this time, was comfortably provided with two millions of dollars for the use of the Spaniards, and from him Baird was forced to borrow for the necessities of his English soldiers!

Again, after Sir Arthur's first successful campaign in Portugal, the same ministers, having 90,000 superb soldiers disposable for offensive operations, allowed Sir Arthur Wellesley to commence the campaign with 22,000, while they devoted 40,000 of their finest troops to destruction at Walcheren, and employed 12,000, drawn from Sicily, in an useless descent on the southern extremity of Italy!

And yet, even up to the Battle of Salamanca, Sir Arthur was more than once reminded by Mr. Perceval that the whole responsibility of failure would rest on his head.

These instances, a few among many similar, must be admitted to justify the censure though not the tone. The bitter feeling manifested by Colonel Napier towards Canning and Perceval was occasioned principally by what he considered their base surrender of Sir John Moore's memory to the attacks of his calumniators; but he himself admitted afterwards, in a letter to the son of Mr. Perceval, that some of his expressions were inconsistent with the dignity of history.

As regards the honesty and impartiality of the work there can be but one opinion. Sufficient extracts have been given to show how fearlessly he published political opinions which must have made him an object of suspicion and alarm to both the powerful parties in the state. That he could be impartial in his censure, and could blame as well as praise the Duke of Wellington, on whose personal favour the success of his whole future military career depended, is manifest from the following extract:—

Such were the reasons assigned by the English general for his slack pursuit after the Battle of Vittoria; yet he had commanded that army for five years! Was he then deficient in the first qualification of a general, the art of disciplining and inspiring troops; or was the English military system defective? It is certain he always exacted the confidence of his soldiers as a leader; it is not so certain he gained their affections. The barbarity of the English military code excited public horror, the inequality of promotion created public discontent; yet the general complained he had no adequate power to reward or punish; and he condemned alike the system and the soldiers it produced.

The latter 'were detestable for everything but fighting, and the officers as culpable as the men.' The vehemence of these censures is inconsistent with his celebrated observation, subsequently made, namely, that he thought he could go anywhere and do anything with the army that fought on the Pyrenees; and although it cannot be denied that his complaints were generally too well founded, there were thousands of true and noble soldiers, and zealous worthy officers, who served their country honestly and merited no reproaches. It is enough that they have since been neglected, exactly in proportion to their want of that corrupt aristocratic influence which produced the evils complained of.

The Duke of Wellington, writing to Mr. Dudley Perceval in 1835, stated:

> Notwithstanding my great respect for Colonel Napier and his work, I have never read a line of it, because I wished to avoid being led into a literary controversy, which I should probably find more troublesome than the operations which it is the design of the colonel's work to describe and record.

Yet there is little doubt that through Lord Fitzroy Somerset he made himself well acquainted with both the spirit of the work and with its account of the most important transactions of the war; and the following extract from a letter addressed to the author by Sir N. Trant expresses the Duke's opinion on the subject:—

> Allow me to explain what I meant with regard to Ferguson's expression to me. We were talking of your book, and giving you credit for the spirit of independence with which it is written.

He said he had heard the Duke speak of it in the same sense and in these words:—

'Napier may be somewhat radical, but, by G—, his *History* is the only one which tells truth as to the events of the Peninsular War.'

The obligations laid upon him by his historian, which the Duke could, however, but imperfectly appreciate, are well expressed in the following extract from the *Edinburgh Review*:—

Before Colonel Napier commenced his *History*, few persons had any accurate conceptions respecting either the character of the struggle which he describes, or of the parties by whom it was carried on. The few who did possess a knowledge of the truth were, from various reasons, unwilling to state it. Amongst these the most marked was the Duke of Wellington; and he, as the result has shown, was content with the renown he already possessed, and unwilling, when he desired rest from toil, to recall the recollection of the weakness, folly, and treachery, by which his efforts had been cramped, his victories often rendered of no avail, and his final success almost rendered impossible.

The event was successful, and that was enough: all men were willing to afford him unbounded admiration and applause; and he was not anxious that this admiration and applause should be bestowed in consequence of a perfect conception of the many extraordinary obstacles which his genius and fortitude enabled him to surmount The voice of truth was drowned by the shout of victory. Doubtless, for the personal comfort of the Duke of Wellington, this was a prudent course. For his country and for posterity, however, truth was needed; and even for his own renown it was not unimportant. The vulgar judged him by his success; they who thought, however, but who were necessarily ignorant of the true nature of the contest, underrated his worth; because, judging him by the means which they fancied him to have possessed, they deemed the result hardly adequate to those means.

It was supposed that he was lavishly supplied with money, men, and arms, by the most lavish government the world ever saw; that he wielded, without let or molestation, the whole power of England, Portugal, and Spain; that the ministry at home were at his absolute disposal; that Spain was his enthusiastic, ardent, gallant ally; and that, having, as his obedient supporters, two whole nations burning for independence, and ready with patriot ardour to sacrifice life and fortune in order to attain it—having also the finest army England could furnish, equipped with all that an army needed,—it was no marvellous feat of arms, slowly to win his way in six long years from Lisbon to Toulouse, and to be finally successful only because the army of Napoleon had been buried in the snows of Russia.

The true history of his difficulties was needed to obviate these objections; and now, when this is known, it is found that a greater glory is really his due than that which the ignorant multitude bestowed on him merely because he was successful.

Appendix 1

NOTES OF CONVERSATIONS WITH THE DUKE OF WELLINGTON.

The army embarked at Cork was not intended for South America nor for any especial purpose. Lord Wellington had given this information to Miranda by the direction of the English Ministers, all idea of revolutionizing South America being at an end.

General Anstruther's army had been embarked and had sailed for the coast of Portugal, and he was met by a schooner, sent in search of him by Lord Wellington, and directed upon Macaira (or wherever he landed).

Sir John Moore's army was a welcome and unexpected succour (a Godsend).

General Spencer's army was sent to the Tagus in consequence of the opinion of Sir Charles Cotton that there were only 4000 men in Lisbon. General Spencer was right not to move in the South. All nations give up the war into the hands of the British when joined by them; 4000 men as a principal army would have been ridiculous, Junot would have marched his whole force against him, and some shame always attends a retreat.

BATTLE OF VIMIERA.

The position of Vimiera was very strong, forming a half-circle with its back to the sea, having a strong height in the centre in front of the town, a church and churchyard to cover the left. The left of the army very strong ground, the right also strong.

The French attacked Lord Wellington at Vimiera; their centre column was beat back with great loss very easily; they attacked again on the left feebly, and made another attack in which Brennier was taken. Brennier asked the English whether the reserve had attacked; from which Lord Wellington found out that the whole French army had attacked him. The French were not aware of the ravine between the left and the corps in advance of our centre, and this ruined their combination.

Lord Hill at the end of the battle was two miles nearer Torres Vedras than the enemy.

Lord Wellington's intention was to push his army (Lord Hill following with the rest) along the two roads of Torres Vedras and Mafra to get to Lisbon before the enemy, who must have passed to the other side of Monte Junsa, and could only have got to Lisbon afterwards along the banks of the Tagus. Lord Wellington did not conceive there would have been the least danger in this movement, because with a small portion of his force he had beaten the enemy at Vimiera, fresh troops had since landed, and more were expected under Sir John Moore. Sir Harry Burrard prevented him from putting the plan in execution. Burrard consulted with Lord Wellington on the day before the battle of Vimiera, and then went to the ships. He remained with his army. Sir Harry Burrard was wrong to interfere with him at all; General Murray and General Clinton both supported him in his declining to pursue.

Lord Wellington had intended on the morning of the Battle of Vimiera to march to look out for the French and to attack them, when a German officer of dragoons came galloping in a great fright at midnight informing him that the enemy were advancing to attack the English, and would be there in an hour, 20,000 strong, and saying he had seen them. This was exaggerated by fear, for they did not attack till two hours after day, and had not 20,000 men.

INSURRECTION OF PORTUGAL.

Lord Wellington never thought much of the insurrection in Portugal; in fact there was no insurrection.

It is true that Junot and the French officers thought a great deal of it, and were frightened at it; but it was equally true that the English did not know of their alarm,[1] and did not suspect it, because in fact the insurrection was nothing.

CONVENTION OF CINTRA

General Spencer was the first man who spoke to Lord Wellington about the convention. Sattaro, the Portuguese commissary, told him (Lord Wellington) before the Battle of Vimiera that the French would enter into a convention if they were tried, and then General Spencer

---
1. See Convention of Cintra.

spoke.

Lord Wellington thought the convention quite right, for the following reasons:—the greatest objection made to it was that the articles were bad; Lord Wellington thinks they were badly worded rather than bad in themselves; the French were in possession of a great many fortified places, very strong, and it would have taken a year to get them out of them. It would have been madness to have thought of carrying a battering train to besiege them, from the information received as to the state of the roads, which told so much against them that Sir John Moore was afraid to carry field artillery.

Certainly an able, active general of determined character could have crossed to the other side of the Tagus, or could have gone up in boats to Abrantes, for the English army had never quitted the mountains about Lisbon, and he might with the Russian sailors have formed an army of 33,000 or 34,000 men at least, based upon the fortress of Elvas. The English army at that time, after Sir John Moore's arrival, was not above 24,000 men, consequently it was a great advantage to us to get the French out of the country by a convention, clean, and without loss to ns.[2] Lord Wellington thinks that even if the enemy had been cut off and dispersed after the battle of Vimiera the convention would still have been right. If the sieges had been undertaken they would have given time to Bonaparte to crush the army.

The English people were mad at that time, and gave a proof of it by calling it the Convention of *Cintra*—Cintra having nothing to do with it at any time. No person in the army at that period had any doubt of the propriety of the convention, though many abused it afterwards.

The conduct of the court in the inquiry into the Convention of Cintra was unfair, their report was not luminous, Lord Moira's detailed reasons were ill founded, and Lord Wellington considered himself unjustly used.

General Freire's Advice.

General Barnard Freire wanted Lord Wellington to go into the middle of Beira with his army; he refused, thinking that he should have to trust to the Portuguese, for provisions if he quitted his ships, and that they would not supply him. His object was to strike the blow at the enemy as near to Lisbon as possible.

---

2. For an additional reason see, under the head of 'Insurrection in Portugal,' the opinion of Lord Wellington and of the French on the insurrection.

Moore's Campaign.

Lord Wellington fought the battle of Busaco politically, and looks upon Sir John Moore's advance to Sahagun to have been performed on the same principal.

Sir John Moore was afraid to carry field artillery in consequence of the information he had received on the state of the roads. Lord Wellington thinks he was quite right under such information to send the artillery the way he did; in fact, Lord Wellington's army made the roads which we acted upon afterwards.

Lord Wellington thinks that Sir John Moore could not have fought, as his army was unprepared to fight; but he thinks that he committed a fault in not considering his march upon Sahagun as a movement of retreat, and arranging the march of his columns and all the halts beforehand in case of such retreat; but (adds he), this opinion is formed from great experience in the art of war, and especially in that peculiar war adapted to Spain, and formed "*après coup.*"

Battle of Talavera.

In the plan of campaign for Talavera it was arranged, with the approbation of the Junta, that Venegas with his army, consisting of 25,000 men of the best Spanish troops, should move along the south of the Tagus as high as he could, for instance to Trebleque, in order to draw Sebastiani along the other bank away from the King's army, which last might be attacked by Cuesta and Lord Wellington.

If Sebastiani quitted the Tagus to join the King, Venegas was to cross and enter Madrid.

Lord Wellington and Cuesta acted upon this plan, but the Junta secretly ordered Venegas not to move and not to inform either Cuesta or Lord Wellington of his secret orders. Lord Wellington imagines that their vanity convinced them that he and Cuesta were sufficient, and that they thought it a masterstroke to save Venegas the chance of a defeat.

Cuesta had not more than 35,000 men in the battle of Talavera. The town and convent made the position strong; and Lord Wellington would have manoeuvred with his right, and have driven them upon the mountains if they had forced his left.

Cuesta was an obstinate old fool. Having 35,000 men at first, he lost 5000 by his folly in pursuing Victor with imprudence from Talavera on the 25th and 26th. 10,000 of his men, and all his artillery, fled on the night of the 27th as far as Oropesa, and with them the Adjutant-General O'Donoghue. Cuesta took post between the heights on the French side of the Alberchi and the river, and was with difficulty persuaded by Lord Wellington to quit it. He said he had made that Englishman go down on his knees first.

The Spaniards were posted by Lord Wellington on the right among olives and ditches safe from attack. On the evening of the 27th the British cavalry and advanced guard retired skirmishing to the position. The French deployed their cavalry and skirmished with pistols to make the Spaniards retire. These, to the amount of 10,000, fired and fled, but were not pursued as the night was setting in; the British cavalry were posted on the flank of the road, and the ditches rendered it unsafe at each side. A field entrenched battery was erected at the junction of the allied lines. but, as the artillery all ran away with the infantry, it was not mounted. A large convent was also occupied by the Spaniards between the position and the town.

Lord Wellington thinks his plan was good upon the data he possessed, but he admits that if Jourdan's plan had been followed it would have ruined him, as he could not have got back. (*Vide* Jourdan's plan).

Lord Wellington did not know Soult's force; guessed it was 20,000 men. Lord Wellington was in march to attack him, but was advised by Cuesta that he was too strong; and he passed the Tagus at Arzobispo.

Cuesta lost his guns on the left side of the Tagus; the French did not take them until they were informed of their being there by the trumpeter who went with Gordon as a flag of truce.

Cuesta also left them at the foot of the pass of Mezza de Ibor, although within range of the other side of the Tagus. Lord Wellington persuaded him to remove them.

Almeida and the Coa.

Colonel ——, of Almeida, was very negligent in not putting some men into the windmill in front of the works. It would have delayed the investment, and have given time to General Craufurd to withdraw his division in safety. General Craufurd had proposed to hold his position there, and thought he could do so if Lord Wellington gave him two regiments of *Caçadores* to watch his right and left. Lord Wellington answered that if he thought he could hold it he would give him two divisions, but he was sure he could not, and he desired him not to try it. Lord Wellington's intention was to place him on the Monte Negri, on the left bank of the Coa, intending by that means to hold open the communications with the place, or to force the enemy to invest it with a very large body of troops, but he found General Craufurd so beaten and dispirited by the affair of the Coa that he gave up that idea.

He had some thoughts of moving himself with his whole army up to the Coa, passing the bridges and fords by force and carrying off the garrison. This could have been done, because the enemy had not a great force at the investment, but the affair of the Coa, and the blowing up of the magazine, destroyed this project.

Busaco.

Lord Wellington fought the battle of Busaco politically.

Colonel Squires. Santarem.

Colonel Squires was wrong in thinking that by passing the Tagus and taking up the line of the Zezere Lord Wellington could have shut up Masséna's army at Santarem.

Lord Wellington's plan was to have 10,000 men opposite to Santarem, and to move with the rest of the army by Rio Mayor, attacking the right of the enemy, and throwing him upon the Tagus.

This could have been easily done when he received reinforcements, as Ney's corps spread as far as Tomar; but Sir John Yorke took six weeks instead of six days to get to Lisbon with the reinforcements, and when he arrived Masséna had moved.

Still Lord Wellington thinks he might have carried off his main body if he had attacked him. Colonel Squires' plan would have been good if Lord Wellington had had men enough to keep a corps on the left bank of the Tagus also.

Lord Wellington received an odd report at that time from General Lundey to the following effect:—

> The enemy are about to move either to their front, to their right flank, to their left flank, or to their rear.

Masséna's Plans.

Masséna's great object was to keep a footing in Portugal in order to produce an effect, and for this purpose he took up several positions, particularly one at Guarda, but was turned out of all of them, although he really had a force superior to that by which he was pursued. He could not have crossed the Estrella mountain and come down upon the Tagus as it was said he intended; he could not have passed the mountains, he could not have found subsistence. Soult was too much for Marshal Beresford in the south.

Surrender of General Imas.

General Imas was communicated with by letter by a confidential officer, and by telegraph, and was told that the French had retreated, in spite of which he surrendered 9000 men to about 12,000, and, having made a point of being allowed to march his men through the breach, he was obliged to break down a breach himself in order to do it.

The Cortes would neither shoot him nor break him; his trial lasted through the whole Peninsular war.

Battle of Sabugal.

The divisions were tolerably compact on the evening before the battle of Sabugal.

Marmont in 1811.

When Marmont came down in 1811 Lord Wellington remained with two divisions, and two brigades of cavalry, in position in front of Guinaldo for two days, in order to cover the retreat of the Light Division, compromised by the oddity of General Craufurd, and thus kept in check with less than 14,000 men an army of more than 60,000. When General Craufurd arrived Lord Wellington retired, and it is curious that the French retired on the same night. They afterwards returned and made a sharp attack, but were repulsed with considerable loss.

General Rénaud, the Governor of Ciudad Rodrigo, was taken by Don Julian Sanchez at that time.

Heights of Palmela.

Lord Wellington fortified the heights of Palmela because, although Admiral Berkeley had informed him elaborately that he could at any time take the ships out of the Tagus when the heights of Palmela were occupied by the enemy, yet he afterwards informed Marshal Beresford and some other general that he could not do it. Lord Wellington received this information from Beresford at Pero Negro, and ordered the heights to be strongly fortified, thus seeming Lisbon.

Battle of Salamanca, and subsequent Operations.

Don Carlos d'España had withdrawn the garrison from Alba de Tonnes before the Battle of Salamanca, and did not tell of it when he found out that it was wrong.

Lord Wellington's intention was to retire if Marmont had manoeuvred well, to advance when Marmont retired, and so to keep the French army constantly concentrated, and to relieve the other parts of Spain, ready himself to give battle if a favourable opportunity offered. He thinks that Marmont acted foolishly in passing the Douro; he should have passed at Toro at once, being a day's march in advance, which he lost by retracing his steps to Tordesillas. Lord Wellington thinks that Marmont did not know of the near approach of the King and the dragoons from the north, as Lord Wellington had intercepted all his letters.

The dragoons did not join until two days after the battle, that is four ordinary marches. General Pakenham and the 3rd Division were left at Cabrarisa, in front of Salamanca, to watch a rearguard of Marmont's, and afterwards put into a wood, and hid until the moment of attack, which arrived when Lord Wellington had finished his dinner; he having then observed the separation of the enemy, and Marmont's approach to the high road leading to Ciudad Rodrigo. The enemy could not have kept together if no battle had taken place.

Soult retired from Andalusia the moment he heard of the battle of Salamanca. Lord Wellington remained at Madrid until he heard of his moving past Grenada, and then went to the army opposed to Clausel, who had returned, raised the siege of Zamora, and threatened Astorga. Clausel displayed much ability in taking up positions every day or night in such a manner as to require a flank movement to dislodge him.

If Soult had not quitted Andalusia Lord Wellington intended to have taken 20,000 men from the army, to have, quitted Madrid, leaving what he calls a *"tête de cantonment"* about Toledo, Madrid, &c., and to have marched against Soult in conjunction with Hill.

Lord Wellington stayed too long at Salamanca in November, 1812.

Passage of the Tormes.

Lord Wellington thought that Soult intended to entrench his camp with a *tête de cantonment* after having passed the Alba at Mozarbes, and to operate upon Lord Wellington's communications with Ciudad Rodrigo. Lord Wellington, finding this, passed actually round his left wing, and established himself in the rear of it on the first evening of the retreat; a strange thing for Soult to permit.

Retreat from the Huebra.

In the retreat from the Huebra the generals of division consulted and agreed to disobey Lord Wellington's orders, and to move upon a different road. They did so, and got into a scrape, from which they did not get out until Lord Wellington set them to rights. When he first found them he asked them gravely what they intended to do next, and, as they did not know, hoped that in future they would obey his orders.

Vittoria.

In 1813 the second line moved to pass the Douro; the first line did not stir until the second was up to the river. When the first line moved, the French thought that the whole army was there. General Graham had 40,000 men, and the initiative was taken m much in advance that no danger accrued, as the enemy were surprised; otherwise the manoeuvre was not certain of success, though not very dangerous. Lord Wellington himself quitted Hill and went to the Esla; at the passage of the Douro he threw over his bridge at Pollos, he might have done it at Toro; if prevented at the latter place he had no other way of getting the French out of the line of the Douro, as by the right the country of Avila is very mountainous and difficult.

General Hill had 26,000 men in front of Salamanca. He tried to break the squares of the enemy's infantry (in retreat) with his cavalry, but failed every time.

Lord Wellington thinks it a bad manoeuvre, not to be done without a mass of artillery.

Burgos was not in a state of defence, and therefore the French did right to blow it up, as it would have cost 3000 men to defend it for eight or ten days; and Lord Wellington would have made a point of it, which would have enabled him to intercept the corps moving from Madrid. As soon as it was blown up all the army moved upon the Ebro.

After the battle Clausel should have moved upon Suchet, and, in conjunction with him, have held Saragossa, manoeuvring upon our rear. This would have caused great jealousy on our part. Clausel might have had orders not to do so, as Soult moved as soon as his corps joined him.

Mina pursued him alone after Tudela, and imposed upon him by making him believe that the English were after him. Clausel, thus deceived, destroyed his cannon and baggage. Ciudad Rodrigo and

Badajoz being in our possession left us at liberty to move where we pleased.

Sauroren.

After the defeat of Soult at Sauroren he sent his artillery by the Roncesvalles road, and retired by St. Estevan himself. He halted in that town, and the next evening Lord Wellington came upon the heights overlooking St. Estevan, at the head of the valley, with Lord Hill's corps upon his right, and the 3rd, 4th, and 6th Divisions upon his left. Lord Wellington now expected to be able to capture Soult and his army, as General Graham's corps and the Light Division were moving upon the left of the Bidassoa, and ought to have seized the bridge and to have stopped all egress by the narrow road running between scarped rocks and the right bank of the Bidassoa. Lord Wellington had given orders to keep the troops concealed behind the hills until the Light and General Graham's Divisions had established themselves on the French route.

An *aide-de-camp* told him that four *gendarmes* were in the valley. "Let them alone," was the answer. Soon after, three soldiers of our army who had, contrary to orders, straggled into the valley, were observed to be taken and carried off by the *gendarmes*. No sooner had these men been carried into St. Estevan than the French army began to *débouch* from that town. The Light Division were in sufficient time to have stopped the enemy; so were Longa's corps; but the former was commanded by Charles Alten, whose obstinate stupidity no officer and no representations could overcome. He suffered the French to defile within pistol-shot on the narrow road, where six men could not pass abreast, without attempting to interfere with them.

Longa excused himself as being too weak, although it was impossible for the French to get at him.

Orthez.

At Orthez, Marshal Beresford's corps being across, rendered the passage by the other divisions less dangerous; but still it was a delicate manoeuvre.

Miscellaneous.
Lord Wellington's Command of Spanish Armies.—Ballesteros.

When the command of the Spanish armies was offered to Lord Wellington by the Cortes he did not immediately accept it, as he wished to have it arranged in such a manner as that he should have a corps of Spanish troops constantly in the field in British pay, that is, paid from our subsidy; but that he should have the entire direction of them himself. He was willing to leave any particular body under the direct control of the Cortes. He did not get them settled until after the retreat from Salamanca, when he went to Cadiz for the purpose.

When Ballesteros heard that the Duke was appointed to command he remonstrated with the Cortes, and sent in his resignation to them. Lord Wellington wrote to him to move upon Chinchilla Castle, in order to prevent the army from Valencia from moving the direct road upon Madrid. Ballesteros had 10,000 or 12,000 good troops. He did not answer Lord Wellington, neither did he move, otherwise the French would have had a long detour, and might have been stopped altogether.

(*Note.* Napier. This seems odd, as Hill might have moved there, and stopped them also.)

Galicia

Galicia never did anything for Lord Wellington, but might have done much.

All the meat latterly came out of Galicia.

Soult in 1812.

Lord Wellington would have fought Soult in 1812 if the latter had attacked him; and he thinks he would have beaten him in that position, in which case Madrid would have been his again.

Cadiz.

The ministers were always wishing to occupy Cadiz. Lord Wellington thinks this a folly. It was rather a burthen to him. Either General Spencer or General Anstruther was intended to command the garrison; thinks it was Anstruther; he came out with the appointment.

Frere's plan for Albuquerque in La Mancha.

Mr. Frere's plan for Albuquerque to manoeuvre in La Mancha was taken from a French emigrant, and was calculated upon an idea of mountains being there, which was not a true one.

Portugal.

Portugal is not capable of being defended on the frontier. It may be too easily penetrated in many points. The Portuguese and Lord Wellington separated good friends before Vimiera; and General Trant got some of their troops for him.

Thiébaut, St. Cyr, &c.

Lord Wellington admires Thiébaut's description of Junot's invasion.

St. Cyr's plan of not using his artillery in order to raise the morale of his troops was great nonsense. Every battle has its crisis, in which every effort in your power must be made use of to win, therefore St. Cyr talks nonsense. Battles are dangerous operations, and a trifle may lose them; for instance, being on one side of a ditch instead of another.

Our habit of reconnoitring by single officers is peculiar to us, and admirable.

Carthagena.

Carthagena was occupied for a short time only by us. It was not much in the French line, and was unhealthy.

Waterloo.
Note sent from London, May, 1835.

Wellington would have fought the Battle of Waterloo on the French position instead of his own *if* his cavalry had held their ground the day before.

Appendix 2

QUESTIONS BY COLONEL NAPIER.
ANSWERS BY THE DUKE OF WELLINGTON

1. Was the advance from Coimbra decided, on political grounds, because of the conspiracy in Soult's camp, or on military reasons—or from both?

The operation upon Oporto was undertaken upon military grounds exclusively. See Despatches at the time. I positively refused either to retard, to accelerate, or to check my movement in reference to the communications existing with the disaffected in the French army.

2. Sir John Cradock found great difficulty in getting up the supplies—was any peculiar exertion made by the Duke for that purpose; or did he march, trusting to his own activity and the zeal of the army to overcome difficulties, or to bear privations?

I know nothing of Sir John Craddock's difficulties. We experienced many. But having determined to drive Soult from the north of Portugal, the difficulties of the enterprise were not of a nature to prevent our attempting it.

The transactions of the Commissariat will best show the difficulties of those days.

3. Were any particular measures taken to deceive Soult relative to the intended movement?

It is certainly true that many in the French army knew that we were in force upon the Mondego and the Vouga, and that Soult did not. We turned the enemy's right by the lake of Aveiro, and his left by the operations of Lord Beresford; but the main body advanced along the high road from Coimbra and Oporto. We did not arrive upon the

Vouga till later in the evening before the first attack, in order that the French *videttes* might not see our troops. The Portuguese under General Trant were there, and our intention was to surprise the French cavalry next morning.

We did not succeed in this object; but we only just failed. But the French cavalry must on that day have seen the whole corps, even including the troops which proceeded by the lake Aveiro.

The subsequent operations were pushed on with as much celerity as possible: and in fact, Soult got the last of his troops over the Douro and destroyed the bridge only an hour or two before we were in Villa Nova.

4. was the passage of the Douro attempted because the enemy appeared to be retreating from that town, or from of any reliance on the conspirators in Soult's camp?

The passage of the Douro was attempted because the localities gave great facilities for the performance of the operation. The convent of Serra, in Villa Nova commands all the town and the surrounding country on the opposite bank.

There was immediately opposite to this convent an unfinished building of considerable size, called the Seminary, or Jesuits' College. This was enclosed by a high stone wall, having an iron gate opening upon the high road from Oporto to Vallonga.

There was an easy access from the river to this building. The wall enclosed a considerable space of ground, enough to form in it at least two battalions, or possibly 300 yards long, along the river, and the depth about half the space. The building was within musket-shot of the iron gate. It commanded everything in its neighbourhood, excepting a mound at about the distance of a cannon-shot; which however had not space enough upon its summit to place a gun upon it.

The guns at the convent in Villa Nova commanded the whole enclosure of the Seminary, and they enfiladed and defended the left of its wall, so that an enemy could not attack on that side. The right of the troops which passed over to this Seminary (which in fact made an admirable *tête de pont*) was protected by the passage of the Douro higher up by Lieut.-General Sir John Murray and the King's German Legion, supported by other troops. . . . . .so that in fact the troops in the Seminary could be attacked only by the iron gate from the high road.

The attack was continued for a length of time, but principally to cover the retreat of the enemy from the town; at last, when they evacuated the lower part of the town, there was a general waving of handkerchiefs in the windows, and a hurrah in the town! The boats were sent over from the right bank of the Douro, of which we had but few before, and the troops were carried over in large bodies. The attack was discontinued upon the Seminary by the enemy; our troops formed and moved forward, and the enemy was pressed in his rear.

5. Why did the Duke halt next day?

The halt was made the next day, first, because the whole army had not crossed the Douro, and none of its supplies and baggage; secondly, on account of the great exertion and fatigue of the preceding day, particularly the last; thirdly, because we had no account of Lord Beresford being in possession of Amarante, or even across the Douro, we having in fact outmarched everything; and, fourthly, the horses and animals required a day's rest as well as the men.

6. What was real cause of Beresford's delay at Chaves, when he ought to have been at Villa del Rey before Soult was at Montalegre?

I never knew the cause of Lord Beresford's delay, if there was any. After Soult's escape by the bridge of Misarella, which was accidental, nothing could have stopped him.

I don't recollect what force we had for this operation north of the Mondego. There were some Portuguese militia under Trant, and some Portuguese infantry with me, and some with Lord Beresford, but they were in their infancy. Soult must have been stronger than Lord Beresford and I together.

The relative numbers and the nature of the troops must be considered in all these cases; and this fact moreover, that, excepting to attain a very great object, we could not risk the loss of a corps.

However, Soult suffered very handsomely in his retreat. He lost vast numbers of men and horses, and all the *matériel* of his army.

7. Was not the Duke displeased with Colonel Mayne for destroying the bridge of Alcantara?

Colonel Mayne was ordered to destroy the bridge of Alcantara, but it was under different circumstances. He had not concealed his instructions—the French knew of them; and that the bridge was ready loaded with a mine. General La Pipe was sent with the division to make a false attack upon the bridge, in order to induce Colonel Mayne to blow it up, which he did. The French general had orders, however, to destroy it if Mayne did not.

We were in fault in not sending orders to General Mackenzie not to allow the bridge to be destroyed as soon as we reached the Tagus; but he must have gone there with his whole division. After all, I am not quite certain that the French did not suffer in the end more inconvenience from the want of this communication than we did.

COLONEL NAPIER TO LORD FITZROY SOMERSET.
NOTES AND REPLIES BY THE DUKE OF WELLINGTON.

July 5, 1838.

My dear Lord Fitzroy,

When our army was on the Caya, June and July, 1811, the 1st Division was at Portalegre, Lord Londonderry says it was to be at hand in case the enemy demonstrated towards the Tagus, I do not take such liberties with the mathematics, but I think they must have been kept there: 1st, to be ready to move upon Marvao in case the enemy attempted to turn our left by Albuquerque; and, 2ndly, I think that they would not have been kept there at all if Lord Wellington had not been assured that the French were spreading and not going to attack, otherwise I think it would have been dangerous to keep them at such a distance.

Was not Lord Hill's position beyond the Caya exposed, if Soult had crossed the Guadiana in force by the fords above Jerumenha? It appears to me he might thus have invested Elvas, or obliged us to fight on that side, and that in fact Lord Wellington bullied both him and Marmont,

Yours sincerely,

W. Napier.

July 8, 1833

It would take me some time, and require more reflection than I can at this moment give to the subject, to answer Colonel Napier's Memorandum.

As well as I recollect, our position in 1811 was a "bully." It was very strong however, and supported by Campo Mayor, and by Elvas an its right

The object was to oblige the French to concentrate their forces. If I recollect right, the two armies of Soult and Marmont joined, and both touched us. We then retired. They separated, and each went to his own province.

The 1st Division was at Portalegre, and, as well as I recollect, we had another between Campo Mayor and Portalegre to observe the rear of the position, and the movements of the army of Portugal under Marmont.

When I shall have a little more leisure, I will endeavour to recollect these movements; but I perfectly recollect the position in front of Campo Mayor.

Wellington.

Feb. 1839.

If you can answer the question, I want to know what the march of the 3rd Division was on the 31st July, 1st and 2nd August, because I find that Division ordered on the 30th, in the evening, to march on the 31st from Zubiri towards Roncesvalles. But in the Duke's Despatches he tells O'Donnel he did not know the true state of General Hill's position until after these orders were issued.

Now I find, in a note of conversation; with the Duke many years ago, that he brought the 3rd, 4th, and 6th Divisions upon Soult's left at San Estevan, on the 31st of July in the evening, and that Soult only escaped by an accident, some of our soldiers straggling and giving the alarm.

W. Napier.

PS.—You would be surprised to know the number of persons I have applied to personally and by letter, to ascertain the march of the 3rd Division, and without success. Nobody seems to know anything about it.

I don't recollect the march of the 3rd Division on the days mentioned.

This is true.

We arrived at the *débouché* of the valley of the Bidassoa early in the afternoon of the 31st July. We halted there for an hour. Soult was at Estevan with his army. Three of our men were carried off who were plundering an orchard. Soult marched the moment he received the intelligence.

Wellington.

Battle of Vimiero.

I don't think Sir Harry Burrard landed till the morning of the battle.

I intended to march, but not to attack on the morning of the battle till I went on board the ship on the evening before the battle. I was forbidden to march, and returned to my quarters, intending to obey orders. In the night I heard of the movement of the French; the army was under arms in the morning, and I sent to Sir Harry Burrard who landed in the morning.

Anstruther had joined. I went to Lourinha on the 18th to facilitate his landing and junction.

I think Acland landed either before or during the battle. I believe the former.

I knew on the evening of the Battle of Roliça, on the 17th, that Loison was in movement somewhere in the neighbourhood of the field. I was therefore cautious in my movements on that day; the next morning moved towards Anstruther to secure his landing and junction.

I had reason to believe that, altogether, Junot would have about 18,000 men, which is I believe the number he had.

Wellington.

COLONEL NAPIER TO LORD F. SOMERSET.
ANSWERS BY THE DUKE OF WELLINGTON.

Nov. 1838.

I am somewhat at a loss to ascertain the number of Spanish troops under the Duke's command at the period of the battles in the Pyrenees; and I therefore have set down what I suppose to be nearly the mark, and I shall be much obliged to you to tell me if I am much in error.

1. Part of Mendizabel's people engaged in the siege of Santona	6,000
2. Giron's army, including the remainder of Mendizabel's, Long, &c.	10,000
3. Morillo's Division at Roncesvalles	4,000
4. Abispal's army of reserve at Pampeluna	10,000
5. Carlos d'Españas Division in march for Pampeluna	5,000
6. Mina, Empecinado, Duran, Goyan, &c., &c., Aragon	15,000
Total	50,000

—of which 24,000 were in line during the operations, and the remainder engaged in blockades, sieges, and desultory warfare on the rear and right flank.

I find that the siege of St. Sebastian was not carried on at all in accord with Lord Wellington's views, and that the deviations from his instructions were most injurious to the success of the operation; which I am sorry for, as I am quite tired of pointing out mistakes, but justice must be done, and the saddle put on the right horse, or rather horses, though some of the defaulters are scarcely entitled to be likened to that particular quadruped.

W. Napier.

2. I should say 8000. They never had them under arms.

4. 7000 or 8000 at most.

5. 4000.

There was at that time in Catalonia the first army under Copons, the best of them all; it had 10,000 men.

There was, besides, a division of 4000 men under Colonel Manso in Catalonia.

The 3rd army in Valencia, under the Duke del Parque, afterwards under the Prince of Anglona, in Catalonia, Aragon, and Navarre.

I should think that the 3rd army had 8000 men. It never was brought all into line.

Whittingham and Roche each commanded a division of Spanish infantry, besides the cavalry under the first, say 5000 men each.

These acted under Sir John Murray and Lord William Bentinck. They were paid out of the Spanish subsidy, clothed, and ought to have been an effective army.

We never saw the Empecinado, Goyan, &c., but they were somewhere in Castile.

Mina followed Clausel out to Jaca, and we did not hear much of him afterwards till the winter and spring of 1814.

Wellington.

S.S.   Dec. 24, 1838.

I send answers to Colonel Napier's last questions. In one of his papers he asks about the period of Carlos d'España joining at Pampeluna. He had certainly arrived before the battle was won. I cannot say whether he had before it began. By-the-bye it is certain that Abispal had only 7000 men.

Wellington.

BATTLES OF THE PYRENEES.
QUESTIONS.
ANSWERS BY THE DUKE OF WELLINGTON.

1. Lord Wellington says that Vera and Echallar were indispensable posts to cover the siege of San Sebastian.

Am I right in supposing that, if they were not held, the French army could have been thrown into the Bastan and the valley of the Bidassoa, and then crossing the mountains by the pass of Donna Maria have seized the great road of Irurzun, bringing up left shoulders, and operating on the rear of the besieging army by that road and by the pass of Zubietta at the game time?

In answer to the 1st Question, I should consider the supposed march and the great road impracticable; there being an opposing army in the field.

The height of Vera covers the approach to Lezaca; which was the *débouché* of the communications across the hills with Passages and San Sebastian.

As well as I recollect there was a horse-road from Vera to Irun along the Bidassoa.

It must always be observed that the siege of San Sebastian was not raised till the order of the night of the 25th, or morning of the 26th. The firing was discontinued for want of ammunition after the failure of the storm.

The embarkation of the guns, stores, &c., and the turning of the siege to a blockade, was not ordered till the night.

It was therefore necessary to protect the approaches to Passages and St. Sebastian.

2. Why did the 6th Division remain until the morning of the 27th at San Estevan instead of marching on the evening of the 26th?

Marshal Soult was appointed to command the French army on the frontiers of Spain early in July. He arrived on the 13th. He announced himself to his army on the 23rd. His first measures indicated an intention to operate with his right. He collected bridges at Orogne, &c.

3. Why did that Division march into the valley of Lanz instead of going at once by Lizasso and Marcabain—which last road it was afterwards obliged to take, thus losing time?

The allied army was engaged in the siege of St Sebastian and the blockade of Pampeluna. In order to cover these operations the passes in the Pyrenees were occupied from Roncesvalles to St Sebastian.

Sir John Byng with his brigade at Roncesvalles.

Sir L. Cole with the 4th Division to support him. The 3rd Division at Olagne to support the troops in advance.

General Campbell in the Alduides.

Sir Rowland Hill in the Valley de Bastan and Puerto de Maya communicating by his right with General Campbell.

The 7th Division on the left of the Valley de Bastan, covering Vera and Echallar.

The 6th Division at St Estevan.

An attempt was made to take St. Sebastian by storm on the 25th of July in the morning, and failed.

I went there afterwards. The ammunition having been expended, the discontinuance of the fire upon the place had become necessary, till a supply should be received from England.

On my return to Lezaca I heard of the attack on the Puerto de Maya. It was reported to have failed.

It had succeeded; but the enemy had been subsequently driven off.

In the night accounts were received from Sir Rowland Hill, stating that Sir L. Cole had been attacked at Roncesvalles; and that having retired, he, Sir Rowland, had withdrawn the troops from the Puerto de Maya.

I sent orders immediately to raise the siege of St. Sebastian, to embark the guns and stores, but to maintain the blockade of the place.

I went in the morning of the 26th to Sir Rowland Hill's corps.

Thus then Marshal Soult on the 25th July broke in upon our line, at the same moment that we failed in our attempt to take St Sebastian by storm.

Our right was turned. The troops at Roncevaux retired, and rendered necessary the retreat of Sir Rowland Hill's corps from the Valley de Bastan.

The object was to save the blockade of Pampeluna by collecting as soon as possible the largest body of troops.

Sir Thomas Picton did not stand in any position after Sir L. Cole, with the 4th Division, Byng's and Campbell's brigades, had joined him; and it was not known on the night of the 26th, at Sir Rowland Hill's quarters, what was the precise position of the troops of the right of the army, or the intentions of Sir Thomas Picton.

I ordered Sir Rowland Hill to retire upon Lizasso early on the

27th; and the 6th and 7th Divisions, and all the disposable troops, to move upon Ostiz in the valley of the Lanz.

I did not learn more of Sir Thomas Picton till I reached the quarters of General Long at Ostiz on the morning of the 27th, where I heard that he had fallen back upon the heights of Huarto.

I went on immediately by the valley of the Lanz to join him.

I left orders at Ostiz to the quartermaster-general to wait at Ostiz, and to halt all the troops till I should ascertain the state of things between Ostiz and Sauroren.

The French army were taking up their ground on the heights on the left of the road while I was riding along the valley of the Lanz. It was obvious that no troops could follow by that road.

I wrote the orders to turn everything at Ostiz by the other road, upon the bridge of Sauroren. Lord Fitzroy Somerset carried them, and quitted the village by one road while I joined the army by another, and the detachment of French cavalry entered the village by a third.

Thus then it will be seen that the original intention was to collect the army as soon as possible to avoid false movements; and to move this 6th Division by the valley of the Lanz.

The execution of this design was prevented by the movements of Sir Thomas Picton, and Marshal Soult following him so quickly.

4. Did General Allen lose his way, or did the order to march upon Lecumberri fail to reach him? I ask this because I find that the Light Division wandered very much after quitting Vera, and I suppose that his orders were to cover the right flank of Sir Thomas Graham by guarding, first, the passes of Zubietta and Goritz; and secondly, as this flank advanced on the rights the great road to Irurzun.

I cannot recollect any order to the Light Division. They were placed under the general direction of Sir Thomas Graham.

He may have given them orders.

There was great difficulty in reaching them after the battle. It was wished to bring them down to the Bidassoa to intercept the retreat of the enemy.

5. What was the nature of the intelligence sent to Lord Wellington by Abispal, which induced the former to move some of the 6th Division behind the heights of San Cristoval; that is to say by Berioplana. The intelligence I mean was brought to Lord Wellington by Camac?

I don't recollect any such communication.

The 6th Division were ordered from the valley of the Lanz for the reasons above stated. They arrived on the ground most opportunely on the morning of the 28th.

The armies were so near each other that I saw Marshal Soult; and so distinctly as to know him by sight from that view of his person.

I don't recollect any deviation from the original route from Ostiz.

6. I cannot discover any good reason why Picton did not draw Campbell's brigade from Engui on the night of the 26th, and then with the 17,000 men he could thus have had, disputed the heights of Linzoin with Soult on the 27th. I do not think he could have been forced in front, and Soult could hardly have turned him to any purpose by descending the valley of Urroz, If Picton had held his ground it is probable the 6th Division might have joined him, and perhaps that was the object of its moving into the valley of Lanz.

7. It appears to me that Soult failed in not attacking Sir L. Cole on the evening of the 26th at Linzoin before the 3rd Division joined him from Zubiri.

I cannot give any answer to these questions.

Appendix 3

SELECTION FROM MS. NOTES ON *MÉMOIRES DE NAPOLÉON*.
TEXT WITH NOTES BY COLONEL NAPIER

Les institutions militaires des Anglais sont vicieuses: 1°, ils n'operent leur recrutement qu'à prix d'argent, si ce n'est que fréquemment ils vident leurs prisons dans leur régimens; 2°, leur discipline est cruelle; 3°, l'espèce de leurs soldats est telle, qu'ils ne peuvent en tirer que des sous-officiers médiocres; ce qui les oblige à multiplier les officiers hors de toute proportion; 4°, chacun de leurs bataillons trâine à sa suite des centaines de femmes et d'enfants; aucune armée n'a autant de bagages; 5°, les places d'officiers sont vénales: les lieutenances, les compagnies, les bataillons s'achètent; 6°, un officier est à la fois major dans l'armée et capitaine dans son régiment; bizarrerie fort contraire à tout esprit militaire,—(Mélanges, Montholon, vol. 1.)

This is not sound criticism. The recruiting by money obtains stouter and more willing men. The taking men from prisons was under the extreme pressure of Napoleon's warfare; it had its advantages also: it gave many stout men, saved punishment, and enabled Government to employ the good regiments on service—for the prison men were not, except in a few cases, sent to the regiments of character; moreover the system was soon laid aside, and does not belong to the English military institution. The discipline was cruel, it is so no longer, but is very just. The non-commissioned officers were, and are, excellent. In Spain the baggage was not unreasonably great. The system of purchase is a very difficult question, involving national customs and feelings: I am inclined to think it good, but it should not be pushed too &c. The brevet rank is a consequence of purchase; it opens promotion for long service without money.

No doubt the English military institutions are anomalous, and in some points defective; but all military institutions must be influenced in some degree by national manners and customs. England has sent forth at all times soldiers capable of conquering every enemy; her institutions cannot therefore be very bad, or the soldier himself must be infinitely superior to all other men.

Les officiers des compagnies se dégraderaient s'ils se mêlaient des details du décompte du soldat; its deviendraient sous-officiers; le Sergent-major est propre à ce tervice.—(Mélanges, Montholon, vol. 1.)

This is one of the things that depend on national customs. In the British army the best effects are produced by the rule that officers and not sergeants shall settle personally with their men. The officer's honour is a safeguard for the man, who has besides the right to complain to his commanding officer and to the inspecting general if he is wronged; this practice also brings the officer more in contact with his men, and makes them acquainted with each other's characters: there is nothing a soldier abhors so much as an officer who is mean or tricky about money; hence the love and esteem of the soldier is a premium for honour in the officer. Notwithstanding all these precautions, the soldier is sometimes defrauded by sergeants; what would it be if the latter had entire control of the payments!

The British officer is proud and disdainful; it is good to bring him perforce into contact with the poverty and wants of the poor soldier: the French officer is familiar with his men off duty; it may therefore be proper to keep them asunder in money matters; but I have no doubt, from what I have heard, that the French soldier's security for his pay is not so good as the British soldier's. The conscription also must be considered; the French soldier is often of higher rank in society and better educated than his officer—whence a necessity for keeping the latter from the temptation of defrauding his men. In fine, military institutions are like constitutions, the growth of national manners under different systems of pruning and training. This general rule will, however, be an infallible guide in all services. The soldier cannot have too much reverence and esteem for his officer: the officer cannot be esteemed if he is not just; he may be esteemed without being loved. To be both he must not keep aloof from his men.—W.N,

En Russie nos pertes furent considérables, mais non pas telles qu'on se l'imagine, 400,000 hommes passèrent la Vistule; 160,000 seulement dépassèrent Smolensk pour se porter sur Moskou; 240,000 hommes restèrent en réserve enire la Vistule, le Borysthène, et la Dwina. La moitié de ces 400,000 hommes étaient Autrichiens, Prussiens, Saxes, Polonais, &c. &c. La campagne de 1812 en Russie coûta moins de 50,000 hommes à la France actuelle,—(Mélanges, Montholon, vol. 2.).

I know this to be correct; I have seen the original states of the army; the Emperor's private states, which could not be wrong. I mean as to the 400,000 men. What proportion passed Smolensk I only know from this account.

La mort du Duc d'Enghien doit être attribuée aux personnes qui dirigeaient et commandaient de Londres l'assassinat du Premier Consul . . . . elle doit être attribuée aussi à ceux qui s'efforcèrent, par des rapports et des conjectures, à le présenter comme chef de la conspiration; elle doit être éternellement reprochée enfin à ceux qui, entraînes par un zèle criminel, n'attendirent point les ordres de leur souverain pour exécuter le jugement de la commission militaire. Le Duc d'Enghien périt victime des intrigues d'alors. Sa mort, si injustement reprochée à Napoléon, lui nuisit, et ne lui fut d'aucune utilite politique, Si Napoléon avait été capable d'ordonner un crime, Louis 18me et Ferdinand ne régneraient point aujourd'hui; leur mort, on l'a déjà dit, lui a été proposée, conseillée même à plusieurs reprises.—(Mélanges, Montholon, vol. 2.)

Talleyrand and Fouché.

This is pointed at St. Real, the Grand Judge. He held back the Duke's letter to Napoleon, and also the judgement of the court-martial, which by the law of France is always executed within a certain time without confirmation, unless a superior order forbids it This very curious history was known to Joseph Bonaparte, and it will be probably told some day in his memoirs: it was told by Joseph to a friend of mine, Mr. Cowell. Joseph's story runs thus:—He was at his house at Marfontaine near Paris, when information reached him that some remarkable event had happened. He repaired to the Tuileries, and went towards his brother's room: suddenly Josephine came out of a side-room in her bedgown, and in a hurried manner said "Go to him—be quick—the Duc d'Enghien is a prisoner; the Boiteux (Talleyrand) is with your brother and is giving him bad advice."

Joseph went hastily into the Emperor's room, and there was Talleyrand, who on seeing Joseph left the room, but in passing gave a significant sneering smile. Joseph understood this to mean "You are too late, I have settled the affair."

In this notion he walked straight up to the Emperor, and repeated some lines from a French poet which had been a favourite declamation with both of them when they were boys. Napoleon smiled and replied, "That did very well for boys, but Talleyrand has been putting the matter in its true light; he says the Duke is accused of plotting my assassination and raising a civil war; that any man of less degree would be put to death for this, and there would be neither reason nor justice in permitting the Duke, merely because he is a Bourbon, to commit such crimes with impunity."

Joseph instantly repeated the verses again, the purport being that an enemy in your power ought to be spared. "Ah, yes!" replied Napoleon, "but justice must first be satisfied. The Duke must be tried: the proofs are complete, and he will certainly be found guilty; but then I can pardon him;" and he repeated the verses himself; he added—"I am even anxious to attach him to me, and to give him high command." Satisfied with this assurance, Joseph retired, and that evening went to different "*salons*," principally among the Royalists.

To his astonishment he found the latter willing to urge the Duke's execution. Talleyrand and Fouché had been giving the cue to their opinions and language: they said—"If any of us had been engaged in such an affair, no mercy would be shown us; but because he is of royal blood he is to be pardoned." Joseph told all those who were anxious for his life that he would not be harmed in any way, and he endeavoured to raise a feeling of pity for him; for, trusting to Napoleon's assurances, he wished to soften the angry feeling which Talleyrand and Fouché had raised by their villainous proceedings: they hoped thus to force the Emperor into a bloody course.

Joseph slept that night at Paris, but he was suddenly awakened in the morning by a message from Josephine to say that something dreadful had happened. He hastened to the palace, and had just reached his brother's room when the door opened violently, and the Emperor appeared in a state of uncontrollable passion, pushing St. Real the judge out, and, as Joseph thought, striking him. Joseph went to his brother and sought to soothe him, but he could get no answer from him: he continued to repeat, "He has destroyed the finest moment of my life."

At last he suddenly ceased this exclamation and said, "Well! the wine is drawn—we must drink;" then, assuming a peculiar marble look which belonged to him when his resolution was fixed, he commenced speaking of other subjects, and from that hour to his death Joseph never could obtain any explanation of his violence to St. Real. On quitting Napoleon he learned that the Duke had been shot an hour before. However, in after years when Joseph was an exile in America, he met St Real, then also an exile, and heard from him this explanation

I was troubled to find that the general opinion of the *salons*, and especially of the Royalists, was against the Duke. I knew that Talleyrand and Fouché were at work exciting this feeling. I knew also that the Emperor was inclined to mercy, and that there would be a cry and a faction if the Duke was pardoned: I thought to save the Emperor from this inconvenience, and from the annoyance of deciding; so I kept back the sentence of the court-martial until that sentence had been executed; and you saw the effect on the Emperor.

Napoleon was so firm and proud a man that he would never attempt to clear himself. He knew that if he threw the blame on St. Real the world would only say he sacrificed his tool. Therefore he kept silence, but he has in his *Memoirs* hinted at the truth, using the initial S. for St. Real. This has given rise to the belief that he meant Savary, but it is an error. St Real was the judge whose business it was to bring the judgement to the Emperor for his final determination; and as that was not given, the sentence was executed as a matter of course according to the French law.—W. N,

The Battle of the Nile.

Le projet de l'Amiral était d'attaquer de vaisseau à vaisseau chaque bâtiment Français, jetant l'ancre par l'arrière, et se plaçant en travers de la proue des Français, Le hasard changea cette disposition. Le Culloden, destiné à attaquer le Guerrier, voulant passer entre son gauche et l'île, échoua.

This is true.

Le Goliath, qui le suivait, manoeuvrant pour se mouiller au travers de la proue du Guerrier, fut entraîné par le vent et le courant, et ne jeta l'ancre qu'après avoir dépassé et tourné ce vaisseau. S'apercevant alors que la batterie gauche ne tirait pas, il se plaça bord à bord avec lui, et le désempara en peu de temps. Le Zélé, deuxième vaisseau Anglais, suivit le mouvement du Goliath, et se mouillant bord à bord du Guerrier, qui ne pouvait pas répondre à son feu, il le démâte promptement, &c.—(Gourgaud, vol. 2.)

This is an error. Sir Thomas Foley had an old chart, by which he knew there was water enough inside: the famous manoeuvre and the speech attributed to Nelson are vulgar errors. The first belongs to Foley; the last was not made *before* the fight, at all events. Nelson even told Foley afterwards he did not know what he was at when he saw him passing between the island and the French fleet, and that if he had known he would have stopped him; or if he could have got a signal ready he would have recalled him: it was the last expression, I think. Was Nelson wrong? I believe not.

The attack thus led by Foley was contrary to the principle of battles at sea; Nelson's own plan was better; and if Villeneuve had come up, it would have been found so. Foley and the ships inside the line could not have beaten back against the wind; and to run down the French line in that narrow passage would have been very dangerous: they must have remained and continued their fight.

Meanwhile, Villeneuve, who had only about one mile to beat up with plenty of sea-room, would with fresh ships have placed Nelson and the vessels which followed him on the outside of the French line between two fires, just as Foley had placed the French left: then if Villeneuve was beaten, he would have gone off, as far as sea and wind were concerned; but if Nelson and Foley were beaten, they would have had no retreat. On the other hand, Foley said he trusted to the known habits of the French who seldom got more than one side of their ships cleared for action; and so it was on this occasion.

Sir Thomas Foley, being shown this account of the battle by General Sir C. Napier, admitted that it was generally very accurate, though there were some errors of detail. He was a very simple-minded, brave, and honest man. He cherished the memory of Lord Nelson, and had no vanity. His friends, knowing the share he had in the action, forced an acknowledgment of it in the House of Lords; but Foley never disputed that Nelson's plan might have been better, though he gave the reasons above stated for his own enterprising movement.

Alexandre, Condé, ont pu commander dès leur plus jeune âge: l'art de la guerre de terre est un art de génie d'inspiration; mais ni Alexandre ni Condé, à l'âge de 22 ans, n'eussent commandé une armée navale. Dans celle-ci rien n'est génie ni inspiration; tout y est positif et expérience, Le général de mer n'a besoin que d'une science, celle de la navigation, Celui de terre a besoin de toutes, ou d'un talent qui équivaut à toutes, celui de profiter de toutes les expériences et de toutes les connaissances. Un général de mer n'a rien à deviner; il sait où est son ennemi; il connâit sa force. Un général de terre ne sait jamais rien certainement; ne voit jamais bien son ennemi; ne sait jamais positivement où il est, &c.—(Gourgaud, vol. 2.)

In land operations the natural obstacles are, generally speaking, subordinate to. the efforts of man; at sea they control his powers. A general can move his army anywhere and anyhow, because it is a sentient machine, and the loss of some of its component parts is not irremediable: an admiral can only evade natural obstacles; he cannot overcome them: winds, waves, rocks, are his masters; his army is of wood and iron, non-sentient, and it goes to wreck altogether, or is saved altogether; it cannot lose a part and remain available for service: a ship goes down altogether. A general's genius may rise above impediments of nature; an admiral's genius consists in yielding to them, and hence he cannot give full scope to his natural courage or enterprise. He is always restricted by fear of a master whose orders cannot be contradicted—Nature!

Ces pays (Africa and Asia) étant habités par des hommes de plusieurs coleurs, la polygamie est le seul moyen d'empêcher qu'ils ne se persécutent. Les législateurs ont pensé que, pour que les blancs ne fussent pas ennemis des noirs, les noirs des blancs, les cuivrés des uns et des autres, il fallait les faire tous membres d'une même famille, et lutter ainsi contre ce penchant de l'homme de haïr tout ce qui n'est pas à lui. Mahomet pense qtie quatre femmes étaient suffisantes pour atteindre ce but, parceque chaque home pouvait avoir une blanche, une noire, une cuivrée, et une femme d'une autre couleur. Sans doute il était aussi dans la nature d'une réligion sensuelle de favoriser les passions de ses sectateurs; et en cela la politique et le prophète ont pu se trouver d'accord.— (Gourgaud, vol. 2.)

Perhaps also because the new religion being to be propagated by the sword, the men would be swept away in far greater numbers on both sides, than the women; and it was necessary to sustain the races without a general depravation of morals, by permitting polygamy, though Mahomet's great genius led him to restrict it to four wives. Did he overlook the terrible results of lowering the character and position of women? or was he unable to correct the manners of his people? Probably the latter, for he always treated his own wives with great distinction.

Le Général Hoche mourut dans ce temps subitement à Mayence. Beaucoup de gens ont cru qu'il avait été empoisonné; cette opinion n'est pas fondée.— (Montholon, vol. 4.)

Marshal Soult told me that he was with Hoche when his death happened; that his (Soult's) belief, and Hoche's also, was that he was poisoned by the councils. Soult gave me many strong proofs that this opinion was correct; amongst others, he pointed to the fact that three surgeons opened the body; two were ignorant army surgeons, the other was an eminent person of Mayence: the two first declared against poison; the last positively declared that the traces of poison were evident: the opinion of the two first was published, the opinion of the latter suppressed! Hoche, before he died, told Soult he had been poisoned by agents of the councils.—W. N,

> Mais Pitt redouta le degré de puissance où la France pouvait s'élever si on lui laissait tranquillement établir sa révolution; et il ne songea pas qu'il mettait en péril la destinée de l'Europe entière, s'il parvenait à l'armée contre la liberté Française.—(Montholon, vol. 5.)

An error. Pitt did not want to go to war. He was forced to it by Lords Spencer and Fitzwilliam, who were the chiefs and organs of the aristocracy, or rather of the borough obligarchy of England.

> L'enthousiasme guerrier, et surtout l'enthousiasme révolutionnaire que la France avail déployé depuis la bataille de Jemmappes, dut faire prévoir qu'au moment d'un danger plus sérieux dont l'armée de Clairfayt et celles des émigrés faisaient la menace, une grande démonstration nationale de défense, une insurrection unanime pour l'attaque, se déploiraient dans toute la France.—(Montholon, vol. 5.)

Mr. Fox warned Pitt that it would be so if he turned the French spirit and enthusiasm from internal changes to war; and he added that they would then overrun Europe in the strength of their enthusiasm. He was derided and abused; and Burke, who predicted that France would be blotted from the map of Europe, was listened to and became a prophet in Israel.

> Si les opérations de la Basse Vendée eussent été, comme cela devait être, combinées avec celles de la Haute Vendée où commandait Cathélineau, la République était infailliblement vaincue, mais il manqua toujours un Prince à la tête de la cause Vendéenne, Les Royalistes le demandèrent sans cesse à l'Angleterre, qui le leur montra une seule fois, et ne le leur donna pas; ce qui fut un raffinement nouveau en fait de cruauté politique,—(Montholon, vol. 5.)

This is not a just accusation. It was the extreme cowardice of the French princes that retained them. See Puissaye's *Memoirs*, a scarce work. Joseph de la Puissaye, the great Breton chief, who planned the expedition to Quiberon, himself told me that it was the cowardice of the princes that ruined the affairs of the Royalists. Puissaye also showed me a letter signed by Louis the Eighteenth, directed to the Chief of the Emigrant troops, instructing him to use Puissaye and then assassinate him.

La Puissaye has been abused and I believe most unjustly by the

French Royalists. To me he appeared a very able and very honourable man, calm and dignified in the extreme, and most commanding in manner.—W. N.

ALSO FROM LEONAUR
AVAILABLE IN SOFTCOVER OR HARDCOVER WITH DUST JACKET

THE 9TH—THE KING'S (LIVERPOOL REGIMENT) IN THE GREAT WAR 1914 - 1918 by *Enos H. G. Roberts*—Mersey to mud—war and Liverpool men.

THE GAMBARDIER by *Mark Severn*—The experiences of a battery of Heavy artillery on the Western Front during the First World War.

FROM MESSINES TO THIRD YPRES by *Thomas Floyd*—A personal account of the First World War on the Western front by a 2/5th Lancashire Fusilier.

THE IRISH GUARDS IN THE GREAT WAR - VOLUME 1 by *Rudyard Kipling*—Edited and Compiled from Their Diaries and Papers—The First Battalion.

THE IRISH GUARDS IN THE GREAT WAR - VOLUME 1 by *Rudyard Kipling*—Edited and Compiled from Their Diaries and Papers—The Second Battalion.

ARMOURED CARS IN EDEN by *K. Roosevelt*—An American President's son serving in Rolls Royce armoured cars with the British in Mesopatamia & with the American Artillery in France during the First World War.

CHASSEUR OF 1914 by *Marcel Dupont*—Experiences of the twilight of the French Light Cavalry by a young officer during the early battles of the great war in Europe.

TROOP HORSE & TRENCH by *R.A. Lloyd*—The experiences of a British Lifeguardsman of the household cavalry fighting on the western front during the First World War 1914-18.

THE EAST AFRICAN MOUNTED RIFLES by *C.J. Wilson*—Experiences of the campaign in the East African bush during the First World War.

THE LONG PATROL by *George Berrie*—A Novel of Light Horsemen from Gallipoli to the Palestine campaign of the First World War.

THE FIGHTING CAMELIERS by *Frank Reid*—The exploits of the Imperial Camel Corps in the desert and Palestine campaigns of the First World War.

STEEL CHARIOTS IN THE DESERT by *S. C. Rolls*—The first world war experiences of a Rolls Royce armoured car driver with the Duke of Westminster in Libya and in Arabia with T.E. Lawrence.

WITH THE IMPERIAL CAMEL CORPS IN THE GREAT WAR by *Geoffrey Inchbald*—The story of a serving officer with the British 2nd battalion against the Senussi and during the Palestine campaign.

AVAILABLE ONLINE AT **www.leonaur.com**
AND FROM ALL GOOD BOOK STORES

www.ingramcontent.com/pod-product-compliance
Lightning Source LLC
Chambersburg PA
CBHW030216170426
43201CB00006B/99